CW00351537

YOUNG OFFENDERS
Juvenile Delinquency
1700-2000

YOUNG OFFENDERS

Juvenile Delinquency
1700-2000

PAMELA HORN

AMBERLEY

'Crime, especially that committed by children and young people, seems to have become a leitmotif for a general social malaise, capturing public fears about the moral health of the nation ... Perhaps at the heart of the continuing debate about youth, crime and justice lie two related but separate questions. Firstly, how can we explain the wrong-doing of young people and secondly, how do we best respond to those young people who, as a result of their actions, become involved with the criminal justice system?'

Robert MacDonald,
Youth, Crime and Justice: Editorial Introduction in Youth and Policy, No. 48 (Spring 1995).

Shillings and Pence Conversion Table

Old Money	*Decimal*	*Old Money*	*Decimal*
1*d*	½ p	1*s* 8*d*	8 ½p
2*d* or 3*d*	1p	1*s* 9*d* or 1*s* 10*d*	9p
4*d*	1 ½p	1*s* 11*d*	9 ½p
5*d*	2p	2*s*	10p
6*d*	2 ½p	2*s* 6*d*	12 ½p
1*s*	5p	3*s*	15p
1*s* 1*d*	5½p	5*s*	25p
1*s* 2*d* or 1*s* 3*d*	6p	10*s*	50p
1*s* 6*d*	7½p	20*s*	100p, i.e. £1

First published 2010

Amberley Publishing Plc
Cirencester Road, Chalford,
Stroud, Gloucestershire, GL6 8PE

www.amberley-books.com

Copyright © Pamela Horn 2010

The right of Pamela Horn to be identified as the Author of this work has been asserted in accordance with the Copyrights, Designs and Patents Act 1988.

ISBN 978 1 84868 880 3

British Library Cataloguing in Publication Data.
A catalogue record for this book is available from the British Library.

Typesetting and Origination by FONTHILLDESIGN.
Printed in the UK.

CONTENTS

           Juvenile offending in the First World War   167
           The inter war years: 1919-1938   179

Chapter 7 The Second World War and its aftermath: 1939-1990s   195
           The Second World War: 1939-1945   195
           The Post-War World: 1945-1990s   211

           Conclusion   233
           Endnotes   235
           Bibliography   269
           Index   277

ACKNOWLEDGEMENTS

I should like to thank all who have helped in the preparation of this book, either by providing photographs and documents or in other ways. They include the Archives Office of Tasmania and Bath News and Media. I have received much efficient assistance and guidance from staff in the libraries, archives and record offices where I have worked and to them, too, I should like to express my gratitude. They include Berkshire Record Office; the Bodleian Library, Oxford; the British Library; the British Library Newspaper Library, Colindale; Bristol Local History Library; Cardiff Reference Library; the Centre for Oxfordshire Studies, Oxford; Dorset Record Office; Gloucestershire Archives; the Guildhall Library, London; Hackney Archives; Hampshire Record Office; London Metropolitan Archives; the National Archives, Kew; Oxfordshire Record Office; Portsmouth Record Office; and the Women's Library in London.

As always, I owe a great debt to my late husband for his help and encouragement over the years and for his company on many research 'expeditions'. Without him neither this nor any of my books could have been written.

PAMELA HORN
September, 2009

CHAPTER 1

THE RISE OF JUVENILLE DELINQUENCY

... juvenile delinquency has of late years increased to an unprecedented extent, and is still rapidly and progressively increasing ...

Report of the Committee of the Society for the Improvement of Prison Discipline and for the Reformation of Juvenile Offenders (1818).

Eighteenth-Century Attitudes to Youth Crime

At the beginning of the twenty-first century juvenile crime has become an issue of widespread social and political debate, with government ministers and the news media highlighting the anti-social behaviour of certain groups of young people and the detrimental effect this has on the communities where they live.[1]

In the early 1700s the situation was very different. Then juvenile offending, in a society generally far more violent than our own (especially in the major cities) caused little anxiety. This was partly because about three-quarters of the population still lived in rural areas and even in 1801 around two-thirds did so.[2] Only in London, where about one English person in eight lived in 1700, did the criminal conduct of young people give rise to adverse comment.

When children did break the law few distinctions were made between the treatment accorded them and that of adult criminals. The main differences were that those aged under seven were considered incapable of committing a crime and could not be charged with one, while between seven and fourteen they were given partial legal immunity in that it had to be shown that when they acted feloniously they were motivated by malice and were fully aware of what they had done. At fourteen, in strictly legal terms, they were treated as adults, although in practice youth was regarded as a reason for leniency in many cases. In the early nineteenth century one observer reported that where the offender was 'of tender years' the chance of escaping the full rigours of the law was considerable: 'there is scarcely anyone of common humanity who would not shudder at taking away the life of a child under 16 or 17'.[3] Hence in 1783, magistrates sitting at the Essex quarter sessions refused to try a twelve-year-old girl on the grounds that she was 'an infant under the age of discretion'. In the same year a nine-year-old orphaned chimney sweep was tried at the Old Bailey for housebreaking. He was acquitted of the capital charge, however, when the Judge told the jury: 'His confession should not be allowed, because it was made under fear. It would be too hard to find a boy of his tender age guilty of the burglary'.[4]

This approach was significant in that during the eighteenth century the number of offences carrying the death penalty increased enormously. In 1688 around fifty crimes were punishable by death. That had risen to about 160 by 1765 and then grew further to perhaps 225 by the early nineteenth century. As Michael Ignatieff has pointed out, some of these new statutes made offences capital which had formerly been subjected to lesser penalties, and a number of them involved activities particularly likely to attract children.[5] In 1699, for example, a new Act made shoplifting of goods valued at over 5s an offence punishable by death. Shoplifting remained a capital offence, at least in theory, until the 1820s, although in practice the full penalty was rarely exacted. In 1706 amendments were introduced to allow for sentences of six months to two years in a house of correction to be imposed on those found guilty of a first offence. Again, in 1713 a new act made it a capital offence to steal goods worth 40s or more from a house. In its preamble it was made clear that this was aimed particularly at servants who stole from their masters. The picking of pockets remained a capital offence until 1808, and in other instances actions became criminal which had previously been accepted as communal perquisites, especially in the countryside. These included the gathering of wood for firing, the lopping of trees, and the stealing of fruit from orchards. They were all offences likely to be committed by young people.[6]

In 1744 a new Vagrancy Act gave magistrates power to send 'rogues' and 'vagabonds' – or those classed as such – who had been taken up by paish constables, to the local house of correction, there to be detained until the next quarter sessions. If they were subsequently tried at the sessions as a rogue or vagabond they could be sentenced to between six months and two years in a house of correction, and whipped into the bargain. In addition, any male over the age of twelve years could, before his sentence had expired, be recruited into 'his Majesty's Service, either by sea or land', as the magistrates thought fit.[7] Among those caught up in this legislation was eight-year-old George Colman who, with an older man, probably his father, was committed to the Winchester Bridewell, or house of correction, on 17 July 1802 to await the next quarter sessions.[8] That opened nine days later, but on the appearance of the two Colmans in court they were remanded until the following quarter sessions, held in early October. At that point they were apparently freed, having served, in effect, a term of three months' imprisonment, for no other reason than that they had been found wandering abroad without a settled home.

Frequently, though, both prosecutors and magistrates favoured the use of informal punishments in cases involving offenders under the age of seventeen. In the 1740s the Wiltshire magistrate, William Hunt, acting under legislation passed in the previous century, punished youngsters for the theft of fruit and vegetables by requiring them to recompense the victim for damage caused and to pay a fine. This was to be for the use of the poor. The alternative was a whipping. Quite often Hunt handed part of the fine over to the families of the offenders, if they were known to be impoverished. Thus in July 1744 he granted a warrant against three boys for robbing the orchard of a Mr Flower Sainsbury. The youngsters admitted the theft and a penalty of 5s was imposed on them, or they were to be whipped. They paid over the cash about a fortnight later, with 1s. of the sum set aside for the 'poor'. In this case the beneficiaries were three members of the boys' own families.[9] About eighteen months later Hunt granted a warrant against three boys for wood stealing. On this occasion, upon their 'humbling themselves' to the victim of the crime, 'and ... promising not to offend in like manner any more, they were forgiven by the complainant', and thus escaped other punishment. And in 1783 the justices of the Whitechapel Rotation (or Police) Office in London released a boy, Samuel Smith, on condition that he 'be corrected at school'. A little later the London-based Philanthropic Society declared that 'children ... carried before a magistrate for theft have been discharged not ... in consequence of any doubt respecting their guilt but ... through the unwillingness of the injured party to bring them to trial'.[10]

Early in the nineteenth century the Bedfordshire Justice of the Peace, Samuel Whitbread, adopted similar tactics, punishing childish pranks with a whipping. Boys disturbing the Sunday service in a nonconformist chapel and removing the key (which was not recovered) were ordered to be flogged, 'lesser ones 6, bigger ones 10 stripes', and their parents were to pay the constable's expenses in the case. On another occasion, in November 1811, the three ringleaders of boys from the village of Elstow, accused of breaking a farmer's hedges, were given a whipping, while the rest were made to 'beg pardon'.[11]

Not all youngsters were so fortunate. In the summer of 1802 Hampshire-born Jonas Cooper, aged ten, was found with a quantity of wood in his possession and on his refusing 'to give a satisfactory account how he came by the same', or to pay the penalty imposed upon him, he was sentenced by the clergyman JP who heard the case to a month's imprisonment in the Winchester Bridewell. [12] A shortage of cash may well have prevented him from paying the sum required. In other instances children who were charged on more than one occasion with offences seem to have escaped without formal punishment, other than being remanded in custody to await trial – a stiff enough penalty in itself. This was true of another Hampshire boy, Aaron Wilton, aged twelve. In January 1792 he was accused of having stolen two silver spoons, valued at 3s. When he appeared before the Hampshire Epiphany quarter sessions in 1792 he pleaded not guilty. The jury accepted that plea. The following year he and an older brother were accused of robbing a male victim in a wood at Millbrook in the same county. On this occasion there was a failure to indict either of them and so no charges were pressed. Six months later Aaron, now aged fourteen, was accused of having stolen 'two pieces of a silver tea spoon and the bowl of a silver table spoon' at Nursling. Another older brother, Job, was committed with him to the Bridewell for refusing to enter into a recognisance to appear at the quarter sessions to give evidence against Aaron. The younger boy was committed on 16 April and the case was due to be heard the following July. Once more there was a failure to produce an indictment. In all, Aaron Wilton was remanded to appear before the Hampshire quarter sessions on three occasions between January 1792 and Midsummer 1793. Although he received no specific punishment, he spent several months in prison awaiting trial. In this way recalcitrant youngsters or those regarded as suspect by the magistrates could be pressurised into mending their ways without any formal penalty being imposed upon them. [13]

In all, over the period 1789-95, 564 prisoners appeared before the Hampshire quarter sessions. Of those just twenty-four, or 4.2 per cent, were young people under seventeen. Most of them either had no case to answer or they were acquitted. Just five were given a specific punishment, including William Ashford, aged fifteen, who was sentenced at the Easter sessions in 1791 to one week's imprisonment and to be twice whipped, for stealing a pair of worsted stockings, a pair of leather shoes and some scissors, together valued at 1s 10d. By the time the sentence was passed he had already spent over three months in the Bridewell awaiting trial. [14]

A class element entered into these prosecutions, too, in that offences were often ignored when committed by the sons of the well-to-do which could lead to charges being laid when committed by the children of the poor. Lord Eldon, the Lord Chancellor, confessed in the House of Lords that as a boy he had stolen fruit and gone poaching. If he had been prosecuted instead of having a beating from his father, it is unlikely that he would ever have achieved his subsequent legal eminence. Yet he was insistent that these offences must be rigorously punished when committed by members of the lower orders. The future Essex JP, John Harriott, was the beneficiary of similar clemency as a boy after his raids on local orchards.[15] It was in these circumstances that in 1828 a select Committee on Criminal Commitments and Convictions reported sourly how the 'sons of persons of the highest rank in this country, when at school, often commit offences out of the exuberance of spirits and activity, which the law, if it visited them at all, must visit by sentences of great severity.' Such offences, 'passed over as frolics in the sons of the rich, are treated in the children of the poor as crimes of magnitude.'[16] The dire reputation of prisons at this time doubtless added to the desire of the 'respectable' classes to make sure that members of their family did not experience their contaminating influence.

Meanwhile in major towns like Bristol or Norwich, and especially in London itself, where even in 1800 about one in ten of the population lived, there were large numbers of children who were orphaned or whose parents were unable or unwilling to support them. The large-scale consumption of spirits, especially gin, was blamed for many of the crimes of violence committed by adults and adolescents in the first half of the eighteenth century. That meant numbers of neglected children, 'starved and naked at home', were forced to beg for a subsistence and as they grew up they learned 'to pilfer and steal'.[17] In 1751 Henry Fielding, the pioneer Bow Street magistrate, who did much to initiate police reform in the capital, wrote of that city's crime wave in pessimistic terms:

> There is not a street in [Westminster] which doth not swarm all day with Beggars, and all Night with Thieves ... Great and numerous Gangs ... have for a long time committed the most open Outrages in Defiance of the law.[18]

In the latter part of the century improvements in street lighting, a modest increase in the effectiveness of policing, and the appointment of stipendiary magistrates in seven new public rotation, or police, offices in 1792, led to some reduction in the capital's crime levels. Nevertheless in 1790 visitors to London were still being advised 'never to stop in a crowd or look at the windows of a print-shop, if you would not have your Pocket Picked.'[19] And half the capital's hackney coachmen were said to be in league with thieves.[20]

Against this background early in the eighteenth century the London Workhouse, set up by the newly-established Corporation of the Poor, began receiving youngsters who had pilfered but who would otherwise have gone unpunished, since their victims were unable or unwilling to prosecute them in the courts, perhaps on cost grounds or because they could not identify them, or through a reluctance to apply legal sanctions to such juveniles. The workhouse provided a means of disciplining them as well as offering some industrial training, designed to steer them away from a life of crime. According to a report of 1739, this meant they were fed, clothed, and taught 'both in the Principles of Religion, and to work toward their Support ... who otherwise would have been brought up in the greatest Wickedness'. Among the hundreds of young vagrants and beggars received into the workhouse in the early years of the century were children like Ann Gainsford, aged ten, John Shaw, aged twelve, and James Price, aged fourteen, who had been caught stealing sugar, tobacco and other goods from warehouses and quays along the river Thames. Other youngsters were committed on suspicion of pick pocketing, and they joined the throng of boys and girls taken in after being discovered living rough on the streets. Some were subsequently put out as apprentices, but by the late 1730s a shortage of funds was hampering this rescue mission.[21]

For the remainder of the eighteenth century and beyond, the question of what to do with children living on the streets without family support or a settled home and who were in danger of being corrupted by criminal companions, preoccupied philanthropists and, as we shall see, led to the introduction of various initiatives designed to bring about their reformation and to restore them to a situation of self-dependence and respectability. A mid-century commentator lamented that one of the causes of robberies was the lack of provision *'for maintaining and educating in good principles, and habits of industry, the children of the Poor.'*[22]

At the end of 1755 the London magistrate, Sir John Fielding, was struck by the 'vast number of wretched boys, ragged as colts, abandoned, strangers to beds, and who lay about ... in ruinous houses, in Westminster, and its environs.' Other contemporary observers, like the prison reformer, John Howard, condemned the way in which in the prisons of the 1770s youngsters of twelve or fourteen were confined with adult criminals, who corrupted them with tales of their 'adventures, successes, stratagems, and escapes'. He warned that many children, 'committed for some trifling offence,' were morally ruined as a result.

> I make no scruple to affirm that if it were the wish and aim of the Magistrates to effect the destruction present and future of young delinquents, they could not devise a more effectual method, than to confine them so long in our prisons, those seats and seminaries ... of idleness and every vice. [23]

For this reason, many contemporaries supported the application of informal sanctions to children who had broken the law rather than sending them to gaol. But not all shared that view. In 1785 one critic named Madan, complained of the leniency of juries towards an offender, simply because he 'happens to be young'.[24] A year later Hewling Luson, in stressing the urgent need for new ways to be found to deal with young offenders, nonetheless claimed that thieving had now

> become a *science*; and no sooner are these outcasts of the community arrived at an age to be capable of distinguishing good from evil than they are systematically trained up to it by the most industrious and able proficients ... Long before ... his equals in age can read a lesson with tolerable fluency, the infant thief can pick a pocket with wonderful dexterity; and the transition, from this beginning to higher exploits, is rapid and easy[25].

Luson blamed 'abandoned parents' for training up to a 'life of misery, beggary, prostitution, or plunder' the hundreds of 'wretched children' on the streets. He called for such youngsters to be 'taken under the protection of the public, and placed in some asylum, where ... maintenance, employment and instruction may be provided for them'.[26]

Also blamed for attracting juvenile pilferers was the tempting array of goods displayed at open shop fronts and on stalls in towns and markets. These invited children to steal the merchandise. The ease with which property could be disposed of to receivers added to the problem, with petty traders and sellers of second-hand goods encouraging servants, apprentices and other young people to bring stolen goods to them. One such young thief was twelve-year-old Robert Payworth, who worked for a barber on Fish Street Hill in London and was to have become his apprentice. Robert took a shoe to a cobbler to be mended and the cobbler's wife asked him if he had anything to sell. He answered that he had 'an old whitish handkerchief'. She then responded, 'get whatever you can, I'll buy it for I buy anything'. The result was that the boy was induced to steal his master's property and when he was found out, he was convicted of theft and branded with a cold iron, before being required to give evidence about the reason for his fall from grace.[27] The case was heard in the spring of 1752

In 1816, Sir John Silvester, who was Recorder of the City of London from 1803 to 1822, listed over a hundred people in the capital who 'fenced' stolen articles supplied by children. Among them was a Mrs Franklin of Soho, who, as a front, sold fruit and vegetables from her shop door, located in a cellar under a chandler's business. She had lived there for a number of years and according to Silvester, purchased anything the youngsters brought to her, including meat and loaves of bread. 'This Woman buys the most trifling things from little Boys, telling them they must bring better things next time'. If there were pawnable goods among the booty she told the children to return later and then took these items to a nearby pawnbroker. But she had no scruples about cheating the youngsters when she could. 'for 6 pairs of Ladies Shoes worth £3, she gives £1, 6d. for a Quartern Loaf, 6d. pr. lb for Meat'. Silvester estimated that she acted as a receiver for about sixty boys, almost a third of whom were only nine and ten years old. She also bought from about twelve girls, who provided her with stolen lace, ribbons, gown pieces and other finery. Another woman, a Mrs Jennings of Red Lion Market, combined the receiving of stolen goods with keeping a brothel. She was a 'most notorious Fence', and had secret rooms reached 'by Doors out of cupboards', where she hid the plunder brought to her. 'Innumerable Girls & Boys of the youngest class resort to this House as she makes up more Beds than any other House in that part of the Metropolis ... & the House is thronged every Night.' She encouraged the girls to steal from any 'Strangers whom they can inveigle into the House & whom the Girls will bilk into the bargain'.[28]

But whilst outside observers condemned the receivers for exerting a malign influence on the children, the youngsters themselves saw things differently. To them, such people offered a refuge where they could meet companions in a similar situation to their own and where they could join gangs to go out on pickpocketing and shoplifting expeditions, or with whom they gambled and went to the penny theatres. There is evidence that peer pressure was exerted on some reluctant youngsters to persist with their lawless activities. But others enjoyed the excitement engendered by these escapades. In the early nineteenth century the then chief magistrate at Bow Street, Sir Richard Birnie, described how young offenders carried out their 'depredations' at dusk, 'at the playhouses and at places of public resort.' They went out in groups of three into shopping areas such as the Strand and Bond Street: 'one went first, and with a diamond or coarse nail, cut the window; a second followed, pushed in the piece; and a third (the youngest with the smallest hand), took the article; all that did not occupy above a minute'.[29] This method of stealing from shops was known as 'starring the glaze'.

Another commentator, who served as Upper Marshal of the City of London from the 1790s, described the principal offences children committed:

Picking pockets; taking things, on their hands and knees, from shops, such as haberdashers and linen-drapers; in the winter time, with a knife at the corner of the glass starring it, and taking things out, which has occasioned the trades people having so many guard irons; but still there are shops not so guarded, and they can find opportunities of continually robbing: Boys upon all occasions, where there is anything which excites a crowd, are very active, and many of them extremely clever; they are short and active and generally attended by men … They are trained by thieves who are adepts; these boys are generally apprehended three or four together, but they go in larger gangs than that … Many of them from six to ten.[30]

In the 1830s William Augustus Miles, a long-time investigator of the causes of juvenile crime, also pointed to the way in which the boys herded together so as to make themselves into a separate small community, with few links to bind them to society at large. 'They must eat, so they thieve, having no other means of procuring food – they have no character to recommend them to an employer … Money is useless to them beyond enabling them to supply themselves with food or drink … so in order to get rid of it as quickly as they can, they gamble.'[31] He noted, too, the differing grades or 'castes' among these semi-professional young pilferers, including, at the top, 'a kind of aristocracy':

There is the incipient house-breaker … the pickpocket, a subdivided class, however, for the boy who dives for purses or for watches, would scorn to take a handkerchief. Then, again, there is a class called 'sneaks,' who enter shops slyly, or crawl upon their hands and knees to abstract a till. There is another 'caste' or class called 'bouncers,' who enter a shop, and, while bargaining, contrive to steal property. Another class steals exposed property about shop doors or windows; others break, by means of a nail, the glass in windows in order to abstract goods; some rob from mercers by inserting a jagged wire and drawing silks through the bolt holes. There is one class who ride behind carriages to steal the leather braces, which they can sell for ninepence each pair: but the lowest of all thieves (despised even of his fellows) is the *'pudding snammer.'* These 'pudding snammers' are young urchins whose love of pudding far exceeds all love of work; so they loiter about cook shops, and when customers are departing with plates of beef or pudding, the choice provision and the 'pudding snammers' have vanished like magic! They sell the surplus, after gratifying their own hunger, to other boys or coster-mongers, and then seek a shelter in some nest of crime, where they can be accommodated with a bed for threepence, or a stair to sleep upon for a half-penny!

According to Miles, the different grades would usually 'herd together', with the 'pudding snammer' regarded as the lowest class, 'unworthy of higher fellowship'.[32]

Some were opportunist thieves, like John Wisehammer, born in Gloucestershire at the end of the 1760s. In February 1785 aged fifteen, he was sentenced to be transported for seven years for stealing snuff from a Bristol shop.[33] Then there was fifteen-year-old William Wheeler, who was committed for trial at Berkshire quarter sessions, charged with stealing several items of clothing from a fellow worker on the farm where they both lodged. His victim, Francis Bury, had gone out for the day on Sunday, 3 July, 1791, leaving some of the articles in his sleeping quarters above the stable and others locked up in a corn bin for safe keeping. But young Wheeler, who had only been hired about ten days before, managed to get hold of them. Later in the day his employer, farmer John Warren of Uffington, saw him walking through some standing corn with a bundle. Warren's curiosity was aroused and he followed the lad. When he caught up with him he forced the boy to reveal the contents of the bundle and found they contained Bury's clothes. William admitted the theft and was taken before a magistrate, who remanded him to Reading Bridewell to await trial. Another young prisoner in the Bridewell at that date was thirteen-year-old Sarah Kenting, also an opportunist thief, who was accused of taking a linen shift from the garden of a labourer in the village of Swallowfield, presumably after it had been washed and hung out to dry.[34]

It was in the 1780s and 1790s that concern began to grow about the issue of youth crime, and efforts were made to curb it in a more determined fashion than had applied earlier in the century. In practice, though, the number of youngsters charged before the courts remained relatively low. Peter King has calculated that, on the basis of gaol calendars and assize and quarter sessions records, over the period 1782 to 1793 only around one in ten property offenders brought before the courts in Shropshire, Berkshire, London and Middlesex were aged up to seventeen, although in Bristol, with its important commercial and trading links, the total was over a quarter. But, as King points out, only a tiny fraction of offenders were actually being indicted at that date.[35] In consequence just a small increase in the proportion of victims prepared to prosecute youngsters rather than to use informal alternative punishments could produce a large rise in the number of recorded crimes. This began to take place, partly out of a growing desire to discipline the poor and partly as a result of a changing attitude towards childhood itself. The petty scavenging and pilfering lifestyle of youngsters growing up without education, religious instruction, or moral training, and lacking the means to obtain lawful future employment, conflicted with new middle-class ideals about 'a protected, home-centred, constantly nurtured childhood … [The] street children's apparent freedom challenged the ordered, hierarchical notions within which middle-class childhood was constructed.'[36]

The increasing percentage of children and young people in the population, which peaked at around 39 per cent under the age of fourteen in 1821, added to this unease. As Sir John Silvester commented in 1816, when questioned about the advance in juvenile crime, although such offences had risen, 'when you consider the proportion of children, I do not think they have increased in proportion'.[37] However, to many better-off members of society youth crime was a symbol of a wider insubordination among the lower orders, which was itself being fuelled from the late 1780s by the disturbing influence of the French revolution. In the industrial areas, too, there were those who blamed the role of the factories and the decline in residential apprenticeships for a failure to provide a firm structure to the lives of young people during their leisure hours. In Manchester, for example, where the cotton industry was expanding rapidly in the late eighteenth and early nineteenth centuries, nearly a quarter of the total population in 1821 was aged from ten to nineteen years. Perhaps because of need during times of economic difficulty or out of youthful exuberance during periods of recreation, by 1820-22, 46.7 per cent of all property offenders in the town were youngsters under the age of twenty, according to official records. This compares with 39.7 per cent of property offenders falling into that age group within Lancashire as a whole and 31.6 per cent in London and Middlesex. Only Bristol, with 46.1 per cent of property offenders in that youthful group in 1820-22, came close to the Manchester figure.[38]

In 1819 when the prison reformer, Elizabeth Fry and her brother, J. J. Gurney, visited the Midlands and the North, they argued that it was the destruction of small workshops and the rise of the new factories which had increased crime in the area. Unlike small employers, they declared, 'the factory owners did not bother to supervise their youthful workers after hours, and in the weaving sheds and spinning rooms they allowed boys and girls to inflame each other with criminal desires.'[39]

This was an exaggeration and, in any case, contemporary accounts show that many eighteenth-century apprentices who <u>lived in</u> and worked in small businesses were allowed a good deal of freedom. Francis Place, who was bound apprentice to a leather breeches maker in London in the 1780s, recalled that when he first took up the apprenticeship he was required to be in his master's house by 10 p.m. but that was soon extended to 11 p.m. and then he was allowed to do much as he pleased:

Like most of my companions I was a member of a cutter club, smoked my pipe. sang my song and rowed in the eight-oared boat ... Our club was no better than many others, most of the members either robbed their masters or other persons to supply means for their extravagance.

According to Place, his master exerted little control over him, 'neither did he care much about me, or what became of me so that I did the work he required'.[40]

As Joan Lane points out, small-scale cheating of customers and petty pilfering were 'fairly common crimes by apprentices against their masters, as was the theft of craft implements' by those who absconded. That included a barber-surgeon's apprentice who ran away to sea taking with him a number of his master's surgical instruments, presumably in the hope of setting up in practice on his own account.[41] Advertisements in the press inserted by aggrieved masters often warned prospective employers not to take on youngsters who had broken their apprenticeship contract. In March 1779, for example, Thomas Read, a glover and breeches-maker of Broad Chalke in Wiltshire, advertised for his sixteen-year-old apprentice, John Philpot, who had absconded. Philpot was 'five feet high, pale complexion, strait (sic) dark hair, and stammers in his speech; had on when he went away, a garnet-coloured coat and waistcoat, a blue surtout coat, and a pair of doeskin breeches: This is to caution all persons not to employ or detain him, as they will be prosecuted without further notice, but give information to his master.'[42] Some masters accepted the absconders back, if they were traced, but others punished them by taking them to court and having them imprisoned.[43]

Recalcitrant apprentices could be penalised for not obeying their master's instructions, like the two apprentices of a London calenderer who refused to work on a Sunday 'when there was urgent necessity'. He complained about their conduct and they were both committed to Bridewell for three days.[44]

Victims of juvenile crime may have become more ready to take offenders to court at the end of the eighteenth century as a result of administrative changes in the judicial system. In 1778 a new Act allowed the expenses of a prosecutor to be met from official funds, as well as a reasonable sum to be allowed to cover his or her time and trouble in bringing forward the case. In addition, the expenses of poor persons giving evidence in such cases were also to be met.[45] The growing tendency to give conditional pardons to those convicted of capital offences rather than leaving them to hang may also have reduced the reluctance to prosecute in certain cases. As a consequence, instead of large numbers of young criminals being allowed to continue their depredations unscathed, there was a new willingness among victims to institute prosecutions, especially in London and in growing towns like Manchester. Improvements in policing in some of the larger urban areas also played a part in enabling the perpetrators of crimes to be caught.

Ironically, as juvenile prosecution levels rose, the sense of social unease intensified. There was alarm about a possible future upsurge of idleness, insubordination, and 'family degeneration' among sections of the growing urban working class, at a time when industry and the labour force itself were in transition from the old-style handicraft system of manufacture to a new, mass-production era.[46] This led to the development of two different policy strands designed to tackle youth crime. The first was based on philanthropic endeavour, designed to rescue youngsters from the lawless life they had embarked upon and to set them on the path to becoming useful and law-abiding members of society. That might mean separating them from the community in which they had grown up and which had brought them to their current plight. 'Every child, brought up in the resort of vicious and profligate people must almost inevitably imbibe the contagion of moral turpitude, and become an enemy to those laws on which the general good depends', declared one of the best known of these organisations, the Philanthropic Society, in its first report in 1789. If necessary that could mean restricting parental access to the children being cared for, to prevent the society's work being undermined by unsatisfactory family influences .[47]

The second approach took the form of an examination of the causes of crime and the drawing up of a broad strategic plan to deal with them. It is to the role of the philanthropists that we must turn first.

The Agencies of Reform

Even in the early 1700s efforts were made to rescue homeless and neglected youngsters by offering them shelter and training. This was one of the tasks undertaken by the London Workhouse at the beginning of the eighteenth century. In the 1750s came two other initiatives. The first was the Lambeth Asylum, opened in 1758 to give support and protection to young girls left on their own in London and in danger of becoming prostitutes. It offered religious and vocational training to equip them with the skills needed to become superior domestic servants. It was set up in the belief that it was 'easier to save girls from sin than to rehabilitate them once they had fallen'.[48]

The second venture was the establishment of the Marine Society in 1756, to cater for boys. Its aim was to cleanse, feed and clothe some of 'the vast shoals of shoplifters, pilferers and pickpockets' aged between twelve and sixteen, found on the streets of London, and to send them to sea.[49] At this time England was at war with France and Spain and the Society intended to send 'stout, active boys, properly clothed' to serve on board naval ships as servants to the captains and other officers. Magistrates were encouraged to send delinquent boys to the Marine Society rather than incarcerating them in prison. On occasion, even after youngsters had been committed to gaol they were released to the Society. From the time it was set up in 1756 until the end of the war in 1763, this 'nursery of seamen', as it was labelled, fitted out 5,174 poor boys as officers' servants in the Royal Navy, at a cost of nearly £24,000.[50] When hostilities ended, however, the Society for a time suspended operations and according to Radzinowicz and Hood, 'swarms of begging, pilfering boys returned, the "black fountain" of professional crime.'[51] When it resumed recruitment in the early 1770s its reputation was sufficiently high for the courts to send boys to it who were guilty of minor offences, rather than confining them in prison. In practice, however, the Society itself was now less enthusiastic about accepting them and was anxious instead to train only lads of good character for the sea service. Its role in reclaiming delinquent youngsters was, therefore, much diminished by the final quarter of the eighteenth century.[52]

This reduced commitment contrasted with the ambitious programme put forward by the Philanthropic Society, formed in September 1788 by a group of reformers anxious to improve the morals of the poor and to ameliorate the lot of some of London's vagrant and destitute children. To this end, however, they sought to operate 'rather on principles of police than of charity', since they regarded many charitable ventures as likely to demoralise the needy by encouraging a spirit of dependency. According to a notice issued by the founders, its aim was to prevent 'crimes ... [by] seeking out, and ... training up to virtue and usefulness in life the children of Vagrants and criminals, and such who are in the Paths of Vice and Infamy'.[53] The first children it took under its wing were sent to foster parents, but when the number recruited had reached twelve the Society rented a small house in Hackney for £10 a year, with a matron in charge and the young inmates taught to knit stockings and to make lace. Further houses were acquired as the numbers grew and specialist tradesmen and their wives were given the care of the children. One house was controlled by a shoemaker, another by a tailor, and a third by a carpenter. Each was to train the boys in his house in his particular craft. The girls were instructed in domestic skills, with the intention of preparing them to become 'menial' servants. It was firmly stated that no female could be admitted or retained who gave any appearance of 'unchaste manners'.[54] Prostitution was always seen as the likely fate of delinquent girls, just as thieving was regarded as the commonest kind of wrongdoing among delinquent boys. The austere and distant approach adopted by the Society in dealing with its young charges in these early days was underlined by the practice of referring to them in official reports as 'objects' rather than children.

Among the youngsters directed to the Society by the courts was eleven-year-old Charles Richmond, found guilty at the Old Bailey in December

1791 of stealing three cotton gowns, an apron and a muslin handkerchief, together valued at about 28s. They were the property of two maids who lived in a nearby property. Young Richmond was apprenticed to a Mr Murray and one Sunday he absconded, only to return on the following Tuesday. As a punishment, Murray locked the boy in his room, but nothing daunted the youngster climbed up the chimney and managed to get into the attic of the house next door but one. There he came down the chimney and stole the articles of clothing which he found lying on the bed. He then returned the way he had come. According to one of the maids: 'It was from a small hand [print] against the wall' that she first discovered the robbery. Presumably the boy's hand had been coated with soot.

On his master coming into the room to release him the lad declared he had 'something which would be of use to [his] wife; the first thing he shewed me was this gown; he shewed me all the things ... I sent my wife to make enquiry where these things were lost from'.[55] Richmond's victims were identified and when he was tried at the Old Bailey the jury found him guilty. He was sentenced to be whipped and then dispatched to the Philanthropic Society.

Other children cared for by the Society in its early days included thirteen-year-old Margaret Bell, who had been deserted by her parents and was found begging on the streets and selling matches, while when Roger, John and Michael Connor were admitted, their father was under sentence of death in Newgate prison. Their mother lived in Carrier street, a location where, according to the Society, 'few but persons of the most abandoned character reside.'[56] A list of fifty-two young inmates issued in 1799 revealed that just over 36 per cent of them had been guilty of criminal offences; the rest were the offspring of convicts, deserted children, or orphans. Among the lawbreakers was a thirteen-year-old who had begun his criminal career by stealing candles from a church in Cornhill. As a result he was punished in Bridewell, but soon after his release he ran away from home, taking with him a canvas bag containing candles, matches, flint and steel. He attempted to rob a house in the neighbourhood but was found concealed in the cellar by the maid. He was taken before a magistrate and confessed that his intention had been to let in some thieves to rob the house. He was tried for the crime but the evidence 'not being complete' he was recommended for admission to the Philanthropic.[57]

In 1792 the Society opened a central institution at St George's Fields, Southwark for the boys, with a separate establishment for the girls. At first children like young Richmond, with a criminal record, were housed with those who were merely the offspring of convicts or were unfortunates like Margaret Bell, who had been left to fend for themselves and had committed no crime. Soon punishment cells had to be provided where those who broke the rules were kept on a bread and water diet. But the possibility of 'contamination' to which this policy gave rise led in 1802 to the opening of a separate reform institute in Bermondsey, to accommodate the young male criminals. The original institution was now known as the Manufactory and was used for the rest of the male inmates. In the Reform the youngsters were instructed in religion and morality and were kept under strict supervision. Out of school hours they were set to pick oakum, so that they would not acquire 'habits of idleness'. Only when they had shown themselves ready to be reformed and rehabilitated were they sent to the Manufactory. There they and the other children learned various trades, such as shoemaking, tailoring and printing.[58]

In these early years the Society's impact was very limited. By 1796 it was reported that a total of 176 boys and 60 girls had been admitted. Of these, 51 boys and five girls had absconded. Seventeen of the boys had gone to sea. Five had been sent to the Marine Society, three had been expelled, ten had returned to their families, seven were in employment, and three had died. The rest were still in the institution. Of the fifty-one male absconders, thirty-one had been aged thirteen or above when they were admitted, and it was proposed that since at that age they were 'so far advanced in years as affording little chance of their being reclaimed', recruitment should in future be restricted to younger children. By the early 1820s strict age limits had been imposed, whereby no boy or girl, the child of a convict, could be admitted after thirteen years of age, while for criminal boys the upper age limit was twelve years. Criminal girls were excluded entirely from the year 1817 and for all of the children the minimum age of admission became nine.[59]

Discipline problems nonetheless persisted, with strict controls introduced to prevent the boys from absconding. That included having porters to sleep in their dormitories. Some indication of the difficulties faced may be gleaned from an order issued in June 1793 requiring that

> the boys be not permitted to go into the country for a holiday unless the superintendent and masters see that they have no weapons as guns, pistols, etc., of any sort, and that they behave themselves with the greatest regularity and never enter into any gardens, orchards, pleasure grounds. etc., by which they could give offence or do any mischief and that they be always present with some of the masters.[60]

The girls, too, proved difficult to control, with riots and absconding reported in the early nineteenth century. They also made attempts to get in touch with the boys, who were accommodated on the same site, despite the high wall which separated the male and female institutions. After thirteen girls had run away in one year the sub-matron was dismissed and it was decided not to admit females with a criminal record for the future. But another seventeen girls escaped shortly afterwards, and a committee of enquiry found that this was due to the severe 'restraint' imposed on them. It was decided, therefore, to relax the discipline somewhat, so as to allow the girls to go out with the matron from time to time and occasionally to visit their relatives.[61] In 1845 the Society resolved to exclude girls permanently, and to concentrate its efforts on reforming young male criminals. The children of convicts were no longer accepted. In 1848 it was decided to move the institution to the country and in its new location at Redhill in Surrey it became a Farm School. There it was destined to pioneer a new phase in the rehabilitation of juvenile delinquents, to enable them to return to mainstream society. Its role as part of this new Reformatory movement will be examined in a later Chapter.

Throughout these years the Philanthropic Society provided instruction in useful skills to its inmates to enable them to gain an honest livelihood when they left, sometimes arranging for them to be apprenticed to suitable masters outside the institution or preparing them for life overseas in one of the colonies. However, as late as 1840 a special committee of the Society lamented that the boys were 'not benefiting morally or generally from their training', and fresh efforts were made to tighten discipline. That meant, if necessary, the expulsion of particularly 'bad boys'.[62] In 1848 the annual report claimed it was giving 'the means and opportunity of repentance and reform to upwards of a hundred boys a-year; and actually rescuing about two thirds of them from the grasp of their criminal and vicious habits, and restoring them to paths of virtue, utility and happiness'. In that year there were 135 youngsters in the institution, of whom twenty-eight had been admitted on payment of £16 a year by associations of magistrates and others, anxious to keep them out of prison. Others were admitted in consideration of subscribers' donations or with small weekly payments from parents. Most of the remainder were either on the Society's 'free' list, or were beneficiaries of government grants towards their maintenance and the expense of their outfit when they left. Of ninety-six boys admitted in 1847, seventy had been received from prison – forty-seven of them having been imprisoned on at least one previous occasion.[63]

From its inception the Philanthropic Society sought to rescue children before they had become inured to a life of crime. Another reforming organisation set up in 1804, the Refuge for the Destitute, targeted youngsters who had served a prison term and were likely, on grounds of poverty, to resume a life of crime on their release because they lacked any other means of supporting themselves. It also received a few children who had 'forfeited their character by dishonest practices' and were 'desirous of returning to the paths of industry and rectitude.' [64] As with the Philanthropic Society, young inmates were taught to avoid the 'polluting influence of evil associates' and to adopt the principles of 'religion, industry, and subordination'. Separate institutions were set up for the boys and girls respectively, with the former learning shoemaking, tailoring and the like, and the girls taught laundrywork, needlework and general 'household business.' The laundrywork proved particularly lucrative, with public contracts undertaken for the London Orphan Asylum and the City of London Tavern, among others. In 1817 alone, the female institution received nearly £1,300 for its laundrywork, while the male institution earned just over £600 for the work it undertook. Over half of that was earned from shoemaking and another substantial portion came from firewood sales. [65]

When first admitted the boys were set to work chopping wood, this being seen as the equivalent of 'hard labour' in a prison and as a means of disciplining them, as well as providing a useful income for the Refuge. After they had conducted themselves properly for two or three months they were allowed to learn a trade. If they misbehaved they were sent back to wood chopping as a punishment. For more serious offences they were confined in a separate punishment cell in the dark for some days. [66]

In recognition of the value of its work with young prisoners the Refuge received grants from the government. These amounted to £2,000 in 1818, rising to £5,000 by 1820. In 1827 that had fallen to £4,000 and in 1828 to £3,000 but clearly the payments were a valuable boost to its work. [67]

A Temporary Refuge was set up in June 1818 at the expense of another reformist organisation, the society for the Improvement of Prison Discipline and for the Reformation of Juvenile Offenders. This aimed to provide short-term care to youngsters released from prison but who had no other means of shelter. In it they were fed, clothed and, where possible, reconciled with their family and friends, or found appropriate employment. That might include supplying them with working tools. In recompense they were expected to chop wood. Should these arrangements prove unsuccessful, they were helped to return to their place of legal settlement under the poor law, where they would be eligible to receive parish relief. [68]

Among those aided in this way was fifteen-year-old W. R., committed to Newgate prison for stealing a loaf of bread, which he had taken to keep himself from starving. He was sentenced to be flogged and was then discharged. He entered the Temporary Refuge, and remained there for three months before he was found a post with a 'reputable family'. There he was later said to be behaving 'with much propriety'. [69]

Sometimes applications were made on behalf of youngsters in danger of breaking the law by parents who claimed that their children were out of control. But like all charitable institutions working in this field, the committee of the Refuge was wary of encouraging feckless families to pass over their parental responsibilities to someone else. One such case involved thirteen-year-old Mary Coleman. In August 1812 application was made for her admission, with her mother claiming she was 'a very naughty &disobedient girl and not at all manageable by her, whose employment as a Basket-woman [that is a street trader] prevented her from being at home with her family'. The appeal was turned down. Also unsuccessful was a petition on behalf of sixteen-year-old Frances Milton of Egham in Surrey, made by the local clergyman on unspecified grounds. In this case the girl's own attitude was a decisive factor, the committee noting acidly that she 'did not seem conscious that her conduct needed reformation, or that her admission into the Refuge would be any more than into any common place of Service'.[70] Successful candidates were clearly expected to show an appropriate spirit of repentance, humility and gratitude. Hence Isabella Dalcourt, aged fifteen, from Westminster was regarded with favour. She had lost her place as a domestic servant as a result of stealing £10 from a lodger in her employer's house. 'She seemed very penitent &desirous of retrieving her reputation', the committee noted approvingly, 'and was consequently admitted.'[71]

By July 1820 the Refuge claimed it had admitted 922 females and 378 males to its permanent establishments since its establishment in 1804. Most of the girls, when they left, were either returned to their family and friends or sent to 'respectable service'. Among the males, apprenticeships or other suitable employment were the favoured options, although a trickle went to sea or enlisted in the East India Company's service.[72] A minority of youngsters emigrated, nine boys being sent as new settlers to Algoa Bay in South Africa in 1819. Later it was Canada that was to prove the chosen destination.[73] Emigration was seen as a way of giving the youngsters a fresh start in life away from their former 'contaminating' environment. It was an approach to juvenile reform adopted by many penal reformers concerned with rehabilitating children abandoned by their family and friends in the nineteenth century.

Although most of the rescue agencies in the late eighteenth and early nineteenth centuries were based in London, where the problem of child delinquency was regarded as particularly serious, the ideas espoused by the Philanthropic Society and the Refuge for the Destitute were taken up elsewhere. One of the best-known of the early ventures was set up in Warwickshire in 1817. It was established as a result of an appeal by Mr Justice Dallas at the opening of the Warwick Summer Assizes in 1816, when he called on the county's magistrates to do something to improve the lot of the many young offenders 'scarcely … able to distinguish Right from Wrong or ... trained and tutored by those to whose control and command they [were] subject, to confound the one with the other'. What was needed, he declared, was an institution 'to open the Mind – to amend the Heart ... to scatter the principles of subordination and Order, of Industry and Application'.[74] Led by Sir John Eardley-Wilmot, the county's JPs responded by hiring a farmhouse and a small tract of land in the village of Stretton-on-Dunsmoor, with the first inmates being accepted in 1817. By 1835, 179 juveniles had been received into this Warwick County Asylum, of whom 114 were said to have become reformed characters and to be 'respectably settled in Society'. Twenty-seven were admitted without being sent to prison and it was noted by the Asylum's superintendents that the reform of such youths was always much quicker and easier than was the case with those who had been committed to prison and were then sent after their sentence had expired. On admission, the boys were formally hired as servants in Husbandry and Handicraft by the master of the Asylum, with the aim of ensuring that should they run away, they could be brought before the magistrates for a breach of their employment contract and punished. If they misbehaved they were sent to the house of correction for a short period, to be kept in solitary confinement.[75] Recreation periods were allowed and instruction was given in religion and morality, as well as in reading, writing and arithmetic. The boys were engaged in making shoes and doing tailoring work. 'We do not wish to receive them under fourteen Years of Age.' declared the Asylum's secretary in 1835, 'because it is too expensive for our Establishment to keep them till they are fit for regular Employment ... We do not receive them after Seventeen, unless in some particular instances'.[76]

The scale of the Warwick County Asylum was modest, largely because of a shortage of funds, but it enjoyed a good reputation among penal reformers, and led to a similar establishment being set up in Glasgow.[77] Radzinowicz and Hood consider it was the only 'English venture to compare, in its own small way, with the most advanced continental reformatories,' through its regime of emphasising the importance of 'small groups ... personal contact ... and a 'family' atmosphere'. The aim was to interest the boys and to respect their independence rather than cramping them by the imposition of restrictions.[78] Over the period from 1818 to the beginning of 1846, 243 of the inmates completed their stint at the Asylum and of those, 134 were considered 'reformed', and established in 'respectable' positions in life.[79] Unfortunately the Asylum's perennial cash shortage eventually led to its closure in 1851, just when a new phase in the reformatory movement was getting under way.

These early initiatives to 'rescue' juvenile delinquents were essentially small in scale and limited in their effectiveness. But they opened up the question of how best to treat child offenders, so as to bring about their rehabilitation rather than merely consigning them to prison and accepting that many would reoffend soon after their release. It was this debate over the merits of reform versus punishment in a penal institution which was to inform discussions on the reformatories of the 1840s and 1850s. It is also echoed today in the arguments over the merits of confining delinquents in young offender institutions as opposed to involving them in community service and restorative justice.

The Analysis of Child Offending

At the beginning of the nineteenth century, and especially after the end of the war with Napoleonic France in 1815, there was increasing anxiety about rising crime rates and the part played in these by juveniles. In 1819, the poet and pamphleteer, W. L. Bowles, attributed the increase in crime to 'the alteration in the reasonings, feelings and habits of mind, particularly in the fermenting populous districts, in consequence of the French Revolution'.[80] In the country at large it was a time of social unrest, economic difficulty and political discontent, with concern also expressed about the inadequacies of the education system, the poor standard of policing, and the unsatisfactory nature of parish relief for the needy.[81] As Heather Shore has stated, in the arguments about 'debilitating environments, wretched poverty, minimal literacy and education', the 'role of the juvenile offender, as both the progeny and progenitor of criminals was central. Juvenile criminals were … for many commentators, the genesis of the professional criminal'.[82] Some expressed sympathy with the plight of these youngsters. Mr Justice Dallas in 1816, for example, referred to the 'swarms of youthful offenders who infest our Streets and invade our Dwellings' and who were being 'almost hourly' punished for their misdeeds. Yet who could 'withhold compassion from their fate?... For what … is the intrinsic Guilt of a miserable Boy or Girl, brought up from Infancy so as scarcely to be able to distinguish Right from Wrong...?'[83] Others saw them as members of an alien breed, who threatened the harmony and well-being of the community. In 1839, William Augustus Miles, for example, referred to 'a youthful population in the Metropolis devoted to crime, trained to it from infancy … and whom no Punishment can deter; a race … different from the rest of Society, not only in thoughts, habits, and manners, but even in appearance, possessing, moreover, a language exclusively … their own'.[84]

It was against this background that social investigators sought to identify the causes of juvenile offending and to find remedies for them. Some did so in connection with their own philanthropic activities; others supplied evidence to the parliamentary inquiries on policing matters which proliferated in the 1810s and 1820s. In these early investigations, London was the focus of attention because it was there that criminality was at its most obvious. Henry Fielding's comments of 1751 still largely applied, when he noted that the city's 'immense number of Lanes, Alleys, Courts and Bye-places' seemed as if they had 'been intended for the very Purpose of Concealment … Upon such a View, the whole appears as a vast Wood or Forest, in which a thief may harbour with as great Security, as wild Beasts do in the Deserts of Africa or Arabia'.[85]

The first serious attempt to examine the problem of child offending appeared in May 1816 in the *Report of the Committee for investigating the causes of the Alarming Increase of Juvenile Delinquency in the Metropolis*.[86] The Committee started work in 1815 making contact with around eight or nine hundred boys who were either in prison or were confederates of such youngsters. As a result of its interviews and investigations, it identified four principal factors pre-disposing juveniles to embark on a life of crime. These were the 'improper conduct of parents', and their readiness to neglect or mistreat their offspring; 'the want of education;' the shortage of suitable employment, which applied to both parents and the children themselves; and the lack of reverence for the Sabbath, including especially the habit of 'gambling in the public streets'. Three subsidiary issues were also identified, namely the severity of the criminal code; the defective state of policing; and deficiencies in the existing system of prison discipline.[87] As regards the criminal code, it pointed to the fact that the death penalty was attached to over two hundred offences, yet the 'humanity of the present age' prevented the application of 'the greater part of these laws'. That, claimed the Committee, encouraged the young to behave recklessly, since offenders calculated that even if they were caught and convicted they would receive a mitigated sentence. The stringency of the law thus failed to curb crime.

The inadequacies in prison discipline arose from the indiscriminate association of criminals of all ages and dispositions. The report quoted the conclusion of an eminent contemporary that in gaols and houses of correction, 'emulation is excited only to excel in crime, and all are soon raised to an equality therein'.[88] It deplored the way in which during their incarceration youngsters were exposed to 'the temptations of idle hours and corrupt society'.

These conclusions led members of the Committee to form the Society for the Improvement of Prison Discipline and for the Reformation of Juvenile Offenders. In its first report, issued in 1818, the new body argued that it had been inspired to act because of the 'alarming increase of Crime, more especially amongst Children and Youth of both sexes'; the 'disgraceful condition' of many gaols; and 'the destructive consequences … following from the neglect of prison discipline'. Over the following years it devoted itself to exposing the flaws in the criminal code and the unsatisfactory conditions in individual prisons. As we have seen, it also provided temporary aid, in association with the Refuge for the Destitute, to youngsters who had recently left prison and were destitute. Among those assisted in 1822 were eight boys released from Newgate prison on the same day. They had been sentenced to a flogging and this had been carried out, as was customary, on the day they were discharged. 'The boys were … immediately turned into the streets with their backs sore from the flagellation and in such a state that two … who were received by the Committee into the "temporary Refuge", were obliged, immediately on their admission, to be placed in the infirmary; one of them, a lad of fifteen, having received seventy lashes.'[89]

William Augustus Miles was another investigator who gave evidence to the 1835 Select Committee on Gaols and Houses of Correction. In this he pinpointed poverty and homelessness as being frequent causes of juvenile offending:

> To Boys so lost and so destitute what is a Prison but a Blessing; an Asylum greatly to be coveted; a Shelter, however, which will destroy whatever of Good may remain in their Dispositions, as it introduces them to the confirmed in Crime, who teach them that to thieve advantageously is the best means to better their forlorn condition. Whatever a Boy can contrive to steal in this Metropolis he can immediately convert into money … If we consider the number of Youths who are left without the least Restraint, the great number whose Parents daily send them forth to live as they can, and to bring Money home at Night, under the Penalty of a severe Beating if they fail; if we add to this list the number who, being idly and extravagantly disposed, plunder unknown to their Parents; … we cannot feel surprised at the Increase in the Number of juvenile Delinquents.[90]

Two years later, in a pamphlet addressed to the Home Secretary, Lord John Russell, Miles declared that the three prime causes of children's crimes were; 'The Congregating of the poorest classes in … low neighbourhoods'; the neglect of parents; and the 'facilities of selling every sort of stolen property' to a multiplicity of receivers.[91] He called for 'the parental solicitude of Government' to be extended to these children, by the provision of some other refuge than a prison.

In reaching his conclusions, Miles had carried out extensive interviews with a number of young criminals, many of them guilty of serious offences and under sentence of transportation as convicts to New South Wales. These interviews, however, revealed a more complex picture of the reasons for offending than Miles had himself put forward in his analysis. It is clear that for many of the boys crime offered not merely a livelihood but excitement and companionship. Nor did all the boys have neglectful or dissolute parents. Heather Shore has calculated that of thirty-two lads interviewed by Miles in the mid-1830s, fifteen had parents 'in reduced but respectable situations'.[92] Their motives for breaking the law were mixed. For some, as Miles suggested, it was dire necessity; but for others it was a desire to get cash to gamble or to visit the penny theatres, or to buy alcohol. In many cases they were egged on by companions or by the receivers of stolen property, who encouraged them to bring goods to them.

One such persistent offender was George Hickman, a Clerkenwell boy, aged sixteen when interviewed by Miles. He had been in prison several times but was now under sentence of seven years' transportation. His mother was a nurse and his father a working jeweller, and they were both described as 'sober persons'. He also had four sisters. According to his own account he had been three years

> on the town stealing anything I can lay my hands upon – I used to gamble all I got – play Heads & tails for a Shilling each time … I like cards best. Thieves are playing cards all day long … I generally robbed in company with the same boy … and also with Robinson [who was imprisoned with him] … I never have worked since I began thieving – I generally sold my Plunder to two sisters, Jewesses in Field Lane – they keep 'a Handkerchief Shop' and give 2/- for a good one … The richest purse I ever stole contained £15, and I once sold a Watch of some value to a Jew in Field Lane … Young thieves brag to each other of the amount they have stolen – they never think of Punishment when at liberty – some dread a flogging – some prefer it to a month's imprisonment. [93]

Another young interviewee was Samuel Holmes from Stepney, aged thirteen, who had already been in prison four times. His mother was dead and his father was a waterman and a heavy drinker. Samuel had stolen goods from shops and had also run away with the tills. He, too, spent money on gambling at pitch and toss and skittles. 'Young thieves drink much, almost everyone keeps his girl', he declared. He had begun his career by playing around in the streets and his father had tried to keep him at home by taking away his clothes and tying him to a bed post. But 'the Boys used to come round the House at night & whistle & entice me to go out thieving again with them – They once got some cloathes, got in at the window in the back parlour where I was tied up naked, dressed me

Oliver Twist entering Fagin's thieves' kitchen – the kind of surroundings familiar to some of the youngsters interviewed by Miles in the 1830s.

in them & I went away with them'. Eventually he ran off with two of the lads and went to a lodging house. There the landlord agreed to provide him with bed and board for 2s 6d a week, 'provided I brought & sold to him all that I might steal'. There were about thirteen boys in the house, living on the same terms, and the landlord also had an adjoining property, with communicating doors into it. 'The back kitchen is fitted up with trap doors to help escape – and in a corner of one of the back kitchens is a sliding floor underneath' where the loot was hidden. 'A coat is hung up in the kitchen or public room & Boys practise how to pick the pockets, the Men in the House show them how to manage'. Young Samuel himself had about a fortnight's training in pickpocketing before he was allowed to go out with some of the other lads. 'In a short time I went out on my own account, as I soon saw how they did it … the landlord lends money to a Boy of his House if he has been unlucky at tossing … If thieves are unlucky they can always get money – can borrow it any time & are always sure of being able to repay it the next day'.[94]

Miles concluded that with boys of this kind prison sentences and whippings were useless as deterrents. 'It is in prisons that boys form acquaintances more mischievous than themselves. Many lads have owned to me that they learned more in a gaol than out of one.'[95] Yet in the 1830s and 1840s prison was increasingly the destination of large numbers of young offenders, for whom the informal punishments applied in the eighteenth century were no longer considered proper. As Sir Thomas Baring lamented in 1828, whereas formerly the custom had been 'that if a boy of twelve or fourteen years of age committed any petty offence … he was corrected on the spot … now it is impossible to do so; an information would immediately be laid against the person so inflicting summary punishment, and he would be indicted for an assault. But I think, if the Magistrate were to order the Constable in such cases to inflict summary punishment in the way I have mentioned, it would deter from the commission of the offence much more, and would prevent our prisons being filled with juvenile offenders.'[96]

It is the issue of punishment and the way that it was administered to the criminal young that we must now consider. At the same time it is important to remember that many of the anxieties and debates about how best to deal with teenage delinquents in the early twenty-first century, including the role of parents and the influence of peer pressure on the young, were preoccupying our ancestors two hundred years ago. They, too, struggled to find solutions to the social problems they faced.

CHAPTER 2

THE ROLE OF PUBLIC PUNISHMENTS AND IMPRISONMENTS:1700-1830s

Disorder and neglect were the dominant features of the eighteenth-century prison. On entering the jail, one was confronted with the noise and smell of the place. It was seldom easy to distinguish those who belonged in the prison from those who did not. Only the presence of irons differentiated the felons from the visitors or from the debtors and their families ... Eighteenth-century English Justice employed a wide variety of measures to punish crime. For misdemeanours, English courts typically imposed fines or resorted to public and symbolic inflictions such as the pillory or whipping. Offenders were sometimes encouraged to join the military ... The hierarchy of punishments climaxed in the drama of the gallows ...

Randall McGowen, 'The Well-Ordered Prison. England, 1780-1865' in Norval Morris and David J. Rothman ed., *The Oxford History of the Prison* (New York and Oxford, 1995), pp. 79-80.

Public Punishments

Before the 1770s imprisonment was rarely used as a punishment in its own right, either for adults or for children, but especially for the latter.[1] When it was employed it was normally in respect of such misdemeanours as vagrancy, disobedience to a master, leaving service without giving due notice, or for minor thefts and game offences. In such cases its duration was usually brief, although offenders could spend weeks and even months remanded in custody as they awaited trial at the assizes or quarter sessions. Indeed, this pre-trial confinement could exceed the length of the eventual sentence. Of twenty-four juvenile prisoners tried before Hampshire quarter sessions between 1789 and 1795, eighteen were eventually acquitted or had no case to answer when the trial came on. Yet more than half of the twenty-four had been remanded in custody for around two or three months. Only six spent less than a month in prison before the trial.[2] Of the six youngsters who were found guilty, one received a whipping, one was imprisoned for a week and was whipped, one was imprisoned for a month; only three received penalties lasting longer than a month.

Sometimes punishments took the form of a public whipping, while for the more serious offenders, there was transportation. This was first to America, until it was brought to an end by the outbreak of the American War of Independence in 1775. Then, from the later 1780s, it was to Australia. Fines were imposed on a minority of wrongdoers and if these were not paid, offenders might be imprisoned instead. Finally, there were public executions, when a capital sentence was passed. These continued until 1868, when the public aspect was ended. In practice, few juveniles were hanged even in the eighteenth century and fewer still in the nineteenth, although it was not until the 1908 Children Act that it became illegal to execute youngsters under the age of sixteen.[4]

From the early nineteenth century there was an ongoing debate about the interplay of punishment and reform, with some stressing the need for retribution and others for rehabilitation. There were also discussions on what kind of punishment was most likely to prove effective in achieving this latter end. Commentators like Sir Richard Birnie recommended 'a little flogging at a certain age' as desirable, with the young offenders then discharged rather than imprisoned.[5] Many contemporaries agreed with Samuel Hoare's contention that 'the indiscriminate confinement' of a child 'committed for trial on some small offence' was 'the most certain method that can be devised of increasing the number of delinquents. Few that know anything of the interior of a gaol, will expose an ignorant child, for a small offence to its most baneful contamination'.[6] In London in 1816 it was claimed that the Lord Mayor was reluctant to send children to the notorious Newgate gaol if he could find 'anybody that will answer for them, and give them employment ... For it is a bad school'.[7] In these circumstances, as late as 1817 juveniles formed only 6 per cent of total prison inmates, and their limited share in that population was confirmed by individual prisons, like the New Bailey at Salford. There boys and girls aged seventeen and under who had been committed to gaol for a felony comprised just 10.6 per cent of the total in 1809 and 14.8 per cent in 1815.[8]

With the ending of the war with Napoleonic France in the latter year, however, there was a change of attitude towards the prosecution of children and, between 1808 and the 1830s, an easing of the capital code itself. These factors led to a rise in juvenile imprisonment. In 1821, almost a third (32.1 per cent) of the committals for felony at the New Bailey,

Salford, involved youngsters aged seventeen or under. Over the next few years that fell back a little but it remained around 25 per cent even in 1826. In the nation at large by 1847, 18 per cent of the prison population comprised juveniles below seventeen years, and at that date around three quarters of all convicted youngsters were being imprisoned rather than dealt with in any other way.[9]

In the eighteenth century, the approach had been very different. As we saw in the last Chapter, there was at that time a wide use of alternative penalties, with many youngsters caught committing minor illegal acts being dealt with on the spot informally, perhaps by a cuffing or beating rather than being charged before a magistrate. When they did appear before JPs they might be sentenced to a public whipping, perhaps accompanied by a brief prison term. This applied to Andrew White, aged fifteen, charged at the Hampshire quarter sessions in January 1819 with stealing clothes from a house at Fareham in that county. He was imprisoned for six months with hard labour and was also to be publicly whipped in Fareham. Similarly, sixteen-year-old John Garns, appearing before the same quarter sessions for a like offence, was to be imprisoned in Odiham Bridewell (or house of correction) for three months and to be 'publicly whipped on a market day at Odiham for the space of 100 yards'.[10] By the early 1820s, however, public whippings were falling out of favour because it was considered that humiliating offenders in this way reduced their chance of obtaining future employment, thereby driving them back into criminality. Private whipping, by contrast, was used widely to punish boys for years to come, and was generally accepted as an appropriate option.

An alternative penalty for young men, especially during periods of war, was for their impressment into the armed forces, rather than facing other sanctions, such as transportation or imprisonment. In the 1770s the private papers of the anti-slavery campaigner, Granville Sharp, show that when he caught a young London pickpocket trying to steal his handkerchief, he took the lad before the Lord Mayor's court and forced him to enlist in the Royal Navy.[11] But impressment could only be used for boys above the age of twelve and applied to a small minority of young offenders anyway, usually during years when the Royal Navy was short of manpower.

Sometimes victims put pressure on youngsters to enlist without bringing them to court. In 1796 the Suffolk merchant, James Oakes, noted that he had caught a boy named William Penburey stealing cash from him: 'I had for some time suspected him of these petty thefts & by marking Money, wch being mised & found upon him, brot the fact clearly to his charge'. Oakes sent for the lad's mother and his Uncle Prigg, and 'instead of presenting him [before a magistrate] mean, if possible, sending him to Sea'.[13] The ploy seems to have been successful. But where a youngster was guilty of a minor offence unlikely to attract a severe punishment such as transportation, the boy might refuse to co-operate. In 1770, a fourteen-year-old Essex lad who had been accused of stealing rabbits, was 'examined several times during the time he was awaiting trial in the Barking house of Correction so that the "father might send him to sea".' But he firmly resisted all pressure and was eventually sentenced at the next quarter sessions to a whipping. He doubtless felt that his stubborn refusal to enlist had been fully vindicated.[14]

On occasion members of the public took matters into their own hands by physically attacking young wrongdoers. In December 1771, Richard Wyatt, a Surrey magistrate, noted that the Chertsey blacksmith had gone to the farmyard of Edward Tickner and had there picked up a large cart whip, with which he proceeded to flog a ten-year-old labourer employed there. He accused the boy of killing his geese but the beating was so severe that the farmer supported the boy's charge of assault against the blacksmith. As a result the latter was bound over in the sum of £40, with two recognizances at £20 each, to appear at the next quarter sessions. When these began, however, the case was not mentioned, so presumably the parties had reconciled their differences.[15]

Victims might also refer young offenders to others to punish, as the Somerset parson, William Holland did, when he discovered his neighbour's seventeen-year-old son stealing plums from his tree. He told the lad's father about it, so he could administer the required beating. [16]

Volatile urban crowds, too, sometimes exacted their own vengeance on pickpockets and thieves. This might involve ducking them in a pond or throwing stones and dirt at them. Peter King quotes the case of a sixteen-year-old London pickpocket who died after undergoing a 'severe set of duckings in a pond off the Tottenham Court Road' in 1785.[17]

One of the most striking public spectacles associated with the administration of justice during this period was the arrival of judges in an assize town in order to conduct court proceedings. The assizes were held twice a year and in 1820, the French visitor, Cottu, described how the judges were ceremoniously greeted by the sheriff as they approached their destination. 'They enter the town with bells ringing and trumpets playing, preceded by the sheriff's men ... in full dress, armed with javelins', and with a large crowd of spectators watching the impressive ritual.[18]

On occasion, as in Surrey, the assizes were held in relatively small court rooms, with members of the public crammed in, in close proximity not only to the judge and jury but to the accused and the witnesses as well. In these circumstances proceedings could become disorderly and emotional, with hissing and booing greeting unpopular verdicts. For a child charged with a serious offence in such a court, it must have been a bewildering and terrifying experience; some diminutive prisoners were scarcely able to peer over the rim of the dock. This perhaps applied in Dorset in March 1801, when twelve-year-old Peter Burbidge was charged with stealing a quantity of oats and was eventually sentenced by the judge to six calendar months' imprisonment with hard labour, and a fine of 6d.[19] Then there was John Row, aged eleven, charged in July of that year with breaking and entering a mill and bakehouse at Charmouth in Dorset, and stealing loaves of bread, a knife, a wood screw box, 'and a quantity of bad half pence'. He, too, was sentenced to six calendar months in prison with hard labour, and a fine of 6d at the assizes.[20]

Not all young prisoners were intimidated by the formal court ritual. Richard Winders, aged seventeen, was charged at the Epiphany quarter sessions in Gloucestershire in 1818 with stealing a turkey. He had previously served a month in prison for the theft of a pair of leather breeches, and on this second occasion be was sentenced to be transported for seven years. Before he left the dock he turned to the chairman of the bench, smiled and declared defiantly: 'I wish thou mightest be sitting there till I come back and then I'll be with thee again'.[21]

George Lisley, aged fifteen, was a plough boy who had been earning 5s 6d a week when he was convicted at High Wycombe of stealing a whip, valued at 6s. He was sentenced to serve ten days' imprisonment with hard labour in Aylesbury Gaol. He was received in the gaol on 18 October 1871, and the chaplain noted: 'Prisoner has been at work since 9 years. For last year drove plough from 6 a.m. to 2 p.m. and works from 4 a.m. to 4 p.m.' Perhaps the long hours accounted for his drawn face.

A contemporary critic complained of the way in which the 'low rabble' all too often filled the court room, thereby detracting from its solemnity, while a modern historian, John Beattie has commented drily:

> We have perhaps been in some danger of exaggerating the dignity and order of the eighteenth-century courts and perhaps of overemphasising their success as theatre – taking the robes, full-bottom wigs, and black caps as guarantees ... that the solemnity and hushed seriousness the judges would have wanted was in fact always achieved. There is ... a good deal of evidence that the courts were often crowded and noisy.[22]

Children under seven could, of course, not be charged with a felony and therefore could not be tried for a capital offence. Between the ages of seven and fourteen they might be executed, if malicious intent could be proved. But there was, in practice, widespread reluctance to hang young people, even when they were above the age of fourteen. In September 1785 *The Times* reported disapprovingly the execution in Dublin of an 'unfortunate wretch ... in the front of the New Prison'. He 'was not above seventeen years old, a mere slender lad', and to add to the horror of the occasion, through some mismanagement on the scaffold 'he remained ten minutes convulsed in agonies, which is too often the case in this late mode of execution'.[23] Around two and a half years later the same newspaper expressed its approval of a decision by the Recorder at the Old Bailey in London to ensure that a ten-year-old boy who had committed a capital offence by stealing a set of valuable mathematical instruments, escaped any possibility of a death sentence.[24] It praised the Recorder's 'humanity'.

There were, nonetheless, a few cases, especially in the early eighteenth century, when children were executed. Thus in July 1716, Mary Hickes and her eleven-year-old daughter, Elizabeth, were hanged for witchcraft at Huntingdon.[25] Eight years before Michael Hammond, aged eleven, and his seven-year-old sister were executed at Kings Lynn in Norfolk, for an unspecified felony.[26] Elizabeth Marsh was only fifteen when she was hanged in 1794 at Dorchester in Dorset for the murder of her grandfather.[27]

The heart searching to which this use of the death penalty gave rise when children of 'tender' years were involved, was exemplified in 1748 by the case of ten-year-old William York. He was condemned at Bury assizes for the murder of Ann Mayhew, aged five. Both William and Ann were parish children and while their guardians were working in the fields he took the little girl into the farmyard and stabbed her to death, apparently because he disliked her sulky manner and her habit of fouling the bed. He hid the body in a dung heap and then cleaned himself up as well as he could. When the crime was discovered he at first denied any involvement, before eventually breaking down and confessing in tears. It appeared to the court that the boy had had 'malicious' intent and the death sentence was duly pronounced. But his youth led the presiding judge to consult other members of the judiciary as to whether hanging was appropriate in this case. A stay of execution was granted and as the consultation dragged on, there were further reprieves – four in all. Finally, at the summer assizes in 1757, nine years after the original verdict, the now nineteen-year-old youth was given a royal pardon, on condition of his 'entering immediately into the sea service'.[28]

On occasion the hostility displayed by the court room spectators might influence a judge's sentence. After Baron Hotham had capitally convicted a ten-year-old Essex boy in 1800 for stealing notes at Chelmsford post office, on the grounds that he had 'art and contrivance beyond his years', the angry reaction to the verdict led him to reconsider the decision. When the boy appeared before the court he was dressed in a pinafore and looked so much an 'absolute child' that, as the judge told the Home Office, 'the scene was so dreadful, on [my] passing sentence'. Following the expression of public outrage at the verdict he hastily indicated that 'the case [would be] open to the royal clemency'. Eventually the boy was transported to labour in Grenada for fourteen years instead of being hanged.[29]

In the early nineteenth century the death sentence continued to be pronounced on children, with 103 cases identified at the Old Bailey alone in which juveniles were convicted, although none was executed. As a contemporary sourly observed, boys under the age of fourteen sentenced to death in this way and then sent back to Newgate prison to await their punishment were 'treated like all other prisoners of their own age … They and the officers of the prison know that they will not be executed; and the sentence passed on them [is] a mere formal lie'. He claimed, indeed, to know one young prisoner, who, on being given a death sentence, expressed his delight at the verdict because this gave him added prestige in the eyes of his fellow prisoners.[30]

In 1837 William Augustus Miles similarly maintained that boys in Newgate who had been condemned to death, knew that the sentence would not be carried out but nonetheless conducted themselves

> as boys of a superior class to the transport lads. The boy under sentence of transportation for life is of greater consequence than the boy who is sentenced to seven years, while the lad whose sentence is a short imprisonment is not deemed worthy to associate or converse with them: in short, the daring offender is a member of the prison aristocracy … and severity of punishment is by them converted into a scale of merit. The pomp and panoply of justice only gives to these lads a feeling of self-importance: they never [have] any feeling of shame or disgrace[31].

This sense of importance was compounded, in Miles's opinion, when children not in their 'teens' were placed 'behind large iron bars, strong enough to restrain an elephant'. The boy could only conclude that he 'must be a very clever lad to require such barricades, and that society had a great dread of his talents'.[32]

Usually when the death sentence was commuted a period of transportation was substituted. But sometimes when the sentence was respited it was replaced by what seems to be a bizarrely short period of imprisonment, in view of the severity of the original punishment. Thus at the Lent assizes in Dorset in March 1812 Elizabeth Young, aged fifteen, was sentenced to death for breaking and entering the house of a Marnhull widow and stealing a one pound county bank note, some silver coins of the value of five shillings and sixpence each, and a gold coin valued at seven shillings. But within a short time she was reprieved and was instead required to serve just two years in prison, with hard labour. A year later a sixteen-year-old boy was capitally convicted at the Dorset assizes of stealing from 'a small pocket book', after breaking and entering two houses in Whitechurch

Joseph Bellingham, an errand boy, aged fourteen; height 4 ft 9 in. Convicted at Bedfordshire Quarter Sessions in October 1861 for stealing a horse and van in Woolwich and being found with them at Studham in Bedfordshire. Sentenced to fourteen days' hard labour in Bedford County Gaol and four years in Bedfordshire Reformatory.

Canonicorum. Again he was granted a speedy reprieve, but in this case he was required to serve only one year in prison, with hard labour.[33]

Nevertheless on rare occasions juveniles were hanged for their crimes even in the early nineteenth century. That included a boy of fourteen executed at Newport in 1814 for theft.[34] But one of the best-known examples of child executions involved John Any Bird Bell, aged fourteen, who was hanged at Maidstone in 1831 for the murder of another lad, aged thirteen. He and his younger brother had lured their victim into a wood, as the latter was returning home with the family's weekly parish relief payment of 9s. John slit the boy's throat and then the two lads hid the body in the wood. After the crime the elder brother washed his hands and the knife in a pond, and the two then carried on as it nothing had happened. Eventually the body was discovered and the murder was traced to John Bell. During his subsequent trial, according to newspaper accounts, he displayed no emotion, not even when the death sentence was pronounced. Only later, when he returned to his cell, did he break down in tears. According to the *Annual Register* he was 'remarkably short in stature', although thick-set and strongly built, 'with an almost infantine complexion, being ... exceedingly fair'. The jury, in returning their guilty verdict, recommended him to mercy because of his youth and the 'unnatural manner in which he had been brought up', by a family living on the fringes of respectable society. But the judge overrode the recommendation and on the Monday following the trial, John walked stoically to the scaffold, with the chaplain in attendance. After the rope had been placed round his neck he exclaimed in a loud voice, 'Lord have mercy upon us ... All people before me take warning by me'.[35] As was then the custom at public executions, the hanging was witnessed by a large crowd and this kind of expression of repentance intended as a lesson to the onlookers, was part of the expected ritual. Often, such events took on something of the atmosphere of a carnival rather than a solemn judicial procedure. Food was offered for sale, ballad singers hawked pictures of the murderer or sold copies of his 'last confession', and there was a general buzz of excitement and anticipation.

Increasingly, however, such spectacles were condemned as morally repugnant. In the 1840s Charles Dickens was one who called for an end to these events, not out of compassion for the victim but to deny the crowd an opportunity for its 'odious' levity.[36] In 1841 a hanging at Shrewsbury led a contemporary to complain of the merrymaking that accompanied it: 'The country people flocked in their holiday dresses ... The whole town was a scene of drunkenness and debauchery of every kind'.[37] Yet despite these expressions of disapproval it was not until 1868 that public executions were ended.

More than thirty years earlier, Edward Gibbon Wakefield, in evidence
before the Select Committee on Metropolitan Police Offices, claimed that
boys who went with older criminals to witness the 'singing and talking'
and the noisy proceedings which took place before Newgate prison at
public executions, were themselves thereby led into crime. They were
undeterred by the 'putting to death [of] a fellow creature in cold blood and
in public'. Indeed, according to him, it was 'common practice' for young
prisoners within Newgate itself to conduct a mock ceremony 'in derision
of an execution, and sometimes on the very day when an execution had
taken place, one of them playing the part of the sheriff and another the
part of the reverend ordinary [that is, the chaplain], a third the part of the
hangman, and a fourth the part of a culprit, with a rope'. [38]

Paradoxically the existence of England's 'bloody code', with over two
hundred capital offences on the statute book at the beginning of the
nineteenth century, served to discourage certain would-be prosecutors
from pursuing a case in the courts because it might result in the offender
being condemned to death. In following that course they sometimes
received the tacit backing of the magistrates. In 1819, James Jennings told
the Select Committee on Criminal Laws that he had lived near Bridgwater
in Somerset for more than sixteen years and had suffered much pilfering
from his shop. Eventually he caught two girls, one aged fourteen and the
other eleven, stealing some material. According to him, when he brought
them before the quarter sessions there was 'a strong impression in the
bench in favour of the youngest girl, that I should not offer evidence
against her at all. I did not; and although our evidence against the girl of
fourteen was completely full, yet, upon consulting with the bench, I did not
adduce evidence against her, and she was in consequence acquitted'. Public
opinion was such, he declared, that 'except for murder', it was felt that the
law was too severe and, as a consequence, offenders escaped unscathed
and traders suffered very much from 'those depredations'. [39]

Mr Yardley, clerk to the police office in Worship Street, London, likewise
commented on the reluctance to prosecute in capital cases, except for
murder. When larcenies were involved he had often heard prosecutors,
'especially females, say "I hope it is not a hanging matter".' [40] In 1816, a
London magistrate frankly admitted to a parliamentary committee that
when a child was committed for further examination, he and his fellow JPs
did not speak to the prosecutor openly on the matter but found a means of
giving him a hint, 'that if he does not wish to prosecute he may afford us
an opportunity of discharging him, being fully aware that it would be the
ruin of that child'. [41]

In some cases the friends and relatives of a convicted prisoner might
petition the judiciary and the Home Office for a pardon, or a reduction

in sentence. This power to bestow or withhold clemency pleased those in authority since it demonstrated their power and influence, and their ability to impose an exemplary punishment should it be their wish to deter other potential wrongdoers. When petitions were organised on behalf of juveniles it was common to draw attention to their youth as a mitigating factor, and also the fact that they had allegedly been led astray by 'bad company' or older companions. Another favourable point might be if the youngster concerned could show that someone of good character was prepared to take him or her into service. This applied in 1786 to William Smart, who was recommended by the judge for a pardon not only because he was 'a very young boy' but because a 'man of character' was willing to take him as an apprentice. [42] The judge himself occasionally took the initiative, too, in recommending a young offender for a pardon. This happened in the case of twelve-year-old Thomas Evans. He was tried at the Salisbury assizes early in 1788 on a charge of stealing a canvas bag containing twelve guineas. The seriousness of the charge was reduced to larceny only, but since the trial the judge had

> received various testimonials of his Parents' character, and honesty, and that it was the boy's first offence, that he was seduced from his home, by a Man with a puppet show, going to a fair, where the theft was committed.

Young Thomas had been in prison for six months when the judge wrote his letter recommending clemency, and he clearly considered this had been sufficient punishment.[43]

Sometimes petitions were backed by respected members of the offender's community, who claimed to have known him or her for years and to attest that he or she had always borne a good character. That was the case with young Samuel Cole of Manningtree in Essex, found guilty at Chelmsford assizes in March 1787 of stealing eight guineas from a local miller. A petition on his behalf was signed by twenty-two local people, including the rector of Manningtree, who had been one of the justices committing the boy for trial. It was stated that not only was he very young, being but thirteen years of age, and hitherto a lad of good character, but he had the offer of an apprenticeship for seven years to a 'Gentleman'. This proved to be a local mariner, who agreed to take him should he be pardoned. During his confinement in prison he had shown remorse and 'a fixed determination should he again be admitted into society, to behave himself as a good and worthy member thereof'. The judge's report suggests that it was the opportunity to make a fresh start by way of an apprenticeship to a respectable occupation that turned the decision in Samuel's favour.[44]

As we shall see in Chapter 3, these petitions became increasingly urgent and emotional when the youngster concerned was sentenced to be transported to Australia, with petitioners stressing their despair at being unlikely ever to see the prisoner again, even if the banishment were limited to a period of seven years.

However, many thousands of offenders did not have the benefit of petitions being organised on their behalf. Instead they had to accept the punishment dispensed to them in court. Only in the case of the death penalty was a reprieve likely to be forthcoming for a child criminal through the customary judicial machinery.

The Role of Imprisonment

The ending of transportation to America in the mid-1770s, and the consequent build up of prisoner numbers, profoundly influenced attitudes towards the use of imprisonment as a judicial instrument. Initially its large-scale adoption was seen as a temporary expedient until transportation could be resumed, but soon it came to be seen as having merits in its own right. Among these was its flexibility, which enabled a penalty to be adjusted in length and severity according to the nature of the crime or the character of the offender and his or her previous record of convictions, or whether anyone of repute would speak in his or her favour, at a time when the exercise of patronage was of major importance.[45] However, that had the disadvantage of creating wide variations in the punishments imposed, according to the views of individual judges or benches of magistrates. It could also mean that penalties of markedly different severity were imposed by the courts for similar – and, in some cases, the same – crime. One such example occurred in Kent in 1825, when William Powell, aged thirteen, and James Francis, aged twelve, were tried jointly at West Kent Summer sessions with stealing four weights, valued at 3s, from a shop in Deptford. The boys had subsequently sold them for 5d to a marine store dealer. Both were found guilty yet while Powell was sentenced to seven years' transportation for the theft, Francis was given just one month's imprisonment with hard labour in the house of correction, plus a whipping.[46]

In other cases, too, punishments seemed disproportionately severe, as in the case of Ann Braker, aged thirteen, who was sentenced to six months' hard labour at the Dorset Epiphany quarter sessions in 1810, for stealing 'a chop of pork', while the same quarter sessions in January 1806 sentenced a twelve-year-old boy and his seven-year-old brother to hard labour for two calendar months each for stealing 'a quantity of faggot wood'.[47] Elsewhere brief prison terms only were imposed, far too short to bring about the

Joseph Lewis, No. 5248, aged eleven from Rotherhithe. Sentenced in 1873 to one calendar month's imprisonment for stealing 28 lbs of iron, valued at 3s. His sentence was served in Wandsworth Prison in London.

prisoner's 'reform' or to achieve anything beyond habituating him or her to the vagaries of the custodial system.

As prison conditions improved in the nineteenth century a term in gaol came to be seen by some homeless youngsters as offering a welcome break from the harsh conditions of life on the streets. This was particularly true of those without parents or who had lost touch with their families. In the 1830s William Augustus Miles recorded the perhaps apocryphal story of a sixteen-year-old chimney sweep who was without either shoes or stockings when he was sent to prison for a trifling offence.

> The warm bath into which he was put much delighted him, but nothing could exceed his astonishment on being told to put on shoes and stockings. 'And am I to wear them? and this?...' he said as each article of dress was given to him. His joy was complete when they took him to his cell, he turned down the bedclothes with great delight, and half doubting his good fortune, hesitatingly asked if he was really to sleep in the bed![48]

Subsequently he told the governor that with such conditions he would be 'd--d if I ever do another stroke of work!' According to Miles, he kept his word and 'was ultimately transported'.

Around the same time a London magistrate recounted the case of Thomas M'Nelly, aged fourteen. Thomas was an orphan and without a settled home, so whenever he left the house of correction, it was 'natural to suppose that he must go to thieving again'. His recorded criminal career began on 15 April, 1836, when he was sentenced to seven days' imprisonment for breaking several panes of glass in a church window. On 30 April he was charged with sleeping in the open air, thereby falling foul of the vagrancy laws, and on this occasion he was discharged. On 29 May he stole 14 lbs of coal from a barge and received a month's imprisonment. On 6 July, a few days after leaving prison he was sentenced to three months' imprisonment for stealing a bag containing brushes and other articles. Further offences followed over the succeeding months and fresh terms of imprisonment were served. In all from 15 April 1836 to 29 April 1837, Thomas was charged eight times with sundry offences, and for six out of the eight was imprisoned for varying periods. In total these amounted to almost nine months and, as the magistrate drily commented, in his case there was clear 'practical proof' that prison had 'worked no reformation in that boy; in all probability it had done the contrary'.[49]

For most of the eighteenth century prisons had a grim reputation as unhealthy and morally bankrupt institutions likely to encourage future wrongdoing even among relatively innocent inmates because of the indiscriminate manner in which young and old, persistent offenders and those entering prison for the first time were mixed together. William Smith, a London medical man, made clear his concern in 1776 when he discussed conditions in the capital's prisons:

> To suffer children to remain in gaol is very impolitic for many reasons; ... it not only corrupts their morals, but injures their health, stops their growth, hurts their looks, and endangers their lives ... In gaol they serve a regular apprenticeship, and finish their education at Newgate ... little thieves are there taught to become proficients in vice ... Parents sometimes suffer an extravagant son to be some time confined in gaol, in order to reclaim him. This is a very dangerous and erroneous practice. Satan will rebuke sin when reformation is brought about in a gaol.[50]

John Howard, in his seminal work, *The State of the Prisons*, first published in 1777, agreed with Smith's gloomy comments and drew attention to other evils as well. He pointed out that in many bridewells or houses of correction, prisoners were kept short of food and were without proper bedding. Even the straw on which they lay was rarely changed, being kept until it was filthy and reduced almost to dust. Some inmates lay upon rags and others upon the bare floors. There were fatal outbreaks of gaol fever, with more prisoners dying from this cause than by public execution. Many, especially in the leading London prison, Newgate, had nothing but rags to wear and when

Howard visited there in 1779 he claimed there were several boys of twelve or fourteen years of age on the men's side of the prison 'almost naked'.[51]

Bridewells were supposed to provide employment for prisoners as part of their sentence and to aid their rehabilitation, but according to Howard this was rarely done. 'The prisoners have neither tools nor materials of any kind; but spend their time in sloth, profaneness and debauchery'.[52] Some prisons required inmates to wear chains, since this was a cheap way of preventing them from escaping, and that included children. At Bristol gaol in 1815, John Harford described how he had seen

> the irons put on a little boy only ten years old, who had just been brought into Prison for stealing a pound and a half of sugar ... As soon as the irons were put on this little fellow, he was introduced into the Felons' court, which was crowded with a set of wretches, several of whom are said to be among the most abandoned of the class of Felons. Sad to say, there were four other young lads, mingled in the crowd.[53]

Three years later another visitor to that prison reported caustically that there were then eleven children confined, 'hardly old enough to be released from the nursery – hardly competent to understand the principles of moral obligation'. All convicted felons or those charged with felony were 'in heavy irons – almost all were in rags – almost all were filthy in the extreme – almost all exhibited the appearance of ill health.'[54]

In a few places individual initiatives were put in hand to achieve reform and to ameliorate the conditions experienced by young offenders. At Warwick gaol, Esther Tatnall, wife of the governor, early in the nineteenth century set up a school for child inmates of both sexes, where they learnt to read, recite the catechism, and to acquire skill in needlework in the case of the girls. To occupy the time not devoted to schooling it was arranged that the boys would be employed in pinmaking. According to Mrs Tatnall, these efforts led to a high proportion of the youngsters being 'permanently reformed,' so that many years later they were 'getting an honest livelihood in trade or service'.[55]

In the late eighteenth century the gaols themselves varied widely, ranging from dungeons in medieval castles to 'in small market towns ... little more than strong rooms above a shop or an inn'.[56] The largest institutions were in London, which in 1776 contained over a quarter of the total prison population of England and Wales. Newgate was the biggest of them all. In the early nineteenth century it had accommodation for around 427 prisoners of all ages, but on occasion, when prisoners were brought in from elsewhere shortly before the opening of an Old Bailey sessions, numbers could soar to double that number and even more.[57]

Newgate was a warren of dark, damp wards, yards, privies and staircases, a place that one historian has described as 'synonymous with misery, despair, wickedness and death'.[58] Visitors and relatives were allowed to come and go to see the prisoners and to bring them food. Among them were prostitutes, posing as relatives. Drunkenness and gambling were endemic and a critic claimed that so lax was the discipline that 'burglaries and robberies were plotted ... notes were forged and coining ... carried on within its gloomy walls'.[59] There was a strong inmate sub-culture, and widespread bullying and corruption. That included the practice of 'garnish', by which an incoming prisoner was required to hand over a sum of money for the use of his fellows, to be spent on drink, food or fuel. Any prisoner unable, or unwilling, to pay would be beaten up or attacked by the rest, and perhaps have his clothes stolen from off his back.[60]

In August 1814 a 'school' was opened at Newgate for the youngest boys, to separate them from the older men and youths, and with an adult prisoner acting as schoolmaster. But the segregation was incomplete. Years later some boys were still found in the men's wards and the girls were, in any case, housed with the adult women.[61] Furthermore, among the boys themselves there was 'bullying and extortion, with the more experienced or the more violent intimidating the weaker lads. The failure to recognise that it was not only adults who threatened the wellbeing of less robust youngsters but those in their own age group as well, was to undermine the value of any application of prisoner classification based on age alone.

In the mid-1830s the annual report of the first prison inspectors drew attention to these faults and the way in which within the Newgate 'school'

> Boys committed for their first offence, and those whose guilt is doubtful, have no means of avoiding the society of hardened and atrocious offenders. There is no restraint on conversation ... Instruction is given in reading, during part of the day; but, except at these intervals, there is no kind of employment, and the nature of the confinement is calculated altogether to counteract any benefit which might, under other circumstances, be derived from the School.[62]

Around a decade earlier the Newgate ordinary, or chaplain, had also complained about the generally poor provision made for younger prisoners, as on 8 November 1823, when he noted 'two boys in a very ragged & dirty condition, without shoes, stockings or shirts, which I represented to the Keeper, who gave the necessary orders'. Two days later he commented on the 'very offensive' condition of the water closets at the boys' school. They had been out of order for weeks.[63] On 18 December 1824, he was shocked to discover that the inmates of the school included 'an infant of eight years of age committed, with another of ten, for stealing pots! Surely such a proceeding could never have been contemplated by the legislation'. Later he visited the women's side and found there a 'female infant committed with the above for the same offence. There are at this moment, in the Prison, two female children of very tender years under sentence of death, in the women's condemned cell, & this one, for trial – and these facts are recorded in the year 1824 in the Metropolis of England'.[64] A week later, on visiting the boys' school he discovered that the eight-year-old was 'still without stockings'.

Despite some modest reforms, Newgate remained a depressing and unsatisfactory institution even in the middle of the nineteenth century. [65]

Elsewhere reformers were beginning to act to tackle the problem of the 'contamination' of one prisoner by another. One way this was done was by the classification of inmates but, as at Reading Bridewell in the 1790s, the categories chosen were often too broad. Although there were divisions on gender lines, no distinction was made on grounds of age, though they did distinguish between those accused of felony or of misdemeanours and those convicted of these offences. [66] Gaming was forbidden, no alcoholic drinks were to be consumed, the levying of 'garnish' was prohibited, and all those convicted were to wear a prison uniform made up of two different colours 'for the better detection of the Prisoners in case of escape'.[67] Hygiene matters were attended to by demanding that inmates 'wash their hands, face and feet, when required so to do by the Governor or Keeper,' and that they 'bathe as often as directed by the Surgeon or Apothecary'.[68]

How far these rules were implemented is difficult to assess. Certainly in late eighteenth-century Lancaster prison, rules calling for the provision of cheap and useful uniforms, 'so contrived as to prevent escapes', had still not been put into effect twenty-six years later, in 1812. At Lancaster a particular source of trouble among the inmates was said to be provided by the boys, who exchanged some of their bread with older male prisoners in return for receiving protection from the other convicts. But, as the head turnkey complained in 1843, that meant that these 'protectors' sided with the boys even when they behaved badly, while according to one prisoner, the men induced 'the boys to commit faults'. Another prisoner had asked to be put in solitary confinement because he was ruptured 'and the boys are always jeering ... about it'.[69]

On a national basis as early as the 1770s pressure from reformers had brought about changes in two aspects of prison administration, namely those relating to religion and to health. In 1773 magistrates were authorised to appoint paid chaplains to gaols and a year later surgeons, too, could be chosen to attend to the prisoners. More attention was also given to the punishment process itself, with the use of solitary confinement suggested as one means of avoiding 'contamination' and bringing about prisoner repentance. In 1776 Jonas Hanway examined this question in his *Solitude in Imprisonment*, in which he emphasised that rehabilitation, especially of the young, needed to be achieved through religious conversion. For this to succeed solitary confinement was an essential element, by enabling the young prisoner to contemplate his moral shortcomings and to benefit from visits by the chaplain.[70]

Initially these ideas were taken up locally on an *ad hoc* basis. Thus at Horsham in Sussex in 1775, each prisoner was provided with a separate cell equipped with a bed and blankets, and with much attention paid to hygiene and religious instruction.[71] At Gloucester prison, too, a policy of 'unremitting solitude' and strict discipline was implemented. In 1828, Thomas Cunningham, keeper of Gloucester gaol for around thirty-seven years, noted that all prisoners sentenced to a month's imprisonment were kept in solitude, on a bread and water diet. He often had boys confined in the gaol for a month, and they were treated in this way. He also favoured their being whipped as part of their punishment.[72]

In London in 1794, Coldbath Fields house of correction was set up along similar lines to Gloucester. However, the penitentiary discipline proposed soon broke down, partly because of the corruption of the first governor but also because the prison rapidly became overcrowded. Within three years all attempt to introduce solitary confinement had to be abandoned.[73]

The passage of the 1779 Penitentiary Act was partly a response to this new mood but it was encouraged by the effects of the suspension of transportation. Its aim was the setting up of prisons with single cells, where the inmates would be kept at hard labour. The penal servitude thus served would be a substitute for the term of transportation to which they had been sentenced, and the act envisaged a tariff to cover this. Thus if a prisoner had been sentenced to seven years' transportation he or she might serve up to five years in a penitentiary instead; those sentenced to be transported for fourteen years, were to serve 'not less than two years, nor exceeding seven years' in lieu. Prisoners pardoned from a capital offence could also be sent, and the hard labour envisaged involved such tasks as helping to clean up the Thames.[74]

The cost of the proposed building programme, however, and the pressure of prisoner numbers meant that little was done to introduce the penitentiary principle in the eighteenth century. Not until the construction of Millbank, between 1812 and 1821 was a national prison along these lines established. This envisaged the accommodation of around one thousand two hundred convicts of all ages, accommodated in six pentagonal ranges, which converged on the chapel as the centre of the whole complex. Each prisoner had his own cell, where he slept and worked. Reading material was confined to religious texts. However, it proved impossible to impose cellular isolation in full measure because a small amount of communal work was carried out, and the need for exercise also prevented the achievement of complete separation. Furthermore, 'increasing insanity among the prisoners' necessitated some modification to this attempt at total isolation.[75] It was found difficult to implement the hard labour aspect of the punishment, too, before the introduction of the tread wheel, which was invented by Cubitt in 1818. Oakum picking, that is the pulling to pieces of old tarry ropes for use in caulking wooden ships or to be re-used as new ropes, was one early option. But its adoption was dismissed by critics like Samuel Hoare, as 'a mere apology for idleness'. The tread wheel, by contrast, comprised a series of steps on a giant wheel which was propelled by the prisoners' own climbing motion. It deprived convicts of all independence in regulating their labour and by 1824 it had been adopted in some fifty-four prisons.[76]

Initially officials greeted the tread wheels with enthusiasm, claiming prisoners disliked them so much that they were staying away from crime as a result. That was soon seen to be erroneous, as prisoner numbers continued to mount, and in the meantime concern was expressed by reformers about their suitability as a punishment for younger prisoners and women. In 1843 the Prison Inspectors' General Survey concluded that it was 'an improper punishment for females and boys under fourteen years of age'. But, as Jeannie Duckworth comments, no mention was made 'of boys not working other forms of hard labour.' Up to 1865 these included 'the crank, capstan and stone crushing. The crank was a wheel with a counting device fitted into a box of gravel which the prisoner had to turn by handle for a given number of rotations; it was [a] useless activity which did nothing but move gravel in a box'.[77] In certain prisons gaolers developed a system whereby a convict, either juvenile or adult, was only allowed to eat or drink when he had completed a certain number of revolutions on the crank. In at least one case this led to the suicide of a fifteen-year-old boy who had been repeatedly denied food for failing to achieve his target, and for his general resistance to the punishment. [78]

When young people underwent solitary confinement it was sometimes restricted to a brief period only, perhaps as part of a longer sentence. At the Epiphany quarter sessions in Hampshire in January 1819, for example, Ann Harding, aged fourteen, who had stolen laundry from a washerwoman, was sentenced to a month's imprisonment, the last week of which was to be in solitary confinement. Presumably this was to enable her to contemplate her past wrongdoing without any distractions. [79] Similarly in July 1829 at the Berkshire sessions, John Whittick, aged fifteen, who had stolen a punt pole, a halser cord, some stockings and a silk handkerchief, was sentenced to two months imprisonment with hard labour and like Ann Harding, his last week was to be spent in a solitary cell.[80]

But when the solitary system was introduced at Wakefield gaol it soon had to be discontinued for juveniles because it apparently caused 'debility and contraction of the joints; premonitory symptoms of sluggishness and feeble-mindedness appeared and there was evident danger to their minds'.[81]

Nonetheless, solitary confinement continued to have its supporters as a means of achieving the reform of young prisoners. Or as Samuel Hoare, chairman of the committee of the Prison Discipline Society, put it in 1828: 'Being a long time locked up in solitude during the night would have the happiest effect'.[82] The Prison Inspectors, too, gave cautious support to the concept, considering it 'preferable to the mischievous association which prevails in ordinary prisons ... for very short periods ... we know of no other kind of discipline that is calculated to produce any beneficial impression upon either young or old'. But they emphasised that for 'protracted periods ... a plan of individual separation' was 'wholly inapplicable to the feelings, habits and character of young persons'.[83]

Elsewhere, as at Coldbath Fields and the Westminster house of correction at Tothill Fields, prisoner numbers and a shortage of solitary cells led to the adoption of the 'silent system', with prisoners forbidden to communicate with one another, under a regime of severe discipline and strict surveillance. Yet, despite the stringency of these arrangements, covert communication between prisoners working together or employed on the tread wheel, did take place. The Prison Inspectors dismissed the silent system as a 'defective and objectionable policy' and as imposing 'unnatural restraint on the elasticity of youth. It presents a constant temptation to disobedience, while the frequency of punishment necessarily excites resentment. It ... keeps alive a feeling of irritation, instead of encouraging that resignation to the sentence of the law, which is the first step towards amendment.[84] Despite the criticisms, it was nonetheless retained at both of these prisons, and at others, for some years to come.

Young Samuel Holmes from Stepney confirmed that prisoners could engage in clandestine communication with one another. In the mid-1830s he confessed to having been in prison four times, three of them in the house of correction at Coldbath Fields and once at Ilford. He preferred Ilford 'because they are under less restraint – they steal one another's bread'. The house of correction was 'stricter, but they do talk to each other, altho' it is not allowed – they tell each other what they have done and what they will do'.[85] George Hickman, from Clerkenwell had served nine prison terms during his sixteen years, four of them at Coldbath Fields, twice

BOYS EXERCISING AT TOTHILL FIELDS PRISON.

Boys exercising at Tothill Fields Prison in London, *c*.1860.

in the New Prison, Clerkenwell, once at Brixton and twice in Newgate, which he preferred 'in every respect except sleeping because they can see their friends, can play, talk and do as they like'.[86] Another sixteen-year-old named Thompson, who had been in prison twice before, preferred Tothill Fields house of correction to Coldbath Fields 'because the food is better and the work is less'.[87]

On a wider front, however, reforms were being introduced, notably by the 1823 Gaols Act and its successors, which introduced a national system of classification into prisons and required educational facilities and religious instruction to be provided. No prisoner was to be put in irons by the keeper of any prison 'except in case of urgent and absolute necessity', as the Act put it, and the particulars of this were to be entered in the keeper's journal. Gaming, the system of garnish, and the consumption of alcohol were all forbidden, while a 'competent Number' of cells for solitary confinement were to be supplied 'for the Punishment of refractory prisoners, or for those sentenced to a term in solitude'.[88]

Demands were also made for the establishment of a separate prison for juveniles only. These were initially put forward in 1828 but a further decade elapsed before the plan was put into operation with the establishment of Parkhurst on the Isle of Wight. At first the emphasis was placed on its 'reformatory' role, but there was a belief that severe discipline was needed to achieve this. As the Prison Inspectors declared in 1837, such an institution should be 'in every sense of the word, a prison'.[89] A year later they returned to the subject, stating firmly,

> An institution for criminal boys which has no penal aspect, but in which they are comfortably fed and clothed, and subjected to but little, if any corrective discipline, holds out the strongest inducements to indigent parents to abandon their children, and instigate them to commit crimes for the sake of placing them in such an establishment.

Parkhurst was intended to accommodate about 320 boys, of whom two hundred would be aged twelve and above and 120 under that age. Instruction was provided in moral and religious duties and in 'industrious occupations of various descriptions', such as tailoring, shoemaking, ropemaking, and carpentry, as well as agricultural labour. Eighty acres of land were attached to the prison, and the boys were to cultivate these, with the aim of fitting them 'to emigrate to a distant colony at the expiration of their imprisonment'.[90]

In 1839, the Inspectors defined Parkhurst's objective as to bring about the 'penal correction of the boy with a view to … deter, not himself only, but juvenile offenders generally, from the commission of crime' and to achieve the 'moral reformation of the culprit.' Nothing should be done 'to weaken the terrors of the law, or to lessen in the minds of the juvenile population at large (or their parents) the dread of being committed to a prison'.[91]

Between 26 December 1838 and 23 May 1839, 102 prisoners were received at the new prison from a variety of other penal institutions. They ranged in age from seventeen to eight, with thirty-eight of them under twelve years. Most had been sentenced to transportation, with only eight sentenced to be imprisoned in Britain itself. After they had served a term at Parkhurst it was intended they would be sent overseas, so that they could make a fresh start. Unlike the ordinary transportees, they would not be sent to a penal colony, and in the early days New Zealand proved a favoured destination. [92] Parkhurst's role in the settlement of youngsters overseas, and its eventual failure to achieve the reforms intended will be discussed in the next Chapter, when the issues of transportation and the compulsory emigration of young offenders are examined.

In the prison's early days the severe discipline imposed included requiring the young inmates to wear a leg iron as well as a distinctively marked uniform. Their diet was 'reduced to its minimum'. Silence was to be enforced 'on all occasions of instruction and duty and an uninterrupted surveillance by officers' was to take place. By February 1839, however, the Home Office instructed the governor that the leg irons could be removed for good conduct, and in September 1840 they were abolished for all the prisoners.[93]

Despite the restrictions – or because of them – a number of boys attempted to abscond each year, and the numbers sent to the Refractory Ward grew. 'In spite of solitary confinement, bread and water, extra drill and whipping,' writes Julius Carlebach, 'some boys proved too tough to handle and were either transported as convicts or returned to ordinary prisons'.[94] They included William Howard, who was aged fourteen when he arrived at Parkhurst in December 1838. He had been charged with larceny from the person and had already been imprisoned on five previous occasions. He was a mask maker by trade, but had been sentenced to ten years' transportation before coming to the Isle of Wight. Less than three months later he was 'Removed ... by order of the Secretary of State' for attempting to escape and was returned to his previous place of confinement. Then there was John Maguire, aged thirteen, found guilty of 'stealing from the person' at Manchester in January 1838. He was described as a 'Factory boy' and was sentenced to seven years' transportation. He had been imprisoned once before. But his stay at Parkhurst was brief. After arriving on 28 December, 1838, he was removed the following 19 February as 'Incorrigible'.[95]

Over the years discipline problems continued and in 1849 the prison received much criticism in the press when thirty-four of the boys attempted to escape while working on the land outside the prison walls. To allay public anxiety, a small military guard was temporarily provided to check such escapes. The following year, five boys set fire to a ward dormitory, thereby destroying 158 cells, and later in that same year some younger boys attempted to set fire to their quarters, this time without success.[96]

These difficulties were compounded by the adverse comments of prison reformers, who disliked the *state's* involvement in what was, at least initially, classed as a reformatory institution. By the mid-nineteenth century voluntary reformatories were springing up all over the country, and the boys being sent to Parkhurst at that time were described as 'almost all of the worst character, the reformatory establishments ... receiving the better class'. By the early 1860s the number of youngsters being sent to the prison was declining, and in April 1864 its juvenile section was closed, with the last seventy-eight inmates escorted to Dartmoor.[97]

At the end of the 1830s, therefore, there was still no clear strategy in gaol administration to deal with juvenile offenders. There were prisons

Two Victorian
child prisoners
with a prison
warder.

like Newgate, where there continued to be a mixture of inmates, despite
attempts at reform; there was a specialist institution like Parkhurst which
catered for children and young people only; and there were other prisons
where a policy of solitary confinement was applied. In others again, such
as Coldbath Fields and Tothill Fields, the 'silent' system was adopted as a
means of preventing prisoner 'contamination'. Many children were sent
to prison for very short periods only, thereby achieving little more than
giving them the stigma of having been sent to gaol. These were all matters
with which the mid-century advocates of voluntary reformatories were to
grapple.

The Hulks

The pressures created by the ending of transportation to America in the mid-1770s not only led to overcrowded gaols and houses of correction and, indeed, to a changing attitude towards imprisonment itself as an instrument of punishment, but, encouraged the development of alternative kinds of custodial institutions. These included plans, from the late 1770s, to build penitentiaries and, from 1776, the introduction of a new type of prison – the hulks. These were created by converting old naval vessels that were no longer seaworthy. The initiative was intended as a short-term measure to accommodate some of the prisoners still being sentenced by the courts to transportation, until they could be sent overseas. Even when transportation revived in the late 1780s, however, prisoner numbers continued to mount, so that what had been conceived as a temporary expedient was destined to survive, at least in an attenuated form, until the 1850s.[98]

Prisoners sent to the hulks were required to perform 'hard labour', such as cleaning and banking the river Thames and working in the naval dockyards or other military installations. They were moored in the Thames estuary and at Chatham, Sheerness and Portsmouth. The first, the *Justitia*, was anchored at Woolwich in 1776. However, the harsh, damp and insanitary conditions in which the convicts were kept, coupled with an insufficient diet, infestations of vermin, and the onset of disease, led to high mortality. From August 1776, when the convicts first went on board the *Justitia*, until 26 March, 1778, 166 of the first 632 prisoners died. [99] A public inquiry followed and led to some improvements, but criticisms of the overcrowded, unhealthy and violent conditions on board the hulks persisted throughout their history. As Sidney and Beatrice Webb wrote in 1922: 'Of all the places of confinement that British history records, the hulks were apparently the most brutalising, the most demoralising and the most horrible'.[100]

Meanwhile the number of hulks increased, together with their convict population, this latter rising from 526 in 1779 to 1,931 in 1783.[101] In 1815 when there were five hulks in use, based at Woolwich and Sheerness plus three in or near Portsmouth harbour, the number of prisoners on board had risen to 2,038. By 1828, these totals had risen further, to ten hulks and 4,446 convicts on board them in England alone.[102]

From the start, juveniles sentenced to transportation formed a small proportion of the prisoners confined on board. In 1788, when John Howard visited the *Lion* hulk at Portsmouth he found several boys among the 273 convicts, some of them only ten years old. In 1815, out of 2,038 convicts on the hulks, 112 were said to be under twenty, with twenty-one of those below the age of seventeen.[103]

At first no special provision was made for them, so they were mixed up with the adult males. Apart from the time the prisoners spent on shore at 'hard labour' little supervision was exercised by the officers over their daily activities. As Radzinowicz and Hood point out, 'The Sunday service was the only form of "instruction". At night and for 16 hours of a winter's day, convicts of all ages and descriptions were confined in the lower decks. No officer dared enter there, though it was well known that prisoners passed their leisure in 'gambling, drinking and ... "abominable practices"' by which was meant physical and sexual abuse.[104] According to one former hulk inmate, interviewed in the 1830s, the prisoners spent their time below decks, singing, dancing, smoking and talking. When asked if the youngest boys were separated from the men, he stated that they were not: 'There are some boys 12 and 13 with the men, sleep in the same place ... They live with the men, drink tea and sleep all in one place'.[105]

When they first came on board the hulks it was customary to shackle them, so as to prevent absconding. In 1816 instructions issued to John Henry Capper, the recently appointed superintendent of the hulks, laid down: 'No convict is to be allowed to go about the hulk without an iron upon one or both lege'.[106] In practice, these precautions failed to prevent escape attempts and some of these were successful. Thus in December 1785, George Dunstan, then aged about thirteen, was found guilty of breaking into a hosier's shop and stealing several pairs of stockings, valued at over £4. Initially he was sentenced to death but, on account of his age, this was commuted to seven years' transportation, and in October 1787, he was sent from Newgate to the Thames hulk *Stanislaus*, where he was set to work on shore at Woolwich. On 28 November he absconded and remained at large for about six months, living with his family in London, until he was recognised in the street by a constable who had earlier escorted him to the hulk. In May 1788 he was again tried at the Old Bailey and was once more sentenced to death. Not until September 1789 was he reprieved and a sentence of transportation for life substituted. Around two months later he was sent from Newgate gaol to the *Scarborough* transport, for his journey to New South Wales.[107]

Even when being taken to the hulks it was common for the prisoners to be put in irons. In 1819 the Hon. Henry Grey Bennet, a Member of Parliament and a penal reformer, complained to the Home Secretary about the way in which they travelled from the prisons where they had been confined. Some were

> chained on the tops of coaches; others, as from London, travel in an open caravan, exposed to the inclemency of the weather, the gaze of the idle and the taunts and mockeries of the cruel ... Men and boys, children

just emerging from infancy, as young in vice as in years, are fettered together, and … paraded through the kingdom … Some years back I saw … a considerable number of convicts who were on the road to the hulks. Among them were several children all heavily fettered, ragged and sickly, and carrying in their countenance proofs of the miseries they had undergone.[108]

Bennet also condemned the practice of double ironing the prisoners when they first reached the hulks. 'Upon what principle double irons are used I was unable to discover; it could not be for security; for one of the convicts so fettered was a very little boy 13 years of age … There is here no classification that can be so called … [The] young and the old, the boys and the men … are all associated together.' When he boarded the *Leviathan* at Portsmouth in December 1817 he found around five hundred convicts present, of whom thirty-five were under twenty years of age, the youngest being a boy of thirteen. He came from Bristol, had been convicted of grand larceny in 1812, when he was about eight years old, and was sentenced to seven years' transportation.[109]

By this time, however, there were moves to bring about reform. Already in 1816 the superintendent of the hulks, John Capper, favoured having a separate vessel for juvenile prisoners.[110] Two years later the Revd Thomas Price, chaplain of the hulk *Retribution* also recommended the allocation of a juvenile vessel to cater for youngsters from the various penal institutions. With 'proper overlookers (and everything would depend upon the choice of such persons), many of these poor children might be reclaimed. Let one part of the ship be allotted for their habitation, and other parts of the ship be appropriated for schools and places of instruction in different branches of trade … let it be remembered that they are at present children, and so situated as to claim our sympathetic concern'.[111] By this time some rudimentary schooling was being provided on many hulks, with one of the prisoners acting as instructor, and a degree of separation had been achieved on certain of them. Thus by 1818 Henry Grey Bennet reported that boys on board the *Leviathan* were now being accommodated away from the men and were learning trades. They did not go ashore to work as the men did. Similarly on the *Bellerophon*, with 474 prisoners on board, the boys aged fifteen and under were separated from the adults, in four wards in the middle deck, close to the chapel, which was itself also being used for a school. They were being trained in shoemaking, tailoring and the like. They, too, were not allowed on shore, but followed their trades on the hulk – something which must have reinforced their sense of isolation from the outside world. There were fifty-two boys on board at the time of Bennet's visit, twenty-seven of them under sentence of transportation for life.[112]

Not until 1823, however, was a hulk specifically allocated to juvenile prisoners. This was the *Bellerophon*, moored at Sheerness. Initially over three hundred boys were sent to it, all under the age of fifteen. They were engaged in making clothing, shoes and other articles for the convicts on the other hulks, and during 1825 alone they were said to have produced 'upwards of 6,000 pairs of shoes; 15,500 garments, and various articles of cooperage and bedding'. They were accommodated in forty separate housing bays in the underdecks, each of which held eight or ten inmates. There were also central corridors patrolled by the guards assigned to below-decks duty at night. According to the chaplain, although the boys made good progress in their trade training, the situation was less satisfactory as regards their character reform. 'Their propensity to lying is … I am sorry to say, such, that scarce any confidence can be placed in anything they say'.[113] He emphasised the importance of religious instruction, in the hope that this would induce repentance. To that end he noted that 144 of the three hundred and fifty boys on board in early July 1824 could repeat the Church Catechism … During Divine service, owing to a very strict vigilance kept up they conduct themselves very well'.

The poor condition of the *Bellerophon*, with its damp, rotting timbers, meant that it served as a juvenile hulk for only about two years. In 1825 a much smaller vessel, the *Euryalus* was converted for juvenile use. Unfortunately from the beginning it was overcrowded, with no system of classifying the prisoners, and this, combined with a regime of harsh discipline, inadequate diet, monotonous work, and bullying, led to unrest and even mutinies among the young inmates. The chaplain, Thomas Price, a conscientious man, nonetheless reported wryly that when he entered on this new duty, 'it was represented to me, that … such was the depravity of the Boys, that every attempt to moralise them would only terminate in disappointment. I find much reason for the remark'. By 1827 John Capper himself was admitting that during the previous year the boys had 'upon two or three occasions, been refractory, and committed outrages on the persons of some of the Officers'.[114] During 1826 there were on average, more than 380 boys on the *Euryalus*, but the ship was too small to permit 'proper classification … which is absolutely requisite for keeping them in a proper state of subjection', declared Capper. That remained true throughout the *Euryalus's* history, despite half-hearted attempts to separate the worst offenders from the less vicious boys.

To add to the discontent on the hulk there was a poor diet and soon after the boys went on board there were outbreaks of scurvy and opthalmia. To maintain discipline the 'silent system' was applied, with the boys forbidden to talk either when they were working or when they were exercising on deck. Breaches of the rules led to beatings, a reduced diet and, on occasion, confinement in a dark cell.[115]

The *Euryalus* soon gained an unenviable reputation as a 'nursery' of vice. The boys were not allowed to go ashore, but they did have lessons in reading and writing, as well as religious instruction. The trade training was now confined to make clothing for the rest of the convict establishment. Their day began at 5 a.m. when they rose, opened the portholes, lowered and lashed up the hammocks in which they slept, washed, and had their bedding inspected. Morning prayers and breakfast then followed, the latter comprising a small piece of cheese and a hunk of brown bread. After this the boys began work, making jackets and other items. At 9 a.m. any prisoners whose conduct had given cause for complaint were brought before the commander and given appropriate punishment. That included stopping their dinner, correcting them 'moderately' with the cane, or imposing solitary confinement on bread and water for a period 'not exceeding Seven Days'. [116]

Dinner at noon usually consisted of boiled beef or oatmeal gruel, and after this had been consumed the boys went on deck for air and exercise, tramping around for about an hour in total silence. They then returned to their work, although around a third of them were excused this for three hours on weekday afternoons so that they could have lessons. Supper was at 5.30 p.m., followed by another brief break on deck, before they went below to let their hammocks down. At 7 p.m. there were evening prayers in the chapel and they then went to bed. Each week, on Saturdays, they were 'washed all over in tepid water and soap'. [117] According to John Capper, by 9 p.m. each day there was 'profound' silence throughout the ship.

But if that were the official picture of life aboard the *Euryalus* the reality was very different. According to Thomas Dexter, a convict who had served as a nurse on the juvenile hospital ship which took boys from the hulk, and who had himself been on board in the course of his duties, violence and bullying among the boys were endemic. As he told the 1835 House of Lords Select Committee on Gaols and Houses of Correction, if he read in a newspaper that a judge had sentenced a boy 'out of Mercy to him to the Hulks, I have made the observation that was it a Child of mine I would rather see him dead at my feet than see him sent to that Place'. [118] The brutality and the strong inmate sub-culture led some of the weaker or younger boys to self-harm in an effort to get a spell in the hospital away from the *Euryalus*:

There are what they call Nobs, perhaps little Boys that were not higher than the table. I have seen them myself take a Broomstick and strike a Boy over the Arm, almost to break his Arm, and the other dare not say a single word to him ... the Nobs have got such an Ascendancy, and they were so liked by the Majority of the Boys, that anybody that dared to

say a Word against them was sure to be pitched upon by all hands; ... I
have known the Boys take an old Copper Button and apply it hot to the
Skin, and then apply Soap and Rum to a sore occasioned by a hot Button
and wrap it up for two or three Days, and then show that Wound to the
Doctor, and then come to the Hospital in a State piteous to behold; ... I
have known several Cases in which they have broken their Arms to get
into the Hospital; they held their Arms upon a Form, and let the edge of
the Table drop upon them, to break them in two. They would get other
Boys to do it for them, and then the Excuse was, that they had tumbled
down the Ladder.[119]

Sometimes three or four boys had to be locked up in a cell by themselves
so as to protect them against attack by the others. They were nicknamed
'Noseys', because they were suspected of having told the officers what was
going on. The 'Noseys' were 'particularly pointed out by the Majority of
Prisoners on whom to wreak their Vengeance'. The Nobs also deprived
the weaker lads of part of their scanty rations. According to Dexter, some
had told him they had 'not tasted Meat for Three Weeks together' because
they had been forced to surrender their ration to the 'Nobs'. Instead
they had dined on gruel and the parings of potatoes. One of the benefits
they anticipated from being in hospital was that they would have proper
meals.

The atmosphere of violence and abuse was confirmed by William
Johnson, who arrived with a party of other boys from Newgate prison in
January 1833. He had been found guilty of 'stealing from the person' and
sentenced to seven years' transportation. When he was interviewed about
two years and nine months later on board the *Euryalus* he confessed that
four of the boys who came with him had been in the habit of bullying
him when he was in Newgate. Two of them, John Plumpton, who was
thirteen, the same age as William himself, and Henry Houldsworth, who
was fourteen, were placed in the same cell on the hulk as he. They already
knew other boys on board and encouraged these to beat and ill treat him.
He dared not complain for fear of being further 'knocked about by the
other Boys'. In the end he decided to try to get into hospital by putting pins
into his hand, presumably in the hope that the wound would turn septic.
There were eighteen lads in his cell and he confided his plan to some of
them. The word got back to Plumpton and Houldsworth, who persuaded
him that he could get removed at less pain to himself if he injured his eyes.
To this he agreed. But the next morning, about half an hour before he
rose, the two boys came up to him as he lay in his hammock and began
to prick his eyes with a needle, holding the eyes open while they jagged
the needle three or four times into each of them.[120] William did not report

the attack for two days for fear of incurring further violence. Instead he stayed in the corner of his cell until a guard found him and took him to the captain. By then he had lost the sight of one eye and from the other was only able to see the 'shadow of a person – can see Daylight'. [121] Plumpton and Houldsworth were punished, one by being beaten with a cane and the other by being put in 'the black hole'. But the investigation was brief and superficial, taking only about ten minutes. Nonetheless both of the offending lads were sent away soon after, Plumpton being transported in March 1833 and Houldsworth the following May. [122] Meanwhile William's parents petitioned the Home Secretary, asking for a pardon and pointing to the 'misfortune of his losing one eye, with the probable decay of the other, and his sickly habit of body'. They did not mention how these injuries were sustained. Eventually their efforts were successful, for he was granted a free pardon, although the precise date of this cannot be identified, as the entry in the *Euryalus* register is illegible. [123]

Heather Shore mentions the case of another boy, Nicholas White, who was only nine when he was sent to the *Euryalus*. He, too, referred to the atmosphere of fear and abuse which existed on board. Like William Johnson he noted that many of the boys had known one another before their arrival on the hulk and they were thus able to form liaisons to intimidate the smaller and weaker prisoners. [124]

Some children spent their entire sentence on the *Euryalus* or on one of the other hulks and were never transported. Either, like William Johnson, they gained a free pardon before their time was up, or like nine-year-old John Scott from Leeds, sentenced in January 1825 to seven years' transportation, they spent their time on the hulk. John was finally discharged in January 1832, having served his seven-year term. A few, like ten-year-old Samuel Jones, found guilty of stealing ten combs, died on board. Samuel had served about four and a half years of his sentence at the time of his death. [125]

Most of the boy's sentenced to be transported were, however, sent away sooner or later, and many, like ten-year-old Samuel Ogilby, were anxious to go overseas. Samuel had been on the *Euryalus* for twenty months when he was interviewed by the 1835 Select Committee on Gaols and Houses of Correction. He and his brother, Henry, who was two years his senior, had been found guilty of breaking into a house and stealing some hinges and articles of clothing. This was not his first offence. Before he was eight years of age he had been caught stealing wood and taken before a magistrate, but had received no punishment. Soon after he stole two trowels and was again allowed to go free. His parents had tried to curb his thieving habits by beating him and locking him up in a room. After the second offence, they had even taken away his clothes for a few days. But it was in vain, and in October 1833 Samuel and Henry were both tried at the Old Bailey and were sentenced to seven years' transportation. When asked by the Select Committee if he would like to go to Botany Bay, he quickly replied, 'Yes … I do not like this Place'. By that he meant the *Euryalus*. His wish was speedily granted for a month or two after the interview both Ogilby brothers were dispatched to New South Wales on the *John Barry*, which departed on 31 August 1835. By 1837 they were located in the settlement of Bathurst.[126]

Other boys were sent away even more quickly than the Ogilby boys. James Gavagan, aged twelve, was sentenced to seven years' transportation at the Old Bailey on 2 March 1835 for stealing twenty-one umbrellas. James arrived at the *Euryalus* soon after and was, sent to Van Diemen's Land (as Tasmania was then known) in the following October, travelling on board the *Asia* transport. When he arrived at the penal settlement it seems that his problems persisted, for the records show that he was repeatedly beaten for continued absenteeism.[127] His parents were fruit hawkers in London and he had spent three years in a workhouse before committing the crime which had led to his transportation.

After hearing evidence about life aboard the *Euryalus* the 1835 Select Committee recommended that this 'Hotbed of Vice' be abandoned 'with the least possible Delay'. But, as Radzinowicz and Hood point out, that was not done: 'another seven years and 2,100 children passed through the *Euryalus* before it was closed for good in 1843 by the then Home Secretary'.[128] It had been a disastrous experiment failing to rehabilitate the youngsters consigned to it and, unable to provide basic protection for the weakest and most vulnerable of its inmates. Even John Capper, the superintendent, had to admit as early as 1828 that the results of confinement on the hulks were discouraging. When asked for information on the conduct of boys who had been released, he declared: 'I am sorry to have to say it has been very indifferent for eight out of ten that have been liberated returned to their old careers'. At that time, too, it was recommended that hulks should no longer be used for boys but this was ignored.[129]

Not all young convicts sent to the hulks went to the *Euryalus*. The first fifty-one prisoners admitted to Parkhurst Prison in December 1838 and January 1839 came from the *York* hulk; not until March 1839 was the first consignment of twelve received from the *Euryalus*.[130] The *York* continued in service at Portsmouth until 1852, when it was returned to the Admiralty to be broken up.[131] Even in the 1850s, therefore, a few young convicts were being sent to the dwindling number of hulks, with one estimate suggesting that in 1854, one hundred and fifty juveniles were passing through the Woolwich establishment in that year.[132] But by then this form of imprisonment was virtually at an end for men and boys alike. For adults it was finally phased out, at least in England, in 1856-57.[133]

CHAPTER 3

THE OVERSEAS DIMENSION: 1700-1840s

The idea of sending children off to a new start in the colonies was in many ways a thinly veiled extension of transportation. However, as in the fraught relationship between punishment and reformation debated in parliament, these two forms of emigration shared an equally symbiotic relationship. Firstly, transportation was a punishment. However, there was more than a whiff of reformatory idealism in the air, especially in the case of young offenders. There was some feeling that once a boy had worked his assignment for a while, and had got his ticket-of-leave, then he too could strike out on his own. Similarly, compulsory emigration could easily be seen as a punishment. This depended very much on the place that a child was assigned to, some children being treated as little more than slave labour ... Yet transportation was more than a policy of removal. Whether through altruism or self-interest, there was a growing feeling that it should provide a new start, a chance to break free from the environment and companions that, it was believed, were a strong inducement to crime.

Heather Shore, *Artful Dodgers. Youth and Crime in Early Nineteenth Century – London* (Woodbridge, 1995), p. 110.

Transportation

To punish offenders by banishing them overseas had been a policy pursued in a limited way since a law of 1597 allowed for 'obdurate idlers' to be treated in this fashion. In addition, during the seventeenth century some political prisoners and a number of convicts whose death sentence had been commuted were sent to the newly-settled American colonies to provide much-needed labour, particularly on the tobacco plantations of Virginia.[1]

These were mainly adults, since juveniles lacked the physical strength required for the heavy work and harsh conditions involved in developing the new territory. However, in 1618 a group of orphaned and destitute children were sent to Richmond, Virginia, apparently on the grounds that they were 'idle young people, who though they have been twise punished still continue to follow the same, havving noe employment'.[2]

Nevertheless it was only following the passage of the 1718 Transportation Act that a coherent transportation system was developed. It offered an alternative not merely to capital punishment but to such lesser penalties as public whipping and branding on the hand.[3] The Act was introduced at a time of anxiety about mounting crime levels, particularly in London, and as a response to the increasing demand for labour 'in the Colonies and Plantations in America'.[4] Both aims were made clear in the preamble to the 1718 legislation. For lesser offences the punishment was to be seven years' transportation but for those whose death sentence had been commuted there was a minimum term of fourteen years. Anyone who returned before the end of his or her sentence without receiving a royal pardon faced the death penalty.

The government funded the transportation of convicts who were sent from London and the Home Counties through commercial contracts drawn up with shipping firms. The payment amounted to £3 per head from London and £5 from other places, although after 1727 £5 was paid for all transportees from the London area. Outside this region, the courts had to make their own arrangements for the conveyance of the prisoners. In the case of Gloucestershire, for example, £4 per convict seems to have been the going rate between 1727 and 1773, except for a brief period in the 1730s and 1740s when the payment was slightly lower.[5]

In this way, as a contemporary commented, a number of 'threatening offenders' whose lawbreaking could not be cured by milder means were being sent away 'to prevent their doing further mischiefs'. Juries, too, welcomed transportation as an alternative to the death penalty, while it was felt that the felons themselves would gain by experiencing the discipline of honest work, away from the malign influence of former companions, who had contributed to their current plight. Yet there were critics, both then and later, who considered that transportation was not a sufficiently stringent penalty for offenders. In 1773, for instance, a Scottish magistrate complained that in his district it was an inadequate deterrent to criminality and had begun 'to lose every Characteristick of punishment'.[6] In 1810, when transportation to Australia was well under way, Lord Ellenborough, the Lord Chief Justice, even described it as 'a summer excursion, an easy migration to a happier and better climate'.[7] That it certainly was not, as events showed.

Between 1718 and 1775 perhaps forty to fifty thousand felons were carried across the Atlantic from all parts of the British Isles. At that point the outbreak of the American War of Independence brought the whole procedure to a halt. Of those, around nineteen thousand came from London, Middlesex, Buckinghamshire and the Home Counties, while a further eleven thousand or so were from other parts of England.[8] By the 1760s, however, a number of the colonies were growing reluctant to act as a permanent dumping ground for convicts, especially when, in the case of the plantations, they had access to the labour of slaves of African origin. By 1770 only Maryland was still accepting transported prisoners, due to a continuing shortage of labour. Of the convicts dispatched in this way, up to 80 per cent went to the Chesapeake region, where they worked alongside African slaves.[9]

It was part of the arrangement that the shipping contractors were allowed to sell the labour of the transportees to the highest bidder for personal profit. Hence benefactors were anxious to accept only those convicts who were readily disposable and that meant that juveniles were not particularly attractive. In 1755, for example, a census in Maryland showed that only 4.4 per cent of the colony's convicts were under sixteen years of age.[10] Some youngsters were nevertheless dispatched, and contemporary newspapers urged 'the thief takers' to concentrate on 'the young fry of pick pockets … who swarm about the Playhouses and other Places and by an early Removal of them to our Plantations … prevent their growing up here fit for the commission of Burglaries and Robberies on the Highways',[11] Certainly Peter Williamson, who seems to have been transported as a young boy to Pennsylvania as a 'vagrant', was able to establish after his return that his 'kidnap' had been connived at by the authorities in Aberdeen.[12]

For the prisoners the journey across the Atlantic was a traumatic experience, and there were reports that on arrival in port many looked half starved and were clad in ragged clothes or almost naked – features unlikely to appeal to future masters, who were expected to bid for their services. Incidentally, should they be given a royal pardon and thereby be allowed to return home before the expiry of their original sentence they had to compensate their master for his loss of their labour before they could depart.

At least one youngster, fourteen-year-old Matthew MacDonald from County Durham, took drastic action to avoid being sent overseas. He was found guilty of a minor theft at the quarter sessions in 1757 and sentenced to seven years transportation to the American plantations. In response he claimed to have seen his father and another man burying the body of an unknown person and when a search proved abortive, 'he confessed that he had lied to the authorities in the hope of evading transportation or effecting his escape from the gaol.' As Gwenda Morgan and Peter Rushton drily comment, 'He managed the first but not the second'[13]

Meanwhile concern was being expressed in Britain at the large number of convicts who were returning from America after their sentence was completed and who were 'made more desperate than before' by their experience.[14] One of the attractions of transportation to Australia when it commenced in the late 1780s was that its location on the other side of the world made return from there much less likely, even after a sentence had expired.

The ending of transportation to America in the mid-1770s quickly led, as we saw in the last chapter, to prisons becoming overcrowded. The establishment of the hulks from 1776 to accommodate those awaiting removal proved an inadequate alternative, even in the short term. Initially it had been hoped that the American War would be speedily won and transportation across the Atlantic resumed once more. When that option fell through, the search began in the mid-1780s to find an alternative venue. Three candidates were considered. The first was the island of Lemaine, an unhealthy spot about four hundred miles up the Gambia River in West Africa. It was argued that although many 'would perish in this African grave … the survivors would turn into planters'.[15] However the outcry against the proposal was such that it was soon rejected. As the *Daily Universal Register* of 13 April 1785, commented; 'To transport capital felons to Africa, who have received his Majesty's pardon is undoubtedly just; but as it has ever been held a point of law that the order cannot encrease punishments, sending persons convicted of larcenies to Africa, which is one high road to eternity does not appear … consistent with the principles of the British constitution'.[16] The second alternative was Das Voltas Bay, by the mouth of the Orange River in South-West Africa, and initially this was seen as a likely choice. Indeed, some prisoners who were subsequently sent to New South Wales were initially sentenced to be transported to Africa. They included Mary Branham, who was tried at the Old Bailey in December 1784 and found guilty of stealing clothing from her mistress while the latter was out of the house. Mary was about fourteen at the time and she was ordered to be transported to Africa in March 1785. In the end nothing came of it and in the spring of 1787, along with a large number of other convicts, she was sent to Australia instead.[17] Meanwhile Das Voltas Bay was rejected because closer investigation revealed that it was too dry and sterile to be settled. That left only the third possibility – Botany Bay in New South Wales. Little was known about it, but in the absence of other candidates it was this which was decided upon.

Plans were soon in hand to arrange the shipment of the first batch of prisoners and their guards. The location had the advantage of giving

Britain a foothold in a new continent, albeit one not on her usual trading routes, and, most importantly, it permitted the removal from the country of what a contemporary called 'a Dreadful banditti'.[18] Eleven vessels were commissioned, mostly merchant ships, and they were to carry a total of around 1,500 people, of whom just under 750 were convicts. About 190 of these were females and nearly, 560 were males.[19] They included a sprinkling of juveniles, for of the 262 convicts whose ages are known, at least five were under the age of seventeen when they sailed. The youngest males included John Hudson, a former chimney sweep, who was sentenced at the age of nine at the Old Bailey, in December 1783, for breaking into a house at night and stealing some clothes and a pistol. He was subsequently discovered at a pawnbroker's with the clothing. Ironically the lad seems to have been given a sentence of seven years' transportation from a desire on the judge's part 'to snatch such a boy, if one possibly could, from destruction, for he will only return to the same kind of life which he has led before, and will be an instrument in the hands of very bad people, who make use of boys of that sort to rob houses.'[20] He was discharged from the *Dunkirk* hulk in March 1787 to go aboard the *Friendship* transport in readiness for the journey to New South Wales. He was just thirteen.

The youngest of the females to be despatched in this First Fleet was Elizabeth Hayward, who was thirteen years of age when she stole a linen gown, a silk bonnet and a cloak from Thomas Cross, to whom she was apprenticed. The gown was discovered in a pawnshop and Elizabeth was sentenced at the Old Bailey in January 1787 to seven years' transportation. In her case, removal to the transport vessel, the *Lady Penrhyn*, was speedy, taking place within days of the sentence being pronounced.[21]

The condition of some of the women and girls when they came on board ship, however, was such that the leader of the expedition and the future governor of New South Wales, Captain Arthur Phillip, complained they were so filthy, as well as almost naked, that 'nothing but clothing them could have prevented them from perishing'. He also lamented the 'many venereal complaints' from which they were suffering.[22]

In the early years there was no attempt to cater for the special needs of young offenders on the transport ships. They were mixed in with the adults, with all the dangers of moral 'contamination' and physical and sexual abuse that this offered during a lengthy voyage. In the case of the First Fleet the journey lasted eight months, with the vessels finally leaving Portsmouth in May 1787 and arriving at Botany Bay early in the following January. On the way lengthy stops were made at Rio de Janeiro and Cape Town, so that fresh supplies could be taken on board. Many of the youngest prisoners must have found the experience terrifying, travelling to a destination about which they knew nothing, subjected to harsh discipline, surrounded by violent adult convicts, and with severe storms or enervating heat to contend with. The journal of Arthur Bowes, surgeon of the *Lady Penrhyn*, described the bad weather they encountered, as on 24 September 1787, when there was a 'heavy gale & a good swell of Sea ... Many of the Convict women rec'd Hurts & Bruises from falls'. But it was their moral condition that disturbed him most:

> I ... believe I may venture to assert there never was a more abandon'd set of Wretches collected in one Place, at any Period than are to be met with in this Ship & I am credibly inform'd the comparison holds good in respect to all the Convicts in the fleet ... [T]hey are perpetually thieving the Cloaths from each other; nay almost from off their Backs & this may be rank'd among the least of their crimes ... The Oaths and imprecations they daily make use of in their common conversations & disputes with each other, are shocking ... far exceeding anything of the kind to be met with I shd suppose among the most abandoned Wretches in London.[23]

Punishments included the use of thumb screws as well as fetters to their wrists, 'and sometimes their Hair is cut off & their Heads shav'd, which latter they seem more to dislike than any other', At first they were 'flogg'd with a Catt of Nine tails on their naked Breech' for misconduct, but this was considered to offend against common decency and was subsequently abandoned.[24] These were the conditions under which young Elizabeth Hayward travelled to New South Wales.

Among the male prisoners, discipline was still more severe. Nevertheless, despite the discomfort of the journey, mortality rates on the First Fleet convoy remained low. That was not to be the case with some of the subsequent transports, and especially the Second Fleet. Overall, however, between 1787 and 1868, when transportation finally ended, around 162,000 prisoners were dispatched to Australia; at the peak of the system, the average death rate from illness on board was slightly above 1 per cent.[25]

The next vessel to be sent left Plymouth at the end of July 1789 with 244 female convicts on board. This was the *Lady Juliana* and of the 230 prisoners whose ages were recorded, fifty-one were aged between ten and nineteen, thirteen of them being under seventeen when they set sail. The youngest of them, Mary Wade, was eleven at the time of departure and had been sentenced, together with a fellow prisoner, Jane Whiting, aged fourteen, to seven years' transportation for luring a little girl into a 'necessary' and there stripping her of all her clothes. This was the second time that Mary had stripped a child of her clothing and on the previous occasion she had thrown her young victim into a ditch. Initially the two youngsters were sentenced to death but this was commuted to transportation for life.[26]

Another young transportee was Jane Forbes, who was aged fourteen, and had been twelve when she was convicted of pickpocketing, at the Old Bailey. She was sentenced to seven years' transportation. However, what made the *Lady Juliana's* voyage notorious was the way that most of the seamen took 'wives' from among the women prisoners. As John Nicol, a steward on board the vessel, declared, 'When we were fairly out at sea, every man on board took a wife from among the convicts, they nothing loath'.[27] This has led to the *Lady Juliana* being labelled the 'floating Brothel'. Jane Forbes was the youngest of these 'ship wives'. She was taken into the hammock of seaman William Carlo, and when the vessel arrived in Sydney Cove, Australia on 3 June 1790, she was nursing a baby.[28] Another young mother who had formed a shipboard liaison was Ann Bryant, aged sixteen when she boarded the *Lady Juliana*. She had been convicted at Kent Lent Assizes in 1789, along with others, of stealing muslin and linen cloth. She was sentenced to seven years' transportation and was taken as a partner by seaman William Hughes. [29]

Despite the moral shortcomings apparent on the *Lady Juliana* during its long voyage, mortality rates remained low. That was not true of what was to be labelled the Second Fleet. It departed from England in January 1790, and comprised three main vessels, the *Neptune*, the *Scarborough* and the *Surprise*. Together they carried 1,026 convicts, of whom just seventy-eight were female. These all travelled on the *Neptune*, along with 421 males. During the five-month journey the convicts were cheated out of their rations, so that many suffered from scurvy and other diseases. To add to the horror of the voyage, they were also chained two and two together and confined in the hold during the long trip. When they reached Australia it emerged that the *Neptune* had a 31 per cent death rate; the *Scarborough* a 27 per cent one, and the *Surprise* a 14 per cent rate. Of the 1,026 convicts who had embarked on the three ships, therefore, 267 had died before they reached New South Wales and a further 124 perished soon after they came ashore, mainly as a result of scurvy, fever or dysentry. All were filthy and a number were unable to walk as a result of weakness and their prolonged confinement in shackles.[30] It was the most disastrous voyage in the history of transportation and led to the laying down of rules for the carriage of convicts in order to avoid such a catastrophe in the future. These included giving gratuities to captains who ran healthy ships and appointing naval surgeons to each ship, with captains made subject to them in matters connected with the convicts' health. [31] Of the 836 male convicts on the Second Fleet whose ages have been established, forty-six, or 5.5 per cent, were under sixteen. A further 194 or 23.2 per cent were aged sixteen to twenty inclusive.[32] Among the survivors of this nightmare journey was George Dunstan, who had escaped from the hulk *Stanislaus* in November 1787, when he was about fifteen, and was then picked up as an absconder on the streets of London, in April 1788. At first he was sentenced to death but this was later commuted to transportation for life. On arrival in Australia he seems for a time to have followed his father's trade of shoemaker, and in 1800-1801 was shown as self-employed in that trade in the Sydney area.[33]

Despite the improvement in shipping conditions which took place, however, children and adults continued to be transported together on the same vessels. During the years 1812 to 1817, for example, nearly 3 per cent of the convicts carried were under sixteen years of age.[34] From 1817 an attempt was made to divide the below decks prison into three sections by the use of open iron railings, which did not impede the flow of air but made possible the separation of 'more or less hardened offenders' from the younger and more innocent. But men and boys were still allowed to mix on deck. The only way of minimising 'contamination' was to make the voyage as direct and as brief as possible.[35] Nonetheless until 1833 boys were still being shipped with adult males on some of the transports. Not until 1836, partly as a result of pressure from the Australian authorities, was it decided to carry male juveniles in separate vessels. The girls were still shipped with the adult women.

The children's own attitude towards transportation varied widely. The MP and prison reformer, Henry Grey Bennet, claimed some youngsters actually volunteered to be sent to New South Wales. He quoted the evidence of Mr Cotton, the ordinary (or chaplain) of Newgate, who informed the Select Committee on the Police of the Metropolis in 1816, that many who were to be transported considered it 'a party of pleasure – as going out to see the world'. According to Bennet, one group sent from Newgate at that time, on being put 'into the caravan, shouted and huzzaed and were very joyous; several of them called out to the keepers who were there in the yard, the first fine Sunday we will have a glorious Kangaroo hunt at the Bay, [Botany bay] seeming to anticipate a great deal of pleasure'.[36] On the other hand, Thomas Galloway, a naval surgeon who acted as superintendent on five convict ships, considered that until the early 1830s most looked on transportation as 'a severe punishment'. After that they got to know what a 'fine country they were to go to ... I believe many of them got themselves into scrapes for the purpose of being transported'.[37]

A year or two later, when William Augustus Miles interviewed several of the boys on the *Euryalus* hulk who were awaiting transportation to Australia, they, too, seemed generally to favour going away. James McCartney, a fifteen-year-old Scots lad, who had started thieving in order to get cash to visit playhouses, was one of them, declaring; 'If I were to go back again I should turn bad so I would rather go abroad than join my

old companions for they would only bring me into worse trouble'.[38] Then
there was the young Whitechapel orphan, William Cook, who had been
in prison at least fifteen times for stealing meat and picking pockets. He,
too, 'would rather go abroad – I have no friends and if I was to get into a
place I should be enticed away again'.[39] Others, like a sixteen-year-old boy
named Thompson, were philosophical, declaring that transportation was
'looked upon by each thief as an event which must occur some time or
another, and the only point is to keep from it as long as they can'.[40] A few,
like thirteen-year-old Thomas O'Donnell from London were afraid 'of
going to the Bay'. He would 'prefer the House of Correction' in England.[41]
In the event he was sent to Australia in January 1836.

For parents the prospects of separation often caused anguish, for they
had little hope of ever seeing their offspring again, once they were shipped
off. In 1829, for example, Peter Daniels, a London basketmaker, petitioned
the Home Secretary to mitigate the sentence of transportation for life
pronounced on his sixteen-year-old son, David, who had been found guilty
of robbery. 'I most humbly implore your honor's kindness, to send him to
any place where you may think proper but New South Wales', he wrote, 'as
I shall never have a ray of hope of ever seeing him again if sent there, the
thought of which, Sir, causes me the most poignant feelings'. The petition
was refused.[42] Then there was the seventy-three-year-old former soldier,
Michael Hallman, who in 1833, pleaded for a remission of the sentence on
his daughter, Margaret, aged fifteen. She had been found guilty of stealing
some china plates and was to be transported for seven years. Michael not
only pointed out that he himself had served 'his King and Country 25 Years
during which he was ... twice severely wounded', but his wife, Margaret's
mother, was 'in a State of Illness bordering on distraction and her Life
almost despaired of'. A petition on Margaret's behalf was also presented
by the prosecutor herself and by tradesmen from Old Brentford, where the
family lived. Once again, it was in vain.[43]

There were, of course, some 'vicious, malicious parents', as Heather
Shore points out, whose aim was to divest themselves of responsibility
for their offspring by arranging for their transportation or imprisonment.
One such was the father of Henry Wells, aged fifteen and under sentence
of transportation in 1834. Henry was convicted at the Old Bailey of
stealing from his father a gown that had belonged to his late mother. She
had died the previous May, leaving six children to the tender mercies of a
neglectful and cruel father. The father quickly remarried and, according to
Henry, he had only taken the gown at the express wish of his late mother.
She had wanted her clothing to be destroyed rather than that it should
come into the possession of the woman who was to become Henry's
stepmother. The author of a letter supporting the boy, Louisa Skeene, was

also anxious to stress his misfortune and the role played in his downfall by his father. A former employer of Henry likewise declared that on the Monday preceding the boy's trial he had gone to try to hire him to work in his business again. But the father was adamant that 'he would transport' his son if possible 'and threatened to turn the elder brother out of doors as he would not support him'. As Heather Shore comments, the father was obviously concerned only with 'his own survival, with a new wife and the possibility of a new family to support.'[44] But such cases as this were few and far between. In most instances parents were in despair at the thought of being separated from their children, probably forever, in view of the vast distances involved.

The first of the ships to carry juvenile convicts only was the *Frances Charlotte*, which left England on 1 January 1837, carrying about 140 boys. The surgeon-superintendent, Alexander Nisbit, who was in charge of them, left a detailed account of the voyage, and of the attempts made not only to ensure their health and good behaviour but to inculcate the correct religious and moral sentiments. Ten adult convicts accompanied them, their task being to supervise the boys. Two of them took charge of the schools which were organised for the journey, as well as caring for the sick; one man had the general superintendence both of the boys and the adult prisoners, and received his orders from the surgeon-superintendent himself. The boys were divided into messes of eight, with a monitor appointed to each. It was his duty to look after the conduct of the mess and to report 'any improper conduct or language on the part of any individual belonging to this mess'; when the boys were in bed a monitor was nominated for each sleeping berth of four, and he was held accountable for any noise or disturbance that occurred after they went to bed.

Schooling began once the ship had cleared the 'cold tempestuous weather' in the channel, with the youngsters being instructed for one and a half hours a day to read, spell and do simple arithmetic. Each Saturday tests were held and prizes awarded to those who had made most progress. These took the form of fruit, books and other 'indulgencies' according to Nisbit:

While one-third of the boys were at school the remainder were ... on deck, where they were allowed and encouraged to amuse themselves in all sorts of games, and as we had a violin-player on board, dancing was permitted after school-hours ... I did not attempt to inculcate any particular religious doctrine, for which I feel myself unequal, but endeavoured to lay the foundation on which a religious superstructure might be raised.

Each day the boys rose at dawn and were mustered on deck, clad only in their trousers, which were rolled up to the knees. They then had a wash in a large tub of salt water, after which they returned below, dressed themselves, made up their beds, which were stowed on deck, and swept out the prison. This was followed by breakfast, with further cleaning duties or schooling next carried out. 'Dinner was always, in fine weather, taken on deck, and usually occupied about half an hour, when the school resumed, and continued as long as they could see below; all hands then came on deck, beds were sent below and made up, and free egress allowed until dark.' The prison gates were closed for the night at 8 p.m. However, because some of the seamen had turned mutinous and refused to work when the ship left England, Nisbit allowed a watch of eight boys to be kept during the night. 'It was an object of great ambition to be enrolled in the watch, and was used to reward monitors and other of the stoutest boys.'[45]

When they first came on board and had left behind the discipline of the hulks, the surgeon-superintendent described their behaviour as 'exceedingly unruly and indecorous, tainted also with many acts of petty theft', though they were never 'of such magnitude as to require the use of corporal punishment'. But as the voyage advanced their conduct improved, with theft becoming 'exceedingly rare; immoral language or behaviour had entirely disappeared, at least in public, and the offences generally which were then committed seemed more to depend on the ebullition of youthful feeling than on any inherent depravity'.[46]

The ship took 134 days to reach Hobart in Van Diemen's Land (present-day Tasmania) and all the boys arrived safely. The experiment had been a success and the surgeon-superintendent believed that the way in which the prisoners had been disposed of when they reached the colony seemed 'to bid fair … to complete what had been contemplated – to withdraw them from the fangs of vice and render them useful members of society'.[48]

The voyage led to at least eight more juvenile convict ships being sent to Australia between 1837 and 1842, the last of them, the *Elphinstone*, leaving England on 19 March 1842 and arriving in Hobart on the following 28 July.[49] Some of the surgeons-superintendent reported having to deal with 'refractory boys', as was the case with Daniel Ritchie. He wrote of the voyage of the *Egyptian*, during which young troublemakers were 'assigned to the cleaning of the ladders, the hatchways, deck and prison quarters'. Those punishments were directed particularly at lads who 'stole, sold, exchanged or gave away food at meal times'. He also had problems with boys in some of the messes 'skylarking by throwing pieces of biscuit at one another at night.' He concluded gloomily that 'boys are not the least dangerous class of criminals. Their physical weakness is in proportion to the vigour of their moral depravity'. Like many of the other surgeons-superintendent, Ritchie made extensive use of the 'solitary box', an isolation cell placed on deck, which although it did not have the brutality of flogging, nonetheless exerted psychological pressure on the prisoners and was greatly feared by them.[50]

William Jones, the surgeon-superintendent on the *Elphinstone*, which sailed from Sheerness in 1842, made clear to his young charges at the outset that he would report to the lieutenant-governor of Van Diemen's Land on their conduct during the journey. They could expect 'severe punishment' should they behave ill: 'I shall be most rigid in my punishment on board likewise. Bread & Water; solitary confinement, is my mode, and the Cat of Nine Tails'. Rules and regulations were drawn up, including threats of harsh penalties in cases of swearing, fighting, stealing, or disputes. All boys must remove their headgear at meal times, and there was to be no buying, selling, or 'trafficking with provisions'. In his report on the journey he emphasised the importance of strict cleanliness and of the distribution of lime juice and wine to ward off disease. He stressed the need for personal supervision at dinner time, to ensure that each boy got his fair share of the food, and every Sunday a medical inspection was carried out.[51] In all, 223 boys, with seven adult convicts to help supervise them, were on board. Jones's report mentioned the illnesses from which the youngsters suffered on the journey, with one boy dying, the need to issue shoes and clothing as required, and the fact that sodomy did not merely involve adult men and boys. One thirteen-year-old lad reported that his bedmate, Thomas Robinson, had attempted 'the unnatural crime upon his person' during the night. Investigation proved the truth of the allegation, Robinson admitting his guilt. As a result he was 'placed in irons' by the surgeon-superintendents a fitting punishment for actions that Jones described as 'diabolical'.[52]

The transportation of prisoners to New South Wales came to an end in 1840, as a result of resistance from the settlers in what was a rapidly expanding colony. After that date prisoners were sent to Van Diemen's Land, which from its opening up in 1803 had been used largely for prisoners who had proved particularly refractory or who had committed the most serious offences. But in 1853 it, too, ceased to receive convicts. By now prison building in Britain itself and a changing philosophy towards punishment, particularly of the young, had undermined belief in transportation as an appropriate penalty for offenders. During the 1860s some adult male convicts were despatched to Western Australia, before the system finally ended in 1868.[53] However, no juveniles were sent to Australia as transportees after the early 1850s although, as we shall see, many thousands were to be despatched as 'emigrants' under various schemes into the twentieth century.

In the meantime, how did the young convicts fare when they reached Australia and what fate awaited them?

Life in Australia

Robert Hughes has labelled the initial period of settlement in Australia the 'starvation years' and has written of 'stony, grasping men, who robbed one another like jackals snarling over a carcase and cheated the government blind whenever they could'.[54] In the late 1780s the inability to raise adequate local supplies of essential foodstuffs in the unfamiliar terrain and the lengthy intervals which elapsed between the ships bringing in produce from outside led to severe shortages, especially of meat and flour. Rations for the convicts were repeatedly cut, so that by April 1790 the amount they received was only about half that issued when the First Fleet arrived in 1788. The effect of this, as Wilfrid Oldham points out, was to reduce the men's capability of carrying out heavy manual tasks, clearing the land for cultivation, carrying out construction work, and creating dock facilities. The removal of the large gum trees itself was a task that taxed the strength and resolution of those engaged upon it.[55] The most common illnesses suffered in the settlements were scurvy and debility. The scarcity also encouraged thefts of food by the more daring or the more desperate, willing to risk the severe punishments imposed if they were detected. The main preoccupation at this stage was the colony's survival.[56]

Discipline was stringent and over time special penal colonies were established in Van Diemen's Land and, most particularly, on Norfolk Island for those who proved especially difficult to handle or who committed further crimes in Australia itself. Floggings were commonplace and were administered to young offenders as well as to the adult convicts. Hence thirteen-year-old Elizabeth Hayward, about a month after arrival, was ordered thirty lashes for insolence. In March 1790 she was sent to Norfolk Island, where by 1805 she had borne three children. When she left in 1813 to go to Van Diemen's Land she was recorded as the wife of a Joseph Lowe.[57]

John Hudson, too, was despatched to Norfolk Island in March 1790 and less than a year later, in February 1791, received fifty lashes 'for been out of his hut after nine o'clock'.[58] Significantly a return of corporal punishment inflicted upon prisoners from Hyde Park Barracks in Sydney between 4 and 30 September 1833, revealed that seven of the twenty-nine males beaten were boys. They included John Tree, punished for 'neglect of duty by feigning sickness.' He was given thirty-six 'lashes on the breech'. According to the superintendent of the Barracks, who witnessed the punishment, at the '11th stroke the blood appeared, and continued running; he cried out loudly at every lash; this was the first time of corporal punishment. This boy suffered most severely; and, in my opinion, 12 lashes would have been sufficient for him.'[59] Most of the reports of beatings administered to the other youngsters followed a similar pattern.

One lad, John Dowlan, who had absconded, was given fifty lashes when he was recaptured. The superintendent noted that he had been flogged six months before and on this occasion 'cried out at the 1st lash; the skin was lacerated at the 13th lash; the blood came at the 19th lash, and ran down at the 24th lash. Twelve lashes would have been sufficient punishment.'[60] Clearly he found the barbarity of the whole procedure shocking.

Juvenile male prisoners were difficult to assign for employment purposes, either as labourers allocated to the free settlers or as part of the government's own work force. They were not strong enough to carry out the heavy manual tasks necessary. By contrast, many of the girls were set to work as domestic servants or else were sent to the factory establishment opened at Parramatta in 1804. There they were engaged in ropemaking and textile production while they waited to be assigned. Many were accused of prostitution. [61] Female convicts were, however, always in the minority throughout the period of transportation between 1787 and 1868, accounting for only about 15 per cent of the 162,000 or so convicts despatched.[62]

In 1803 the authorities attempted to tackle the problem of juvenile male unemployment by developing an apprenticeship system. At this stage, however, it proved as unsuccessful as most of the earlier efforts to assign their labour had been.[63]

Other developments in the early years included from 1801 the issuing of 'tickets-of-leave' to prisoners who had completed part of their sentence satisfactorily. These allowed the recipients to seek paid employment on their own account, although they were permitted to work only within a designated area of Australia, and the tickets had to be renewed annually until the sentence was completed and they were at liberty, or until an official pardon had been granted. Along with tickets-of-leave the 1801 reforms introduced the principle of conditional and absolute pardons. The former gave citizenship rights in the colony, as well as freedom to seek employment, but did not permit the erstwhile prisoner to return to Great Britain. Absolute pardons not only bestowed full citizenship rights but granted a right to return to Great Britain if that were desired. These were issued in a limited number of cases only.[64]

At first no special accommodation was provided for young prisoners employed on government projects or awaiting assignment. Then between 1820 and 1833 the separate Carter's Barracks were opened in Sydney to house around a hundred and fifty young prisoners.[65] There they learnt a trade and an attempt to classify them was also made. One room was allotted to youngsters who had misbehaved, and they were punished by being given an inferior diet and worse bedding than their more co-operative colleagues. For example, while the latter slept on beds with mattresses and ordinary blankets, the former had to make do with sleeping on boards covered only by a thin blanket. They had shorter rations, too, than the more amenable lads.[66] One aim of the Carter's Barracks was to prevent the boys from being corrupted by adult prisoners and to protect them against sexual abuse, at a time when sodomy was widespread among the male-dominated convict labour force. Unfortunately the boys themselves, when gathered together in one place, soon acquired such a bad reputation that private employers were reluctant to hire them. Eventually in 1832 a system of semi-apprenticeship was drawn up, with the boys allocated to their new masters immediately on arrival in Australia and remaining with them for a full seven-year term. From December 1833 boys of sixteen were assigned in the same way as adult labourers and under these circumstances, Carter's Barracks were closed.[67] Once again New South Wales was without any special institution for juveniles. Those who for some reason did not become apprentices or who were returned by their masters, were accommodated again with the adult male prisoners. As before, there were allegations of sexual abuse of the boys, many of whom were given female names like 'Kitty' or 'Nanny'. James Mudie, a New South Wales landowner, claimed 'every species of vice' was indulged in: 'it is the glory of men convicts to corrupt a boy; in fact they could not live if they resisted ... I should say that there is no species of crime that they would not glory in'.[68]

Ernest Slade, who was for a time superintendent of the main Hyde Park barracks in Sydney confirmed in 1837 that sodomy was so widespread that the boys complained 'that they could not remain in the rooms with the men ... young hands have frequently made a complaint to me of improper liberties taken with them by those men'.[69] His efforts to stamp out what was an illegal practice proved abortive.

Nor was the problem confined to New South Wales. The situation was as bad or worse in Van Diemen's Land and on Norfolk Island, with the former colony being used on an increasing scale between 1803 and 1853 to take in young offenders. In 1837 the Revd. William Ullathorne, the Roman Catholic vicar-general of New Holland and Van Diemen's Land, lamented that although the boys were separated from the men in the barracks for sleeping purposes, they mixed freely during the recreation periods:

> the moral contamination upon the boys is very great indeed; I observe that generally there are from 16 to 20 arrive in a ship with the men; I used to caution particularly young boys, on the very day of arrival, of the temptations to which they would be subject in the barracks; and I remember in one instance being told by one boy, a very young boy, he could not be more than 10 or 12 at the most, that that very morning he had been attacked by a man in the barracks, and the boy observed, very simply, that such crimes were never known in Ireland, whence he came.[70]

During the 1820s and 1830s the number of children shipped to Van Diemen's Land rose sharply. One estimate suggests that of the 65,000 convicts sent to the colony between 1803 and 1853, at least 15 per cent were eighteen years of age or under, and in the 1830s that proportion rose to about 20 per cent.[71] In these circumstances the governor, Colonel George Arthur, sent a gloomy despatch to the Colonial Under-Secretary in London in 1833. In it he drew attention to the 'unusual number of Boys ... sent out; it is utterly impossible to imagine a more corrupt fraternity of little depraved felons ... but all are the objects of compassion'.[72] It was impossible to assign them since they were too small and underfed to be set to work on tasks required of pioneers, such as felling trees, making roads, quarrying stone, and mining coal. It was therefore decided to open a special prison for them called Point Puer on Tasman's Peninsula in the vicinity of the penal settlement of Port Arthur. There they would learn a trade, receive some schooling, and be offered moral and religious guidance, under conditions of strict discipline, so as to prepare them for future employment. They were put under the charge of Captain O'Hara Booth, the commandant of Port Arthur and a stern taskmaster.[73]

In December 1833, sixty boys were sent from the prisoners' barracks at Hobart Town to the new juvenile prison. They were the advance guard of many hundreds of youngsters, since during the fifteen years or so that followed, until Point Puer was closed in 1849, around two thousand boys passed through the establishment. At its peak in 1842-43 it had almost eight hundred inmates, and this led to much overcrowding. However, by 1849, around the time of its Closure, that had slumped to about one hundred and sixty.[74]

The location of Point Puer was good from a security standpoint since escape was virtually impossible, but from almost every other angle it was totally unsuitable. As a later commandant of Port Arthur declared in 1844, it was 'a wretched, bleak, barren spot, without water, wood for fuel, or an inch of soil that [was] not for agricultural purposes utterly valueless; ... at present it will grow nothing.'[75] The buildings had been hastily constructed and oversight of the boys was largely the responsibility of adult ticket-of-leave men or former convicts. The day began at 5 a.m. when the youngsters rose, rolled up their hammocks, stowed them away, and then washed in tanks in the yard. This was followed by prayers, breakfast, a general muster and then a spell in the workshops. The instruction given to the trade groups included carpentry, tailoring, shoemaking, gardening, baking, blacksmithing, boat building and even stone masonry, although for these two latter tasks the teaching took place in Port Arthur itself.[76] When they first arrived, the young prisoners were sent to labouring gangs, engaged in breaking up new ground, cultivating the garden, carrying timber, splitting it for firewood, and performing various domestic chores. When these tasks had been completed satisfactorily the boys were allowed to join the trade classes. These activities took up almost six hours a day, while schooling occupied between one hour and two hours, and the rest of the time was taken up with meals, sleeping, and such varied duties as musters, assemblies, religious services, and prayers as well as some recreation.[77]

Discipline was strict, as O'Hara Booth took the view that there could be no laxity if the boys were to be rehabilitated and made into useful citizens:

The most trivial crime or irregularity is not permitted to pass without punishment in proportion to the degree or nature of the offence, which consists in confinement to the muster ground during cessation from labour, where no amusement is allowed, and the boys so confined are required to do the duties of scavengers. The next grade of punishment, where a more refractory spirit is evinced, is to be placed in a cell immediately labour ceases, and receive their meals therein, where no talking or noise is permitted; they also sleep in them, but attend school, and are confined until they manifest a disposition to amendment. The next grade of punishment is confinement in a cell on bread and water; ... in cases of more determined violation of the regulations, the offender is sentenced to punishment on the breech. This measure is never resorted to until every other means to reform have been tried. [78]

A return of punishments administered at Point Puer during the half-year ending 30 June 1837 revealed, however, that 64.4 per cent of those penalised were given two or three days in solitary confinement on bread and water, while a further 13.2 per cent were punished by beating, with between twelve and twenty-five stripes given, according to the seriousness of the offence.[79] For the most incorrigible there were bricked yards divided into stalls with a chain running through them. There the particularly violent or vicious were chained to carry out stone breaking.[80]

When he was depressed Booth had doubts about this disciplinary regime. 'Sick at Heart from the number of Boys obliged to punish,' he wrote in his journal in 1838, after a particularly difficult day among the Point Puer prisoners. 'Would that we had persons to work the system – with firmness but temper and Patience to witness the result of perseverance'.[81] In 1840 out of a total of 494 boys, 351 were punished for a total of 1,011 offences.[82]

Among those sent to Point Puer was Samuel Holmes, who was interviewed in 1835 by William Augustus Miles on the *Euryalus*, while awaiting transportation in England. He was despatched to Van Diemen's Land in 1836 and on arrival at Point Puer he was punished with three days' solitary confinement on a 'strong suspicion of pilfering buttons from off Government clothing'. Around three weeks later, on 5 December 1836, he had a further three days in solitary confinement for 'making use of blasphemous language on the Sabbath', and about a month after that he received fifteen lashes for 'gross insolence to the superintendent'. This was to be the pattern of his first years in the prison, with regular punishments for insolence, refusing to work, and absenting himself from his labour gang. He received numerous beatings, including twenty-five lashes for 'striking Thomas Preston'. In 1839 he was transferred to the Green Ponds Probation Station, but his misconduct continued and in 1840 his sentence was apparently increased by a further two years.[83]

George Hickman, another of Miles's 1835 interviewees, recorded a similar catalogue of repeat offending. He, too, was transported in 1836 and was initially assigned to a Mr Giblin. However, within weeks he was being punished for absenting himself from duty and the assignment was ended. His spells of punishment were served either at the Green Ponds Probation Station or on road parties. His penalties, like those of Samuel Holmes, included hard labour and solitary confinement, until 1838 when he began to behave even more badly, receiving a 'dozen lashes' for general misconduct and thirty-six lashes for violently assaulting another prisoner. Soon after he received a further thirty-six lashes for 'general misconduct'.[84] He completed his sentence, however, and in the early 1840s was given a 'free certificate', which allowed him to become a full citizen. In 1846 he was still living in the colony.[85]

Bullying was endemic at Point Puer, with the older lads imposing their will on the younger and smaller prisoners. Booth himself wrote of 'the tyranny of public opinion amongst themselves to which every boy in the place must submit as a slave almost at peril of his life'.[86] It was part of the inner life of Point Puer which the authorities were unable to eradicate or even control.

On rare occasions the violence spilled over into murder. One such case occurred early in July 1843 when an overseer was killed by two fourteen-year-old boys who had already been put into the 'crime class', a category designed for those who repeatedly refused to obey orders or who stole from other boys. The overseer's body was found in the exercise yard, he having been beaten over the head. Although no boy was sentenced to death at Point Puer, between 1843 and 1848, thirteen lads, including these two were 'removed to Port Arthur', where they probably suffered the 'utmost severity the law could inflict'. Other less serious attacks included dousing overseers with tubs of urine as they patrolled the dormitories during the night.[87]

In 1843 Point Puer was visited by a British prisons inspector, Benjamin Horne. He found much to criticise, both as regards the poor educational provision for the boys and the unsatisfactory state of the facilities generally. He also considered they were allowed an excessive amount of recreation and condemned the use of ticket-of-leave men to act as instructors and overseers, declaring that 'a slave in power becomes an intolerable tyrant'.[88] He recommended the setting up of a new establishment along lines similar to those at Parkhurst. But although plans were drawn up for the new prison and some construction work was commenced, the scheme ultimately fell through, following the closure of Point Puer itself.[89] Nonetheless reforms were introduced as a result of Horne's visit, with each boy given 2½ hours of education daily and with 7¼ hours a day now devoted to labour. No play hours were specified, so that recreation had to be fitted into meal breaks. Professional teachers were employed to replace the convict labour.[90]

From 1840 New South Wales refused to accept transportees of any age and by the mid-1840s fewer boys were in any case being sentenced to transportation. So while in 1845 around 20 per cent of the convicts arriving in Van Diemen's Land were lads under the age of eighteen, by 1847 that had fallen to below 10 per cent, and in 1849 it was under 1 per cent. [91] New methods of punishing juvenile delinquents were being tried in Britain itself, and in Australia growing resistance to the transportation system was becoming apparent.

When the boys had spent about four years in training at Point Puer and were considered able to earn their own living, they were normally granted a ticket-of-leave and, in later years, were sent along to a new probation station for juveniles, from where they could seek employment on their own account.[92] Some were eventually able to set up in business for themselves, and many more achieved respectability as tradesmen, shopworkers and labourers in Australia. A few went on to greater things. They included the Scots-born Andrew Thomson, who was transported to New South Wales at the end of the eighteenth century, when he was sixteen. He came from a family of hawkers and on arriving in the colony he worked as a labourer in a stone-mason's gang. When his sentence expired he set up as a shopkeeper in the settlement of Windsor. Subsequently he financed the building of small ships which were used for local trading, and acted as superintendant of some of the convict labourers in government employ at Windsor. Later he turned to farming, as well as setting up a salt-making plant. Alongside his official posts he used his newly won prosperity to give financial aid to some of his neighbours when they were hit by severe floods. These activities led to his appointment as a magistrate in 1810, despite opposition from many of the free settlers, who felt that his elevation – and that of other former convicts – undermined their own status in the community.

Thomson became a friend of the then Governor, Lachlan Macquarie, and when he died a few months after becoming a magistrate, the Governor paid a warm tribute to his role in Australian community life.[93]

A more modest success story involved William Wilkes, who was transported for life in 1833 at the age of sixteen for stealing cash from the home of a neighbour. Despite the fact that the money taken was immediately repaid, he was sent to New South Wales shortly after the trial. On arrival he was employed on surveying work for the government and later recounted how on one occasion when in charge of a party of convicts he had 'succeeded without bloodshed in warding off a determined attack made on the camp by hostile Aboriginal Natives.' This feat was subsequently notified to the authorities by his superior. When he obtained his ticket-of-leave he took up a clerical post and subsequently had a temporary appointment as 'Clerk of the Bench and Post Master' at Brisbane, having by that time obtained a conditional pardon. This gave him rights of citizenship but did not permit him to leave Australia. Later he became editor of a local newspaper and in 1855 he applied for an absolute pardon, having, as he pointed out, been in Australia for twenty-two years. In his appeal he mentioned that he had married and had three daughters, 'whose prospects in life may be seriously affected, should the petitioner die, without the last brand of criminality being erased from his character'.[94] His application was passed to the Home Secretary, Sir George Grey, in London. It was finally approved in July 1856, Grey noting that taking into account Wilkes's age when the offence was committed and the fact that the governor of New South Wales had recommended him 'for the grant of a Free Pardon … this might be granted'.[95] Wilkes was now able to return to Britain should he so desire.

Another youngster who went on to achieve modest prosperity was Thomas Crapper of Oxford. Early in December 1843, Thomas, then aged fourteen, and his twelve-year-old cousin, Richard Crapper, were sentenced at the winter assizes to ten years' transportation for burglary. Both boys were sent first to Millbank prison, where they arrived on 22 January 1844, and from there they went to Parkhurst, where Richard died in February 1846. Thomas, meanwhile, was trained as a shoemaker and in June 1846 he sailed on the *Maitland* for Port Philip in Australia. On arrival he received a conditional pardon and was able to obtain paid employment as a shoemaker. Later he became a gold digger, and in October 1859 he married Alice Kenny. They had nine children and in the interim Thomas took over a hotel and store. Later he became a farmer and acquired extensive property in the Neilborough district, as well as owning a blacksmith's shop. He died in Australia in October 1909, aged eighty.[96]

Yet while some transportees were able to achieve success in Australia, or at least to make a comfortable life for themselves, there were many others who were less fortunate. In part, for those who were assigned, it could depend on the character of their master or mistress, with some treating their convict labour with harshness, while others offered their workers a chance to make good. Only in Van Diemen's Land, under the governorship of George Arthur (1824-36) was an attempt made to distribute the convicts according to the character of the master and mistress, the order and discipline they maintained in their establishment, and the occupation they pursued. Innkeepers and former convicts, were among the people forbidden to receive assigned labour by Arthur.[97]

Among those unfortunates whose life in Australia was not a happy one was young Jane Forbes, who had come out with the *Lady Juliana*. She had been taken as a 'ship wife' by the seaman William Carlo, and soon after her arrival in the summer of 1790 she was sent to Parramatta, where her daughter was baptised in November 1790. Less than three months later the little girl died and about six weeks after that Jane married one of the First Fleet convicts, William Butler. They had their first child, a daughter, a year or so after, but she died at the age of one, while a son was born in October 1893. The couple moved to a 50-acre farm in July 1791 and exactly four years after that Jane died at the age of twenty-two. While she was preparing the family breakfast she accidentally fell into the fire and was so severely burnt that she died. Her surviving child may also have died, as Butler was recorded as being without children in 1800.[98]

Then there was James Grace, who as a boy of eleven was sentenced to seven years' transportation for breaking into a shop and stealing a pair of silk stockings and ten yards of ribbon. In 1787, aged about fourteen, he embarked on the *Friendship*, one of the First Fleet transports. In March 1790 he was sent to Norfolk Island where he was shown as subsisting on a small plot of land and sharing ownership of a sow provided by the government, with two other convicts. It was a precarious livelihood and by February 1792 he seems to have been working for other settlers. He died on 15 November, 1793 on Norfolk Island at the age of twenty or twenty-one.[99]

So while the hopes of those who saw transportation as a device for reform as well as punishment were sustained by cases like those of Andrew Thomson, William Wilkes and Thomas Crapper, it is clear that many more fell by the wayside, or by re-offending in Australia faced harsh punishment in one of the penal settlements, or even death. In 1853 the system largely came to an end, although a few prisoners continued to be despatched for another fifteen years. By that time doubts about the value of transportation were being widely voiced. As early as 1838 this had been made clear when the *Report of the Select Committee on Transportation* denounced the whole concept:

> Transportation is not merely inefficient in producing the moral reformation of an offender; it is efficient in demoralising those, whom accidental circumstances, more than a really vicious nature, have seduced into crime. It is hardly needful to point out, how this must necessarily be the result of crowding together multitudes of offenders during the idleness of a long voyage; of a life in a colony, where vice is the rule and virtue the exception; where every description of offender and profligate finds himself kept in countenance by a majority, and where there is free interchange of every kind of vicious instruction.[100]

The Committee concluded that transportation should be discontinued as soon as possible, and that those crimes which were punished in that way should 'in future be punished by confinement with hard labour ... for periods varying from two to fifteen years'.[101] Despite these forceful comments three more decades were to elapse before the last vestiges of the system came to an end.

But if there were doubts about transportation itself, that did not undermine the more general belief that a new start in a fresh environment could bring about the reform of errant youth. As well as transportation, therefore, a significant emigration movement was developed, designed to rescue the destitute and rehabilitate the potentially criminal. It was a cause taken up by some of the philanthropic organisations working with young offenders at the beginning of the nineteenth century and beyond, as well as by the promoters of Parkhurst juvenile prison. As the Marlborough Street magistrate, Henry Moreton Dyer, commented in March 1828: 'I am so strongly impressed with the expediency of this removal of criminals, that I cannot help thinking it might be highly expedient for His Majesty's government to adopt and encourage some system of voluntary emigration for those who are detected in offences, and yet have not advanced so far as to bring themselves, under the existing law, within the pale of transportation. I feel convinced, that many persons who now derive a precarious subsistence from their depredations on the public ... would be glad to take advantage of the means of finding an occupation in another country'.[102]

Colonial Emigration

As we have seen, in the early nineteenth century there was growing anxiety about the large number of vagrant children wandering the streets of London and other expanding urban areas, without any obvious means of subsistence. Clad in ragged clothes, with 'filthy matted hair, and red, chilblained feet' during the winter months, they snatched a living where they could.[103] In 1816 William Fielding, one of the capital's magistrates, spoke of the numerous 'vagabond boys' who were appearing before him from the parish of St Martin's in the Fields. 'To send them to prison would be cruel; and there is no way of providing for them; but if there was a mode of sending them either to America, to the Cape of Good Hope, or to the West Indian Islands ... I am sure the magistrates could very speedily supply these places with inhabitants if they were wanted'.[104] A decade later Robert Chambers, another of the capital's magistrates, echoed these views, declaring that 'such a system of emigration' would be highly beneficial. 'I conceive that London has got too full of children.' He was concerned about their lack of employment and considered that youngsters aged between twelve and twenty would gain from an overseas initiative of this kind.[105]

These comments underline the ambiguous motives of philanthropists and the state as they sought to promote juvenile emigration throughout the nineteenth century and, indeed, up to the First World War and beyond. It was never clear whether the main beneficiaries were to be the children themselves, who would be given a fresh start in life away from the temptations of British urban society, or whether it was the community at large that would gain by having removed from the streets unwanted and impoverished children, who were seen as potential criminals. This dichotomy was expressed by Captain Edward Brenton, an early supporter of emigration and founder of the Society for the Suppression of Juvenile Vagrancy, set up in 1830. In 1834 it adopted the more emollient title of The Children's Friend Society, although its objectives were unchanged. As Brenton himself declared, it sought to rescue 'from early depravity children who are ... running wild about the streets, daily progressing in crime'. In his case, as with most of the other philanthropists involved in the emigration cause, poverty, homelessness and criminality were inextricably interlinked. The view that a youngster could be destitute and yet honest did not enter into their calculations. To meet the needs of such children, the new Society was to establish 'Agricultural Workhouses' at a 'convenient distance from the Metropolis', where training in 'habits of industry' would be given to fit them for future employment. At the same time 'the most scrupulous attention' would be given to the inmates' religious and moral duties.[106] 'Any boy guilty of a falsehood or improper language [was] to be placed in solitary confinement for a short period', but, interestingly, the corporal punishment of wrongdoers was 'strictly forbidden'. If at the end of their training, there was no employment for them in Britain itself, then 'facilities will be given to them to proceed to our Colonies, where there is a great demand for their labour'. To prepare for this they were not only to spend several hours a day in field labour but were to learn other relevant skills, such as how to grow their own vegetables, cook their food, wash and mend their clothes, carry out simple building work, and even grind their corn in hand mills.[107]

The first group of boys instructed at the Society's Hackney Wick Asylum were sent to the Cape of Good Hope in 1833. There they were to be apprenticed to masters who would provide them with a home and additional training. To ensure that the correct procedures were followed and appropriate places were found, local commissioners were appointed in South Africa to co-ordinate the operation. In 1834, in a letter to the *Morning Herald* Brenton described the whole venture as the 'transplanting of young people to a more open and less occupied field'. This was 'as necessary in human society, as it is in the vegetable kingdom, and the effect is as beneficial in the one case as in the other'.[108] In all, between 1833 and 1841, when the Society ceased its emigration campaign, it was to 'rescue' 2,000 children from the London streets and to ship 1,158 of them overseas, with about 840 going to South Africa alone.[109] Of the rest, around seventy-four went to Australia, five to Mauritius and the remainder went to Canada.

However, although Edward Brenton's efforts were to provide a major focus for the juvenile emigration movement in the 1830s, his organisation was not the first in the field. Already in 1819 the Refuge for the Destitute, in its efforts to rehabilitate young criminals, began to send a few boys to South Africa. This policy continued on a small scale into the 1840s. Thus of eighty-five young males who left the Refuge's Hoxton base in 1841, nineteen emigrated to Upper Canada.[110] These initiatives were praised in 1836 in the *First Report of the Inspectors of Prisons*. The Inspectors also gave support to the emigration movement in general. 'In the Canadas, and at the Cape', they declared,

> many lads ... Sent out by the 'Refuge for the Destitute' have readily found employment; and we submit that what this institution has desultorily effected on a small scale, might, with the aid of the Colonial Government be extended to youthful offenders generally, with the best effects.

However, they also warned that it was essential to draw a distinction between emigration, which was a voluntary process – at least in theory – and transportation:

> The one should be regarded as a preventive, the other a punishment for crime. It will therefore be necessary to establish a broad distinction in the treatment of the emigrant, and the transport-boy. This distinction may consist in the selection of the colony to which they are sent, their

treatment on their arrival, the terms and period of their apprenticeship, and in the prospective advantage to be enjoyed at its expiration.[111]

Nonetheless in the 1830s it was the Children's Friend Society which remained to the fore in the promotion of juvenile emigration. The choice of South Africa as a major destination for its young charges was significant because it came at a time when the ending of slave apprenticeships among the black population in the Cape Colony was leading to fears of a labour shortage. (These apprenticeships finally ended in December 1838). However, despite the selection of local commissioners to ensure that the children were properly looked after, that did not always prove an effective safeguard. According to their apprenticeship indentures, the industrial training the children were to receive, their living conditions, their remuneration and their religious and moral instruction were all covered. But experience showed that those conditions were not always observed. George Waddilove, for example, was apprenticed as a shepherd to a farmer in the Cape Town area in 1836. Three years later he complained of not having enough to eat and being required to sleep 'in the chaff-house', where he had 'a blanket, but no bed. I get soap and wash my clothes ... I am sometimes punished for neglect'. Although he had a father in England he was not able to contact him.[112] Then there was John Gunn, who was aged about seventeen in 1839 and was apprenticed with two other boys at Great Drakenstein. 'I never go to church; am employed taking care of horses grazing; I and the other two apprentices sleep in the same bed, in an outhouse; I am in good health, get enough to eat, but have no clothes but these on me, and have, to wash my shirt every Sunday'. According to the magistrate who visited the three lads, they had 'but one ragged suit each' and their condition was described as generally 'deplorable'.[113]

Many of the children were sent to Dutch-speaking families on remote farmsteads, and some even began to forget their own language. Their employment in such dead-end jobs as cattle herding, looking after sheep and watching over horses was also criticised. It was said that such a youngster spent his time 'during the heat of the day, either in sleeping under a bush, or in strolling, sluggard-like, after the cattle; his only associate some stray Hottentot, and his only attainment indolent and slovenly habits.'[114]

As well as preparing boys for colonial life at its Hackney Wick Asylum, The Children's Friend Society set up a centre for girls at Chiswick in 1834. There they learnt household skills in preparation for apprenticeship as domestic servants in colonial families. Brenton's slogan was: 'The Bible and spade for the boy; the Bible, broom and needle for the girl'.[115]

The plan was for the children to receive at least three months' training in England, thereby giving them 'full time to make up their minds' as to whether they wanted to emigrate.[116] But it seems those rules too were not always observed. Sarah Ballot, who was working as a maid for a doctor in Paarl, South Africa, claimed in 1839 that prior to being sent overseas she had attended the parish school at St Martin's in London. She had been 'sent out here without my sister's knowledge or my own consent', and she wished to return to her sister, who was married and lived in London.[117]

Apart from the youngsters the Society itself gathered together, it was also prepared to accept poor law children sent by individual parishes, providing a financial contribution was made towards their maintenance while they were undergoing training and to help meet the cost of their journey to their colonial destination. Normally their future masters were expected to meet three-fifths of the total transport costs, which in the case of South Africa amounted to £15 per child, while the Society – or, in the case of poor law children, the parish – made up the rest. Some of the children and their families claimed that this meant that the young people were in effect being 'sold' into slavery by the Society.[118]

Inevitably the well-being of individual migrants depended on the character of their master and mistress. So while William Tozer praised Philip Botha as being more like a father to him than a master, others were less fortunate. Already by 1836 there were reports of examples of 'undue severity or blameable neglect' in the treatment of some young apprentices, particularly in the Cape Colony.[119] These ranged from a failure to pay the apprentices the paltry pocket money they were owed, so that they became in effect unpaid labourers, to a more damaging omission to provide proper food and clothing, and an excessive use of corporal punishment for even trivial misdemeanours.

These issues surfaced in the British press, notably in *The Times*, in April 1839, when among other reports about the doings of the Children's Friend Society in South Africa, the newspaper reproduced a letter allegedly written by one young emigrant, William Henry Bay, to his mother. In this he complained he was 'learning no trade', but was treated as 'only a servant'. He had

> not the best of masters. I am neither found in caps nor shoes, from which I feel great inconvenience; ... I am placed amongst a parcel of slaves, and not thought much better of by the master nor by the slaves themselves, as there is no difference made between us ... My master is a Dutchman, ... a farmer ...

He asked his mother not to let anyone know that he had written in this vein as it would 'make bad worse, and will be of no use; ... I am only 12 miles from Cape-town, and will look for a ship which will convey me home much better and sooner than all the trouble you can take for me'.[120] In the furore that followed this and similar allegations, *The Times* scathingly referred to the Children's Friend Society as the 'Children's "Kidnapping Society"', and condemned its general emigration strategy and, in particular, the activities of Captain Brenton himself. In the midst of the controversy, Brenton suddenly died. The Government then intervened, with the Colonial Secretary ordering an inquiry to be undertaken in South Africa to ascertain the conditions under which the children were apprenticed. This was instituted under the direction of the Governor, Sir George Napier, and was conducted by four Cape magistrates. They reported back at the end of 1839. In total, 434 apprentices were investigated under the direction of one of the magistrates. Although he condemned the policy whereby many children had been sent to remote farms run by Boer families, where they were employed on tasks with few prospects, such as herding cattle, he pointed out that the Society itself was partly responsible for this. For it had repeatedly urged the local commissioners, in seeking masters 'not to be too urgent to select tradesmen in towns ... to apprentice their wards to'. It was considered more desirable to place them in the country under a careful master, 'than to indenture them where they would be exposed to temptations, or fall in with bad companions'. Hence of the 434 apprentices considered only about sixty were learning a trade. A further twenty were employed as gardeners and ten worked as clerks or in stores. The rest were either farm servants or house servants.[121] Another of the magistrates was concerned at the cultural effect where the apprentices worked for Dutch-speaking farmers who knew no English. They were 'fast losing their religion and language, and gradually, I fear, falling into the immoral habits and customs of the coloured population'.[122] There seems little doubt that racism and the fact that many of the apprentices were performing tasks formerly carried out by black slaves contributed to the low esteem in which they were held by many of their masters.

Nonetheless the reports showed that the wilder accusations levelled at the Society regarding their alleged connivance at the ill-treatment of the children were wide of the mark.[123] But by then the damage had been done. In South Africa the local commissioners refused to accept any more emigrants sent by the Society, and in England the bad publicity which had arisen from the events of 1839 led to a drying up of funds. The last boatload of migrants, twenty-three boys, arrived at Cape Town in May 1841, and it was with great difficulty the youngsters were placed in families.[124] By 1843 The Children's Friend Society had itself been dissolved.

However, the unfortunate events surrounding the Brenton initiative did not prevent others venturing into the field of juvenile emigration. For a belief in the benefits of moving deprived and semi-criminal children to a new and purer agrarian environment overseas still had powerful resonances. In the late 1840s, therefore, the Philanthropic Society began to send a trickle of youngsters overseas. Prior to its move to its new Farm School at Redhill in Surrey in 1849 it had despatched fifty-five youngsters. This increased in the early 1850s to around fifty children a year. The boys were sent to North America, Australia and the Cape Colony. Each was consigned to an individual master, for whom they were expected to work for at least twelve months upon arrival. Their voyage was arranged through reputable agents in London, and the boys went out as independent emigrants.[125] The opportunity to move overseas in this way was held out as a reward for good conduct by the Philanthropic Society, and a similar attitude was adopted by the Ragged School Union. This was set up in 1840 to provide a modicum of education and help for destitute children in London. It was established under the leadership of Lord Ashley (later the Earl of Shaftesbury) and in 1848 he was able to persuade the Government to provide funding for one hundred and fifty of the best pupils to be sent to Australia, where they would be employed as shepherds. The boys chosen were to be at least fourteen years of age, while any girls sent out were to go as servants. By this means the colonies would be supplied with much-needed labour and Britain itself would gain 'by the transplantation of thousands of children untainted by crime' since they would be 'rescued from pernicious vagrancy' and would 'rejoice in the fruits of honest labour'. The girls would be 'saved altogether from prostitution'.[126]

Ashley himself claimed the venture was a success but others were less sure. One MP in June 1850 argued that the young migrants had not turned out as well as expected: 'it was to be regretted that several of them on their arrival there, sustained themselves by petty pilfering'.[127] Ashley strongly denied this, but in the event the Government provided no more funds, and the Ragged School Union scheme for emigrating children had to proceed on a voluntary basis. In the 1850s it sent a mixed population of paupers and convicted children to Australia and Canada.[128]

Neither the Ragged School Union nor the Philanthropic Society had a major impact on juvenile emigration during these years. More significant was the attempt at Parkhurst prison to turn boys originally sentenced to transportation into emigrants, free from the taint of criminality. To this end efforts were made at first to send the children to areas away from the penal colonies in New South Wales and Van Diemen's Land, and to provide them with pardons or tickets-of-leave to enable them to make a fresh start. Hence of the first 102 boys admitted to Parkhurst in 1838-39, exactly half were sent to New Zealand, either as emigrants or, in the case of the younger boys, as apprentices. But there they received a cool reception, the editor of the *Southern Cross* newspaper, for example, declaring angrily:

'We can scarcely think of anything more heartlessly cruel or infamously immoral and unjust than the conduct of the Home Government in this colony ... They have sent the seeds of crime and immorality to be scattered in the shape of young convicts from the penitentiary of Parkhurst'.[129] On arrival they were taken in hand by the Harbour Master and Immigration Officer in Auckland, David Rough, who did not rate their trade skills very highly. He tendered them for work as farm labourers by an advertisement in the *Government Gazette*. Nevertheless, despite this hostile reception it was to the boys' credit that over a third of them were said to have done well. Despite Rough's intervention, most seem to have gone into the tailoring and bootmaking trades, with a few only going on to the farms. Eight ended up in gaol.[130] However, the difficulty experienced in finding masters for the boys meant that after 1843 no more were sent to New Zealand.

Similarly when Parkhurst attempted to send some of its charges to the Cape Colony, the Governor, Sir George Napier, wrote in protest: 'The young delinquents ... will instruct their less civilised associates in those vices which have been the cause of their introduction into the colony'.[131]

Efforts to settle the boys in Western Australia proved more successful, with the colonial government appointing a Guardian of Juvenile Immigrants to look after them. At Parkhurst itself, as with the Philanthropic Society's young migrants, the opportunity to emigrate was held out as a reward to those who behaved well, and the Governor of Parkhurst took pride in the favourable reports he received of them.[132] One such was Joshua Strickland, who came to Western Australia in 1842 and was apprenticed to a baker for five years. 'On the very day of his discharge he entered as journeyman the service of the principal baker in Perth at the wage of £3 a month besides which he boards with the family and has comfortable lodgings'.[133] Even in 1861 a Western Australian farmer named Burgess, who had had some Parkhurst boys working for him, was warm in his praise, claiming they had turned out well: 'some of them are now respectable men, and merchants in the place'.[134] In all, 231 boys went to the colony from Parkhurst between 1842 and 1849.[135]

Inevitably there were a trickle of failures, like the young Scotsman, James Nimmo, who was described by the Guardian of Juvenile Immigrants as 'a notorious liar, insolent and idle, cunning and hardened to punishment and I fear very dishonest'.[136] He was unable to find any master prepared to keep the lad. But most of the Parkhurst boys relished the opportunity to gain their liberty by moving overseas. In all, 1,498 boys were sent from the prison to the colonies between 1842 and 1853, when the scheme ended with the disappearance of the ticket-of-leave system itself.[137] The Governor of Parkhurst claimed this change of policy caused discontent among the boys still in the prison, as they saw a potential escape route to a new life overseas snatched away from them.[138]

In the second half of the nineteenth century the emigration movement concentrated on pauper children rather than juvenile delinquents, on the abandoned and the destitute rather than the criminal. As such it falls outside the scope of this study.[139]

CHAPTER 4

THE SPIRIT OF REFORM: 1840-1900

That part of the community which we are to consider, consists of those who have not yet fallen into actual crime, but who are almost certain from their ignorance, destitution, and the circumstances in which they are growing up, to do so, if a helping hand be not extended to raise them; – these form the perishing classes: – and of those who have already received the prison brand, or … are notoriously living by plunder, – … whose hand is against every man, for they know not that any man is their brother; – these form the dangerous classes. Look at them in the streets, where, to the eye of the worldly man, they all appear the scum of the populace, fit only to be swept as vermin from the face of the earth; … Behold them when the hand of wisdom and of love has shown them a better way, and purified and softened their outward demeanour and their inner spirit, in Schools well adapted to themselves, and you hardly believe them to be separated by any distinct boundary from the children who frequent the National and British Schools.

Mary Carpenter, *Reformatory Schools For the Children of the Perishing and Dangerous Classes and for Juvenile Offenders* (London, 1851), pp. 2-3.

The Juvenile Offenders Act, 1847

During the 1840s concern was expressed about what seemed a rapid rise in juvenile crime, and about the need 'for special treatment for juvenile offenders to prevent them growing up into hardened criminals.' In 1851, the penal reformer, Mary Carpenter, described the 'enormity and amount of juvenile depravity' as an issue which currently 'most painfully' engaged the public attention.[1] In the same year another reformer, Matthew Davenport Hill, the recorder of Birmingham, called juvenile delinquency 'the headspring of that ever-flowing river of crime, which spreads its corrupt and corrupting waters through the land'.[2] All this resulted in what two modern writers have labelled 'a deluge of "speech and pamphlet Philanthropy"' sweeping the country, demanding fundamental reform in the way young criminals were treated.[3]

At the same time it was widely recognised that many of the offences the children committed were trivial, such as minor thefts of food or fuel, and that for this they were brought to court to face the full ritual of a jury trial. In 1847 Lord Denman referred to petty thieves who had stolen 'a faggot or an egg' and who were then remanded in custody for several months before their trial came on.[4]

Yet, although the admittedly flawed returns relating to prisoners tried at assizes and quarter sessions, or convicted at petty sessions, do show a rise in juvenile offending during the period, the increase was scarcely as dramatic as some commentators suggested. Thus in 1839, 10,368 young people under the age of seventeen were punished under those three jurisdictions, and by 1847 that had risen to 12,082 so punished; this was an advance of just 1,714 or 16.5 per cent over the nine years in question.[5] Furthermore, closer examination reveals that almost all of the rise was accounted for by young males in the age group fourteen to seventeen. In 1839, 1,761 lads in this category had been tried at assizes or quarter sessions, compared to 2,251 so tried in 1847, a rise of 590. Of those convicted summarily by magistrates, the increase was from 6,184 in 1839 to 7,196 in 1847, up by 1,012. So of the 1,714 extra juveniles charged in 1847, around 1,600 of them comprised youngsters in this narrow fourteen to seventeen age group.

Against this background in 1847 a radical change in sentencing policy towards the young was introduced through the Juvenile Offenders Act. This allowed all children under the age of fourteen who had committed simple larcenies up to a value of five shillings to be tried summarily before two magistrates in petty sessions, providing they or their guardians consented, instead of being sent for trial by jury at the assizes or quarter sessions. The Act also set a maximum of three months on the time magistrates could imprison children, though that could include hard labour and a whipping as well. They could also dismiss a case if they deemed it appropriate, or merely order the young offender to be whipped and then released. As David Philips points out, the use of whipping as a punishment increased as a result of this legislation.[6]

In 1850 the age limit of youngsters covered by the legislation was raised to sixteen, although the provision regarding whipping was excluded as a possible punishment for that older group. Margaret May has stressed the importance of this and other mid-century initiatives in that for 'the first time in a legislative enactment Parliament recognised juvenile delinquents as a distinct social phenomenon ... Thus children coming before the courts were no longer regarded as 'little adults' but as beings in their own right entitled to special care' because they lacked full responsibility for their actions.[7]

The reform movement had a further success in 1879 in that from then on all indictable offences committed by children under twelve, except for homicide, could be tried at petty sessions, subject to parental consent. The range of offences for which those aged between twelve and sixteen could be tried summarily, with their agreement, was likewise extended beyond simple larceny to include more serious crimes, such as larceny from the person, embezzlement by a clerk or servant, and receiving stolen goods.[8]

There were several reasons behind the 1847 policy breakthrough. First and foremost was the desire to cut the time youngsters spent in prison while awaiting trial by jury. As one MP pointed out disapprovingly in a debate on the Bill, under the current arrangements those awaiting a hearing at quarter sessions 'might remain in gaol for two or three months after commitment before they were tried, it being almost impossible for them to procure bail'.[9] Under the new system the case would be heard within days, sometimes, indeed, on the day the offence was committed, and that would avoid the possibility of young children, especially first offenders, being 'contaminated' by an unnecessary spell in gaol. It was also a far cheaper option. David Philips estimates it could easily cost £20 to maintain the accused in prison awaiting trial, to say nothing of perhaps £10 for the cost of prosecution, all to deal with 'a theft of the value of 6*d*.'[10] In addition the 1847 Act provided for payment of appropriate expenses to prosecutors and witnesses for the prosecution, to encourage them to bring forward cases they might otherwise have ignored because of the expense, time and trouble involved in bringing a minor offender to a jury trial. The new arrangement had a further advantage in that the case would be tried in the town of the petty sessional district where the offence had been committed, thereby eliminating the transport and accommodation costs that would have been incurred had it been heard in the county town. For the accused, there was the advantage of having the matter dealt with speedily. It is, therefore, not surprising that most of those accused of thefts amounting to less than 5*s* in value chose to be tried summarily.[11]

But if the Juvenile Offenders Act had aimed to expedite the administration of justice to young delinquents and to make the judicial process less formal and intimidating, it had the unexpected result of increasing greatly the number of children brought to court. Clearly many victims of petty thefts had in the past been reluctant to pursue minor cases at quarter sessions or assizes but now felt free to do so when a simpler and less costly means of prosecution became available. Consequently although there was a decline in the number of juvenile cases heard before quarter sessions in some parts of the country, the total of children and young people tried summarily rose sharply, thereby fuelling fears of an explosion in youth crime. In Lancashire, for example, while the number of youngsters convicted after a trial at quarter sessions or assizes rose from fifty in 1850 to eighty-one in 1852, the number convicted at petty sessions under the Juvenile Offenders Act jumped from 131 to 216 over the same period. Similarly in Derbyshire, where just four young offenders had been convicted after a jury trial in 1850, that had risen to eleven in 1852, plus an advance in the number convicted summarily under the Juvenile Offenders legislation from nil at the earlier date to thirteen at the later. In just three years, therefore, the number of juveniles imprisoned in Derbyshire rose from four to twenty-four.[12] In Staffordshire, David Philips has identified an even more spectacular rise, with seventeen young people convicted under the Juvenile Offenders Act in 1847 increasing to 159 so convicted in 1859, although the total then fell back a little to 120 in 1860, the last year for which Philips has produced figures.[13]

These legislative changes meant, therefore, that whereas about 10,000 young people (including 1,400 girls) had been sent to prison in 1840, that had jumped to 13,981 by 1856. It was in those circumstances that Mary Carpenter in her pioneering book *Reformatory Schools* (1851), referred bitterly to the way in which hopes that the new measures would 'diminish crime by saving young criminals from the brand of public prosecution' had been frustrated by such developments. She quoted statistics collected by John Adams, a leading member of the legal profession that showed juvenile committals to the various London prisons after the Act had risen by 107 in the first year and 173 in the second. According to Adams, many people who would have hesitated to brand a child a felon had decided to prosecute since the Act was introduced, 'thus familiarising the young with the interior of the gaol'.[14] A large proportion of those imprisoned during these mid-century years were sent for very short periods only, in part, apparently, to ensure that they received the lowest scale of prison diet, as a deterrent. But this, too, had what the governor of Edinburgh prison called 'the most mischievous effect possible; it inures them to imprisonment by slow degrees, till it becomes no punishment at all'.[15] At the same time the fact that a boy had been imprisoned at all went 'far to ruin him for life'.

The anxiety about the brevity of sentences and the often trivial nature of offences dealt with by magistrates under the Juvenile Offenders Acts of 1847 and 1850 is understandable if specimen cases brought before London's police courts are examined. Thus in the period 13 September 1847 to 26 February 1848, out of eighty-four youngsters convicted, no less than 59.5 per cent were imprisoned for from one to three days only, usually accompanied by

Oliver Twist watched with horror as the 'Artful Dodger' picked a pocket.

hard labour and a whipping.[16] A further 15.5 per cent were imprisoned for between four and seven days with hard labour, so that three quarters of those convicted served a week or less in prison; a mere 4.8 per cent of the offenders were gaoled for two months. Furthermore, of the eighty-four convicted, twenty-five were found guilty of stealing small quantities of food. They included Robert Cole, who on 18 January 1848, was sentenced by Thames Police Court to two days' hard labour and a whipping for stealing two buns, valued at twopence, from Elizabeth Delve. Then there were William Major and James McCue, who were each sentenced at Hammersmith to seven days' hard labour and a whipping for stealing half a loaf, valued at 4*d* from Elizabeth Coutts in Kensington. Ironically, John Cronan, who had seemingly engaged in pickpocketing, taking a purse and 5*s* in cash from a female victim, was sentenced by the Thames Police Court on the same day as Robert Cole to an identical sentence – two days' imprisonment with hard labour and a whipping – despite the more serious nature of his offence.

Some children appeared more than once before the courts. They included Edward Toghill, sentenced to one day's imprisonment and a whipping for stealing a loaf in September 1847. About three months after, he appeared again before Marylebone Police Court, on a charge of stealing seven silk handkerchiefs of the value of 19s. This time he was imprisoned for a month, with hard labour, and was again to be whipped.[17]

Around five years later, between June and December 1853, a further sample of fifty-eight young offenders reveals that prison sentences had increased somewhat, so that now none of the youngsters was imprisoned for less than four days, and 7.6 per cent only were sentenced to between four days and a week.[18] In all, about six out of ten were being gaoled for a month or less, compared to more than nine out of ten so punished in 1847-48. Of those sentenced in 1853, none imprisoned for more than seven days was given a whipping. Again thefts of food, wine and poultry feature prominently, with just one in five in 1853 offending in this way. They included Robert Allcock, imprisoned for a month with hard labour by Westminster Police Court for stealing a loaf valued at 5¼d. Then there was William Williams, who on 16 November was charged before Westminster Police Court with stealing a tin can valued at 1s 6d. He was given the option of paying a fine of 5s or being imprisoned in the Westminster House of Correction for fourteen days. Presumably he paid up, for on 24 November he committed a further offence, taking 3 lbs of bacon, valued at 2s. This time he was less fortunate, being sent to the Westminster House of Correction for six weeks.[19]

In the 1860s imprisonment for trivial offences continued, so that among the prisoners in the Sussex county prison in 1864 was a nine-year-old boy serving two months' hard labour for stealing 1s 8d. Another lad, aged fifteen, was sentenced to seven days' hard labour for 'wilful damage', which in his case amounted to plucking a flower, worth one penny, from a garden.[20] Not until the 1880s did the Home Office begin to intervene to remit or reduce what were considered inappropriate sentences. By the 1890s a check was kept on magistrates through reports of their sentences being sent by the prison boards to the Home Office. As a result, a magistrate's sentence was occasionally overruled. Gertrude Tuckwell quotes the case of a boy sentenced to a month's imprisonment for stealing fruit but whose punishment was reduced to seven days by direction of the Home Office.

These kinds of offences may have been inspired by mischief or by hunger and destitution, but they hardly amounted to the 'depravity' that contemporary commentators apparently feared.

Many post-1847 judgements aroused the anger of Mary Carpenter. Her own work in promoting a ragged school for needy children in Bristol had led her to argue that youthful criminality was almost always the result of social and environmental factors. She had 'no place for notions of heredity, physical or mental disposition or inherent wickedness'.[22] Instead she blamed the low moral condition of parents, their failure to train their children, the temptations to crime held out by pawnbrokers and the like, and the influence of the workhouse and of the gaol when once the children had been sent to them. She firmly believed that through kindness and appropriate education and training such youngsters could be reformed and turned into worthwhile members of society. That was what she set out to demonstrate, with different remedies for those she classed as the 'perishing' classes, who had not actually committed any crime but by reason of their circumstances were likely to do so, and the 'dangerous' classes, who had already lapsed into criminality.[23] Unless they were saved by reformatory training their 'moral destruction' was imminent.

The notion of reformatory training and rehabilitatory care was not new. In the eighteenth century this had been one of the objectives of the Philanthropic Society, but in the mid-nineteenth century the issue was to become more acute. As the Marquess of Westminster declared in the House of Lords in June 1847, what was needed was 'some change in the treatment of juvenile offenders, so that they might be instructed and reclaimed as far as possible.[24] Already on the continent of Europe various agricultural reform schools and colonies had been established and two of these particularly attracted the attention of English penal reformers. The first, the Rauhe Haus, had been set up near Hamburg in 1833. It adopted a 'family-style' organisation, with a trained and religiously motivated staff dedicated to the welfare of the young inmates. The second, established at Mettray near Tours at the end of 1839, was to prove especially attractive to English reformers. It, too, adopted a family structure, with the four to five hundred residents divided into units of forty boys each. Sydney Turner, chaplain and superintendent of the Philanthropic Society's London settlement, visited Mettray in 1846 at the request of the Committee of the Society, and was much impressed by what he saw.

The groups of boys lived in separate houses under a master and two assistants, and this close association between master and boys encouraged 'higher moral' feelings in the young inmates, who were drawn from French prisons. They were engaged in agricultural labour and were kept so continuously employed that at the end of the day they 'collapsed exhausted into bed'. They lived a spartan like existence, with fires rarely allowed, food and clothing of the simplest kind provided, and with the rules rigidly enforced, so that 'the least fault [was] punished'. But discipline was maintained not merely by punishment but by the offering of rewards, in the form of tools, articles of dress, pictures and religious emblems. And to ensure that the reform process did not give advantages to the inmates that were unavailable to non-criminal lads, their education was limited to 'as much as the average agricultural and other labourers acquire; viz. to read, to write and to cypher'.[25] The basis of the institution's success was considered to be the 'voluntary zeal' of its promoters and their sense of religious mission.

It was the Mettray example that largely inspired the early British reformatory school movement. Yet there was a degree of ambivalence about the whole issue of setting up reformatory institutions in this country. On the one hand there was concern that offenders should not receive an education and training superior to anything available to their non-criminal counterparts, much as had been the case in Mettray. On the other, there was a belief that an element of punishment as well as rehabilitation should form part of the sentences handed down. As an offence had been committed many felt that a term of imprisonment should be imposed, since it was not the business of a reformatory school to punish. A preliminary spell in gaol might also have the merit of supplying a 'calming period' to the young offender after the 'high excitement' which would inevitably have accompanied his trial. That would help to create the proper frame of mind to make the offender receptive to what the reformatory had to offer.[26]

Among those holding these views was the Gloucestershire landowner. Thomas Lloyd Baker, who was a prison visitor, a magistrate and a poor law guardian and who took a long-term interest in the reform of criminal children. In 1852 he set up a reformatory school at Hardwicke on his estate, and even in the 1880s was still advocating 'a short imprisonment before a reformatory, not ... to ... wipe off the debt due to society, for this cannot be done except by a voluntary course of good conduct while at liberty, but to impress on the boy's mind the feeling that he has done wrong, and to prepare him to receive readily the milder discipline of the reformatory.' Likewise, Jelinger Symonds, a schools inspector, argued that it was dangerous to allow criminals, even juvenile offenders, to go unpunished. This was needed for 'the protection of society'.[27]

Mary Carpenter found such attitudes unacceptable, although she did concede that for some older and hardened lawbreakers a spell in gaol might be justified. Ultimately the policy of prior imprisonment before entry to a reformatory triumphed. Only in 1899 was the obligation to serve a brief period in prison before going to a reformatory school finally ended. However, from 1893 magistrates had the option of avoiding a prior prison sentence if they so wished.[28]

It is to the formation of reformatory and industrial schools to cater for Mary Carpenter's 'dangerous' and 'perishing' classes of children and young people, that we must now turn.

Reformatory and Industrial Schools

The government's first move to establish a reformatory-style institution came, ironically, in 1838 with the setting up of Parkhurst juvenile prison on the Isle of Wight. In many respects its creation underlined the tensions which arose between the desire to punish young offenders and the wish to rehabilitate them. Its prime purpose was to equip youngsters under sentence of transportation, for life in the colonies. But the punitive aspects of its regime dominated, with the adoption of a general philosophy that nothing should be done 'to counteract the wholesome restraints of corrective discipline' in its day-to-day running.[29] As a *state* initiative it aroused the bitter hostility of supporters of the voluntary reform movement, like Mary Carpenter. She insisted that it was 'utterly vain to look for any real reformation where the heart is not touched ... this cannot possibly be done for children under the mechanical and military discipline of Parkhurst'.[30] Ultimately, with the cessation of juvenile transportation in the 1850s and the expansion of the voluntary reformatory movement, Parkhurst came under increasing pressure. By the 1860s it was receiving boys of the 'very worst character' only, while the reformatory schools received 'the better class'.[31] As we saw in an earlier chapter, it was closed as a juvenile prison in 1864, when the last of its inmates were transferred to Dartmoor.

The first true reformatory of this new era, therefore, was the Philanthropic Society's Farm School at Redhill in Surrey. It opened in 1849 and was modelled on the Mettray establishment in France. The chaplain and superintendent, Sydney Turner, considered outdoor occupations for the inmates to be essential, to 'prevent the constant communication and intercourse which could scarcely be avoided when the boys are collected together in sedentary trades'.[32] Agriculture and gardening thus formed an essential part of the curriculum. Much emphasis was also placed on the importance of a family-type organisation and on the inculcation of appropriate religious and moral values. Turner himself defined the principles to be applied at the Farm School as 'Religious Influence – Personal Kindness – Exact Justice and Constant Employment'.[33] Where possible the boys were to be encouraged to emigrate once they had completed their stint at the school. Hence in 1863, the school's annual report noted that of one hundred boys who had been discharged over the preceding twelve months, forty-five had emigrated, compared to twenty-eight who had returned to their 'friends', and nineteen who had been sent out on licence prior to their formal release. Four had absconded. But it lamented that more had not chosen the emigration option.[34] In that year of 251 youngsters resident in the school, 157 were working as 'farm boys', fourteen were 'cow house boys', three were in the stables, ten in the garden and sixteen were in the brickfield. The remaining fifty-one were employed as tailors, shoemakers, carpenters, blacksmiths, bakers, house boys, cook's boys and one bricklayer's labourer.[35] The general argument was that 'every emigrant should know how to plough, clean a horse, and milk a cow'.[36]

In its early years Redhill accepted not merely boys sent by the courts with a conditional pardon but those who were sponsored by parents or other interested parties. In 1849, for example, the Earl of Radnor approached the reformatory about the admission of a teenage boy, David Bunce, who was currently imprisoned in Reading gaol 'for running away with Workhouse clothing'.[37] Turner agreed to accept him provided the Earl paid 4s a week towards his maintenance. If possible, Bunce was also to obtain a conditional pardon from the Home Office requiring him to go to Redhill or another reformatory when he left gaol. The reason for this, Turner noted, was that the

> Pardon wd. give us a more complete hold over him in case of his proving wayward & capricious ... He must come here to *work* & *obey* & not idle or play the fool ... We have no *Walls* or *Locks* – or Warders. The Boys are restrained by influence and attachment only.[38]

Radnor agreed to the terms, a conditional pardon was forthcoming, and Bunce was duly despatched to Redhill on 25 January, 1850. The initial impression he created was not favourable. He was described as having 'a very stubborn & hard spirit – & seems to especially dislike the regular *labor* (sic) required from him ... Mr Turner hopes that as he finds it useless to "kick against the prick" – he may become more contented – & thence in time more willing & more interested in his own improvement'.[39] By the following July that seems to have happened. 'His disposition has certainly altered for the better of late', wrote Turner. 'He was very obstinate & restive – & at one time I think meant to run away from the School – & give himself up to the *certainty* of fresh misconduct & fresh punishment.'[40] In October of that year he and six other lads were judged to have improved sufficiently to be sent to Australia. There young Bunce was to be 'consigned to the care of a kind & influential friend ... who has interested himself heartily in our work'.[41]

A major aim of the Redhill reformatory in Turner's view was to strengthen each boy's self-control and to instil regular habits. As part of the process the lads were allowed to earn a few pence each week for their work, and could then spend this pocket money on 'sundry little luxuries', such as coffee for breakfast, treacle with their pudding, sweets, fruit, postage stamps and the like. Misconduct was punished by fines, but if this use of the reward system failed or the misbehaviour was serious lads

were sent to unheated cells on a bread and water diet for a period ranging
from a few hours to a few days. In the most extreme cases, such as those
involving indecency, cruelty, insolence and defiance of a master, corporal
punishment was administered.[42] As far as possible the work carried out by
the young inmates was to resemble that of ordinary farm labourers.

Thomas Barwick Lloyd Baker, another pioneer, like Turner favoured
agricultural employment, careful religious and moral guidance, and
spartan living conditions at the Hardwicke reformatory he opened with a
friend in March 1852. He argued that an 'element of punishment' should
never be 'divorced from the practice of reformation' and considered one
of his main tasks was 'to calm the over-stimulated city boy'. 'I know of
no employment which will allay the excitement and tranquilize the mind,
so as to prepare it to be acted upon by a firm kindness like steady hard
digging', he declared.[43] An underlying factor, for those contemplating a
return to a life of crime, was that the years spent in tilling the soil would
have roughened the hands so much that pickpocketing at least would no
longer be possible.[44]

Baker set a minimum entrance age of eleven or twelve for his reformatory,
since this would enable the boys to carry out the hard physical labour
required of them. Fifteen was considered the appropriate upper limit for

Boys working in the school garden at Hardwicke Reformatory School,
Gloucestershire, under the eye of the superintendent, William Robinson, c.1902.

reformative training to be effective. Schooling was given for two hours each evening, and religious instruction was provided at the daily morning prayers. Living conditions were austere. In the early days twenty boys had to share a small dormitory and this allowed a space of only about three feet by six feet for each of them. That left 'a narrow passage down the centre of the room' and there was little more than a bare space 'for their hammocks, on each of which is a straw-stuffed bed, a pair of sheets, a blanket, and a counterpane'.[45] The diet included much dry bread, supplemented by vegetables grown on the school premises, a little meat and cheese, and with soup or suet puddings also served as main dishes at the midday dinner. Unsweetened cocoa was provided at breakfast and supper, the only exception being that on Sundays a little sugar was allowed, as well as butter for the bread. But the receiving of these 'concessions' depended on the boy's 'general good conduct'.[46] Baths were allowed once a fortnight, but during the summer the boys were permitted to bathe in the nearby canal, where they learnt to swim. Punishments were similar to those at Redhill, with 'a light use' of the cane, short spells in solitary confinement on a bread and water diet, and fines being the order of the day. Only on rare occasions, involving the most serious offences, were public beatings administered with a birch rod.[47]

The school uniform comprised a suit of corduroy, but on working days the jacket was replaced by a short smock of duck, worn over the sleeved waistcoat. Cash rewards were offered to encourage good work, but these were not to exceed a maximum of sixpence a week, and the money could be used to pay fines for misbehaviour or put to the boy's account for later expenditure. As at Redhill, extra luxuries at meals could also be secured.[48] Like all of the reformatory institutions, the working day began very early, with the boys rising at 5.30 a.m. to 6 a.m. and retiring to bed around 8 p.m., after communal prayers.

Many of the Hardwicke boys came from Gloucestershire and its environs, including Bristol. In 1860 the first Inspector of Reformatory Schools even attributed the decline in juvenile crime in the county during the previous five or six years to the influence of Hardwicke. But Lloyd Baker himself was under no illusions about the difficulty of the task. In a letter to the chairman of the Gloucestershire quarter sessions, he wrote: 'we do not propose to be infallible in turning bad boys into good. We may bend nature but we cannot transform it. Some boys have minds hopelessly deformed and the evil principle at the end of two years is only suppressed but smouldering and ready to break out again at any moment'.[49]

Mary Carpenter was another reformatory school pioneer, setting up Kingswood at Bristol also in 1852. She began with ten boys and five girls, aged between eight and fourteen years. Some were related to one another

Boys in the schoolroom at Hardwicke Reformatory School in the late nineteenth century. Note the bareness of the surroundings.

and all had been sent with the permission of their parents or guardians since, as yet, magistrates had no legal power to commit them. The youngest boy had been given a six-year prison sentence for housebreaking but at the other extreme was thirteen-year-old William, who had been sent by a father and step-mother who disliked him. He was half-starved and afraid when he arrived, and ran away on several occasions. In the end Mary found him lodgings with 'a homely family'.[50] At Kingswood the boys worked in the garden as well as receiving some schooling. Later they took up brick and tile making as well.[51] The girls, perhaps inevitably, were trained in domestic duties, designed to make them efficient servants, and good wives and mothers in the future. The children also kept chickens, pigs and pet rabbits, for whose care they had to take responsibility.

Sadly Mary Carpenter's dream of recreating family life in a mixed reformatory school was soon shattered, with the girls, in particular, causing trouble. In March 1853 six of them absconded, apparently because they had had their hair cut by the matron against their will. They were eventually taken to a local police station, from where Mary had to collect them. But in the interim they had created a general disturbance, screaming and shouting so that the police superintendent declared 'he had never seen such girls'. They eventually calmed down and were taken by Mary back to Kingswood. Within an hour, one of them had again run off, only to be recaptured shortly afterwards and once more returned.[52]

Three days later there was a still more serious incident, when the children rioted and ran out into the nearby countryside. They were caught by local inhabitants, who tied them up and took them into the cellars of some of the houses to await collection by Miss Carpenter and her friends.[53]

As a result of these disturbances and of the girls' defiant attitude, the Kingswood management committee refused to retain them any longer and in 1854 Mary set up the first girls' reformatory at Red Lodge, also in her native Bristol.[54]

Although Miss Carpenter still believed in the merits of a family-based system in the running of her institutions, and in the importance of providing religious and moral guidance for children who had been spiritually damaged by their upbringing, it is clear that she had lost some of her early optimism. In an account of her work published in 1875, she lamented that the girls sent to her school were 'usually found to be entirely devoid of any good principles of action; accustomed to the uncontrolled exercise of their will; particularly addicted to deceit both in word and actions; of fair, but misdirected powers; of violent passions; extremely sensitive to imagined injury, and equally sensible to kindness'.[55] She refused to accept what were called 'penitentiary' cases, however, that is those who had had sexual experience. Mary saw as the first step towards the girls' reformation the need to awaken 'a feeling of confidence in their instructors, and to prove to them the anxiety for their welfare that is felt for them; they should be made ... to feel that they must yield to a control which will be kindly but firmly exercised'. Her dilemma about how best to rehabilitate the difficult and often disruptive young people in her care was to be shared by other reformatory school promoters for the rest of the century and beyond.

In the meantime, while voluntary reformatories such as Redhill, Hardwicke, and Kingswood in England and the Glasgow Boys' House of Refuge in Scotland were becoming part of the machinery for dealing with juvenile delinquency, the state had, as yet, remained largely outside the system. That changed in 1854 when the Youthful Offenders Act offered official certification to approved institutions. Under the legislation a partnership was established between the government and the voluntary bodies running the schools, with judges and magistrates empowered to sentence children under sixteen who were found guilty of a punishable offence to reformatory training for between two and five years.[56] This was to be preceded by a prison sentence of at least fourteen days, though that was reduced in 1866 to ten days, and was finally abolished in 1899. In 1893, however, magistrates were given discretion in dispensing with that preliminary period of imprisonment, and in that same year the minimum age

Eliza Smith, aged sixteen, from Southwark, sentenced to one month's hard labour in Wandsworth prison in December 1872, followed by three years in a Reformatory School. Her offence was the theft of three sacks.

of entry to a reformatory was raised from ten to twelve years. Maintenance costs were to be met by the state and by parental contributions of up to 5s per child per week, according to means. The religious affiliation of the child was also to be taken into account in deciding to which reformatory he or she was to be sent, and the Home Secretary could transfer an inmate to another school at any time. In 1857 local authorities were authorised to contribute to the financing of reformatories, both in regard to their establishment and to the upkeep of children in them. In that same year the first inspector of reformatory schools, Sydney Turner from Redhill, was appointed. Margaret May sees the importance of the new legislation as arising from the fact that

> Children for the first time were accepted as wards of state and new rights of enforcing parental responsibility were asserted. The legal age of delinquency was set at sixteen ... and corrective detention in the Reformatory ensured a 'child's punishment for a child's crime'.[57]

At the same time it was an attempt to impose 'middle-class standards of child-rearing on lower-class parents'.[58]

However the 1854 Act was only permissive and some magistrates continued to send young offenders to prison rather than adopting the more expensive and, as yet, largely unproven alternative of rehabilitation in a reformatory. There was a feeling, too, that such a move might encourage feckless parents to let their children commit crimes so they could be free from the expense of maintaining them, since the parental contributions imposed by magistrates were often below the 5s a week maximum laid down, and in many cases proved difficult to collect. Indeed, as the Inspector of Reformatory and Industrial Schools pointed out sourly in 1870, some magistrates failed to impose any payment, and even if they did, parents were easily able to evade the charge by moving house.[59] This was an issue that Lloyd Baker felt strongly about, seeing it as essential for parents to make a contribution towards their child's support. But an examination of the Hardwicke reformatory records shows how difficult this could be in practice. Thus in July 1885 the Minute Book shows that the Inspector had to be approached concerning the failure of the step-father of one of the boys to make a payment for him, as was required. A month later it was noted that although the stepfather had 'been ordered to contribute' he had 'fled the country'.[60] Few errant parents took such an extreme step as this; for most, it was sufficient to move to another neighbourhood or, in large towns, merely to another street. In 1882 out of 2,564 parents who actually made contributions towards the maintenance of their child in a reformatory just fourteen were paying 5s a week, with a further fifteen contributing between 4s and 5s a week; by contrast, 1,674 were remitting between 1s and 2s a week, and 251 less than 1s. So that even those who did pay up were required to make a relatively small outlay.[61]

As a result of the 1854 legislation and its subsequent amendments the number of certified reformatory schools in Great Britain increased rapidly from seven in 1854 to fifty-nine in 1859, and sixty-one in 1882. Already by the end of 1860 they had 3,712 inmates, excluding those youngsters who were out on licence working, prior to their formal discharge.[62] In fact by that date, the Inspector, Sydney Turner, was expressing concern at the extent to which the courts were despatching youngsters to reformatories. During 1860 he calculated that two-sevenths of the children being sent were under the age of twelve, and four-sevenths were received on their first conviction – something which was generally frowned upon. This was not only proving costly to the Treasury, which had to meet a large proportion of the children's maintenance costs, but still more importantly:

> I cannot think ... that it is just or morally expedient to mix together in the same school the mere half-trained child, who has pilfered a few pence, or stolen some sweets or pastry, with the astute experienced

young thief, whose depredations have been systematically carried on, as a chosen means of livelihood.[63]

It was a point to which he returned on more than one occasion, although, as he ruefully conceded, there was little that could be done in that committal was left 'entirely to the discretion of the ... magistrate'. [64] Sometimes, however, reformatory school managers refused to accept cases they considered trivial, such as boys 'sent down' for stealing bread, fruit or cake, which they subsequently ate. Instead they decided that the money needed to keep such children in a reformatory for several years could be better spent 'on more vicious children'.[65]

The Inspector did, however, point out in 1860 that there had been a sharp fall in the number of juveniles being imprisoned in England and Wales since the 1854 certification process had been introduced. In 1856 the total had been 13,981 and that had fallen to 8,029 in 1860. Unfortunately his optimism about the trend was somewhat premature in that during the 1860s prisoner numbers again began to mount, reaching 9,640 in 1865 and 10,314 in 1869.[66] Only in the final quarter of the nineteenth century did the number of juvenile prisoners move strongly and permanently down.

George Purcell, aged thirteen, an agricultural labourer. Found guilty of housebreaking at Newport Pagnell, Buckinghamshire, and of stealing 85s in cash among other things. He was convicted in 1872 and sentenced to four months' imprisonment with hard labour. He was discharged from Aylesbury Gaol on 30 April 1872. It was noted he had never attended school.

Not all of the reformatory schools were land based. The majority were but by the mid-1870s there were seven reformatory training ships as well. They were established in redundant naval vessels but without the regrettable penal overtones of the earlier prison hulks. They included the *Akbar*, set up on the Mersey in January 1856. Boys were admitted to the ship from all parts of the country, including from other reformatories, which considered they needed harsh discipline because of their recalcitrant attitude. There were also pleas for help from parents who were unable to control their children. Among them was a London surgeon who asked for the admission of 'his over-indulged rascally son of 13 years, in order to improve his ways'.[67]

To be eligible for entry to one of the floating reformatories lads had to be relatively strong, so that they could carry out the scrubbing and cleaning duties required of them. On the *Akbar* they were also expected to make and repair their own clothes and footwear, as well as carry out tailoring contracts for other institutions.[68] Life was hard, extremes of temperature had to be endured, and the poor diet led to ill health. In the early days their winter employment included having to pick oakum. The general philosophy was that expressed by the governor of the Glasgow House of Refuge in 1855 when he declared: 'Idleness is the bane of the juvenile population and almost inevitably leads to crime'. To counter any such tendency the inmates of reformatories were kept fully occupied. Nonetheless leisure time was allocated, with the *Akbar* boys playing draughts or bagatelle by the light of oil lamps and reading the improving magazines which were supplied. There were magic lantern shows, too, and lectures on temperance. Eventually a 'full brass band developed and its excellence made it a popular attraction at local church bazaars and other functions', as well as offering band members a welcome break from life aboard the *Akbar*.[69]

Although the ship was moored about a third of a mile off shore, a small number of lads tried to escape. If they were caught, punishment included a bread and water diet and solitary confinement in the ship's cell, plus a beating. Or they might be brought before a magistrate and sentenced to up to three months in prison, as provided in the 1854 reformatory schools legislation. A few lads drowned as they attempted to swim ashore.

Instruction in seamanship was given on board and a number of the boys subsequently joined the merchant marine or found their way into the Royal Navy as stokers.[70] Furthermore, as Joan Rimmer points out, boys of exemplary conduct were allowed leave of absence for a short period once they had completed a year's detention. In 1857, thirty-one country boys were permitted home leave for between ten and fourteen days, while of 126 Liverpool lads due for turns of one-day leave, two of them had the privilege withdrawn because of their unsatisfactory behaviour. By 1896 some youngsters were even being sent on errands ashore to 'test their moral courage and powers of self-control', but in their blue uniforms with shaved heads 'they were closely observed and the slightest hint of bad manners ... was reported by the public'.[71]

In such a confined space, there was inevitably bullying and unrest, as in September 1887 when a mutiny broke out on board the *Akbar*. It was led by a small group of 'evil-disposed' lads who suddenly downed tools and refused to obey orders. They persuaded others to join them and to arm themselves with sticks, pieces of wood and anything else that came to hand. Some broke into the captain's cabin and stole items of his wife's jewellery. There was further trouble in the following months, with thirteen lads absconding in dense fog in January 1888 and having to be rescued by a passing ship. After spending a week on remand in prison, nine were sentenced to three months' hard labour and the remainder were sent back to the *Akbar* for punishment. Not until the following July had things quietened down, with the Inspector then reporting the boys were 'under firm and kindly discipline. There is a good tone prevailing'.[72]

The difficulties on board the *Akbar* were insignificant when compared to those on its Roman Catholic sister ship, the *Clarence*. This, too, was moored in the Mersey and had been borrowed from the Admiralty in 1864. It had accommodation for up to two hundred and fifty lads, and its curriculum and timetable were similar to those on the *Akbar*. In January 1884, however, six of the young inmates set fire to the ship and destroyed her. No lives were lost, but the boys concerned were sentenced to five years penal servitude. Temporary accommodation was found for the rest of the inmates until a new *Clarence* was commissioned in November 1885. However, discipline problems persisted, with a serious mutiny taking place as the lads challenged the ship's harsh disciplinary regime. Eventually in July 1899, the new ship, too, was set ablaze by some of the inmates after weeks of preparation, during which they had carried oily waste into the bowels of the ship. The fire spread so rapidly that nothing could be saved. This time its replacement, a nautical training school, was established ashore.[73]

Other training ships had similar problems, with the *Daily Telegraph* referring to an 'epidemic of discontent and insubordination' on the *Mars*, which was in Scotland. Eleven lads absconded and managed to row ashore before they were caught. They confessed that if they had not managed to escape they would have set fire to the ship.[74] In 1889 another Scottish training ship the *Cumberland* was totally destroyed by four of the boys.[75]

But the land-based reformatory schools had their difficulties as well, as in April 1878 when a serious riot broke out at the Glasgow Boys'

INDUSTRIAL TRAINING SHIP BOY.

A Manchester boy sent to an
Industrial Training ship, *c.*1905.

reformatory school. During the disturbance the acting governor was
attacked and wounded, while many windows were broken and furniture
smashed. 'Having armed themselves with broken pieces of furniture, the
rioters kept possession of the building until the police arrived ... The cause
of the break out [was] ... the punishment of one of the boys.[76] In January
1882 further trouble occurred at the same reformatory, with fifty out of
one hundred and thirty boys taking part, breaking windows, smashing
crockery, and destroying other property. 'A strong detachment of police
was required' to restore order and guard the institution. Again, on 13
November 1875 at Mount St Bernard Roman Catholic reformatory in
Leicestershire, 160 of the 200 inmates managed to escape during a mutiny.
All were recaptured the next day.[77] Small wonder reformatory managers
claimed that the success of a school relied on 'Deterrence, Reformation
and Detention'. As can be seen, the last of these three provisos was not
always easy to achieve.[78]

Reformatory schools were designed to cater for youngsters whom
Mary Carpenter had labelled members of the 'dangerous' classes. Those
whom she called the 'perishing classes', the deprived and the destitute,
were to be cared for in a different way, through the creation of industrial
schools. These were pioneered in Scotland by William Watson, who as

Sheriff-Substitute of Aberdeen, in 1841 instructed the local police to bring all vagrant children to the city's poorhouse, where a room was set aside to serve as an industrial school. As an incentive to attend the children were provided with food. The movement was so successful that by 1851 Aberdeen had four industrial schools, and other Scottish towns quickly followed suit.[79]

In England the industrial school movement started with the setting up of Feltham school, opened in 1854 by progressive Middlesex magistrates and promoted by a private act of parliament. Its purpose was to receive and detain vagrant boys aged from seven to fourteen from the county.[80] However, from 1859 it extended its remit to provide for the 'care, reformation and education' of juvenile offenders from the area, and in that way became a mixture of industrial school and reformatory. Numbers grew rapidly, with 710 boys under detention at the end of the 1860s.[81] At that date around half of the new entrants were 'destitute', that is they were the vagrants and needy for whom the institution was originally formed, and the other half were those who had been 'criminally convicted'.

Among lads who made a success of their stay at Feltham was H. C., who came in January 1861 and left three years later. He was admitted after stealing bacon, and it was his first offence. But in November 1867 he was reported to be doing well as a woollen draper in New Zealand. Then there was W. S. who came to Feltham at almost the same time as H. C., having stolen 1s 4d. He, too, was a first offender, and in November 1867, more than three years after leaving Feltham, was working successfully as a 'messenger and porter'.[82]

But not all succeeded in breaking with their past. Of thirty-one boys discharged in January and February 1864, after completing their stint at the school, seven were said to have 'relapsed' by 1867; in other words, they had again committed a criminal offence. One was dead and one was 'unascertained'.[83]

The state became involved in the industrial school movement in 1857, when the Industrial Schools Act of that year introduced a certification process similar to that in respect of the reformatories. It also empowered magistrates to sentence children aged between seven and fourteen, charged with vagrancy, to such a school for any period up to their fifteenth birthday.[84] In theory this could mean that they were incarcerated for a longer period than applied to a child sent to a reformatory, since this carried a five-year maximum sentence. A seven-year-old sent to an industrial school could be detained there for as long as seven to eight years if the maximum sentence were imposed. Voluntary management was combined with state aid, with parents, too, being required to contribute towards the child's maintenance. Initially this was set at a maximum of

3s a week, although that limit was subsequently raised to 5s. At first the schools were under the control of the Education Department but in 1860 the Home Office assumed oversight, and henceforth they were reported upon by the same Inspector as visited the reformatories.

At first the 1857 Act had little impact, since the charge of vagrancy proved difficult to apply. In 1861, however, the legislation was modified so that the children covered included not merely those found begging or convicted of vagrancy, but those frequenting 'the Company of reputed Thieves'. Youngsters under the age of twelve who had committed an offence punishable by imprisonment but who, on account of age, were deemed suitable for an industrial school rather than the harsher atmosphere of a reformatory, were also covered. Children whose parents claimed they were unable to control them were similarly included. In the latter case, however, the parents had to agree to pay 'all Expenses incurred for the Maintenance of such Child at School'.[85] Already the difference between a reformatory and an industrial school was being blurred, in that children under twelve who had committed minor crimes could receive their punishment in an industrial school. This was confirmed in a consolidatory Act passed in 1866, which also raised the maximum age of detention to sixteen. As a result of these developments, as John Springhall comments, 'a new category of children, those "in need of care and protection", was introduced into English law for the first time'.[86] That aspect was extended further in 1880, when magistrates were authorised to send any children under fourteen found living in a brothel or residing with a reputed prostitute (including their own mother) to an industrial school. In practice, however, many industrial school managers were reluctant to take brothel cases when girls were involved. It was feared they would corrupt other children in the school.[89] Nevertheless the measure was a further example of the way in which the authorities were now prepared to intervene in family life, and to require parents to fulfill their duties in a proper manner, or risk losing control of their child. Stephen Humphries has labelled this as an example of the general mood of 'social imperialism' which was growing up at that time.[88]

Some industrial school managers were keen to emphasise that their young inmates were not 'criminals', in the way that those in reformatories were. Hence when the *Empress* industrial school training ship issued discharge certificates to its young inmates it described itself as 'established for the education of children of poor parentage; not a reformatory; therefore no criminals are admitted or retained'. Another training ship, the *Clio* advertised itself as catering for 'homeless, destitute and poor respectable boys'.[89] But as early as 1870 the Inspector of Reformatories and Industrial Schools had declared that certified industrial schools had 'now become so completely assimilated to reformatories in their necessary arrangements and regulations and the main features of their management' that it was difficult 'to establish any real distinction between them'. The only real point of difference was 'that the industrial schools [dealt] with the younger and the less criminal portion of the class which reformatory schools receive ... They are houses of detention for the young vagabond and petty misdemeanant'.[90] This view was confirmed in 1896 by the Report of a Departmental Committee investigating reformatory and industrial schools when it declared: 'the children in the two institutions are, in the main, of the same class; and, as a fact, there is no substantial difference in the discipline and regime beyond what can be accounted for by difference of age'.[91]

Youngsters who attended industrial schools certainly seem to have found the discipline and conditions just as stringent as those encountered by their reformatory counterparts. Sam Jenkins, who was committed to an industrial school training ship around the beginning of the twentieth century, recalled the sharp blows with the cane he received from the schoolmaster and the fact that he was always hungry:

> Had biscuits, no bread, never had bread ... When we had a bath, they were like horse troughs in this barrack room, and we all stripped naked and there was an officer sitting down in a chair and a man alongside of him with a big tub of soft soap and as he went by he slapped a dollop on the top of your nut ... Tell you my number, 3747, and that was me official number, same as a convict.[92]

He learned to swim while on board and made an attempt to escape, but one of the ship's boats caught up with him and brought him back. 'I got twelve strokes with the birch then'.[93]

Mark Benney, who attended an industrial school a few years later, remembered the bullying that went on, with 'the biggest boys ... making the smallest boys dance by whipping their legs with hazel switches.' But the real sign of distinction 'was to have lackies who were indeed lackies: to have frightened younger boys so thoroughly that they would clean your shoes, make your bed, do your morning task work, run your errands and even give you their weekly pocket money rather than risk your displeasure'. That was real power. Benney himself was beaten up and he remembered the pervasive violence and brutality. It was part of the inner life of the institution. 'In the dormitories, at the meal-tables, at work and at play, the atmosphere was tense with pugnacities'.[94]

Outsiders, too, regarded boys from reformatories and industrial schools as being in much the same category. Daisy Wintle of Bristol, for example,

referred to 'reformatory' boys when she probably meant the lads from
Clifton certified industrial school. She recalled looking down into the yard
'where the boys used to have to do their drill ... and their band practice
... We were never allowed to talk to them ... if you went to speak to a
reformatory boy, father would say, "They're bad boys, you're not to talk
to them ..." Industrial Reformatory School they used to call it, because
they used to make shoes and make all kinds of things, they used to have to
work'.[95]

Daisy Wintle's reminiscences related to the early twentieth century, but
by then, at least in official circles, attitudes were changing as regards the role
played by reformatories and industrial schools. The 1896 Departmental
Committee report on the schools was critical of the training provided
by many of them, and the fact that managements were often concerned
with money-making activities rather than with instruction designed to
be useful to their charges in later life. The chopping of wood, to be sold
in bundles as kindling, and the making of matchboxes were particularly
criticised, as was the running of commercial laundries as an occupation
for the girls.[96] The work was condemned as hard and laborious and, as
Joan Rimmer points out, it could also be dangerous. At the Mount Vernon
Green girls' reformatory in Liverpool the laundry had a lucrative business
washing ladies' finery, but the working conditions were unpleasant, with
the floor constantly awash with soapy water. As a consequence, many of
the girls slipped and broke limbs, while the harsh soap peeled the skin off
chilblained hands. The damp atmosphere and the fumes 'took [their] toll
on constitutionally weakened lungs and rheumaticky limbs'.[97] In 1890, the
Inspector visited the school and commented that while the work had 'its
practical value ... it should not be carried on at the expense of the moral
and intellectual cultivation of the girls. They want more outdoor exercise,
and not quite so much devotion to the washing tub'.[98]

Even those many reformatories and industrial schools that concentrated
on farming had their exploitative side. The young inmates were hired out
to local farmers, as was the case with boys from Hardwicke, while some
youngsters were sent as far afield as Wales, to the financial benefit of the
institution. Again, many of the lads from the Industrial school for Boys
at Heaton on Merseyside went out as 'half-timers as assistant gardeners
in the numerous villas in the neighbourhood,' as well as cultivating a
'large and productive garden' on the school site. In November 1890 the
Reformatory and Refuge Journal commented critically on the fact that
boys from the Wiltshire Reformatory School were spending so much time
away from the institution, working on farms that it was 'difficult to see
how the Superintendent and his staff [could] exercise ... Reformatory
training upon the lads, who are miles away from them during the whole

of the day'. 'The School Farm [of 30 acres] is too often neglected during the busiest part of the year, while the boys have miles to walk to and from their work, and may not be too well fed.' But it recognised that the venture was profitable, 'only subject to a deduction for extra wear and tear of clothing', and that was clearly the decisive factor.[99]

Indeed, despite repeated criticisms of firewood sales, many institutions persisted with these, and even advertised their wares. In October 1890, for example, the Surrey Reformatory and Friendless Boys' Home in Wandsworth, offered bundles of wood, '500 bundles and upwards delivered in London at 3/6 [3s 6d] per 100, largest size'.[100] During the same month the London Female Preventive and Reformatory Institution in Euston Road offered to take in laundry work; 'List of prices charged may be obtained on application to the Secretary', while York Certified Industrial Boys' School promoted its inmates' skills as turners. 'Cricket bats and wickets, tennis racquets (plain and polished), croquet mallets, &c.' were obtainable on application to the superintendent.[101]

Elsewhere, as at Feltham, instruction was given in carpentry, and gardening, while there was a nautical class of a hundred boys in the mid-

Boys in the Smith's Shop at Feltham Industrial School, *c.*1900.

1870s to prepare boys for the merchant navy.[102] The industrial training given here was classed as 'well organised'.

But it was not only the industrial training given that came under question in the later nineteenth century. Discipline, too, began to be criticised where it was unnecessarily repressive. The 1896 Departmental Committee considered that the rules 'for obligatory silence' were carried further than applied in ordinary schools and 'in many cases, further than there is any occasion for. At meals, for instance, we think that children, instead of being compelled to abstain from talking, should be habituated to talk to one another without making a noise ... We consider that excessive discipline, constantly enforced in these little everyday matters, is vexatious and does no good'.[103] It praised the system at Clifton school whereby 'deserving boys' were granted eight days' leave at mid-summer and Christmas, to enable them to visit their families. 'It keeps up the parental tie, and has a beneficial effect on the parents, seeing their boys returned to them so much improved under the influence of good food and better surroundings, added to the school discipline'. In addition, it was 'an incentive to good behaviour'.[104]

Sporting activities were encouraged, and camping expeditions undertaken. At Kingswood, for example, the annual report for 1902 referred with pride to the cricketing and athletic prowess of its young charges, as well as the success of its brass band. 'Army Bandmasters seek eagerly for fresh hands from the musicians of the School, and officers welcome recruits [to] the ranks from a training ground so good', it declared. Then there was the annual camp, which in 1902 was held for a fortnight at Bossington in Porlock Bay.[105]

Significantly, in 1898 the Inspector of Reformatory and Industrial Schools described the instruction given in gymnastics and other sports as being 'as important as that of the schoolroom or shop' in securing the children's welfare. He also commended the change of air and scene that resulted through many of the schools arranging camping expeditions.[106] It was a notable softening of approach compared to the repressive regime of earlier years, although much emphasis continued to be placed on the importance of firm discipline.

The change of attitude was apparent, too, in the reduced number of young people being sent to prison, and the way in which, on occasion, juvenile offenders were punished by being given a short spell in a workhouse rather than a gaol. This was the case with one lad from Bedminster near Bristol in the mid-1890s. He and some other boys went into a hardware shop and stole cash from the till. They were seen by the owner and after appearing in court they were sent to Stapleton workhouse for a week. There they picked oakum. An 'old pauper' was put in charge of them and he gave them 'plenty of wallopings ... We were put in a room with a high wall and we couldn't see anything ... I was up at six and worked nearly all day, we ate bread and marge with some porridge ... After a week in Stapleton workhouse I never repeated the offence'. In addition to the week in the workhouse, each boy received an official caution and had to pay a fine of four shillings.[107]

However, while these changes were under way in the final quarter of the nineteenth century, the issue of compulsory school attendance, imposed on elementary scholars between 1870 and 1880, was creating a new class of deviants – persistent truants. Truancy cases not only swelled the ranks of the existing industrial schools but led to the creation of new institutions, namely truant schools and day industrial schools, to cater for them. They were set up by education authorities, however, rather than by private individuals, as was the case with most of the existing reformatory establishments.

Overall, it is difficult to assess the true success of these residential reformatory and industrial schools during the Victorian period. As Gordon Rose comments, although records were kept of the proportion of successes, like many other nineteenth-century returns they were open to question. Nonetheless, probably two-thirds to three-quarters of children passing through the system could be regarded as successes. Rose considers this 'no mean achievement', even if much of it was attributable to the fact that the schools removed children from an adverse environment and allowed them to grow up and develop under more favourable circumstances.[108] At the same time, for many young inmates the rigid discipline they experienced and the restrictions imposed upon them created a bitterness and sense of social alienation which lasted into their adult years.

The Problems of School Attendance

Between 1870 and 1880 successive education acts imposed compulsory attendance on all children between the ages of five and ten and thereafter to thirteen (or fourteen), as local bye-laws laid down, unless they could pass an agreed leaving examination or gain exemption in some other way. The 1870 Education Act was also significant in that it created rate-aided school boards to provide places for children in areas where there was a deficiency in existing voluntary school provision (usually supplied by the churches but sometimes by private individuals or charities).[109] This meant that from the early 1870s most major towns and cities had their own school board, with attendance officers to see that the bye-laws relating to school attendance were being observed. In 1876 this was extended to the voluntary sector so that districts without school boards now had to set up special attendance committees to supervise schooling in their locality. The 1876 Act had further significance in that it empowered education authorities to set up their own specialist institutions to tackle the truancy issue.[110]

The introduction of compulsory attendance created particular problems in the many urban areas where slum children were drawn into the school net for the first time. Hitherto, as Wendy Prahms notes of Newcastle, sending children to school had been a parental decision only: 'children had home duties and sometimes paid work; education was a luxury for easy times.'[111] There was also reluctance to find the few pence required each week as fees for attendance at elementary schools. Admittedly the poorest families could obtain free education by applying to the school authorities, or later the poor law, for assistance but that involved a bureaucratic process many were reluctant to pursue. Among some children, too, there was an unwillingness to accept the restrictions, rules and disciplined daily routine involved in going to school. Many elementary teachers, for their part, were reluctant to accept dirty, ragged, ill-mannered children, fearful this would alienate their more 'respectable' pupils, to say nothing of the discipline difficulties they would cause. Yet, where parents failed to send their children to school they could be fined and in the long run the courts imposed attendance orders requiring the children to go to a particular school. If they failed to conform, they could be ordered to enter an industrial school for several years, with their parents required to pay a maintenance grant towards the cost of this. If the parents failed to do that, further prosecutions followed. It was in these circumstances that at the turn of the century the young Londoner, Sam Jenkins, was sent to a training ship anchored in the Thames. 'I was always one for running away from school ... Because I kept hopping the wag, playing hookey ... I was sent to the training ship. Took me there, they put me in uniform and read the riot act out to me'.[112]

These developments meant that education authorities in the major cities became swamped with truants, and when a number of them were sent to the existing industrial schools their presence provided a disruptive element there, too. Many youngsters, for example, were sent when they were already eleven or twelve years of age and were only in residence at the school for a brief period. These 'ins-and-outs' unsettled the other pupils, who might be staying for some years. Their numbers could also be very large. According to Jo Manton, the London School Board alone had placed 1,281 truants in industrial schools by March 1874, so that all the schools in and around the capital were becoming overcrowded. At a conference on the working of the industrial schools held in May of that year, many of those present argued that in any case it was wrong to remove children from their families in this way unless it were absolutely essential:

> The Superintendent at the Middlesex Industrial School at Feltham admitted frankly that many of his boys were not the homeless vagabonds for whom the school was intended. They had homes where 'the father goes out to work and the mother goes out charing. They are simply children who will not go of their own accord to school'.[113]

At the same meeting Mary Carpenter claimed that it was not only expensive to send so many children away from home for failing to go to school but that it was cruel, as well as damaging to family relationships, to deprive them of contact with their parents and siblings in this way.[114]

As a result of these concerns the 1876 Education Act allowed school boards to establish institutions to deal specifically with the attendance question. They were, of course, only feasible in places where large numbers of children needed their special provisions. In smaller towns and rural areas recourse continued to be had to the traditional industrial schools, if parental fines and the pressures exerted by attendance officers failed to bring about an improvement in attendance.

Two new solutions to the truancy issue were, therefore, produced. These were residential truant industrial schools, where a strict disciplinary regime applied and the youngsters were required to live in for around three months, before being 'licensed' to return to their family and to attend a specified elementary school in their home locality. If they again lapsed the licence was withdrawn and they returned to the truant school for a longer and harsher taste of disciplinary medicine before being licensed once more. The second alternative was the day industrial school, where the pupils lived at home but spent their days in the school and had most of their meals there. They were described as 'an intermediate and cheaper form' of industrial school, or, more accurately, 'day-feeding schools, in which the children [were] employed, educated and partially fed, but not lodged or clothed'.[115] The Inspector of Reformatory and Industrial Schools praised their contribution, noting the 'motherly care' taken of most of the pupils by the school staff, and the way in which second-hand clothing was provided for some of them through charitable ventures, such as the special police clothing funds. But not all of those connected with the reform movement shared his enthusiasm. *The Reformatory and Refuge Journal* for one was dubious about their long-term effect in so far as 'whatever preventive or reformatory influence they may exercise upon the children is largely counteracted by their nightly return to their so called homes – in not a few instances, dens of misery and wretchedness and worse'.[116] It preferred the long-term referral of the youngsters to one of the old-style industrial schools, where they were kept away from undesirable family influences.

The number of both of the new kinds of institution remained limited, with fourteen truant schools in existence in 1898 and twenty-four day industrial schools, of which twenty were in England and Wales and four in Scotland (three of these being in Glasgow, where they had been set up under a special Act).[117] All of the truant schools catered for boys only.

Liverpool school board pioneered the opening of the truant establishments, with the first being set up at Hightown in 1878. Its disciplinary regime was severe, with the youngsters locked up in a separate bedroom or cell for the first four nights of their stay and for a portion of each of the first four days. In 1884 the Royal Commission on Reformatories and Industrial Schools was highly critical of this policy of isolation, declaring that such a mode of treating truant boys, who were 'often of tender age' was 'open to serious objection'.[118] Despite these and other criticisms, the system was still in operation, largely unchanged, more than a decade later.[119]

The main aim of truant schools was to keep the children constantly employed with educational activities, domestic chores, industrial tasks and a good deal of drill. Its purpose was to create a punitive regime so unpleasant that it would deter young inmates from further acts of truancy. The ethos adopted was described in 1893 in connection with the school set up in Plymouth:

> the distinct object of the managers is to make residence in the school irksome and distasteful, so that rather than stay, and still less to return to it, the truant boy will give up truanting, and steadily attend school. The boys are well fed ... They are well cared for as to health, cleanliness, and dress ... But the discipline is strict, continuous, and inexorable. They are there because they love play better than work; and therefore they are kept at work almost all the day long, from 6 in the morning until 8 at night ... Household work, school, drill, industrial training, with very brief intervals of rest, occupy the whole day. There is little opportunity for the mischief which idle hands so readily find to do.[120]

In some schools it was customary to beat every boy who was readmitted for breaking the terms of his 'license'. In others, including the two truant schools set up in London by the 1890s, corporal punishment was administered only if, after inquiry, it was found that readmission was the result of the child's own waywardness rather than of parental neglect or family pressure.[121]

At Upton House, one of the London schools, the boys rose at 6 a.m. They made their beds and washed in total silence, and at 7 a.m. carried out domestic chores, cleaning the house and the school. During this 'quiet conversation' was allowed. That was followed at 8 a.m. by breakfast and prayers, when total silence was again imposed. The pupils were then divided into two groups for schooling or industrial training, respectively. This lasted for three hours, between 9 a.m. and noon, after which came fifty minutes for drill, followed by dinner at 1 p.m. This, like breakfast, was consumed in total silence. So the day continued until they retired to bed at 8 p.m. According to the 1896 Departmental Committee Report on Reformatory and Industrial Schools, the boys had one hour and twenty minutes of drill daily, and during the whole period they attended they were only allowed half an hour a day when they could play or talk freely.[122]

The Committee condemned the methods applied in the schools and expressed doubt about their long-term success. It was pointed out that up to 31 December, 1894, of 19,767 children who had been licensed from them over the years, more than two out of five were readmitted, with one in four being readmitted once and one in ten readmitted twice. A very small number were admitted as many as four times or more.[123] This meant that, almost always, boys who had been in the schools before were in a majority. Thus at Highbury, London's second truant school, on one day in 1896, of 193 boys present, 111 were readmissions. This not only damaged the 'atmosphere' of the school but undermined its deterrent effect. There were other factors, too, to explain why children who experienced the harsh routine of a truant school returned for more. In the Committee's view it was simply that they were unable to help themselves. They were so neglected by their parents, 'so abandoned to a life in the streets', that they were unable to go to school regularly unless they were helped. 'In our opinion it is contrary to right principles of education that a governor or teacher should have imposed upon him as a duty to cause his scholars to be uncomfortable every day from the first to the last that they are with him, or that little children ... should be kept, as it were, in disgrace for a continuous period of months'.[124] William Inglis, the Inspector of Reformatory and Industrial Schools, also protested at the repressive regime applied when he declared in 1894: 'Useful schools they are, but though I could name two or three that have always been conducted on moderate or sensible lines, there have been others which I have never entered without feeling more sympathy for the inmates than for the truant system'.[125]

Because of the brief time most youngsters spent in the schools at any one period the industrial training given was limited to simple and laborious tasks, including wood chopping to make bundles of kindling, or helping with the domestic chores of the house, and perhaps working in the garden. At Upton House in London, for example, wood-chopping was the principal winter work and gardening took up the summer months. 'The boys do most of the work in kitchen, laundry, and house'.[126] The aim was to keep them constantly active rather than to teach them a trade.

Pupils' records reveal the kind of children caught up in the truant school system. They included Arthur Wren, who was aged 11 years and 8 months when he was admitted to Highbury Truant School in London during April 1891. His father was a 'carman' and the boy's problems were partly attributed to the fact that he had got 'with bad boys'. However, the main cause of his being sent to Highbury was the fact that he had run away from home for six weeks, sleeping rough in fields around Finsbury Park because he so disliked school. After two months at Highbury he was licensed out and remained at liberty, presumably making satisfactory attendances at school, for over a year, until 8 August 1892, when he was readmitted, three more months then elapsed before his licence was renewed and this time he remained at large until August 1893, when he was old enough to go to work.[127]

More problematic was the career of James Faulkner, a fellow pupil, aged ten years and seven months when he entered Highbury a day after Arthur Wren. He began truanting allegedly because he had been late in getting to school and had been caned. As a result he 'refused to go again'. His mother declared unsympathetically that his plight was 'entirely his own fault' and perhaps not surprisingly, given this home background he proved a repeat offender. He was licensed out on the first occasion after three months at Highbury, but returned about three months after that. In all he was readmitted to the school in disgrace on three occasions to receive further disciplinary treatment, once coming back after he had been at liberty just eighteen days. He finally left school at fourteen in 1894.[128]

As might be expected, some youngsters attempted to abscond, although few were successful in remaining free for more than a day or so. At Sheffield's truant school, set up in a converted workhouse, one lad ran away immediately after consuming his Christmas dinner but was recaptured within a mile of the school. A ten-year-old Nottingham boy, who had been sent to the Sheffield school, made one fruitless attempt to escape before he succeeded in slipping away through a thick moorland mist. Although not immediately found he was picked up by the police in Nottingham after two days. On his return to the school he was given nine strokes with the cane, followed by three days in solitary confinement. At Sheffield this involved being set to pick oakum and only being allowed to mix with the other boys at mealtimes, during school hours, and at prayers. The industrial training at this school consisted of market gardening, with some manufacture of hurdle fencing and a brief, unsuccessful attempt at livestock farming.[129]

Despite the criticisms levelled at them, truant schools remained in existence into the twentieth century, although their numbers diminished. In 1906 there were only twelve of them. The Sheffield school, however, survived until 1926, when it was transferred to Sheffield Corporation for use with mentally handicapped children.[130]

Truant schools, then, were one method adopted by school authorities to counter persistent attendance difficulties. The second solution, the day industrial school, offered a milder disciplinary regime with the children being allowed to return to their families in the evening. Parents had to contribute towards their maintenance while they were in attendance, and most pupils were required to remain at the school for three years. In practice, however, a majority of them were licensed out in a few weeks, once it was felt they could be trusted to go to an ordinary elementary school on a regular basis. If they failed to do so, they were returned to the school for further instruction and training. Sometimes, however, a day industrial school became the permanent venue for the poorest children, whose ragged condition made it difficult for them to attend other establishments. On occasion, as at Drury Lane Day Industrial School in London, the head appealed directly for charitable help in supplying footwear and clothing for the most destitute.[131] Similarly in November 1901 the head of Brunswick Road Day Industrial School, also in London,

Boys learning to make and repair shoes at Brunswick Road Industrial School, London, 1908.

commented on the 'sadly neglected' condition of his pupils, 'their feet being badly cut, mainly because of the bad state of the boots'.[132]

Attempts were made to improve the children's lot in life, so that by the 1890s many schools had swimming baths, with the pupils allowed to go for a swim before the school day began. The doors were usually opened at 6 a.m. so those whose parents went to work very early could come to school rather than wander around the streets and get into 'bad' company. The official school day began at 8 a.m. Three meals a day were supplied, beginning with breakfast, and the children were also washed, when necessary, before they began their schooling. The day ended with a tea served at around 5 p.m., before they went home at 6 p.m.

Apart from the less punitive atmosphere that pervaded them, compared to the other correctional institutions, they had the merit in the eyes of their supporters of not separating the child from his or her family. As the governor of Drury Lane School commented in April 1896, even 'a baddish home' was better than sending the child to a residential school. 'Of course, the children have ... to battle with the temptations incident to their circumstances, and there can be no doubt that they are influenced, more or less, by their evil surroundings; but the good habits acquired are far more likely to be permanent if acquired under the conditions of a large measure of home life'.[133] He was speaking from experience in that prior to moving to Drury Lane he had worked at the residential Brentwood Industrial School for several years.[134]

The dire poverty and the difficulties faced by many of the pupils is shown in their school records. Thus George Finch, admitted to Brunswick Road school in October 1901, aged eleven, was described as being 'very delicate, his chest being very weak.' His father was a ship's fireman and there were five other children in the family. He had been sent to the school by Poplar petty sessions because he had been absenting himself from home, 'sleeping in dustbins &c. Led away by elder brother & stayed out all night to avoid thrashing for truancy'.[135] He was eventually discharged from the school in July 1904, when he was fourteen. Then there was Frederick Miles, described as being 'beyond control' by his father, at the tender age of eight. He entered Brunswick Road in November 1901 and within weeks the head was expressing anxiety about him: 'unless he received more vigorous support from the parents in keeping the boy in at night he was afraid that, owing to the boy's thieving propensity he would have to ask the Committee to transfer him to an ordinary Industrial School'. The problems continued, with repeated complaints about his unsatisfactory conduct and 'thieving habits'. In May 1902 he was charged at Poplar petty sessions and was sent to the workhouse pending his removal to a residential industrial school. He was discharged from Brunswick Road on 12 May.[136]

In Glasgow, the industrial school set up in 1878 was seen as a 'place of protection' where the children would be cared for, rather than as a centre for punishment. It was used not only for truants but by single parents who had to work and therefore could not guarantee their children's regular attendance at school.[137]

Day industrial schools, then offered education and basic nutrition to children from poor families, as well as to persistent truants. Parents often resented the interference, and the financial penalty, that their offspring's attendance at them represented. But they provided a structured daily routine for youngsters whose home life was often chaotic, and in many cases they enabled children to take their place as 'respectable' members of society when they grew up. For the school providers, there was the ulterior motive that they were preventing the recalcitrant young from lapsing into criminality, as well as providing help to the most needy. As the Inspector of Reformatory and Industrial Schools commented in the early 1880s: 'The first thing for a superintendent [of a day industrial school] to recollect is "that while discipline must be enforced, kindness should be the guiding principle"'.[138]

CHAPTER 5

NEW OFFENCES AND NEW REMEDIES, 1880-1914

The decline in the numerical strength of the criminal classes is going on so fast and so continuously that a century hence the thief may be as rare as is the highwayman ... There is a diminution in almost all kinds of larceny ... The same is true of forgery and coining. But in regard to offences against the person and offences against property accompanied with violence there is a tendency to a distinct increase ... The break-up or impairment of old ideas of discipline or order and the life of great cities create occasions for some varieties of crime. The pickpocket is dying out; the Hooligan replaces him.

The Times, 6 February 1899.

Street Offences and Street Gangs

It was a paradox of late Victorian and Edwardian Britain that at a time when overall crime levels were falling there was increasing apprehension about the amount of violence within society and, in particular, about the growth of hooliganism among the young. Adolescence itself came to be seen as a stage in life when, unless strict discipline were applied, high spirits would lead to misbehaviour by all classes of youngsters and not merely those of the lower orders.[1] Significantly, committals for indictable offences per 100,000 of the population of England and Wales fell from an annual average of 226.1 in 1881-85 to 163.7 in 1896-1900.[2] Typical of many was the comment in January 1892 by the chairman of Salford quarter sessions when he pointed to a 'very remarkable' diminution in crime over recent years. He attributed this in both Salford and the wider community to the improvements in educational provision which had followed the passage of the 1870 Education Act. 'They could hardly expect that as education progressed there would come a day when there would be no crime. We could hardly expect the millennium just yet ... still, it was a matter of congratulation that crime had so sensibly diminished'.[3]

Official statistics, admittedly, did not necessarily reflect the true level of criminality, in that some offences went unreported and in other cases they might be ignored by the police or dealt with informally. This was especially likely to apply to juveniles. In Oxford, during the 1880s and 1890s Fred Bickerton remembered the local policeman 'generally had a stick with which he punished offenders on the spot. I dare say it was thoroughly illegal for this to be done ... We knew the risks we ran – and kept a sharp look-out accordingly. Even so, many was the time when I was caught at the forbidden pastime of climbing lamp-posts and provided a vulnerable target'.[4]

However, even if the statistics underestimated the true amount of wrongdoing, they did suggest that much of the anxiety about levels of crime in the country was misconceived. This applied also to youngsters. Figures from the Juvenile Courts set up under the 1908 Children Act, to deal with offenders up to the age of sixteen, reveal that between 1910 and 1914 the number of young people tried remained steady or, on the immediate eve of the First World War, actually declined.[5] They show, too, that the offences which they committed were, to a considerable extent, larcenies, much as they had always been, rather than anything more sinister. Often the thefts were relatively trivial, like the 'little sneak thief urchins' recalled by Walter Southgate in Bethnal Green during the 1890s. They slyly moved among the stalls at East End street markets on Saturday nights, '"lifting" anything edible within their grasp'.[6] Then there were the two twelve-year-olds in Salford who in late 1892 slipped into school cloakrooms while the pupils were at their lessons and stole some of the coats. These were pawned and the money spent 'in toffee, turnovers, and at the circus'. When they were charged with the offence and found guilty, the court ordered that they each receive six strokes with the birch rod.[7] A young Londoner, Arthur Harding, also went out with one or two friends to steal fruit from market stalls. But in their case this was combined with a more vicious side, as when they pinned a sheet of paper to the back of an unsuspecting person and set fire to it. At the very least that damaged the victim's clothing and might have caused more serious injury.[8]

In the country at large, meanwhile, there was a feeling that young people had become too independent and were more indisciplined than had once been the case, despite the influence of elementary schooling. A late Victorian magistrate found it 'melancholy ... that some parents [were] not ashamed to confess that children of seven years [were] entirely beyond their control'.[9] Helen Bosanquet, writing in 1906 was struck by the way youngsters displayed 'a prevailing and increasing want of respect towards their elders ... especially, perhaps, towards their parents'.[10] Three years later the economic historian, R. H. Tawney, blamed the casual and irregular nature of much of the work taken up by school leavers, engaged as errand boys, van boys, porters, and the like, for leading them into criminality.[11]

Critics felt, too, that the punishments imposed on wrongdoers were weak and ineffective, and that sterner measures were required. Mr Loveland, vice-chairman of the County of London Sessions, was not alone when in August 1899 he expressed a wish that in dealing with street violence he could order the perpetrators 'to be whipped; prison life only hardened them, and reformatories did little good'. He believed 'whipping would be the most effective and deterrent punishment'.[12] Yet the law normally permitted the beating of young offenders as an official penalty only up to the age of fourteen.

Concerns about hooliganism were compounded by events within the wider society. They included serious labour unrest during the 1880s and again in the early twentieth century, as well as perennial political anxieties about the situation in Ireland, and apprehension, on the manufacturing front, about the rise of foreign competition to challenge Britain's former pre-eminence. Bad behaviour and lack of discipline among the young seemed to symbolise a broader malaise and to portend further difficulties in the future 'Our young people have no idea of discipline and subordination', declared Dr T. F. Young of Liverpool in 1904. He particularly condemned the way in which once they started work, they threw off 'all parental authority ... get to congregating about the street corners at night ... become what we call "corner boys", and get drunken habits'.[13]

Parental weaknesses and deficiencies were seen as contributing to this problem of troublesome adolescents, but so was the influence of popular culture. Geoffrey Pearson has pointed to the way in which almost every kind of youthful recreation received hostile scrutiny.

> The music halls, professional football, the "penny dreadful" comics and the "penny bloods" ... were said to be inducements to crime and immorality, the rowdy presence of working-class people at seaside resorts on Bank Holiday excursions, the evening promenade of young people that was ridiculed by their elders as the "monkey parade", the depravity and violence associated with the pub – they all came under attack at different times. Even the ... bicycle was dragged into the act, amidst a blizzard of respectable fears.[14]

On the latter point, lads were accused of riding their bicycles at speed and without consideration for pedestrians or other road users.

A new factor fuelled this sense of alarm, however, in the form of the popular press, as newspaper proprietors from the 1880s onwards realised that sensational stories of juvenile violence and hooligan behaviour boosted circulation. The exploits of street gangs in London and the major industrial towns were particular features of what the *Daily Mail* in August 1898 labelled 'Hooliganiana'.[15] One such dramatic effusion appeared in the *London Echo* of 7 February, 1898, when it warned that

> the young street ruffian and prowler with his heavy belt, treacherous knife and dangerous pistol is amongst us. He is in full evidence in London … The question for every man who cares for streets that are safe after dark, decent when dark, not disgraced by filthy shouts and brutal deeds, is what is to be done with this new development of the city boy and the slum denizen? Not one tenth of the doings of these young rascals gets into the press, not one half is known to the police.[16]

Even *The Times* caught the general mood of pessimism when on 30 October 1900 it declared that, 'Every week some incident shows that certain parts of London are more perilous for the peaceable wayfarer than the remote districts of Calabria, Sicily, or Greece, once the classic haunts of brigands'.[17]

A STREET GROUP.

A young impoverished street gang in London, *c*.1901.

The following month *The Daily Graphic* drew attention to the uniform style of dress being adopted by members of street gangs. The boys wore 'a peculiar muffler twisted around the neck, a cap set rakishly forward, well over the eyes, and trousers very tight at the knee and very loose at the foot. The most characteristic part ... is the substantial leather belt heavily mounted with metal. It is not ornamental, but then it is not intended for ornament'.[18] In fights with other youths the buckle-end of the belt proved a formidable weapon.

Not all contemporaries were persuaded by these dramatic press claims of social breakdown, although most agreed that the activities of the more vicious street gangs were dangerous. However, it was also accepted that the majority of young people were neither hooligans nor juvenile delinquents.[19] In August 1898 a former New Scotland Yard detective, writing in the *South London Chronicle*, accused newspapers of taking the matter up merely as a 'sensational means of filling their columns', while at around the same time Thomas Holmes, a London police court missioner, described the whole campaign as 'press-manufactured Hooliganism'.[20] When young people met together at night on street corners they were more likely to be discussing sport, especially football, or eyeing the girls or talking about jobs and wages than planning nefarious activities.[21]

Some gangs were based on the youngsters' place of work but for most of them it was coming from the same neighbourhood which was the determining factor. Henry Grimshaw, recalling his childhood in early twentieth century Manchester, commented: 'you were born in a gang if you lived in that area ... you didn't realise you were in a gang: you were just playing with children, see. There was the Cogan Gang, the Kendall Street Gang. I was in the Willesden Street Gang'.[22] For older lads the street gang acted 'as a conduit of information about the world at large, as an arena for the shaping of adolescent opinion, and as a convivial club'.[23]

Street-gang culture was derived from the environment in which youngsters grew up, so that in certain districts it was 'hardness' or toughness which was regarded as an essential masculine virtue. Displays of fighting prowess gave boys kudos among their peers as Clarence Rook noted in late nineteenth century London, when he got to know Alf, a member of the Lambeth Walk gang.[24] According to Rook, the leader gained his position by his forceful personality and his exploits in fights with other gangs. This was confirmed by a young Bristolian, Charles Holbrooke, when he described, years later, how he was 'king of one gang ... and there was another kid, 'e was the ganger, the king of the kids from the next street, we 'ad a fight, and I beat this kid and all his mob came over on my side ... he wasn't king of the castle no more'.[25]

But in other, more violent, circles, such as the Lambeth Walk gang Clarence Rook encountered, status was gained through acts of vandalism and criminality carried out within the wider community. Hence the boy who 'kicked in a door can crow over the boy who has merely smashed a window. If you have knocked out your adversary at the little boxing place off the Walk, you will have proved that your friendship is desirable. If it becomes known ... that you have drugged a toff and run through his pockets, or, better still have cracked a crib on your own and planted the stuff, then you are at once surrounded by sycophants. Your position is assured, and you have but to pick and choose those that shall work with you. Your leadership will be recognised'.[26]

In some major industrial towns gang members had their own generic title, such as the 'scuttlers' of Manchester and Salford, the 'peaky blinders' of Birmingham, the Liverpool 'High Rips', and the Glasgow 'Redskins'.[27] Charles Russell saw the emergence of the Manchester 'scuttlers' in the late nineteenth century as a product of young people's boredom and lack of other sources of excitement and bravado. The 'scuttler', he declared, 'loved romance ... But what to do? War was his amusement and his avocation, and he must make war upon his neighbours of the next street. His gang must show its prowess by thrashing all other gangs ... The gravest troubles generally arose from attentions paid to the sweetheart of a member of one gang, by a member of another ... Gangs, twenty or thirty strong, armed sometimes with heavily buckled belts and mineral-water bottles, would ... engage in set combat, in which serious injuries were often inflicted'.[28] This was confirmed by another contemporary observer of the 'scuttler' scene. James Bent was a long-standing police superintendent in Manchester and according to him, in the 1890s an 'eminent medical man' had told him that 'scarcely a day passed without someone being brought into the Manchester Infirmary in consequence of violence used in these "scuttling" affrays'.[29] Sometimes the conflicts, like similar battles in the early twenty-first century, led to fatalities. Jon Savage describes a 'sensational murder case' involving Manchester scuttlers in 1892, when three sixteen-year-old members of the Lime Street gang, knifed a rival gang member in the back. The killer, William Willan, was led away from the court, crying out, 'Oh master, don't, have mercy on me. I'm only sixteen, I'm dying'.[30]

Most of the victims in these skirmishes were gang members, but on occasion by-standers were injured. In March 1897, a clash between the City-road gang and the Broadway (Hackney) gang in London broke out when the City-road youths went to Hackney to search for their rivals. They were about fifty or sixty strong and were armed with various weapons, including revolvers, which they fired into the air from time to time. In the course of this 'invasion' of their rivals' territory they came across a lad whom they suspected of being one of the 'Broadway chaps'. Five or six shots were fired at him and although they missed their target, a small boy walking along the road was struck in the leg by a bullet, suffering a slight injury. When the police arrived the youths scattered but they managed to catch one of the ringleaders and he and five other lads were subsequently identified as having possessed revolvers. At their trial at the Old Bailey, two were found not guilty but the remaining four were sentenced to terms of imprisonment ranging from two months to six months, all with hard labour. In the course of the court proceedings it emerged that these gang battles had been going on for about two years, although prior to the current case 'in not such an aggravated form'.[31]

In Salford, Robert Roberts remembered how each slum had its 'own cachet and fighting reputation', though care had to be taken with whom clashes took place.

We boys from 'down the gasworks' found our label psychologically useful against the denizens of dockland, say, the Adelphi, or Hulme, but considered twice before taking on a battler from Ancoats, Islington Square, or indeed anyone living in a district closer to the Manchester city centre than our own. Generally, the nearer the heart of things, the older and worse the slum, the tougher its inhabitants.[32]

Manchester newspaper seller, *c.*1903. With his cap pulled forward over his eyes, his muffler and his cigarette, he seems to have been influenced by the city's 'scuttler' gangs.

Roberts also described the dress of the Salford scuttlers. The boys wore bell-bottomed trousers, a heavy leather belt, pricked out in fancy designs with a large steel buckle and thick, iron-shod clogs. Their girl friends were usually dressed in 'clogs and a shawl and a skirt with vertical stripes'.[33]

Most females were connected with the gangs merely through their relationship with one of the lads belonging to them, but some took part in their own right. The Ordsall Lane gang in Salford, for example, had girl members and in June 1890, when an attack by gang members left a police constable beaten unconscious, three of the eight youngsters subsequently charged with the assault were female. According to a witness, they had largely caused the disturbance; 'they acted like Amazons, and were very active in the fray'.[34] The constable himself declared that when he arrested one of the lads during a fracas outside an Ordsall Lane beerhouse, two of the girls shouted, 'Don't let him take you', before grabbing the constable and beating him about the body. Their intervention, according to the constable, then led to a brutal assault by the rest of the gang. Two of the girls, aged eighteen and seventeen, respectively, were sentenced to three months' imprisonment, but their sixteen-year-old companion was treated more leniently, being sent to prison for just fourteen days. She was told by the presiding magistrate that 'he hoped she would keep better company when she came out'.[35]

Girls were also involved in the intimidation of witnesses. Among those affected was an Ordsall youth who was a major witness of the assault on the police constable. On the day of the first court hearing, he was apparently chased through the streets by a band of young women carrying knives. They stood outside his house shouting, 'Come out, Totty White, and we'll rip you open'. Three fourteen-year-olds were arrested on this occasion and were charged at Salford police court with committing a breach of the peace and with threatening White so as to prevent him from giving evidence. The girls protested their innocence, and the stipendiary magistrate was apparently sufficiently influenced by their youth and sex to bind them over in their parents' recognizances of £10 apiece to keep the peace for six months, rather than imposing a more severe punishment. *The Salford Chronicle* criticised him for his leniency.[36]

On another occasion four female scuttlers from the Adelphi area of Salford attacked a former gang member who had been forbidden by her mother to associate with them any more. She was condemned for having broken her 'oath of allegiance' to her former companions. The girls who attacked her were aged between fifteen and twenty-one but again the stipendiary magistrate decided on a light penalty, releasing them either on their own or on their parents' recognizances, after they had promised not to go near their victim's home again or 'loiter in the streets'. This decision, writes Andrew Davies, was surprising in that two of the four prisoners had been convicted at the same court within the previous two months. 'Seventeen-year-old Elizabeth Dugan had been fined five shillings for being drunk and disorderly, while Alice Cullen aged sixteen, had been fined ten shillings for assault.' Furthermore, Alice Cullen was to renew her acquaintance with the court six weeks later, when she was arrested for being drunk and disorderly in the early hours of Christmas morning. On this occasion she was fined ten shillings, with the alternative of seven days' imprisonment. She opted for gaol.[37]

Ultimately it was determined police action that put an end to the worst excesses of the scuttler gangs. At the close of the Victorian period Robert Roberts recalled how scuttlers 'appeared in droves before the courts, often to receive savage sentences'. In the early twentieth century the mass violence had diminished, although street battles 'on a smaller scale continued to recur spasmodically ... until the early days of the first world war.'[38]

Nevertheless, such brutal behaviour was not typical of most gang activities. These were based largely on a desire for companionship and a wish to show solidarity with their friends. Charles Russell, a Manchester youth worker, even praised the scuttlers for their 'sense of comradeship'. He blamed society for failing to provide them with 'a proper outlet for their energy'. Even now, he wrote in 1905, 'we do not sufficiently provide for it, though the many lads' clubs of the city are doing ... increasing service in this direction'.[39] That, of course, begs the question whether would-be scuttlers would have wanted to be organised in boys' clubs anyway.

The actions of young members of street gangs undoubtedly created alarm in some communities, and brought a number of youngsters into conflict with the law. What Matthew Arnold described as 'outbreaks of rowdyism' tended to become more frequent and less trivial over the years, thereby threatening what Arnold called 'the profound ... settled order of security'.[40] But another, less threatening, cause of juvenile wrongdoing arose from changing attitudes on the part of officialdom to activities which had once been tolerated but which in the late nineteenth century were classed as offences under bye-laws drawn up by local councils. It was a development condemned by *The Times* when it commented sourly on the 'multiplication of petty offences' that resulted and the way in which Parliament was constantly swelling their list,

saying this shall be punishable by fine, that by imprisonment, and what is a still more fruitful source of so-called crime, Parliament authorising public bodies to make by-laws which convert into crime what does not necessarily shock the consciences of ordinary citizens ... It satisfies the pride of municipalities and public bodies to be able to fine or imprison all who do not observe their behests. It saves trouble to stamp as a crime that which is intrinsically trivial; but it is a mischievous perversion of the objects of criminal law.[41]

Many of the new bye-laws particularly affected the recreational activities of young people, so that playing football in the street now became a punishable offence. A Bolton girl remembered that when the boys played, she and other 'younger elements – had to be on guard for the bobby coming because ... you were liable to be fined for playing football in the street ... And so we were placed at different corners to watch out ... and we used to give the call ... if we saw a bobby approaching and then of course the lads all scattered in all directions.' On Sundays they used to play at pitch and toss, which as a gambling game, was also prohibited. They congregated at the corner of a back street, 'tossing a penny into the circle, and again that was supposed to be our job, they called it "nicksing" for the police ... I remember they were often fined, and on one occasion they had to go to court, my brothers were in it, and they were fined five shillings each and ... the whole neighbourhood clubbed to pay the fines and they went and took it all down in ha'pennies'.[42]

Street Arabs: 'UM, WHAT'S THE USE O' WACCINATIN' THEM? THEY NEVER CATCHES NUFFIN'!'

'Street Arabs'.

Not all young gamblers got away so lightly. In March 1880 four lads playing pitch and toss in Binsey Lane, Oxford, were caught by the local constable and appeared before Oxford Police Court a few days later. Two of them were given the option of paying a 5s fine and 9s costs or serving seven days' imprisonment with hard labour, but the remaining two had no such opportunity. Instead they were sentenced to fourteen days' imprisonment with hard labour.[43]

These police interventions embittered many lads. Bert Teague from Bristol was caught playing football and refused to give his name to the policeman. This soon led to further difficulties: 'somethin' was said an' he hit me across the head with the bloody truncheon. I went for him and he went for me, and out came the people. Anyway, I got sent down Stapleton Road police station and put inside. I didn't give a bugger 'bout anyone … Anyway … I got a summons. I got told off and fined about two bob [2s] an' people had a collection for me. I was done for breach of the peace, footballing in the street'.[44] Years later the incident still rankled.

In Oxford, young people were brought to court for still more trivial offences, such as sliding on bridges and bathing in the river Thames in the nude. By 1900 swimming was restricted either to a certain public area where regulation bathing dress had to be worn or to a place called

HIGHLAND GAMES IN LONDON.
PORTRAIT OF THE BOY WHO WON THE PRIZE FOR "PUTTING A STONE"
THROUGH A WINDOW.

'Highland games in London'. A boy arrested for 'putting a stone' through a window.

Parson's Pleasure, which charged a fee for nude bathing. 'Boys defended their traditional bathing-places', writes John Gillis, 'by posting look-outs and driving off the disapproving passer-by with a barrage of abusive language'.[45] Sometimes prohibition only added spice to the mischief, as when Thomas Houslow of St Clement's in Oxford tried to stop boys playing games outside his house. The lads' response when Mr Houslow spoke to them was 'insolence and door-knocking', thereby leading him to write to Oxford City Watch and Ward Committee to complain of the annoyance he had suffered.[46]

Even some of the newly formed youth organisations played their part indirectly by causing young people to appear before the courts through the rebuffs they gave to well-meaning club organisers. In the early twentieth century the leaders of Balliol College Boys' Club in Oxford on occasion had to call upon the police to restore order:

> It required all the skill of the officer of the day to establish even tolerable discipline. The chief object for discussion ... was which boys should be turned out. Perhaps [the] decision was coloured by the knowledge that whoever was turned out would probably retaliate by throwing a stone through the window from outside during prayers.[47]

Later the 'unclubables' were simply expelled or kept out by the levying of a fee which they could not, or would not, pay.

In Manchester, too, a lads' club called the Adelphi was set up in 1888 and soon proved popular. But that did not mean it was without its problems. When an attempt was made to hold a singing class the voices of those within the club were drowned by the 'catcalls of the urchins without, shouting through the boards put up to replace the windows they had already broken. Sometimes the roughs broke in and had to be bodily ejected'.[48]

However, perhaps the most significant effect of the new bye-laws drawn up by local authorities related to the issue of street trading. Under pressure from the London Society for the Prevention of Cruelty to Children (later the National Society for the Prevention of Cruelty to Children) legislation was passed in 1889 which prohibited any boy under fourteen or girl under sixteen from offering goods for sale in the streets between 10 p.m. and 5 a.m. Children under ten were prohibited from carrying on these activities at any time. The restrictions particularly affected young newspaper vendors and the sellers of trifles like matches and bootlaces, as well as those helping parents to sell flowers and fruit in the streets. This kind of casual employment was condemned not only for encouraging truancy but for its adverse effect, both physically and morally, on the children themselves. In

1882, the Revd James Nugent, Roman Catholic chaplain of the Borough Gaol in Liverpool, considered that street trading was, more than anything else, responsible for encouraging prostitution amongst young girls in the city. 'I am sure that at the present moment at the very least, in a day, I could count from 200 to 300 girls in certain localities in Liverpool, under 14 years of age, trading on the streets ... Not only basket trading, but selling newspapers and fuzees [matches]; if anything could be done to check this trading of girls under 15 years of age, I am sure it would dry up the sources of prostitution in Liverpool more than anything else'.[49]

But juvenile trading proved difficult to eliminate. Despite a further tightening of the legislation in 1894, enforcement was a problem even in cities like Liverpool and Manchester which introduced a system of licensing for young traders. Indeed, after 1904 the policy of arresting children found trading without a licence in Liverpool was virtually abandoned. Instead they were brought before the city's Street Trading Sub-Committee and cautioned.[50] Elsewhere, as in Bradford, there were complaints that even when children were charged with illicit trading the magistrates failed to take action. In March 1896 the Bradford Watch Committee lamented that in '27 cases out of 38 in the past year' when child street hawkers were brought to court, they were 'discharged by the magistrates'.[51]

Nonetheless the trading prohibitions did bring some children into conflict with the law. In fact even in 1881, before the restrictive legislation of 1889 and 1894 had been introduced, 67 per cent of the youngsters sent to reformatories and industrial schools from Manchester were children who had been street traders. In Leeds the same class provided 60 per cent of the committals to industrial schools in that year.[52]

In 1903 the Employment of Children Act fixed eleven as the minimum age for street vending, while girls were restricted from trading under sixteen, in an effort, very largely, to make juvenile prostitution more difficult. Boys under fourteen were unable to work between 9 p.m. and 6 a.m., and local authorities could reduce these working hours still further should they so desire. Unfortunately, many towns were slow to implement the provisions, partly through fear of incurring expenditure by employing staff for that purpose, also through inertia and a wish not to offend newspaper proprietors and shopkeepers who utilised the children's labour. Hence even in 1913, out of 329 local authorities only 131 had bye-laws restricting juvenile street trading. They included Oxford, where during 1908 twenty-nine boys aged between eleven and sixteen were licensed to sell newspapers and other goods on the city's streets. Each boy had a numbered badge, to be worn on his left arm, as a means of identification. According to the chief constable, there had been 'a marked improvement in the conduct of the boys' since the licensing scheme was introduced.[53] By

1911 their number had fallen to fourteen, but the chief constable favoured still stricter regulations, arguing that once boys took up this kind of occupation, they rarely settled to 'any other regular employment, and the number of news vendors is already very large'. He wanted a complete ban on street trading by lads under fourteen, along lines recently adopted by the London County Council.[54] There was no official reaction to this plea but the number of licensed vendors in Oxford continued to fall. By 1913 only four boys had been given a licence, and these had all lapsed before the end of the year. Three of the lads had found alternative employment, and the fourth had reached sixteen and was, therefore, beyond the age for regulation as a juvenile.[55]

Female Morality

Although girls took part in many criminal acts, including larcenies, their involvement was generally much smaller than that of their male counterparts. Where they did commit thefts, it was often articles of dress they took, either to wear or to pawn. That could even involve stealing from family members. In April 1892 sixteen-year-old Louisa Gostridge from Salford was charged with stealing a shawl and chemise from her mother. She denied all knowledge of the offence until it was proved that she had pawned the articles. The police superintendent described her as an 'unmanageable girl' and when she was found guilty the stipendiary magistrate gave her the choice of going into a 'home' or serving a month in prison before being sent to a reformatory for four years. She was given a few days to decide which option she preferred.[56] That choice was unlikely to have been offered to boys in a similar situation, if cases appearing before the Salford Police Court around that time give any guidance.[57]

Young servants, too, had many opportunities for petty pilfering, and although some employers tolerated this as 'a fairly harmless means of supplementing meagre wages', others regarded it as an infringement of their property rights and took action against it. A number of mistresses tested the honesty and diligence of their maids by leaving coins under the edge of carpets or down the side of upholstered chairs. When they were discovered the maid was expected to hand them over quietly. A Norfolk girl who found several pennies hidden away in this fashion eventually told her father. He informed the mistress that his daughter 'was to pocket any pennies … found among the dirt'. The girl wryly commented: 'I never found another one'.[58]

In 1897, at a time when pressure was being exerted by the Home Office to keep juveniles out of prison wherever possible, the number of girls committed to gaol under the age of sixteen in the nation at large numbered just ninety. That compared with a total of 1,598 boys imprisoned in the same year. But even in 1861, before this anti-gaol campaign was under way, the 1,428 girls committed to prison were outnumbered about five to one by the 7,373 lads.[59]

Yet, though delinquent girls were in such a minority compared to the lads, they were often more difficult to control. According to Lieutenant Colonel Joshua Jebb, chairman of the Directors of Convict Prisons,

> they are not so amenable to punishment, their offences ... depend very much on impulse. If they quarrel one with another they will set to work and break the windows of their cells and tear up their clothes all without assignable reason and then they will sit down and burst out crying.[60]

As with the female scuttlers of Manchester and Salford, girls were sometimes involved in street violence, but the biggest cause of concern for penal reformers was the issue of female morality. It was believed that those who committed offences or who strayed from the path of Victorian respectability were likely to become prostitutes sooner or later. In fact so great was the fear of 'contamination' from such youngsters that managers of reformatory and industrial schools usually refused to receive girls who had been working as prostitutes or who came from a sexually dubious family background.[61] This was a stance supported by the Inspector of Reformatory and Industrial Schools in 1873 when he told the chairman of the Liverpool Committee concerned with the city's reformatories that it was inadvisable to admit 'prostitute cases ... I should steadily refuse ... any who are not certified by the medical authority of the gaol they come from, to be free from venereal disease, and if they were passed on to the school in spite of these precautions under a false or incorrect certificate, I should send them back or apply for their discharge as not eligible under the conditions which have been agreed to. If a girl went wrong, on licence, not criminally but viciously I should apply for her discharge and try to get her into some Magdalene asylum. She would do more harm in returning to the school, than the school could do her good. The school is formed and licensed to reform from thievish propensities and not from vice'.[62]

The restrictions even applied to pupils in day industrial schools. In October 1902, the governor of Brunswick Road day industrial school in London stated that he had intended charging ten-year-old Annie Lloyd with living in a 'house of ill repute', and of sending her away, but that she and her mother and siblings had been admitted to the workhouse, so that no action was needed. Another young pupil, Martha Pendle, was also considered for transfer to a residential school, 'as she is not a fit child to

THE NEW CUT.—EVENING.

Young prostitutes in London in the 1850s. The age of consent for legal sexual intercourse was only raised from twelve to thirteen in 1875 and, after a fierce campaign, to sixteen in 1885.

be with boys'. There she would presumably have been out of the way of temptation. Martha was thirteen, and had been sent to Brunswick Road as 'beyond control' and as setting a 'bad example' to the younger children in the family. In the end she was allowed to remain at the school until her discharge on 27 July, 1903 when she was fourteen.[63]

It was during the final two decades of the nineteenth century that the issue of juvenile prostitution achieved prominence, with the belief that it was now more prevalent in London and the major provincial cities than had been the case in the past. Sexual intercourse with a girl less than twelve years old was illegal until 1875, when that minimum age limit was raised to thirteen. But the precise age of a child prostitute was often impossible to establish even should her potential clients have been anxious to do so. Hence this limited moral protection for the young was ineffective. 'In London', writes Kellow Chesney, 'the openness with which the business was carried on was astonishing … Especially about the Haymarket, but also in parts of the City and elsewhere, little creatures in petticoats could be seen pursuing male pedestrians, plucking at their elbows and trying to excite their interest by all sorts of lewd remarks'.[64] In the Strand, pornographic literature was distributed by children, with 'shoeless, impudent, little girls' pushing their wares into the faces of passers-by.[65] In July 1881, Howard Vincent, director of Criminal Investigations, claimed that juvenile prostitution was 'rampant' in the capital at that date, and that most of the girls lived at home with their parents and not in brothels:

> in the streets about the Haymarket, Waterloo Place, and Piccadilly, from nightfall there are children of 14, 15, and 16 years of age going about openly soliciting prostitution ... I believe ... this prostitution actually takes place with the knowledge and connivance of the mother and to the profit of the household ... they would have no difficulty whatever in going to dozens and dozens of coffee-houses with men and obtaining a bed.

The police, he declared, were powerless to prevent them soliciting in the streets, unless it was to 'the annoyance and obstruction of passengers, and no respectable person is willing to go into a police court and say they were solicited by prostitutes.'[66]

In some cases family poverty and parental neglect were motivating factors; in others it was a lack of alternative employment. In Liverpool, for example, there were few jobs for young girls and those there were, such as dressmaking or domestic service, were poorly paid. Neglected children were allowed to wander around the streets and were picked up by men. They would then be taken down a darkened back alley where sexual intercourse took place, with the girls receiving 'a few pence or 6d' in return. 'I have known a case where one child has kept watch at one end of an entry while a man took another child up for immoral purposes and brought her back again', declared a Liverpool witness in 1882. According to the Roman Catholic Chaplain of Liverpool Borough Gaol, low pay also led girls to take up prostitution. Those who could earn only 2s or 3s a week in 'respectable' employment could go 'to a dancing-room' and pick up a sailor or ship's officer and earn in a week as many pounds as they did in shillings at their former work: 'a girl has no difficulty who goes into this life in getting 2£ or 3£ a week'.[67]

Often, however, it was simply a desire to get nice clothes and to avoid the poorly-paid, drudging life of a domestic servant that led to the girls becoming prostitutes. 'I have watched the progress of some of these children', declared Superintendent Joseph Dunlap of the Metropolitan Police, in 1881. 'They are generally of the low class from Newport Market, Bedfordbury, or Seven Dials; they appear dressed ... with a belcher over their shoulders (one of the coloured handkerchiefs); they come two and two through the streets, and after a few days they are dressed a little more elaborately; and at last you will see them launch out in silks and satins'.[68]

Most girls did not become prostitutes until they were about sixteen years old, but there were exceptions to this, as we have seen. In the early 1880s, the chaplain of one of the prisons compiled statistics relating to 3,076 prostitutes. Of these 292 – or just under one in ten – had been first 'seduced' under the age of sixteen. The three youngest had commenced their career on the streets at the age of eleven.[69] Then there were girls like thirteen-year-old Alice Diver, whose previous employment had been 'nursing children by the day'. She had turned to prostitution and by June 1886 had already spent five weeks in the Middlesex Hospital to be cured of syphilis. She was then taken in by a Salvation Army Refuge for 'fallen' women. Their report noted she had 'a good godly mother but a drunken father' and had been 'led astray' first of all when she was only eleven. She had run away from home on several occasions and it was after one of these escapades that she had been taken to the Refuge. The Salvation Army managed to find Alice's mother and she pleaded with them to 'try and do something for her'. After some weeks they found her a post as a maid in the household of a 'christian woman', but Alice behaved so badly that she was obliged to dismiss the girl after a short time. This was less than six months after her initial entry into the Refuge, and the Salvation Army concluded that she was a 'hopeless case' and returned her to her mother.[70] Presumably she then resumed her life on the streets.

Some procurers specialised in providing child prostitutes for their clients. In Hull one man kept fifteen girls between the ages of twelve and fifteen in a so-called 'infant school', and the police were only able to intervene by prosecuting him for selling intoxicating liquor without a licence. At this point their families were able to take the youngsters away.[71] Similarly in Portsmouth, juvenile prostitutes were provided by some of the shadier publicans and beerhouse-keepers. At the Battle of Inkerman public house in the town the landlord specialised in providing young girls, thus leading to his house, too, being known as the 'infant school'. Young girls also featured prominently at the Good Intent.[72] In London at the beginning of the 1880s, Superintendent Dunlap reported going to arrest a brothel keeper in his division, and finding in each of the rooms in the house

> an elderly gentleman in bed with two of these children. I asked their ages, and got into conversation with them. They knew perfectly well that I could not touch them in the house; and they laughed and joked [with] me ... I questioned them, in the presence of the brothel-keeper, as to what they had paid, and so on. They were to receive 6s each from the gentleman, two of them; and the gentlemen had paid 6s each for the room. It was 4s if there was only one girl, but 6s if there were two girls for the room.[73]

The client paid both the brothel-keeper for the use of the room and the children for their services. Dunlap thought the girls were around fifteen years old.

Anxieties about the amount of juvenile prostitution were also linked to the controversy over the role of the Contagious Diseases legislation passed in the 1860s. This laid down that women and girls in the major military garrison towns and naval seaports, who were suspected by the police of being prostitutes, were required to undergo medical examinations to ascertain whether they had venereal disease. If they refused to be examined or to receive treatment, should they be found to be infected, they could be imprisoned. Thereafter regular medical checks were required. Plain clothes Metropolitan policemen were drafted in to help with the inspection programme and the alleged prostitutes were given no rights against the police, who 'could arrest and humiliate them on whim', as Edward Bristow puts it.[74] The gender inequality of the legislation (since the girls' male clients underwent no such examination) and the general treatment they received led to vociferous condemnation from opponents such as Josephine Butler, who demanded that the Acts be repealed. The measure mainly affected older women, but there were examples of young prostitutes being caught up in its restrictions. In 1871, for example, Mr Bulteel, a surgeon at the Royal Albert Hospital in Devonport claimed that over a two-year period out of about 872 women treated for venereal disease, around nineteen had been under fifteen years of age.[75] Some were sent to hospital several times. The house surgeon at the Lock Hospital, Portsmouth, claimed in March 1871 that he had recently treated a nineteen-year-old girl who claimed to have been in the hospital seventeen times, and who had first become a prostitute at the age of fourteen. He thought there should be a law 'to prevent them going on the town at such an early age as 14'.[76]

Under the 1869 Contagious Diseases Act women and girls suffering from venereal disease could be kept in hospital under a single order for up to nine months, until they were cured.[77] Many naturally resented the confinement and the whole humiliating procedure. Among them was sixteen-year-old Elizabeth Evans, who in the summer of 1873 was charged with disorderly conduct in the 'Lock wards' of the Royal Portsmouth Hospital. She was confined to gaol for two days for having caused a riot in the hospital, along with a number of other inmates. During this, fifty-eight windows had been smashed and a number of other articles broken. When she returned to the hospital, however, she was clearly unrepentant, using bad language to the staff and refusing to observe the rules or to obey the officials. She also disturbed other patients and early the next morning she was removed by the police. When charged in court a second time, Elizabeth was warned that she was liable to be imprisoned for three

Ada Mary Wood, a sixteen-year-old servant, imprisoned in Aylesbury gaol for two months with hard labour for stealing a gold locket from her mistress in 1871.

months. Another patient, aged eighteen, reacted violently to her friend's removal by snatching up a broom and smashing further panes of glass. She was sentenced to fourteen days in gaol with hard labour.[78]

Eventually it became clear that the Contagious Diseases Acts were not achieving their objective of eliminating venereal infections among the military and naval personnel in the garrison towns, while the blatant inequity of the scheme caused outrage among many respectable middle-class women. In part, the legislation failed to meet its goal because of inadequate medical information about the diagnosis and treatment of venereal diseases. Syphilis, for example, comments Edward Bristow, 'often went undetected before the development of the Wasserman test in 1907'. So that even women and girls who co-operated with the inspection regime could 'slip through the surgical examination.' It was discovered, too, that many were being 'released from hospital after primary syphilitic symptoms had cleared but before a cure had been effected. It was also clear that no class of prostitutes had ever complied willingly'. In these circumstances in 1883 it was decided that the medical examination of prostitutes would no longer be compulsory; in other words, the operation of the Acts was suspended. In 1886 they were repealed.[79]

Nonetheless it was during the 1880s that the debate over juvenile prostitution and the issue of the 'white slave trade', whereby girls were allegedly shipped to brothels in France and Belgium, reached a peak. The government responded in 1881 by appointing a Select Committee of the House of Lords to investigate the law regarding the protection of young girls, and to establish the scale of the white slave trade. As regards the latter, it was established that this rarely affected juveniles, and that most of the girls who went abroad were well aware of what was involved. Nevertheless it recommended that it be made a serious misdemeanour for any person to seek to procure a woman to leave the United Kingdom for the purpose of entering a brothel or prostituting herself overseas.[80]

Tackling the problem of juvenile prostitution itself proved more contentious. The first attempt to deal with this had in fact been made in 1880, when under pressure from Ellice Hopkins, a committed social purity campaigner, the Industrial Schools Acts Amendment Act was passed. Under this, any child lodging in a brothel or living with a common or reputed prostitute, even if that were his or her mother, was to be brought to court so that magistrates could make an order for entry to a residential industrial school. The task of enforcing the legislation was given to the school boards. In giving support to the Bill one MP claimed that in four streets in Tower Hamlets there were 'no less than 58 girls of tender age, who were living in common brothels,' and who attended local elementary schools. He hoped that the House 'would not hesitate to grapple with, and, if possible, stamp out this hideous plague spot of juvenile prostitution'.[81] A similar point was made by Lord Norton when the Bill was debated in the Upper House. According to him girls under fourteen years 'were living in great numbers in brothels, in all our great towns, but especially in London.' The new measure would enable magistrates to send them to be boarded in industrial schools and that would benefit not only themselves but 'decently brought up' children with whom they came into contact during classes as a result of the enforcement of compulsory elementary education.[82]

Many school boards and attendance officers, however, were reluctant to intervene in such a delicate area of domestic life and to remove children from their homes, except under the most pressing circumstances, such as when parents were being prosecuted as brothel keepers.[83] Even in Portsmouth, where the school board, after a slow start, began to send children away to residential schools from early in 1882, there were complaints that the action taken was inadequate. In January 1883, a correspondent to the *Hampshire Telegraph*, for example, claimed to know of eight children who had resided for 'some months' in brothels. In response the school board pointed out that between May 1882 and January 1883 alone, twenty-six children had been dealt with on these grounds. Four had been sent away to a local industrial school, one child had been despatched to grandparents in West Bromwich, nine had been removed from the brothels and were being boarded out 'with respectable people', and in twelve cases the parents had voluntarily discontinued the brothels rather than lose their children.[84] In addition from July 1881 a special industrial school was set up with the support of 'many leading men in Portsmouth' to provide accommodation for thirty girls from Portsmouth and Southampton who had been taken away from their families under the terms of the 1880 Industrial Schools legislation.[85]

Elsewhere the reluctance of the authorities to act led Ellice Hopkins to turn to the Reformatory and Refuge Union for help in identifying suitable cases. They appointed an experienced ex-police officer (and later a second) to enforce the legislation. In the early days, these efforts were met with hostility not only from the families concerned but from their neighbours. One such example recounted by Miss Hopkins involved Jane and Mary T., aged 12 and 9, respectively. They were the daughters of brothel keepers in Woolwich. The officer, accompanied by a police constable and a school board official, went to the address and removed the girls to Woolwich Police Court, where they were charged under the 1880 Act with residing in a 'bad house'. When the officer set off with the first girl he was followed by a crowd of about three hundred people, who showered him with flower pots and other missiles. But he considered his action had been justified since at the time of the arrest 'their parents were keeping two bad houses, and had about sixteen prostitutes living with them'.[86] Nonetheless, when the doctor examined the sisters before he signed a certificate for their admission to an industrial school, he stated that he had never seen 'two such fine girls before for their age.' The officer did not seem to understand what a traumatic experience this must have been for the two children, snatched away from their family and home, where they had obviously been well cared for, to be subjected to the regimentation and strict discipline of an industrial school. In many cases it meant they would be kept in the school until they reached the age of sixteen. Some children were very young when they were taken away. In Portsmouth, where the school board intervened in the cases of thirteen children in July 1882, two were aged only five years old and one was just six.[87] Again in April and July 1884, two five-year-olds were sent to a residential school. In each case the board provided a maintenance grant of 2s a week per child. This was its customary rate.

In some instances, however, the children were undoubtedly rescued from a dire home background. This was true of Maria and Mary Perryman, aged nine and five, respectively, when they were removed by the Portsmouth school board from the home they shared with their mother, an aunt, and a mentally handicapped older sister. There were also two brothers, and according to a report submitted to the Portsmouth magistrates, the place where they lived was a perfect den, for house or home it could not be called. The mother was not fit even to be brought into a court of justice, for she was almost destitute of clothing. One broken chair and an old table constituted the entire furniture of the house. Notwithstanding all that, prostitution was carried on there by women who also lived in a state of filth and wretchedness past description.[88]

When an official went to the house he found Mrs Perryman and four of her children lying together in one corner of an upstairs room. A thin partition separated them from a prostitute. In another corner there was a second 'woman of ill-fame. In the coal-hole downstairs there was another woman, who, to keep herself from the ground, had made a bed of bottles, old tins, and brickbats'.[89] When the two girls first appeared before the bench; the magistrates remanded them to the workhouse for seven days pending arrangements being made for their reception into an industrial school. It was later claimed that within weeks of their admission into the school they were 'changed in every respect and, so to speak, "clothed and in their right mind".' But for every example of this kind, there were many others where the children had lived happily and comfortably with their parents, despite the latter's reliance on 'immoral earnings'.

It was with these more favourable cases in mind that one Member of Parliament condemned the school board interventions. Although doubtless undertaken 'with the best intentions on the part of benevolent people' they often resulted in 'a beloved and tender child ... kept in total ignorance of the mother's life', being ruthlessly taken away by a lady 'who had never felt the springs of maternity within her'. Another critic labelled the measure as permitting 'the wholesale kidnapping ... of little girls who may not have perfect domestic surroundings'.[90] In 1896 a Departmental Committee reporting on Reformatory and Industrial Schools criticised the working of the 1880 Act on other grounds. It quoted the manager of one institution which had received 220 children since the passage of the legislation. Of these only ten had not subsequently turned to prostitution. Once they reached the age of sixteen and were released from the school, their parents took them 'straight to the brothels'. The Committee recommended that no girl should be sent to an industrial school over the age of twelve, since if she had grown up in a 'disorderly house' she would be likely to corrupt her fellow pupils.[91]

Despite its reformist intentions, therefore, the Industrial Schools Acts Amendment Act proved an unsatisfactory weapon in the battle against juvenile prostitution. Another, more direct, approach was the attempt to raise the legal age of consent when sexual intercourse was permitted from thirteen to sixteen, as had been recommended in the 1882 Report of the Select Committee on the Law Relating to the Protection of Young Girls. But this proved difficult to achieve. As early as 1874, when attempts were being made to raise the age of consent from twelve to thirteen, there was strong opposition from what Josephine Butler ironically called 'some gentlemen' on the grounds that *their sons would be placed at a great disadvantage*'.⁹² Nonetheless a modest advance to thirteen was achieved in the following year. But efforts to raise the minimum age to sixteen proved far more controversial. Although legislation to that end was passed by the House of Lords in 1883 and 1884, it failed to make progress in the Commons. During 1885 a similar measure was introduced and again seemed likely to fall by the wayside.

It was at that point that W. T. Stead, the fiery editor of the *Pall Mall Gazette* intervened, with a series of articles in the summer of 1885 on 'The Maiden Tribute of Modern Babylon'. This exposed the dark side of prostitution, including the sale, purchase and violation of children, and the procuring of virgins to be raped in brothels.⁹³ 'In and about the Quadrant and Regent street', wrote Stead, 'I have taken or caused to be taken repeatedly to houses of accommodation young girls from thirteen and upwards who have been picked up on the streets; no objection was ever raised by the keepers'⁹⁴. To prove that it could be done, Stead arranged to purchase a girl himself. She was thirteen-year-old Eliza Armstrong and although care was taken that no harm came to her, the account of his actions in the *Pall Mall Gazette* caused an immense furore. It fuelled public demands for a raising of the age of consent, though Stead was subsequently charged with abduction. He was sentenced to three months' imprisonment, a punishment in which he took great pride⁹⁵. In pressing for reform, he had won the support of the leaders of the Salvation Army and of the newly-established London Society for the Prevention of Cruelty to Children⁹⁶.

Against this background of agitation caused by the 'Maiden Tribute' articles, and with MPs deluged with letters from their constituents, on 30 July 1885, the House of Commons resumed its debate on the Criminal Law Amendment Bill, designed, among other reforms, to raise the age of consent. One Member, a Mr Hopwood, opposed the measure on the grounds that it could make young well-to-do men vulnerable to extortion by girls aged from thirteen to sixteen who were 'steeped in depravity'. He believed that if the Bill were passed, 'there would be great danger of young men and even boys being betrayed by designing creatures, whose object was to levy "blackmail". Such cases of extortion had occurred in the past ... Abandoned and profligate fathers and mothers, as well as girls themselves, might make the provisions of this Bill a means of extortion'⁹⁷. Presumably his argument was that youngsters under the age of sixteen would pass themselves off as being of that age, in order to lure young men into having sexual intercourse with them. But his opposition was a minority viewpoint, at least in the Commons debates. Amid some excitement, therefore, the Bill received its third reading on 7 August, when it was approved by 179 votes to 71. Just over a week later a huge demonstration took place in Hyde Park, to demand the enforcement of the legislation, and all over the country social purity groups were formed to achieve the same end.[98]

Under the new Act anyone seeking to have sexual intercourse with a girl under sixteen, whether she consented or not, was liable to a maximum term of two years' imprisonment, with or without hard labour, while anyone who knowingly allowed a girl under sixteen to be on his or her premises for such a purpose could receive a similar punishment[99]. The Act gave the police greater powers to prosecute streetwalkers and brothel-keepers, so that, as Kellow Chesney puts it,

> procuring and brothel-keeping were effectively outlawed. Brothel proprietors and their agents became liable to simple summary proceedings. A £20 fine and three months hard labour could be imposed for a first offence, and £40 and four months for each subsequent conviction.[100]

It also made any act of gross indecency between two male persons a criminal offence, and thus formed the basis of legal proceedings against male homosexuals until 1967.[101]

The 1885 Act did not end juvenile prostitution, as its more optimistic supporters had hoped, but it did offer some protection to the youngest girls, and it brought an end to the most blatant displays of child prostitution on the streets. Henceforward the 'professional bawd' of any age 'had to operate under cover', writes Kellow Chesney, 'and became as unquestionably criminal as the thief or forger. In the whole Victorian underworld no other important field of activity underwent so clear-cut a change.'[102]

New Remedies

The measures adopted for tackling juvenile delinquency in late Victorian and Edwardian England included not merely fresh legislation to deal with particular aspects of wrongdoing, but a fundamental shift in attitude towards the punishment of children. 'The primary assumptions underpinning [the] legislation were that juveniles were less responsible than adults for their actions and should not be subject to the full majesty of the law', writes John Muncie. But, he adds, 'such legislation … can be read as not simply

humanitarian in intent. Whilst separating juvenile from adult justice, it
further cemented the notion that the troublesome young ... constituted an
entirely *new* and *unprecedented* problem for the nation's future.'[103]

The changes ranged from Home Office pressure to avoid sending young
people to gaol where possible, to the creation of various new institutions
designed to bring about their rehabilitation. It culminated in 1914 with
the setting up of the Home Office Children's Branch. The moves, declare
Radzinowicz and Hood, mark 'the beginning of the twentieth century
approach to the treatment of young offenders'.[104]

The first indication of the new philosophy came in 1879 when the Summary
Jurisdiction Act permitted the courts to dismiss with an 'admonition' a
juvenile found guilty of a petty offence. It was intended as an alternative
to imprisonment, or confinement in another correctional establishment.
Disillusion with the effects of short prison sentences and a general unease
about committing children to prison brought this 'admonitory' initiative
into increasing prominence over the following years[105]. It was further
boosted from 1880 by the new Home Secretary, Sir William Harcourt, who
was determined to reduce the number of youngsters still being incarcerated.
As he explained to Queen Victoria, who was concerned about his undue
'tenderness towards offenders' and the frequency with which he remitted
the sentences imposed on young people:

> The child who has been guilty only of some mischievous or thoughtless
> prank which does not partake of the real character of crime finds himself
> committed with adult criminals guilty of heinous offences. In gaol, after a
> week or a fortnight's imprisonment he comes out ... tainted in character
> amongst his former companions ... and he soon lapses into the criminal
> class with whom he has been identified.[106]

Doubts were expressed, too, about the desirability of committing minor
offenders to reformatories or industrial schools for long periods, thereby
not only separating them from their families but institutionalising them as
well. In 1909, John Rose, a Metropolitan police magistrate, condemned the
'tendency to gather up the offending children ... for begging a halfpenny
in the street, and to put them into industrial schools. Personally, I think it
is much to be deprecated that children should be swept up wholesale and
packed off to reformatories and industrial schools ... Often the parents
are very poor, but they are fond of their children'[107].

The alternative punishments which were increasingly being adopted,
therefore, in addition to admonitions, were fines, whipping (in the case of
boys under fourteen), the binding over of offenders to be of good behaviour
under their own, or their parents', recognizances, and the placing of

youngsters under police supervision. On occasion children were formally remanded into the custody of their parents so that they might receive a parental beating. Or, rather than sending young people to a reformatory or industrial school, use was made of refuges, shelters and orphanages set up by philanthropic organisations. This initiative was given legislative backing under the Youthful Offenders Act of 1901, although it was initially used very sparingly. In Liverpool, for example, the stipendiary magistrate stated 'that he was perfectly satisfied with remand to the Workhouse and wanted nothing better'[108].

The way these alternatives worked in practice can be seen in cases which came before the Salford Police Court during the period April to mid-June 1892. During these months there were ten cases involving seventeen juveniles. All except one, Louisa Gostridge, were boys, and three of the cases involved skirmishes in the street, six were minor thefts, and one was for pickpocketing. Of the seventeen youngsters concerned, four were discharged, presumably after receiving an admonition; three were bound over to come up for judgment when called upon; two were birched; six were discharged, on their parents promising to give them 'a sound flogging'; and one was remanded for further enquiries to be made. Only one, Louisa Gostridge, whose case was discussed earlier in the chapter, was given the option of going to prison for a month and then to a reformatory for four years, or being sent to a home.[109]

In 1887, a further boost was given to this non-custodial approach when the Probation of First Offenders Act empowered magistrates to release youngsters guilty of a minor offence, once they had entered into recognizances (with or without sureties) to keep the peace and to be of good behaviour for a period specified by the court[110]. A major weakness of the measure, however, was that it made no provision for official supervision of the probationer, to ensure that the conditions were being met. Unofficial supervision might be provided by newly recruited police court missioners, who were drawn from various philanthropic organisations. These included the Church of England Temperance Society, Discharged Prisoners' Aid Societies and, later on, the National Society for the Prevention of Cruelty to Children, the Church Army and the Salvation Army.[111] The first of the missioners was appointed in 1876 on the initiative of the Church of England Temperance Society, to work at the Southwark, Lambeth and Mansion House Police Courts, in order to assist with the rehabilitation of offenders with a chronic drink problem. But their remit was soon extended and their numbers increased, so that by 1894 there were seventy of them being deployed by courts in different parts of the country. They were used to make enquiries into cases which might be suitable for placement under recognizances, and afterwards to give any offenders allotted to them informal supervision and help. Their motivation, according to Radzinowicz and Hood, was 'deeply religious, to save sinners and bring them to salvation'[112]. They performed a more practical role, too, sometimes helping youngsters to find employment or guiding them into joining boys' clubs and other youth organisations, where they could share in sporting and similar recreational activities.

However, their position was weakened by the fact that they had no official standing. Mr Ferris Pike, who became a police court missioner at Oxford in the 1880s, under the aegis of the Church of England Temperance Society, noted the limitations this placed on the degree of control they could exercise.[113] They had no formal power; 'it was only a moral influence', as Radzinowicz and Hood point out.[114]

Yet despite its deficiencies the initiative was considered sufficiently successful to be placed on a statutory basis. In 1907 the Probation of Offenders Act was passed, designed to give 'reclaimable offenders … opportunity to reform', without experiencing the stigma of imprisonment. It differed from the preceding legislation in that offenders were now conditionally released only under the supervision of a probation officer, who would report back to the court. This official function gave the officer a stronger hold over the offender than before, and thereby gave greater authority to discourage re-offending. But he or, more often, she had other tasks to perform where children were involved. These included paying regular visits to a probationer's home. Miss Lance, a London probation officer, aimed to see the children she was supervising once a week for the first four weeks of their probation and thereafter once a month, for the period specified in the probation order. During her first year and a quarter of employment, from January 1908, when the Act came into force, she had supervised forty-four youngsters, of whom two had subsequently been sent to reformatories and two had resumed stealing. She thought the remainder were 'going on all right'[115]. It was an indication of the new attitude towards offenders that the probation officer's other duties were defined as to 'advise, assist, and befriend' the probationer and 'when necessary, to endeavour to find him suitable employment'[116]. These were tasks Miss Lance had undertaken. When asked if her role was resented by the parents of the children she was supervising, she denied this, stating that they had 'never shown that the visits' were unwelcome. Indeed, they had appreciated her efforts to find the youngsters work: 'the parents say they want someone behind them. They do not know anybody to push them and they are rather glad for that reason to have somebody busy about them'[117]. She thought that the worst cases often came from 'respectable homes … because the children themselves then are bad'. But often the youngsters with whom she had come into contact had offended through a 'spirit of adventure' rather than anything more malign. [118]

Mr Ferris Pike from Oxford also considered that the legislation had had a beneficial effect on the behaviour of other lads. 'I was told the other day in one village where three boys had been put under probation', he commented in 1909, that 'the conduct of the boys in that place was changed from that fact.' They had 'the fear of the Court before them', if they misbehaved. [119]

Some critics, however, saw the new arrangements as offering a soft option to offenders. In the case of children coming from unsatisfactory homes, it was also argued that the efforts of the probation officer were unlikely to improve these. Miss Adler, who spoke on behalf of the Committee on Wage Earning Children, in March 1909 conceded that in cases 'where there is rather more hope in the home we believe probation can do a great deal of good.' But if the home was bad and there were 'drunken parents, or other children ... sent already to industrial schools, or if one of the parents is a person of doubtful character, we think it is better to take the child away entirely'. [120]

Certain magistrates were also reluctant to adopt the new provisions, feeling they offered little benefit over the previous system or they placed an unacceptable limit on their own actions. So although the courts appointed probation officers, some did so on a part-time basis only. As a result there was a great difference between the counties in the use of probation orders. Whereas Lancashire had 330 males and fifty-five females under sixteen on probation in 1908, London had only 150 boys and eighteen girls in that age group on probation, while Northumberland had a mere sixteen males and five females and Cambridgeshire seven males and no females at all under sixteen on probation in that year. Nonetheless, the statistics showed that about one in three of all those against whom probation orders were made in England and Wales in 1908 were under sixteen, with almost a further third in the age group sixteen to twenty-one. [121] Clearly, therefore, where the legislation was being applied it was benefiting young people. During the next few years that trend intensified, so that by 1913, 44 per cent of all those placed on probation were under sixteen, with a further 29 per cent aged between sixteen and twenty-one. [122]

Modern critics have seen the probation system as forming part of a more 'interventionist' style of social control, which sought to inculcate the values of good citizenship and respectability. At the same time it extended judicial surveillance beyond the offender to his or her parents and family. As the leading Liberal politician, Herbert Samuel, put it in 1909, 'the home is put under probation' as well. [123] To Blagg and Wilson, writing three years later, the new arrangements meant the parents 'quite as much as the children' were 'put on probation'. [124]

The probation system, then, was one aspect of the new approach to crime and punishment in the early twentieth century. Another, even more important, influence was the effect of the wide-ranging 1908 Children Act, or 'Children's Charter', as it has been labelled. This covered a large number of welfare issues involving juveniles. On the crime front, the changes it introduced were the raising of the minimum age for capital punishment to sixteen, while children under fourteen were no longer to be sent to prison. A similar principle applied to those between fourteen and sixteen unless the court certified that the young person was 'of so unruly a character that he [could] not be detained in a place of detention … or [was] of so depraved a character that he [was] not a fit person to be so detained.'[125] When a child under the age of sixteen was apprehended and for some reason could not immediately be brought before a court of summary jurisdiction or a senior police officer, then, unless the charge were one of homicide or another grave crime, bail was to be allowed. If that were not possible, and he or she was remanded in custody, the child was to be sent to an approved place of detention and not a prison. In Oxford, for example, the Police Court and Prison Gate Mission established shelters for boys and for women and girls, respectively, in 1909. During the following year, out of forty-seven lads received, twenty-one were remanded by magistrates and a further twelve were brought in by the police.[126]

Finally, and most importantly, the Children Act introduced a system of juvenile courts. These had been pioneered in the United States in the late nineteenth century, but the concept was only taken up in England in 1905, when a children's court was established on an experimental basis in Birmingham. It was composed of certain magistrates who agreed to sit in rotation, and they were aided in their deliberations by a group of men and women who were experienced in working with children.[127] The idea was subsequently adopted by ten other county boroughs over the following months.[128] In 1908 it was incorporated in the Children Act.

Strictly speaking, the courts were criminal courts but their proceedings were modified to take account of the immaturity of the offenders appearing before them. Most importantly, the children were to be kept apart from adult offenders both in a police station and while awaiting trial. The court itself was to be conducted in a separate room or at a separate time from the adult court, and members of the public were excluded, except for accredited newspaper journalists and those who were parties to the case. Special arrangements were to be made in London, with the London County Council, if required, providing suitable accommodation.[129]

Juvenile courts represented a clear recognition of the special position of young offenders but critics complained that they did not go far enough – that, unlike in the United States, the main focus of the proceedings remained the offence committed rather than the welfare of the offender. Cecil Leeson in 1914 condemned the appearance in court of uniformed

Interior of the new Liverpool Juvenile Court, *c*.1925.

police officers and the formality involved, with a plea of guilty or not guilty being entered. This tended 'to destroy in the child that feeling of confidence which the magistrates themselves seek to inspire. The magistrate tells him he is brought there in his own interest; the child sees the policeman, and fails to be convinced'.[130] If he had a sensitive nature the ordeal would frighten him. If not he would brazen the thing out and become 'the hero of his playmates for the rest of his childhood.'

Around the same time a leading Metropolitan magistrate described the procedures as cumbersome, solemn, too complicated for children to understand, and 'too legalistic. The legislation was little more than a device to dissociate young delinquents from adult criminals'.[131] But to the Home Office Children's Branch it was the magistrates themselves who were of vital importance. To a large extent, the future of the child 'and the chance of cure or reformation' depended 'on the way in which the case [was] handled in the Juvenile Court'.[132]

Alongside these initiatives for the reform and rehabilitation of the youngest offenders, steps were taken to deal with those aged between sixteen and twenty-one through the creation of Borstals. These were to be state-run reformatories, unlike the largely philanthropic organisations which had been catering for children since the mid-nineteenth century. Prior to this initiative, young offenders who had reached the age of seventeen had no alternative but prison if they received a custodial sentence. The new Borstals were designed to remedy this, by offering training under conditions of strict discipline. The new institution took its name from the village in Kent where the first Borstal was opened in a special section of an existing convict prison. The idea had been first mooted in the mid-1890s and was based on the fact that the age group sixteen to twenty-one was that which provided the highest number of prisoners. In 1895 a Departmental Committee on Prisons defined the proposed new institution as 'a half-way home between the prison and the reformatory'. It should be located in the countryside, away from urban temptations, and should have a penal and coercive role, as well as a training facility.[133]

A small-scale experimental scheme had been started at Bedford Prison in 1900, with eight young prisoners selected from London gaols. The regime included education, physical exercises, lectures, choir practice, visits by the chaplain, and trade instruction. Within three months the governor of Bedford was reporting that the improvement in all but one of the young inmates had exceeded his expectations. 'The scheme is ... worthy of any trouble and expense the State may incur'.[134]

The following year the transfer to Borstal took place, with the main principles of the scheme defined as strict classification; firm and exact discipline; hard work; and organised supervision on discharge for a period of some months. As at Bedford, physical drill, trade instruction and education were offered, coupled with a system of grades 'through which the inmate gained promotion and increasing small privileges by earning marks for hard work and good conduct'. The supervision given on discharge was intended not merely to help the boys to resettle, but to follow up cases and gather evidence to enable public opinion to judge 'whether the results of the system, as a new means for the prevention of crime, are so good that what is now being tried only as an experiment ... should be made of universal application' It was also decided, after two years' experience, that only lads who had been sentenced to at least twelve months' imprisonment should be sent to Borstal, since six months was 'too short a period' to achieve effective rehabilitation.[135]

In 1908 the experiment was given statutory recognition by the Prevention of Crime Act and from that date the use of the new institution increased steadily, with 271 boys committed in 1910 and 495 in the following year. Under the 1908 legislation offenders were sent to Borstal for between one and three years, although earlier release under licence was possible with the agreement of the Prison Commissioners, once an initial period of six months had been served. This only took place if it were considered there was a 'reasonable probability that the offender [would] abstain from crime and lead a useful and industrious life'. Should he fail to meet these standards, the licence would be revoked and he would return to Borstal. After the expiration of his period of detention, each former inmate remained under the supervision of the Prison Commissioners for a further six months.[136] In 1914 that supervisory period was extended to a year.

In 1911 Feltham became a second Borstal, to cater for the rising number of committals. During these years before the outbreak of the First World War, the new system received favourable publicity. In 1910 *The Times* called it 'the bright spot on the horizon of the future prison administration' and in 1914 the then Home Secretary, Mr McKenna, stressed that Borstal 'was to be developed as an educational system far removed from its prison roots':

> our object is to provide in the Borstal institution a place where the offender will not be imprisoned, but will only be deprived of his liberty to that degree which is necessary to ensure discipline ... It is not a prison. It is, or it should be, far more like a school under severe discipline with a strict industrial training.[137]

To what extent the Borstal initiative realised the more sanguine hopes of its backers in achieving the reform and rehabilitation of young offenders, remains debatable. A survey of 1,454 young men released between 1909 and 1914 revealed that of those who had been at large for as long as four years the failure rate was 35 per cent. But this was still considered a remarkable success for a system which had commenced with limited expectations.[138] By 1921 some commentators were claiming that it had brought about 'a revolution in the prison system and in the attitude of the judiciary and the public to the treatment of the young offender'. As Roger Hood comments, it had accomplished enough to 'ensure public support' for the future. [139]

But the institution had its darker side too. Reform and rehabilitation were certainly not achieved in respect of one early Borstal inmate, Arthur Harding. After serving three months of a twenty-month prison sentence in Wormwood Scrubs, the seventeen-year-old Harding was transferred to the new institution in June 1903. He found the change welcome:

> You weren't kept in a cell. Every day there were physical exercises out of doors and these had a beneficial effect on my health which had suffered from the close confinement of Wormwood Scrubs. And I learnt a good deal of woodwork. I had described myself as a cabinet-maker so I was put into the carpenter's shop – in later years I always went to the carpenter's shop when serving time in jail.
>
> I was discharged from Borstal in September 1904 and went back to Bethnal Green ... Borstal had made me fitter, stronger, taller. I was no longer a kid, and when I went back to my old associates I found that I

was something of a hero ... I had a reputation for being tough. And I was the only one in the younger age group to have done time. They began to look up to me as a sort of leader.[140]

Harding went on to become a significant figure in the East End underworld, taking part in protection rackets, racecourse wars and gang conflicts for territorial supremacy. That was emphatically not the career that the promoters of the Borstal system had had in mind for former inmates.

Within the institutions themselves, too, there was bullying by the older, stronger lads of the weaker and smaller boys. Louis Edward, who was a Borstal 'trainee' after the First World War, found himself, as a small, bespectacled, Jewish nineteen-year-old, a particular target of the bullies' attentions. A youth named Miller was their leader. He was big and powerful, and a good boxer. 'Even his friends feared his violent temper, his cunning, his cruelty ... The Matron gave him new shirts that were specially laundered for him. A tailor pressed his shorts, a little boy cleaned his shoes ... His cronies followed, to stand round his person like courtiers'.[141] Edward did his best to keep out of their way, but to him it 'all seemed so futile. I couldn't understand that this was how the blokes were trained to be decent citizens.'[142]

CHAPTER 6

WAR AND PEACE:
1914-1938

... the 1914-18 war shifted attention away from the penal system. Within a few years of the outbreak of war, the Home Office was facing a sharp increase in juvenile crime and consequent congestion in the industrial and reformatory schools. Hence, with the end of the Great War, under the stimulus of a zeal for 'reconstruction', penal reformers pressed not only for the full implementation of the pre-war legislation but also for improvements to it. While the pace of penal change remained sluggish ... the next two decades were ... to witness far-reaching administrative and legislative changes in the treatment of young offenders.

Victor Bailey, *Delinquency and Citizenship. Reclaiming the Young Offender, 1914-1948* (Oxford, 1987), pp. 7-8.

Juvenile Offending in the First World War

The outbreak of the First World War in August 1914 was followed by a sharp rise in youth offending, thereby leading the Home Office to warn of a 'crime epidemic' among the young. A 1914 total of just under 37,000 children under sixteen charged before juvenile courts in England and Wales had swollen to over 51,000 by 1917, a rise of 39 per cent. Numbers then fell back a little, to about 50,000 in 1918, but it was not until 1921 that the level of offending dropped to around 30,000 cases a year.[1]

The sudden upsurge in lawlessness, coming at a time when serious crime among adults was declining, caused much concern, and explanations were sought as to why it had occurred. As early as May 1916 statistics published in a Home Office circular revealed that in seventeen of the largest towns in the country, there had been an increase of almost 50 per cent in juvenile larceny cases alone, if the three months December 1915 to February 1916 were compared with a similar period from December 1914 to February 1915. There were also more assaults as well as instances of malicious damage, gaming, and offences against the Education Acts, as a result of truancy and illegal employment.[2] Some of this was attributed to the effects of the War itself, with fathers and elder brothers away from home serving in the armed forces or working long hours in munition factories and other areas of war production. Often mothers, too, were in employment. This inevitably led to a 'weakening of parental control'.[3] However, an enquiry carried out by Manchester education authority in 1916 revealed that the influence of war service did not apply in numerous cases. The survey showed that nearly all the heads of families investigated in connection with juvenile offending in the city were men in casual employment rather than in the military. As a consequence numbers of the children took up casual employment themselves when they grew up. The remedies suggested to combat the problem included 'the removal of children from the custody of incompetent parents, "in order that the right ideal of family life should be maintained"; the supervision of certain types of children out of school hours, such as those living in the central areas of the city and those who traded in the streets; and the organised provision of recreation'.[4] Only the latter proposition proved feasible to implement. But it was a symptom of the unease in official circles that the Manchester chief constable declared gloomily in 1916 that the current generation of children had 'neither regard nor respect for their elders, nor any fear of the law. They are well aware they will be treated leniently, with no serious punishment.'[5] It was a comment that would have won the support of elements of the popular press and other critics of juvenile justice in the early twenty-first century.

Among other factors mentioned by the Home Office as contributing to children's wartime misconduct was the ready availability of automatic gaming machines and the illegal use of air guns by young people. This second point was given credence by cases like those tried at Salford in January 1916, when eight boys were charged with firing air guns near a public highway. Two of the lads accidentally injured two other children, one of whom subsequently died. In view of the seriousness of the offence it is surprising that the bench decided merely to impose fines of 5s each on seven of the accused, while in the eighth case the fine was 2s 6d. Even the boy who had fired what proved to be a fatal shot was only fined 5s. However, the court did pass 'some severe strictures about parents allowing their children to possess such guns, and in each instance obtained their consent to have them destroyed'.[6] The *Salford Chronicle* claimed that the guns had cost from 3s 6d to 4s 6d apiece.

The unsuitability of films shown in picture houses, with their glorification of crime and violence, was another factor mentioned in the Home Office's

1916 circular, as was the fact that the work of boys' clubs had been 'crippled by want of staff'. Many of the men who had given time to the clubs, so as to provide recreation for youngsters particularly in the larger towns, were now in the forces or engaged on war work. As a consequence boys had no organised leisure activities and were instead 'running wild' in the streets.[7]

Among contemporaries who shared the Home Office's anxiety at this turn of events was Robert Baden-Powell, the founder of the Boy Scouts. He lamented that 'one serious outcome of the national crisis' had been the 'notable and steady increase of juvenile so-called crime in almost every city of the United Kingdom'.[8] The secretary of the reformist Howard Association, Cecil Leeson, was equally pessimistic when, in 1917, he referred to the 'grave increase in the numbers of juvenile offenders, and especially of juvenile thieves' which had recently occurred. The problem was not confined to any particular area but had 'spread through the country like a Plague'.[9] He considered it no 'minor affair' that thousands of children were jeopardising their future in this way every year. In places as far apart as York, Liverpool, Birmingham, Bristol, Sunderland and Middlesbrough, magistrates and education authorities were co-operating with child welfare organisations to set up special joint committees to 'check the evil' by supplying recreational facilities to divert youngsters from their lawless activities. [10]

In December 1916 the Home Office, too, responded to the challenge by appointing a Central Juvenile Organisations Committee to operate on a national basis and to encourage magistrates and education authorities throughout the country to follow the example of the pioneers.[11]

It was generally agreed that children's misconduct was particularly noticeable during school holidays, when they were left to their own devices, and on Sunday evenings, when the usual amusement outlets were closed. During the winter months restrictions on street lighting, introduced for fuel economy reasons, also encouraged criminality at night, in the darkened streets. Shopkeepers and market stall holders who displayed their wares in the open air were particularly vulnerable to petty thieving, as were delivery vans making their slow, laborious way through the streets. According to Leeson, the 'young marauder' intent on stealing from a shop or stall, approached his intended victim

> under cover of darkness; often the height of the trays or boxes containing the goods is greater than the height of the child, so that the child can screen himself behind them, and having snatched what he desires, he has only to succeed in running a few yards into the surrounding darkness when he is quite out of sight. The darkness not only covers the theft,

but gives the thief greater facility for evading capture; and if to these circumstances be added a shortage in policemen, it is clear that the chief conditions producing delinquency are present.[12]

Among the stallholders experiencing such thefts was Caleb Bisson, who worked in the covered market at Newcastle-under-Lyme in Staffordshire. In January 1915 four boys were charged in the local juvenile court with stealing two purses from his stall. He claimed that he had had trouble with pilfering youngsters for months and that during the previous year he had averaged a loss of 22s 6d a week through thefts from his business. That comment seems to have annoyed the bench, for although they sentenced the eldest boy to five strokes of the birch, and two others, who were said to be 'ailing', to four strokes apiece, subject to medical approval, the youngest boy was dismissed with just a warning. Mr Bisson, however, was reproved by the chairman of the bench for not reporting his previous losses to the police, and when he asked for the payment of his expenses in the case, the application was refused.[13]

Wartime shortages created their own temptations as well. During the winter the shortage of fuel encouraged thefts of coal, and some of the more daring lads earned extra cash by selling their ill-gotten gains to householders. In January 1915, seven Salford boys, aged from eleven to thirteen, were charged with stealing half a hundredweight of coal from a shop in the town. They subsequently sold it for 2½d. to a local housewife, who claimed they had told her they had picked it up in the street. 'They were very persistent,' she declared disarmingly, and she had felt sorry for them, so she had given them the money. She had not realised that the coal had been stolen. The stipendiary magistrate responded sharply that it was 'very dangerous to buy coal from boys. He hoped she would be careful in future and that this would be a warning to her and other women.' The detective-inspector who gave evidence against the lads meanwhile stated that during January alone there had been '21 boys at the court from this particular neighbourhood'. He added drily: 'If there were no receivers there would be no thieves.'[14] All the boys were punished by being sent to a remand home for a week, where it was presumably hoped that the firm discipline and strict routine would deter them from repeating the offence.

Elsewhere, as at Hanley in Staffordshire, boys followed coal wagons as they lumbered along and surreptitiously snatched lumps of coal from them. These they put into buckets they carried with them. They, too, were then sold but, interestingly, in one such case the fact that the two boys involved were described as 'respectable-looking' and that the father of one of them was blind, seems to have persuaded the court to treat them leniently. For his part, the police inspector who gave evidence against them noted that there had been 'many complaints of thefts from carts' in the area. But the magistrates displayed little sympathy, merely commenting that the back-boards of some coal carts were not high enough. As a result, 'coal fell off the carts ... lessening the load and dirtying the streets.' They conceded, however, that this was not applicable in the case in question.[15]

On occasion, as with Jan Jasper in London, youngsters were drawn into criminal activities by adult relatives. Jan's father worked as a timber salesman and he discovered that many of his customers had difficulty in getting hold of screws and glue because of wartime demand. Gerry, Jan's brother-in-law, was employed in a factory making munition boxes, where there were plentiful supplies of both commodities. Gerry suggested that he could steal some of these to supply to his father-in-law, but arrangements would have to be made for their collection. The best time would be when he went out during his afternoon tea break. The items could then be sold by Mr Jasper to his customers, and the profit divided between the two men. Jan was asked to go each day to meet his brother-in-law after school, and reluctantly he agreed. 'I had to take a shopping bag to school with me and then proceed to Bethnal Green Road', where the factory was located. He arrived at about 4 p.m. 'I can't remember the name of the pub where I had to meet Gerry. At the side of the pub there was a gent's toilet that was always open. When Gerry came along I would dive in and he would follow. He would quickly undo his apron and take out packets of screws and packets of dried glue from inside his trousers. He also had his pockets stuffed. They were quickly dropped in the bag and I would walk home. This I had to do every day of the week and Saturday mornings also. The old man would take them on his round and flog them to various small cabinet-makers. On Saturday afternoons they would share out the proceeds'.[16] This continued until Gerry went into the army and, as Jan later commented, 'It's a marvel I didn't grow up a criminal the things I had to do for them'.

In attempting to assess the seriousness of juvenile delinquency during these years, as Cecil Leeson has pointed out, it is important to remember that the terminology in which charges against children were framed, had been designed to cover adult offenders. As such, it often over-dramatised children's lawbreaking. As an example, Leeson quoted the case of a fourteen-year-old boy who was charged with being 'drunk and disorderly', when all he had done was drink two-thirds of a glass of beer and it had 'got into his head'. Again, 'the urchin who steals a penny pie from an itinerant pieman' had committed a felony, 'if, indeed, he [was] not a highway robber out and out'.[17]

The uncertainties and difficulties of the times also made the police and members of the public willing to take youngsters to court for relatively minor offences. In 1917 a Westminster police court probation officer claimed that the streets were currently being more closely controlled than ever before:

> There is a large and increasing army of officials whose duty it is to watch over child life. In many cases it has seemed to me that the zeal of these officers was not always adequately tempered by humanity and expediency. The practical result of their activities has been a systematic increase in the number of charges brought against children.[18]

Perhaps on these grounds the head of the Home Office Children's Branch seemed to take a rather lighter view of the delinquency problem than many of his contemporaries. He attributed it largely to the spirit of adventure engendered among children by news from the War. Hence to a boy pretending to be a combatant, 'an innocent railway wagon, creeping stealthily through a dark, mean street does sometimes prove to be a German convoy, even as the youngsters prove to be British troops – and the van's contents German supplies, and so legitimate spoils of war'.[19]

But others, including Cecil Leeson, were more sceptical. Leeson pointed out drily that small boys had robbed vans before the war, and if there had been darkened streets in peacetime, no doubt an increase in criminality would have taken place then, too.[20] He also argued that at a time of total war, everyone had to play their part: 'The blunt truth is that the state cannot afford juvenile offenders with a population decimated by war.'[21]

The response of the juvenile courts to the rise in youth crime varied from one part of the country to another. Overall, birchings increased, with the 2,415 ordered by the courts in England and Wales during 1914 rising to 5,210 in 1917.[22] The number of youngsters sent to reformatory and industrial schools also grew, from 5,653 in 1914 to 6,602 in 1916, before falling back to 5,209 in 1918.[23] But there were complaints in some places that children and young persons were being placed on probation for offences for which they should have been required to make restitution to their victims as well.[24] Then, too, the shortage of probation officers meant that where fines were imposed it was often impossible to check that they were actually paid. In these circumstances the *Justice of the Peace* journal recommended the creation of a 'disciplinary battalion under military law ... for ... young law breakers. Discipline is all they want ... Compulsory enlistment into this battalion should be the lot of all youthful felons who are not of such a character to come within the Borstal scheme, but whose cases are too bad to be met by binding over or fine, and of all youths persistently making themselves a nuisance in the streets by gambling, using obscene language, and other misconduct. Steady discipline works marvels'.[25] Life in the battalion was to be sufficiently unpleasant to deter other potential offenders. But the proposal seems to have fallen on deaf ears. There is no indication that the Home Office ever contemplated such a measure, since it ran counter to its general philosophy of seeking to reform and rehabilitate youngsters through policies that centred around recreational activities and probation rather than incarceration and repression.

Picture houses, too, were accused of encouraging imitative crimes by the sensational films they showed and for tempting youngsters to steal so as to obtain the few pence needed to gain admission. It was a view shared by many chief constables and magistrates, while Charles Russell, who was now the Chief Inspector of Reformatory and Industrial Schools, in a lecture on *The Problem of Juvenile Crime* (1917) warned that watching films not only caused eye-strain and 'undue excitement' among children but their

> vulgarity and silliness, and the distorted, unreal, Americanised (in the worst sense) view of life presented must have a deteriorating effect, and lead, at the best, to the formation of false ideals[26].

These complaints were given some credence by escapades like those in Paisley during March 1916, when several boys, led by a thirteen-year-old named Michael Feeley, broke into business premises on three successive Sundays, stealing clothing, steel saw blades, and various other things. According to a report of the subsequent court case, Feeley had boasted that he was 'the leader of a gang who called themselves the "Black Hand", and in one of the places which had been broken into he left two post-cards with a crude drawing of a hand and the words "The Black Hand."' His mother, who also gave evidence, claimed that it was 'through going to picture houses that he had come to ... this'.[27] The court sentenced him to receive 'six stripes with the birch rod'.

But other, more sceptical, contemporaries doubted the link between the cinema and juvenile crime. The *Sunday Chronicle* in May 1916 warned against a too ready acceptance of the opinion of chief constables in the matter. What was needed was better parental control rather than scapegoating the 'filming of bad pictures' as a cause of children's wrongdoing.[28] Even the National Council of Public Morals, after carefully considering possible connections between films and juvenile delinquency concluded that it was the wider social and economic uncertainties of the War that were really to blame.[29]

More significant in fuelling the anxieties of the law-abiding about the growth in youth crime, however, was the upsurge in street violence among lads in certain cities, with gang fights taking place, much as they had done in the late Victorian period. A headline in the *Sunday Chronicle* of 21 May, 1916, epitomised many of these fears when it referred to 'The Terrorists of Glasgow – Savagery of Hooligan Gangs':

> each gang outvies the other in savagery and frightfulness. Ladies are held up and robbed; policemen are clubbed or cut with bottles when trying to take some of the ruffians to prison; and old men are beaten and left lying after their pockets have been gone through ... With many districts at night so infested with these brutal ruffians that ladies are afraid to venture out and even men have often to run for their lives, the citizens are demanding that this state of matters must end.[30]

The Glasgow press itself detailed some of these events in chilling detail during the spring of 1916, as when a fifty-eight-year-old carpet weaver was set upon by a band of youths. They knocked him down and kicked him, before making off. He needed hospital treatment for his injuries. In another case a gang of about fifty youths known as the Bloodhound Flying Corps created a disturbance outside the house of a man against whom they had a grudge. They forced their way into the house and only the arrival of the police drove them off. Among the most vicious of the gangs were the Redskins and in April 1916 they engaged in a fight with another gang, known as the Waverleys. This led to assaults on members of the public, with one elderly man being beaten about the head, while bottles and other missiles were freely used, and the windows of a number of houses smashed.[31] In the end the pressures of the War, military recruitment and firm action by the police broke up the Glasgow gangs for a time, although they were to re-emerge with renewed vigour in the post-war period.[32]

In the Ancoats district of Manchester there was the Napoo teenage gang. This established an evil reputation for attacking young women and hacking off their plaits, which were fashionable at that time. According to Larry Goldstone, who remembered their attacks:

> They'd creep up behind girls and women in the street, grab the long plaited hair which hung down the back ... and with a sharp pair of scissors cut off the plaited hair and run off with it as a souvenir. They got bolder and bolder hunting the women with plaited hair. Some used to go upstairs on the trams late at night, and if a woman was sitting on her own, they'd cut off her hair, then, like lightning, dash off without being caught. The idea was probably hatched from the films of Red Indians scalping the whites. The tough would take the plaits to the public house to show how clever he was at hunting.[33]

Members of the Napoo wore a distinctive pink neckerchief and displayed razor blades in waistcoat pockets or in slits in their cloth caps. They caused panic in the streets by charging through them in a group or by starting brawls at public events and dances. According to Henry Grimshaw, another young contemporary, they doubtless enjoyed the feeling of power and sense of excitement that their actions evoked. Rumours abounded about their exploits, and Henry himself shared in the general anxiety. Once, when he was at Heaton Park, he looked round and saw a gang of about fifty or sixty youths running 'like mad ... And there were trams then. They used to run in the park. Well, we made for these trams, and fortunately one was just on its way and I got on. I don't know what happened to those that didn't get on, but everybody started to run'.[34] In the end these violent outbursts caused so much disruption to community life that they invited retaliation. The Napoo were finally overcome 'after a series of attacks on Jewish girls and shops led to the formation of a local Jewish vigilante group, which armed itself with makeshift weapons removed from workshops and factories.' Henry Hoffman, who also witnessed these events, recalled that the youths took heavy rollers and shears from the textile factories and 'went to Oldham Road in Ancoats and battled with 'em. And that ended it, that was ... 1916'.[35]

This street violence was given an added edge by events in the War itself. The sinking of the *Lusitania* liner, with the loss of many lives, in the spring of 1915 led to a sharp increase in attacks on German-owned shops and other property, in which young people as well as adults participated. According to *The Times* in May 1915, at Poplar in London, within an area of a quarter of a mile half a dozen German-owned houses were attacked by mobs. Before the police could disperse them, horse-drawn carts, handcarts and perambulators, as well as 'the unaided arms of men, women and children' had looted all they could from the wrecked homes. Again, in Kentish Town a score of bakers' and confectioners' shops were destroyed and looted by a mob who rushed from shop to shop, stealing whatever they could get.[36] Many other places, including Manchester and Salford, experienced similar outbreaks. In the case of Salford over a two-day period in early May thirty different premises were attacked and goods looted on a vast scale. In the end eighty-nine people were charged in connection with the disturbances, and of these at least twenty-six were youngsters aged sixteen or less. A number of the others were parents (usually mothers) of the children, who were charged with receiving the goods their offspring had taken, knowing them to be stolen. Despite the fact that businesses were destroyed and that some of their German owners had lived in the area for years, none of the accused was imprisoned. Sometimes, as with Maud Arnold, aged eleven, who stole a picture valued at 7s, both she and her mother, who was charged with receiving it, were discharged. The stipendiary magistrate expressed the hope that 'it would be a lesson to them'. Others, like fifteen-year-old Matilda Smith, who had stolen quilts, curtains, and various items of clothing, were fined. In Matilda's case the amount was 6s, while her mother was fined 5s as a receiver. The heaviest fine on a juvenile was imposed on Arthur Wynne, aged fourteen, who had to pay 7s 6d for stealing an armchair, but in this case his mother was discharged without any penalty.[37] A number of the victims were unable to resume their business lives in Salford, and to them the lenient sentences must have been a bitter disappointment. [38]

In 1917, in Leeds, street gangs in the Briggate district behaved violently towards passers-by, who were pushed off the pavement by groups of youths and girls. The *Yorkshire Evening Post* blamed the high wages the young people were earning for their disruptive behaviour. 'Most of the participants', it declared, 'are youths who are earning "good money," and who find themselves with more spare cash than ever they had before. This gives them swollen heads, and arriving in Briggate and mixing with others in a like position they allow their petty sense of importance and independence to get the better of any manners they may have'.[39] Sunday nights in the centre of Leeds became something of a 'bear garden' with gangs of youths jostling strangers and passing insulting comments 'upon all and sundry … to make any reply is simply to "ask for trouble"'. Nor were the girls any better than their male counterparts. Their language was 'amazing in its filthiness, and regrettable as it may appear, it is … the fact that there is little to choose between the sexes in this respect. Nobody can walk down Briggate on these evenings without hearing the most disgusting talk'.[40]

The violence also found expression in anti-Jewish attacks by some of the young hooligans, with fights breaking out between Jewish and non-Jewish gangs. According to the *Yorkshire Evening Post* local youths taunted the Jewish boys with not joining up, even though many had done so, and this led to immediate retaliation. Feelings were further heightened by the circulation of false rumours, including a claim that Jewish lads had beaten up and killed a wounded soldier, using his own crutches.[41] In the end decisive police action, combined with the exposure of the 'wickedly absurd' rumours that had circulated, led to the gang warfare petering out in early June.[42]

Among the girls there was a good deal of clandestine prostitution, and an increase in the incidence of venereal disease. Many of the girls were very young. Cecil Leeson quoted the example of 'Case D', a fourteen-year-old girl who had been arrested 'recently for loitering on a railway station with soldiers.' Yet those who were arrested were usually treated leniently. 'Girls look upon the charge as a joke', declared the chaplain at Manchester prison, expressing a general complaint. 'There is a girl here at the present;

she has three previous convictions of 7, 13 and 25 days respectively.' At Liverpool prison, a major centre for the reception of prostitutes, the governor reported that many of the convicted were 'mere children'. In 1918, the chaplain of London's principal female prison, Holloway, saw a 'great deterioration' in the type of prostitutes being received there. The girls 'for the most part are very young and very ignorant, very vicious and very corrupt. Frequently they come from the provincial towns and country districts. They are distinctly a war product'.[43]

For those youngsters who were sent to reformatory and industrial schools the War also had a profound effect. In some cases boys were licensed to leave early, before the completion of their sentence, so they could enlist. They included youths like thirteen-year-old Horace who was admitted to Liverpool Farm School in June 1916, as a 'nuisance to the neighbourhood and shopkeepers', although he had had no previous convictions. He was licensed in 1918 to an Army band. Then there was fifteen-year-old Hugh who was licensed from the Farm School to enter the Royal Navy after serving a three-year sentence for wilful damage 'by setting fire to a packing case'. Fifteen-year-old Harold from Halifax was sentenced to three years at the Farm School for stealing a purse containing 1½d. He was licensed to the Army and was later reported 'killed in action'.[44]

The Chief Inspector of Reformatory and Industrial Schools, Charles Russell, reported enthusiastically on the military contribution made by the former inmates of these Home Office certified schools, noting that from the outbreak of war to the beginning of March 1916, 29,920 old boys had joined the Army or the Royal Navy and already 1,223 of them had been killed in action, while a further 150 had died of wounds; 3,501 had been wounded, 172 were missing, and 434 were prisoners of war. A number of the boys had also won gallantry medals, including four who had been awarded Victoria Crosses.[45] Russell claimed that as a result of their time in the corrective institutions they had become physically stronger, having been transformed from the 'thin, ill-nourished, stunted specimens of humanity' they had been when they entered the schools. In that condition they 'would have had little chance of serving their country, even had they wished to do so, without the training the Schools [had] given them'.[46] Interestingly, too, at a time when juvenile delinquency was giving rise to so much concern in the nation at large, Russell praised the 'innate qualities and latent grit' of the lads who had been sent to reformatories and industrial schools. These made them 'both ready volunteers, and soldiers of daring and dashing character':

The boy who finds his way to a Reformatory is very often in his rank of life the counterpart of the lively athlete of the Public Schools, but in the great cities from which he usually comes and in the crowded areas in which he has lived the opportunities for expressing his physical energies that are so lavishly afforded to the son of well-to-do parents have not been his.[47]

The long years Russell had spent working with boys in Manchester's lads' clubs and youth organisations had given him an intimate knowledge of their lives and a sympathy with the problems they faced that few other Home Office officials shared.

However, the contribution of youngsters in the certified schools extended beyond their recruitment into the armed forces. While still under confinement they took up war work of various kinds. According to a report produced in August 1915, boys from Mossbank Industrial School, Glasgow, were licensed to work at Messrs. Beardmore's Shell Factory. An inspector who visited them there saw the lads 'drawing red-hot shrapnel cases from the furnaces', something which would seem to have been highly dangerous for such youngsters. Again, fifty-three boys from the Farnworth Nautical School were engaged at the United Alkali Works, Widnes, in operations connected with the manufacture of explosives. Hundreds of lads from Industrial Schools in Ilford, London, Dartford, Chelmsford and Farnborough were employed at Woolwich Arsenal in the production of rifle cartridges, while Redhill Farm School had just completed a contract for 150,000 railway 'thimbles', and was looking forward to receiving a further contract for 120,000 more. At Shadwell Industrial School the boys had soldered thousands of water steriliser tins for the troops and had also made hospital equipment. Nor were the female inmates left out, with the St Elizabeth's Girls' Industrial School, Liverpool, making medical shell-dressing bags, while at Coventry Girls' Industrial School, sheets, pillowcases and men's night wear for military hospitals were made. The girls also rolled bandages. Some went out daily to work at a local wholesale stationers, so as to release regular staff members for munition work. Others again carried out gardening duties.[48] Elsewhere there was a widespread recruitment of youngsters to work on the land, especially at the busy seasons like harvest time.

Nonetheless if these contributions by reformatory and industrial scholars were seen in a positive light by the Home Office inspectorate, the overriding official concern remained to prevent juvenile offending in the first place. By the end of the War, therefore, there was a strong emphasis on finding ways of providing recreational diversions. As Barbara Weinberger notes, boys' clubs were regarded almost as 'a branch of public policy'. The Home Office even applied for the early release of men from the armed forces who had had experience of work in youth organisations, seeing the contribution of these institutions as 'one of the most effective ways of checking juvenile delinquency'.[49]

After the War a high priority was to be given to the issue of child welfare, and to the devising of penal treatments which would seek to 're-educate delinquents in fresh habits and interests.' The aim was to mould the character of the youngsters so as to lead them to respectability and good conduct through the application of 'sympathetic treatment'.[50]

The art was in deciding just what that 'sympathetic treatment' should be.

The Inter-War Years: 1919-1938

During the 1920s and 1930s the more sympathetic attitude towards young offenders demonstrated in the 1908 Children Act was carried a good deal further, culminating in the passage of the 1933 Children and Young Persons Act. This not only raised the age of criminal responsibility from seven to eight years and increased the minimum age for capital punishment to eighteen, but it extended the powers of the juvenile courts to include those up to seventeen. Ten became the minimum age for entry to a Home Office school, and the name of these schools was changed to 'approved',

A more liberal approach to juvenile offending was becoming apparent by the 1920s. A group of youngsters from Home Office Schools on holiday at the seaside, *c.*1925.

in an effort to distance them from their origins as old-style Victorian reformatories and industrial schools. It became the duty of county and county borough councils to provide remand homes, where children could be held while awaiting their appearance in court, and where, as a substitute for imprisonment, a youngster could be committed into custody for a period not exceeding one month. The spirit of the new Act, which remained in operation into the 1960s, was epitomised in its requirement that every court 'in dealing with a child or young persons, either as being in need of care or protection or as an offender or otherwise' was 'to have regard to the welfare of the child or young person'.[51] Throughout the emphasis was to be on reforming and rehabilitating the offender rather than merely administering punishment.

Part of the motive for this urge to promote the welfare of the child lay in a desire to compensate society for the great loss of young men suffered in the First World War. Wider reforms included the creation of an improved education system and the greater provision of school meals and medical inspection. From 1934 the supply of milk to schools was subsidised by the Milk Marketing Board. As a result the daily third of a pint of milk became a feature of school life, and the number of meals served each day rose from 143,000 in 1935 to around 160,000 in 1939.[52] The 1918 Education Act raised the minimum school leaving age to a uniform fourteen years and made elementary education free, since some schools were still charging fees. An increased provision of scholarships opened up secondary education to a wider sector of the child population and led in the 1920s to demands for 'secondary education for all'.[53] The broad aim of the 1918 Act was to create 'a system of education ... which [would] increase the value of every human unit ... in society'.[54]

When applied to young offenders this approach led to a greater willingness, at least in some quarters, to accept that part of the problem of working-class hooliganism arose from the pressures of adolescence itself. One commentator wrote of certain 'primitive instincts which make themselves ... assertive during ... adolescence', while to the London magistrate and youth worker, Basil Henriques, it was 'misdirected ... energy' that led youngsters astray.[55] In order to satisfy their natural desire for excitement and adventure it was essential to find a constructive outlet for that exuberance. This meant the provision of more clubs and associations and more open spaces where organised games could be played. In 1937 Henriques called on fellow JPs to make every effort to ensure that such facilities were made available, so that 'street football and cricket offences, as well as gambling, could be very largely stemmed'. Where there were no play centres, children were led by 'sheer boredom' into 'adventurous crime'. That was particularly true of the new housing estates which were being constructed without proper facilities for leisure pursuits and sporting venues.[56]

Another supporter of the boys' club movement, James Butterworth, shared Henriques' concerns. Butterworth quoted the career of one young recalcitrant, 'Thomas Tiddler', who spent his spare time on the London streets. He probably commenced his evening by throwing a stone or ball through a window:

> Within an hour, and for varied reasons, he will have been chased around several streets, or leaped on every passing vehicle, and may decide to see London 'for nuffin' by jumping on every bus or tram whilst the conductor is upstairs until … he reaches his desired haven … He knows more about sex perversions and crude stories at age thirteen than most people are likely to know at age thirty … unable to resist the appeal of loose railings, he must send the boards outside shops crashing to the ground. Half stuck or well stuck posters on hoardings must be defaced or altered, and if low enough receive a savage kick. He will always appear to be running away from someone.[57]

According to S. F. Hatton, nearly 60 per cent of the lads who spent their time on the London streets, like 'Thomas Tiddler', had no contact with churches, clubs, the scout movement or any other organisation that might give them 'a steadying hand over the difficult period of their adolescence'.[58]

But if some of the causes of juvenile misconduct were attributed to the exuberance of adolescence and the lack of alternative amusements, there was also an acceptance of the need to probe more deeply into the reasons for delinquent behaviour. One of the pioneers in this research was Cyril Burt, who placed much emphasis on the importance of psychological investigation. He recognised that over half of juvenile crime was the result of poverty and overcrowded housing but that alone was not a sufficient explanation. 'With moral disorders as with physical, we must find and fight not symptoms but causes,' he declared.[59] This called for a pre-sentence examination of the mental and physical condition of each offender as well as of his home background and wider social environment.[60]

Burt was anxious to discover why an individual child committed a crime – to ascertain the events that led to the carrying out of a particular act. It might be the by-product of parental laxity or bad companions, but often there was a more precise trigger. Tommy B., for example, was the subject of repeated complaints by shopkeepers and costermongers near to his London home. He regularly stole items of food and when Burt interviewed him he bore all the tell-tale symptoms 'of a half-famished starveling'. It was found that both he and a younger brother were suffering from severe deprivation in a home where there was scant income and their father was dying from tuberculosis. After the father's death, the two orphans were sent to a home in the country and as soon as they were properly fed and cared for, their pilfering stopped.[61] Then there was a respectably dressed girl of fourteen who was brought to Burt after being found guilty of stealing. Up to a year before, her conduct had been 'unimpeachable; then suddenly she was detected in a succession or thefts'. Burt found out that during the War her family had prospered and she had received ample pocket money. In the early 1920s, however, her father's business declined and she was unable to afford the small luxuries to which she had become accustomed. 'When at length her dishonesty had been detected, the moves were not hard to unravel: the coincidence of the twofold change – the decline in home circumstances and the sudden deterioration in personal character, both within the same few months – pointed to the obvious clue'. When her offence was revealed she was withdrawn from school, her pocket money was increased, and she was found a post in an auctioneer's office, where she received a small wage. After that her offending ceased, according to Burt.[62]

Children's involvement in betting and gambling, Burt also claimed, often arose from their being freely used as messengers to carry betting-slips from their parents to illicit bookmakers. This encouraged the boys to begin backing horses themselves, while quite 'tiny boys of eight or nine may be seen in their own backyards playing pitch-and-toss for half-pennies; and bigger schoolboys can be caught playing for money with cards or dominoes behind some sheltering chimney on their tenement roof'.[63] He was more dubious about the allegedly malign influence of the cinema, pointing out that for many youngsters, 'the steady and the healthy-minded,' the picture-house supplied an alternative to less benign activities. 'I could … cite more than one credible instance where the opening of a picture-palace had reduced hooliganism among boys, withdrawn young men from the public-house, and supplied the girls with a safer substitute for lounging with their friends [than] in the alleys or the parks'. [64]

The new shopping centres were a different matter. Some of the large stores with their displays of toys for children and finery for adolescents encouraged juvenile theft, through the careless way they displayed the goods openly on counters and trays.[65] That understanding of the temptations to which children were exposed through these commercial practices was shared by Basil Henriques. He argued that magistrates could help to prevent shoplifting by visiting the multiple shops where the goods were displayed within the reach of youngsters, and make appropriate representations to the management so as 'to have both the goods and the children properly protected':

Again, it seems hardly fair to blame the children from stealing from the backs of lorries, which is such a very common offence ... unless every precaution has been taken, and the magistrates have seen that they have been taken.[66]

Other critics blamed technical innovations like the introduction of cigarette machines, the installation of slot meters for gas and electricity, and the greater use of motor vehicles. The practice of leaving cars unlocked was particularly condemned for encouraging illicit joyriding, while the cigarette and slot machines led to juvenile pilfering. Court cases appear to bear this out to some degree, as when Stanley C., aged fourteen and Albert N., aged thirteen, appeared at Toynbee Hall Juvenile Court in London in March 1930 accused of stealing two packets of cigarettes 'from an automatic machine outside 120 High Street, Shoreditch. They were placed on probation for twelve months, with the younger boy also having to find a surety to the value of £2.[67]

The use of psychology to help explain the causes of juvenile wrongdoing, coupled with a greater willingness to put some of the blame for their misconduct on changes within society at large, had an effect on the courts, too. In particular, it led to more offenders being placed under the supervision of probation officers rather than given custodial sentences. Probation officers were seen as offering friendship, guidance and, where possible, help in improving unsatisfactory home conditions. Probation was favoured, too, because in most cases it allowed the children to remain at home with their families. Unlike in the nineteenth century, when parental contact was often frowned upon, during the inter-war years there was a policy of maintaining family links. That applied even in the case of youngsters sent to the Home Office certified schools. In 1934 the warden of the Philanthropic Society's Farm School at Redhill pointed out that while boys were in residence their parents were encouraged to visit freely; they 'may come when they can'. A decade earlier he had lamented that a majority of mothers and fathers seemed to take little interest in their sons 'until they become wage earners again. Out of 199 boys in the School, 120 received no visits from relatives or friends during the year, and 38 were visited ... once.'[68] Only if home circumstances were especially unsatisfactory or if probation had been shown to fail with an individual youngster was it thought best to send him or her to a residential Home Office school. In 1938 out of 28,116 young people found guilty of indictable offences under the age of seventeen, just 10 per cent were sent to approved schools.[69]

As a consequence, the percentage of children and young persons appearing before juvenile courts who were put on probation rose from 11.9 in 1913

to 13.7 in 1921 and 19.6 in 1924.[70] By 1938 that had risen to 51 per cent
of all those found guilty of indictable offences who were under the age of
seventeen. In a further 24 per cent of the cases the offender was dismissed
under the terms of the probation legislation, while 7.4 per cent were bound
over.[71] In these inter-war years, too, there was a waning belief in the deterrent
effect of corporal punishment. By 1923 only 2 per cent of children coming
before the juvenile courts were sentenced to a whipping. Nonetheless the
issue remained controversial.[72] In 1927 a Departmental Committee on the
Treatment of Young Offenders cautiously concluded that although they
'strongly' deprecated any 'indiscriminate use of whipping', and a medical
examination should in all cases accompany it, the courts should be able
to order a whipping 'in respect of any serious offence committed by a boy
under 17'.[73] Three members of the committee, however, refused to back
this recommendation and instead issued their own Memorandum which
declared: 'We are not satisfied that whipping ordered by a court of law
serves a useful purpose'. So there remained what Victor Bailey calls the
'retributive proponents' of birching and their 'reformative opponents', to
the end of the 1930s. Indeed, in April 1935 the chairman of the Feltham
juvenile court warned parents that magistrates would have to resort to the
birch 'because the court [was] overflowing with boys committing serious
offences'. Yet in 1938 a Departmental Committee set up to examine the
merits of corporal punishment concluded unanimously that as a penalty it
was 'not a suitable or effective remedy for dealing with young offenders'.[74]
Not until 1948 was corporal punishment finally abolished.

To make probation more effective the courts were authorised to impose
conditions on probationers, for example as regards their place of residence
or the leisure activities they pursued during their period of supervision. If
these were breached the probationer would be returned to the court for
further sentencing. Basil Henriques argued that this aspect of the probation
process was under used, and in 1936 the *Justice of the Peace* emphasised
the need for probation to be 'definitely disciplinary as well as friendly, or it
fails in its object'. That could include the youngster making some financial
restitution to his or her victim:

> There may be no desire on the part of the prosecutor for anything of the
> kind. That is not the point. It is the effect upon the offender himself that
> is important; he is made to realise and remember the results of his wrong-
> doing, and, by making good as far as he can, he is doing something to
> rehabilitate himself. It is ... a form of discipline.[75]

Despite these comments, conditions were imposed on probationers in
a minority of cases only. For example, at Toynbee Hall juvenile court

in London in December 1929, Charles H., aged fifteen, found guilty of stealing a bicycle, was bound over in the sum of £2, with one surety, and was placed on probation for a year, on condition that he 'attend evening classes'.[76] Again, in November 1935, the same court found William John H., aged sixteen guilty of playing pitch and toss in Stepney. He, too, was bound over in the sum of £2, and placed on probation for twelve months. In his case, the condition imposed was, appropriately enough, 'no gambling'.[77] Two months after this Alexander P., aged fourteen, was brought before the same juvenile court by his probation officer for failing to observe a condition of his recognizance, namely 'to attend a club as directed by the Probation Officer'. He had originally been found guilty the previous April of stealing a quantity of lead from premises belonging to the Port of London authority. On this occasion his failure to observe the conditions of his probation order led to his being cautioned.[78] Other, less fortunate, youngsters were sent instead to an approved school.

During the 1920s the changing attitude within society towards juvenile offending, led to a sharp drop in the number of cases coming before the courts. From a wartime peak of 51,323 proceeded against in England and Wales in 1917, numbers dropped to 28,769 in 1923 and 25,478 in 1927. The trend continued downwards for some years thereafter.[79] Part of the fall was due to the return of a more stable domestic environment after the war, but other factors included an unwillingness on the part of many victims of minor offences to go to the trouble of taking the case to court. Or perhaps because of what a Home Office report of 1928 labelled 'mistaken leniency', they did not wish 'to brand the child concerned with a conviction'. This was especially true in some larger towns like Leeds, where in the four years 1923-1926 inclusive, the number of juveniles who were not proceeded against because complainants refused to prosecute totalled 173, 207, 130 and 177, respectively. In the same years the corresponding number of young persons who *were* charged before the city's juvenile court amounted to 246, 276, 242 and 249. Elsewhere police cautions were freely issued, so that in Newcastle-on-Tyne during 1923 and 1924, the total of young offenders brought before the magistrates reached 316 and 302, respectively, while police cautions in cases involving trivial offences amounted to 543 and 627. It was an approach that was commended by the Departmental Committee on the Treatment of Young Offenders in 1927 when it commented that 'in trifling cases, especially when it is a first offence, a police officer may properly prefer to turn a blind eye' or merely to issue a warning.[80]

These various factors meant that the number of youngsters sent each year to the certified Home Office schools fell from 3,191 in 1920 to 1,891 in 1924, while the total of school inmates more than halved over the same period, from 15,203 on 31 December, 1920 to 7,463 four years later.[81] To add to the problems of what were still largely voluntary organisations, there was a funding crisis, as cash from private benefactors dried up, while in the immediate post-war period staff were condemned as inefficient and of poor calibre. They sometimes worked their underfed young charges 'as little factory hands in inefficient factories'.[82] They were also encouraged by the Home Office's then Chief Inspector to adopt a policy of early licensing of pupils, to enable them to return as soon as possible to life in the community. That, too, cut inmate numbers. Inevitably as the total of resident pupils dwindled there was spare capacity and over the next few years between thirty and forty schools had to close.[83] Among them was the Hardwicke Reformatory, set up by the Lloyd Baker family in the mid-nineteenth century. A report of its closure in the local newspaper in the spring of 1922 commented on the irony that 'in the cause of national economy, a school that had throughout its career been a model of efficiency and economy should now be closed'.[84] That ignored the fact that the premises themselves were old-fashioned and did not meet new and more exacting standards of accommodation. On the whole it was the smaller and the poorly equipped institutions like Hardwicke that came to an end.

Among the survivors was the Philanthropic Society's Redhill Farm School, which prided itself on the quality of its vocational instruction, and particularly on its agricultural expertise. Even here, however, numbers

Boys on their best behaviour at Hardwicke Reformatory School, *c.*1902. Some are wearing elaborate tam-o'-shanters, while William Robinson, the superintendent, is in his customary boater.

fell, so that in 1923, when thirty-one boys were admitted, sixty-seven were discharged. Of these 'eleven went into the Army, one entered an Army band, eight went into farming, and five became domestic servants. The rest took up a variety of occupations, ranging from carpentry and blacksmithing to tailoring and general labouring; four became shop assistants'.[85] At Redhill much value was attached to sporting prowess and to the benefits of camping holidays, while many of the boys were allowed to go on home 'leave' for one or two weeks 'according to ... seniority'. By 1933 there were 111 boys in the school (compared to 140 a decade earlier) and under the auspices of the 'Seaside Camps for London Lads' association, three separate parties of them went to Walmer to spend a week under canvas. In addition, 109 of the boys were allowed to go home for one or two week breaks. The annual report noted that 'every boy returned honourably from his leave', although one youngster had 'absconded immediately afterwards'.[86] The more relaxed stance taken in the 1930s is indicated by the Redhill warden's comment in 1938 that although it was not uncommon for some new entrants to abscond, 'we say our best lads began as absconders'.[87] When caught they were returned to the school.

The increasing emphasis on the importance of psychology in the treatment of young offenders during these inter-war years and the need for the courts to take this into account when sentencing them did not meet with the approval of all. At Redhill the warden commented tartly in 1938:

Boys from the Redhill Farm School of the Philanthropic Society having a seaside holiday in the 1930s.

The propensity to look for a psychological explanation of juvenile offences should not be allowed to become a prepossession. There is a sufficient explanation, in most cases, in the incomplete home and the entire absence of moral training and religious connections.[88]

On the 'broken home' theme he pointed out that of eighty new admissions to the Farm School over the previous twelve months, six were illegitimate, nine had step-parents, sixteen were from one-parent families, one was an orphan, and five came from homes where 'one of the parents had deserted'. A quarter were 'of poor educational ability and low intelligence'.

More recently, Stephen Humphries, too, has condemned the tendency for biological and psychological interpretations of delinquency to gain dominance during these years, thereby underplaying the 'significance of poverty, inequality and class conflict, as important factors in the production of crime.' He points to the day-to-day experiences of impoverished families and the way in which the older children, in particular, committed minor property thefts in order to obtain fuel and food for the family. One such youngster was Bristol-born Charlie Portingale. He embarked on a series of minor offences during the 1930s to help support the household. 'Being the eldest boy, I was the one that kept the family going'. One of his ploys was to knock over tins of biscuits standing outside a grocer's shop, so that he, or one of his siblings, could go later and ask for cut-price broken biscuits. Another was to steal flowers from the gardens of more affluent houses and then gather them into bunches for subsequent sale. He also crept into a nearby coal yard at night armed with a sack in order to get fuel: 'I'd never get caught, I'd make sure of it. I mean there's many a time we used to sit and have army blankets around us where we was so cold, grate was empty'.[89]

In mining communities the theft of coal from pit heads and slag heaps was not considered a crime by most local people. According to Stephen Humphries, in the interests of social harmony the pit owners and the police rarely prosecuted youngsters who took coal in this way, and for many children it was a daily chore to go to the slag heap in order to collect fuel. Bill Bees, a miner's son from the village of Hanham in South Gloucestershire, remembered it as a dirty and time-consuming task which he had to carry out before going to school. This caused trouble with his teachers, especially if he lacked time to wash properly and so arrived in a scruffy condition. 'They did lead you round the classrooms by your ear an' show the people how much dust or dirt you 'ad up in yer ears. And box you one in the ears an' make you go to the sink an' wash, a proper show up.'[90]

Occasionally there ware prosecutions. One seventeen-year-old girl who persistently stole small quantities of coal for her family was sentenced to three years in Borstal for the offence in 1924, presumably in the hope that this would lead her to mend her ways. In the report on her case it was noted that in her community 'coal lifting' was common: 'everyone more or less does it. Girl very simple and weak, but morally innocent. Feels justified in stealing if family is in need'.[91]

Yet if family necessity provoked some youngsters into breaking the law, others embarked on illicit ventures through associating with young wrongdoers in their neighbourhood. According to the *Justice of the Peace* in June 1936, around two-thirds of the cases which led to children and young persons appearing in juvenile courts charged with indictable offences, involved groups of two or more boys acting together:

> often there is a gang. The gang is often actuated by a spirit of adventure, as the nature of their offences indicates, and there is a light-hearted air about their activities that shows greed or criminality to have had very little to do with them. [92]

Sometimes there were acts of bravado leading to senseless vandalism as one lad egged on another. This was probably the case at Windsor in March 1934, when five youngsters, two of them aged only nine, were concerned 'together in breaking and entering a shed and stealing half a pint of beans and a padlock'. The previous day three of the lads had committed 'mischievous damage to a greenhouse', amounting to £1 3s. Their case was remanded on several occasions, presumably to impress upon them the seriousness of their actions, before on 7 May they were each discharged on a recognizance of 10s and were put on probation for twelve months.[93] In cases involving shopbreaking or shoplifting, it might be a desire to get hold of 'luxury' items like boxes of chocolates or jars of sweets or cigarettes that provided the motive. At Windsor early in 1934, five boys aged between nine and eleven were charged with stealing nine boxes of chocolates. Four were found guilty and were bound over in a recognizance of £2 for two years. The fifth was found not guilty and was discharged.

On occasion these acts were undertaken out of a desire to impress their peers or to emulate the actions of a friend. This seems to have been the case at Liverpool in January 1937 when a sixteen-year-old boy, who had been bound over two days previously, again appeared before the court, along with a seventeen-year-old accomplice. They were charged with shopbreaking and attempted shopbreaking. In the earlier case the boy's then accomplice had been sent to Borstal but he had merely been bound over. So within hours he found another of his friends and they broke into a shop where they were caught with a bizarre collection of loot, including jars of Bovril, tins of condensed milk and various other articles of grocery.

When arrested by a police constable, the boy declared: 'I left the sessions this morning and I want to get back to my mates', by which he meant that he, too, wanted to be sent to Borstal. On hearing this the Liverpool recorder responded sharply, after sentencing him to three years in a Borstal institution, that care must be taken to ensure that he did not go to the same place as his friends. 'It is quite clear that, knowing the others have gone to Borstal, he would like to go with them. We cannot have criminals choosing their own schools ... otherwise they will be doing the same thing again when they come out.'[94] In making that remark the recorder seemed to imply that Borstal was so attractive that youngsters would be anxious to return there once they had completed their sentence. Even in the reformist atmosphere of the 1930s there is little evidence that that was the case. Certainly Bill Bees from Gloucestershire remembered that when one of his friends came out of Borstal he was 'a different young man altogether. Although he would be your best friend, he'd hardly speak to you. And people despised him after, they'd call him the "Borstal boy". He wouldn't discuss it'.[95]

As in earlier years, gang activities involving older youths could take a more sinister turn, especially when they occurred in deprived communities with a high level of unemployment and a well-established neighbourhood gang culture. The authorities referred to 'an epidemic of gangs of idle unemployed youths', who turned to crime as a diversion from hanging about street corners.[96] Sometimes they were associated with sporting events, and especially with football matches. This could lead to trouble on the terraces. In 1921 the boys' section at Bradford Park Avenue was closed down for three months after the referee had been 'pelted with rubbish', while in the early 1920s the rivalry between Arsenal and Tottenham Hotspurs supporters resulted in street battles in which some of the more violent fans armed themselves with iron bars and knives.[97] Similar skirmishes erupted in Glasgow between the followers of the city's two leading clubs, Rangers (supported in the main by Protestants) and Celtic (with a Roman Catholic following). Sectarian animosity added to the tension in this case.

It was, indeed, in Glasgow that gang rivalry was at its most serious. Sectarianism, coupled with severe poverty, chronic overcrowding, and high unemployment bred what Andrew Davies has called 'a catastrophic level of violence in the City's slums'.[98] Gangs defended their own areas against the incursions of other groups, using broken bottles, knives, and, on occasion, razors. Some had their 'junior' sections, as when seventeen-year-old James Tait was fatally stabbed in a fight between the Young Calton Entry, which was the junior part of a prominent gang in the East End of Glasgow, and junior members of the Gorbals-based South Side

Stickers. Six of the 'Stickers' eventually stood trial for murder at the High Court in Glasgow, with sixteen-year-old James McCluskey convicted of culpable homicide. He was sentenced to five years' penal servitude. It was events like these that led to Glasgow being labelled the 'Scottish Chicago', although, as Andrew Davies comments, unlike in the American city, where there were 500 gang-related homicides during the 1920s, Glasgow's gangsters 'seldom inflicted fatalities' and seldom used firearms.[99]

Sometimes the attacks spilled over into the community at large, with innocent passers-by injured. In July 1936, for example, seven young men were tried at the Glasgow Sheriff Court with forming part of a 'riotous mob, committing a breach of the peace and brandishing swords, bayonets and other weapons'.[100] By these means youths who, as individuals, lacked power, prospects, and financial resources, could collectively make themselves into people to be reckoned with. It was also a way of enhancing their status within a society that valued self-assertiveness and physical force as signs of masculinity.[101] For youths in their teens, street gangs offered comradeship, too, much as they had done in Victorian times, as well as protection from rivals. According to Sir Percy Sillitoe, who became chief constable of Glasgow in 1931, most of the bands were based on quite small geographical areas, perhaps centred around a particular street corner or road. Youngsters would sit or sprawl on the pavement, gossiping, wrestling, grumbling and 'inevitably – some of them began to scheme up villainies. People who spoke of a group naturally used their meeting place to describe them, and so such names as "the Beehive Corner Boys" afterwards abbreviated to "the Beehive Gang", were coined'.[102]

In the 1930s religious bigotry saw the rise in the East End of Glasgow of the Protestant 'Billy Boys' and their Catholic opponents based around Norman Street and known as the 'Norman Conquerors'. It was this sectarian violence and animosity that led one Glasgow newspaper to ask what steps the churches were taking to bring an end to the 'uncivilised' behaviour. But it was the criminality that some older gang members engaged in – the robberies and protection rackets they organised – as well as their violent and vicious conduct that precipitated the waging of an energetic campaign by the Glasgow police to end their power. It was led by Percy Sillitoe. His methods succeeded, to the extent that they brought about a decline in the level of gang warfare and put many of the offenders behind bars. But the gang culture itself survived, and there continued to be sporadic conflicts in different parts of the city that the police were unable to prevent. As Andrew Davies points out, in such a city as Glasgow, with its multiplicity of gangs and deep-seated rivalries, police campaigns could never be completely successful: 'Ownership of the streets was too vigorously contested in districts such as the Gorbals, where traditions of gang formation were deeply rooted.' In the end it was the outbreak of the Second World War, and the enlistment of many street gang members which caused a 'more profound disruption to [their] activity in Glasgow than any of the police strategies devised by Sillitoe'.[103]

Yet, while gang conflicts and acts of mass hooliganism aroused alarm in the communities where they were concentrated, it was the upsurge in juvenile crime levels in the mid-1930s which caused more widespread concern. The so-called 'crime wave' followed the passage of the 1933 Children and Young Persons Act, with its more ameliorative approach to offending and its emphasis on the rehabilitation of the wrongdoer rather than on his or her culpability. Significantly the 1927 Report of the Departmental Committee on the Treatment of Young Offenders, which formed the basis of the 1933 legislation, had called for an end to the use of the terms 'conviction' and 'sentence' in juvenile courts. It also recommended the selection of panels of younger magistrates to serve in them. Court business should be conducted in as private and informal a way as possible, and the publication of names, addresses or other details likely to lead to the identification of young offenders should no longer be permitted.[104] When these proposals and the other provisions mentioned earlier were incorporated in the 1933 Act there were soon critics who claimed that its liberal philosophy and the increasing use of probation which accompanied it, were leading youngsters to have scant respect for the law and little fear of its penalties. Sterner responses were needed if the upsurge in child lawlessness was to be stemmed. Mrs Elizabeth Andrews, who chaired a Glamorgan juvenile court, commented in the late 1930s that since the 1933 Act had come into existence 'and juvenile delinquency has apparently increased there has been more talk and argument on birching, as a way out , than at any time than I can remember'.[105] Senior police officers, too, believed that part of the reason for the rise in juvenile crime was that youngsters 'were no longer impressed by their appearance before the juvenile court'.[106] Coupled with this was that perennial scapegoat, lack of parental authority, and only by a greater resort to harsher penalties, especially corporal punishment, could the tide be turned.

Defenders of the legislation, however, pointed out with equal force that although the number of youngsters proceeded against in the juvenile courts on indictable charges was rising, from 14,848 in 1933 to 30,733 in 1937, this could be accounted for by reasons other than a sudden outbreak of child, or rather boy, criminality, since the overwhelming majority of offenders were male.[107] Among these other factors was the larger number of children in their early and mid teens in the population during the mid-1930s as a result of a rise in the birth rate in the immediate aftermath of the First World War. In addition, since greater emphasis was being placed on the need to help young offenders rather than to criminalise them, victims of petty thefts and the like were more willing to bring youngsters to court, in the hope that this would prevent more serious offending in later life. In this way minor crimes that had once gone unrecorded were being added to the national statistics. Changes in police procedure, for example in London, also led to more children caught breaking the law by constables on the beat being brought to court rather than dealt with less formally. Unemployment, too, often led to a decline in domestic discipline, with fathers depressed and demoralised and mothers frequently having to go out to work instead. Among youngsters aged between fourteen and sixteen their own inability to find work created what one commentator called 'young bandits', ready to cause trouble.[108] Finally, since there had always been under-reporting of juvenile offending, the 'crime wave' of the 1930s was probably a sign that more cases were coming to light than had previously occurred.

Early in 1937, the head of the Children's Branch of the Home Office strongly denied alarmist claims of a 'wave' of child delinquency, pointing out that few youngsters below the age of seventeen had consciously 'adopted a life of deliberate dishonesty ... Often ... it was the desire for excitement and adventure, rather than what they expected to get out of a theft, that led young people into trouble'. Past experience showed that 'each time a new statute relating to the young had been passed the immediate effect was an apparent rise in the number of offences. The rise was due not to a sudden efflorescence of iniquity in the community, but to a desire on the part of those in a position to put the law in motion to make use of the new methods of treatment'.[109]

Later that year the Home Secretary, Sir Samuel Hoare, joined in the debate by calling for a thorough investigation of the causes of juvenile offending, but arguing too, that it 'would be a profound mistake to regard the problem of juvenile crime as primarily one to be dealt with by penal methods'. He favoured approved schools becoming part of the educational system of the country rather than of its penal structure. To that end, in supervising these schools the Home Office was working in close co-operation with the Board of Education'.[110]

Within the Home Office schools themselves this approach led to less regimentation than had once been the case. There was some relaxation in the uniforms worn, although in girls' schools these were still considered by the Home Office Children's Branch to be 'rather prim and stereotyped'. Even in the 1920s a greater trust was being shown towards the young inmates, so that in the majority of cases 'the barring of windows, the locking of dormitory doors and the employment of night watchmen had been abandoned ... Many persons visiting the schools for the first time have been surprised to meet boys and girls out for a walk, running errands to the neighbouring town, changing books at the Public Library or spending their pocket-money in the shops'.[111] However, in the second half of the 1930s, as a consequence of the growing number of juveniles coming before the courts, there was also an increase in the total of those being sent to approved schools, thereby reversing the trend of the previous decade. In 1934, 6,905 youngsters were resident in the schools on 31 December and that had risen to 8,754 on 31 December 1938.[112] This necessitated the opening of new establishments in London, Middlesex, Manchester, Staffordshire and Surrey.[113]

In 1937 an anonymous barrister, who was himself a county magistrate and a supporter of the new, less formal, approach to child offending, drily commented in *The Times* on the tendency in some circles to paint an 'alarming picture of the depravity of the youth of the nation. Certain newspapers drew their readers' attention to the "startling increase in juvenile crime." Headlines scream the menace of "boy gangsters." Elderly magistrates deplore the abandonment of their panacea, the birch, and gain a gratifying, if brief, notoriety by gloomy forebodings in the Press of the inevitably disastrous results of the leniency and weakness of the present day'. This 'mistaken belief in the myth of a vast growth of juvenile crime' had led some magistrates to toughen their court procedures and make the surroundings more formal, 'in the evident desire to impress on the boy that he stands before a criminal court and not before two or three justices interested in his conduct and anxious for his welfare'. Yet long experience had shown that even with 'hardened offenders the truth is reached more effectively by informal methods and the appropriate treatment is more surely determined'.[114]

These remarks called forth a hostile response from the deputy chairman of Warwickshire Quarter Sessions. He questioned whether youngsters who had been accused of acts which in an adult would be regarded 'as serious and intolerably unsocial conduct (I carefully avoid the word "crime" lest I should wound the feelings of your sensitive contributor)' would be readily corrected by informal and sympathetic action. 'Is it safe to assume that the admitted increase in the number of juveniles convicted of indictable offences is the obvious consequence of an increasing population and the growing popularity of the juvenile courts? I hope it is, but I fear it is not'.[115]

So the arguments over the best way to deal with young offenders continued to be waged to the end of the 1930s between those whom Victor Bailey has labelled respectively the 'reformers' and the 'reactionaries'.[116] With the outbreak of the Second World War in September 1939 the situation was to change yet again, as new problems and fresh challenges manifested themselves.

CHAPTER 7

THE SECOND WORLD WAR AND ITS AFTERMATH:
1939-1990s

One of the most recurrent types of moral panic in Britain since the war has been associated with the emergence of various forms of youth culture (originally almost exclusively working class, but often recently middle class or student based) whose behaviour is deviant or delinquent. To a greater or lesser degree, these cultures have been associated with violence. The Teddy Boys, the Mods and Rockers, the Hells Angels, the skinheads and the hippies have all been phenomena of this kind. There have been parallel reactions to the drug problem, student militancy, political demonstrations, football hooliganism, vandalism of various kinds and crime and violence in general.

Stanley Cohen, *Folk Devils and Moral Panics* (London, 3rd edn, 2002), p. 1. The book was first published in 1972.

The Second World War: 1939-45

The outbreak of the Second World War in September 1939 was followed, as had been the case in the 1914-18 conflict, by an increase in juvenile offending, particularly among children of school age. During the first year of hostilities there was a 41 per cent rise among the under-fourteens found guilty of criminal offences compared to the pre-war situation. For young people aged between fourteen and seventeen the increase was 22 per cent.[1] In 1941 a further rise occurred, to peak at over 43,000 criminal offences committed by juveniles under seventeen during that year. Numbers then fell back a little, only to rise to a total of nearly 43,000 in 1945. As in earlier years, the offenders were overwhelmingly young males, with girls contributing around 7.5 per cent of the total in 1945, compared to 6.0 per cent in 1939.[2] Thirteen was said to be the peak age for offending, with the number breaking the law declining thereafter for each succeeding year above that.

Much as had been the case in the First World War, the increase was attributed to the effects of the conflict itself. Typical of many was the comment by the Chief Constable of Oxford when he referred in 1940 to the 'distressing feature of moral laxity in time of War' which had led to 'the enormous increase in Juvenile crime'.[3] His counterpart in Brighton claimed that during the same year around a third of the offenders brought to court were children and young persons. 'Sterner measures' than putting them on probation were needed if the upsurge were to be checked.[4] In the country as a whole probation remained the major method of dealing with young lawbreakers between 1939 and 1945.

The disruption to family life caused by the call up of the menfolk and the fact that many mothers were carrying out war work was held responsible for the decline in parental discipline. Darkened streets as a result of the blackout created new opportunities for pilfering and disorderly behaviour, much as in the First World War, while the closure of clubs deprived youngsters of organised leisure pursuits. The excitement and emotional turmoil generated by the conflict likewise played their part in encouraging wrongdoing. A government memorandum published in June 1941, echoed comments made about the earlier World War, when it referred to adolescent boys being 'stirred by stories of deeds at sea, in the field and in the air, and the spirit of adventure this roused'.[5] That applied particularly when air raids began. Among those led astray was a London boy who in the autumn of 1941 pleaded guilty to setting fire to a factory. He had started the blaze in the hope that he could put it out with a stirrup pump and thereby win a George Medal, as was the case with some adult firefighters. But the flames got beyond him, the fire brigade had to be called in, and he found himself in a juvenile court pleading guilty to arson. The magistrates remanded him on bail for some months, on the understanding that he kept in touch with a probation officer and attended a clinic, presumably to receive remedial treatment.[6]

But there were new factors contributing to this upsurge in child criminality, too, notably the effect of evacuation during the early weeks of the War when a million school children were sent out of London and the major industrial cities to billets in safer localities. This not only shattered family life and caused great emotional stress for youngsters removed from their home environment to new places and new people, but it interrupted their education and encouraged truancy. By the spring of 1941 truancy levels in Birmingham were said to be as high as 40 per cent, despite the Board of Education's avowed policy of seeking to provide full-time regular schooling for children in the appropriate age group. According to a Board official, in April 1941 only 7 per cent of children were not able to receive this.[7] But the destruction of school premises in bombing raids or their conversion for war use inevitably affected the situation, for example in London. In parts of the capital emergency schools were opened, but often their capacity only permitted half-time attendance. In a few places half-time schooling continued to operate until March 1945.[8]

Evacuation itself created major problems, too. It was not compulsory, so some children remained behind with their parents, despite the encouragement given for them to move. Those who did leave the poorer areas of big towns, perhaps to go to middle-class homes in the countryside or in small provincial centres, experienced social tensions and many found difficulty in fitting into their new billet. A Blackpool landlady complained of her young charges from the slums that 'if you say two words to them they turn round and swear at you. I've seen a lot of dogs with better manners'.[9] Or they were made to feel 'outsiders' by the family in whose home they were living. One boy sent to Cambridge, for example, apparently had to eat in the kitchen with the maid, much to her annoyance. He was subsequently moved to another household. And a seventeen-year-old 'transplanted North London girl' complained that while a few hosts treated their evacuees as guests 'or as they would their own children ... the majority treated the girls as unpaid maids'.[10] Others never got over the trauma of being selected by the host family in an atmosphere 'like a cattle market', when they first reached the reception areas.[11]

Many of the families, for their part, were shocked at the roughness and the unhygienic habits of the young evacuees, as well as by the obvious deprivation which they had suffered in their home communities. In Scotland as early as mid-September 1939 letters to the *Glasgow Herald* referred to the evacuation of 'disobedient and verminous children', who were 'polluting' country homes.[12]

These factors – separation from their own families and feelings of alienation from the people upon whom they were billeted – led a minority of the evacuees to commit offences, perhaps in order to be moved to another billet or to be allowed to return home. Hermann Mannheim quoted the case of a boy who had been billeted in Cambridge with a lady of over seventy and had, in the opinion of the probation officer, reacted to this by committing wilful damage. He was subsequently placed in an Evacuation Hostel, which was reserved for difficult cases, and where during a stay of eight months, he never received a letter from his mother and only three from his father, nor did he get pocket money or parcels. Eventually he was sent to a Child Guidance Clinic, which advised that he should not be sent home: 'Needs some emotional attachment to some adult; at present inclined to regard all older persons as enemies.' If he were not properly handled he would 'become a delinquent and later a criminal'.[13]

In certain places there was a reluctance to prosecute evacuee children for wrongdoing but in others there were no such inhibitions. Northampton received 17,000 evacuees and its Chief Constable announced that he had taken 'drastic action ... to curb' their 'criminal propensities'. In one week in the autumn of 1939 twenty-two 'intractable' and defiant youngsters were taken to court, mainly for stealing from chain stores.[14] Likewise in Cambridge, which received a large contingent of children from London, there were fifty per cent more juveniles prosecuted in 1940 than in 1939.

Despite the disapproval of the Home Office some magistrates reacted to the juvenile 'crime' wave by resorting to birching as a means of deterrence.[15] The number of such punishments inflicted on boys under fourteen rose from fifty-eight imposed in 1939 to 531 in 1941. However, in 1943 the issue came to the fore when in January, Hereford juvenile court sentenced two boys, aged eleven and thirteen, to four strokes of the birch each for malicious damage. Despite the fact that the parents wanted to appeal against the sentence, the lads were taken to the police station and beaten. A subsequent appeal to the High Court for the sentence to be quashed proved successful, with the Lord Chief Justice declaring that 'fundamental principles of justice had been ignored by the Hereford court'. The issue caused a public outcry and a tribunal of inquiry was then set up by the Home Secretary. Although it absolved the magistrates and the local police force of misconduct, birching itself became the focus of attention. The *Howard Journal* concluded 'that birching and the right of appeal [were] incompatible', and since the 'right of appeal was sacrosanct, whipping would have to go'. In practice the corporal punishment of juveniles was only officially abolished by the 1948 Criminal Justice Act but the number of under-fourteens treated in this fashion fell markedly from 314 in 1942 to just twenty-three in 1945.[16]

As in earlier years there were those who argued that most offences committed by youngsters, particularly by those less than fourteen, were simply mischievous or, at worst, the product of misbehaviour rather than malevolence. In 1941, when Dumbarton County Council expressed alarm at an outbreak of window-breaking by children and condemned the lenient sentences handed down by the juvenile courts on the perpetrators, the Probation Committee reacted by describing the conduct as 'prankish'. It noted that most of the glass had already been damaged in the Blitz. Later in the same year property owners and the police in Glasgow reported an outbreak of 'serious and malicious damage to property by boys, who were generally punished by small fines'.[17] Magistrates responded by pointing out that the damage was mostly caused to sub-standard slum rented property and was a product of the 'inevitable consequences of childhood'. The Home Office, for its part, argued that in the country at large 'the number of delinquents [was] only a small fraction of the number of children and young persons in these age groups who are behaving perfectly well'.[18]

Child evacuees came and went between the major cities and the reception areas during the War years according to the intensity of the bombing, returning to their homes when the opportunity arose. One estimate suggests that by the end of 1940 there were over 80,000 children of school age in London, while in April 1941 Manchester had around 68,000.[19] Some of these ran wild in the streets, either because they were truanting or because they had no school to attend. Like people of all ages in the major cities, they resorted to shelters during air raids and they experienced all the fear, noise and danger of the bombing, as well as witnessing the destruction of people and property going on around them. Bernard Kops, a Jewish boy living in Stepney, remembered going 'underground to get away from the sirens and the bombs ... It was the beginning of an era of utter terror, of fear and horror. I stopped being a child and came face to face with the new reality of the world'.[20] The use of shelters was seen as a further factor undermining parental control, particularly at night, since young people often chose to go to different shelters from their families. There were complaints of youngsters, 'running amok from shelter to shelter, with opportunities for promiscuous sexual relationships, drinking and gambling', many of which were taken.[21]

Even in small cities like Bath some girls elected to sleep out in shelters away from their families. This was true of a thirteen-year-old who appeared before Bath Juvenile Court in April 1944 as 'in need of care and protection'. It was said that on two recent nights she had not been home at all, and on one of those the police had found her in an air raid shelter. A probation officer claimed this was because she was 'unhappy at home'. She was remanded in custody for four weeks.[22] In Glasgow, too, the *Glasgow Herald* in 1942 reported that boy runaways from approved schools were sleeping in air raid shelters, railway carriages and yards in the city while earning cash on the side by carrying luggage at railway stations 'for Polish and Canadian officers'.[23]

Bomb damaged properties encouraged looting, although this was, at least in theory, a capital offence. However, as Donald Thomas drily points out, many looters 'were too young to be shot or hanged'. He quoted a case heard by the East London Juvenile Court in December 1940 in which children were charged with looting toys from a bomb-damaged warehouse. The boys were truants who had not attended school for a year. But as Basil Henriques, chairman of the East London Juvenile Court, commented in March 1941, the casual way in which abandoned goods were left 'lying about', apparently unwanted, might tempt even law-abiding children.[24] Later he pointed out the ease with which shops and warehouses which had

been blitzed could be broken into, especially when the owner no longer
lived on the premises:

> Many of these are very insecure, and it requires little pressure to push in
> boarded-up windows or doors. Playing on the ruins, to a London child,
> is like playing on the rocks on the seashore. The cellars provide scope
> for the most thrilling games or 'camping' ... Getting on the roof of half-
> bombed houses is grand fun. And once there, it is only natural to climb
> along the parapet until, often by accident, the skylight of an occupied
> dwelling is reached. The temptation to look inside and then to get inside
> is too great for them, and once inside it is impossible for them to resist
> stealing.[25]

At the East London Juvenile Court in May 1945, Sidney L., aged sixteen,
was charged with breaching a recognizance he had entered into about a
month before requiring him to reside at a particular hostel for six months.
His original offence had been the theft of a model ship and other articles
'left exposed as a result of war operations'. On the second occasion he
was remanded for a week so that reports could be made on him by a
psychologist and by the superintendent of the remand home.[26]

Viewed nationally, the annual fluctuations in recorded juvenile crime
did not necessarily mean that the amount of offending had itself changed.
Rather the variations indicated that in a number of places the police and the
authorities were adopting a different strategy to deal with the more trivial
cases. In some towns there was an increased issuing of cautions instead
of bringing youngsters to court. Thus Preston's Chief Constable noted in
1944 that a 10 per cent decrease in the number of juvenile offenders in
his area was attributable 'to an increase in the number of cautions' issued
by senior officers.[27] As early as September 1940 the *Police Review* had
warned that 'wartime demanded a different policy from peace. "Some
aspects of the law usually enforced by the Police ought to be given a rest ...
we, would urge once more that the undoubted and well-established Police
discretion to issue cautions instead of applying summonses ... was never so
much in need of use as at the present time"'.[28]

North of the border, too, a policy of using police warnings was applied in
many urban areas, in an effort to keep children out of court. David Smith
claims that the number of juvenile delinquents 'admonished' by the police
nearly doubled when compared with the pre-war situation. In Coatbridge,
for instance, the Chief Constable cautioned in a 'very informal manner
about one-third of the offenders after they had admitted to their offences'.
Police warnings were also considered effective in Glasgow, Dundee and
Kilmarnock, with around 90 per cent of the children so dealt with not re-

offending. These initiatives, coupled with the widely differing economic and social structure of communities led to large differences in reported crime rates between towns. In Scotland, Dunfermline, Kirkcaldy and Edinburgh registered lower than average levels, while Paisley and Motherwell had the highest figures.[29] In England, too, there were variations in the number of officially recorded juvenile offences. Thus in 1943, those under seventeen were responsible for 29.5 per cent of all detected crime in Burnley but in Stockport this proportion rose to 38 per cent and in Hartlepool to 58 per cent. In Bath the figure was just over 17 per cent.[30] In 1942, Manchester's Chief Constable reported that juveniles had accounted for 38.1 per cent of the city's indictable offences. He particularly deplored the appearance in court of 329 children under twelve on such charges, and complained of the extra work these young lawbreakers were imposing on his force:

> it should be unnecessary. The care of youngsters of this age is first and foremost the obligation of the parents, and ways and means should be found for bringing home to them their responsibilities in this respect. This is to some extent a problem for the magistrates ... and the question arises whether the Bench is educated up to its job in this respect.[31]

Elsewhere it was argued that the high wages earned by young workers in war-related industries encouraged them to develop a cavalier attitude towards the property rights of others. According to Dr Brisby, a medical officer at one of HM prisons, access to relatively large sums of money 'without responsibility or the necessity of learning its value' had created a lack of appreciation of property rights and values, both with regard to themselves and to those around them.[32] But that explanation failed to take account of the fact that the sharpest rise in rates of offending was taking place among youngsters of school age rather than among those of fourteen years and above.

As in the earlier years of the century, there were claims that the cinema was encouraging juvenile criminality. Such arguments were fuelled by cases like that which occurred in 1945 when six boys were charged with holding up American soldiers near King's Cross with dummy revolvers. The police became involved when members of the United States military complained of the loss of money and valuables. The boys defended themselves by stating they had got the idea 'from the pictures'. But that excuse did not prevent the court from sending all of them to an approved school.[33] Again in November 1942 the town clerk of Dumfries claimed that children were stealing money to pay for admission to cinemas that were showing 'many undesirable pictures that had bad effects on immature minds'. In Glasgow, it was suggested that at least one young member of a gang had got involved in stealing purely 'to keep [up] appearances' so that he would not be the only one without cash in his pocket to pay for entry to the pictures.[34]

Even Members of Parliament joined in the chorus of disapproval, with the MP for Stretford maintaining that 'the influence of Hollywood on our young people' was 'the major evil ... the more mush they can put on the screen, the greater are the box-office profits'.[35] But the Home Office remained sceptical. In a memorandum written just after the end of the War an official drily commented: 'Each new form of entertainment as it comes into favour tends to be blamed for juvenile delinquency: cinemas and pin table saloons ... have, in turn, been the scapegoat ... There is, in fact, very little evidence that films have contributed directly to juvenile delinquency. On the contrary they have no doubt kept large numbers of juveniles and adolescents happily occupied and out of mischief'.[36] Similar reassurances had been issued for around a quarter of a century but still the picture houses had their critics. Many of the same accusations were to be levelled at television programmes around three decades later, while more recently crime and violent imagery have featured prominently in video games, thereby providing young people with 'vicarious excitement' from activities that critics have regarded as generally damaging'.[37]

Wartime shortages encouraged thefts, too. In May 1945, at a time of strict food rationing, Walter K., aged thirteen and Joseph A., aged ten, were found guilty at East London Juvenile Court of stealing '18 tins of food stuffs and other articles value of 32s' from Montefiore School in London. Each was placed on probation for a year and was required to find a surety of 40s.[38] In Scotland an increase in housebreaking by juveniles was attributed to the general scarcity of household goods. This made it worthwhile to steal them and easier to dispose of them than in the pre-war period.[39]

Petrol rationing and transport restrictions made bicycles more attractive and there were numerous cases of these being stolen by children, either for their own use or for sale. At the beginning of January 1944 two thirteen-year-old boys appeared before Norwich juvenile court charged with bicycle thefts. One admitted that he already had a machine but it had no lights and that was the reason he had taken this second one from a cinema car park. He pleaded guilty to the offence and because he had a good school record the summons against him was dismissed. In the second case the boy declared he had 'always wanted a cycle; that is why I took it'. But according to the police this same lad 'wished two other cases of stealing cycles to be taken into consideration'. They believed he was the leader of a gang of young bicycle thieves in the city, and the other boys 'had already been dealt with'. He was punished by being sent to a remand home for three weeks, where presumably it was hoped that firm discipline and a regimented routine would effect a reform.[40] But this young Norfolk entrepreneur scarcely matched a gang 'tracked down' in Maidstone in 1940 that specialised in bicycle thefts. Its members took the machines to an allotment shed where 'in a matter of minutes' they were 'taken to pieces, parts from other cycles fitted, the "new" machine given a coat of paint and sold.'[41]

Raw materials, especially metals, also increased in value and became tempting targets. One boy, Richie White, recalled how on a trip to Beckenham he and three friends decided to climb on the roof of a bombed-out house, in order to steal lead. They got a large box out of a shed and filled it with square pieces of flat lead. This they dragged home, but 'as we got into the turning' the older brother of one of the boys appeared and asked them what they had. When the younger lad said 'lead' the 'brother belted him and said, "You get in, you'll get nicked, you'll get put away."' The boy immediately made off, and was soon followed by the other two, leaving Richie in sole charge of the box and its contents. He pulled it home and confessed to his mother what he had done. She swore at him but then:

> We put it on a pushchair, rags on top, and took it to Wilson's, the scrap metal dealer down at Lower Sydenham. We got four pounds, which was a lot of money. Wilson never asked no questions. I went to Charlie [one of his friends] and I said, "We got two pounds." So I gave him a pound and me and mum had three. That must have lasted us for ever, three pounds! We never went back for more, though. We were scared after that.[42]

Shoplifting became easier as a result of staff shortages and the restrictions on the amount of lighting that could be used. A headmaster from Portsmouth, evacuated with his pupils to Winchester, discovered that one small boy had been shoplifting in Woolworth's on a major scale. He had even asked a member of staff for a box to carry away his loot and, surprisingly, does not seem to have been caught. The headmaster, tongue in cheek, thought he 'would go far', with such an attitude.[43]

Although gangs continued to operate on a minor scale, as with the groups of young bicycle thieves already mentioned, there was a decline in the overall gang culture in most urban areas, including Glasgow, when older members were called up. As Forbes and Meehan comment of the latter city, the War 'channelled the young Scot's natural aggression into killing Germans instead of his fellow countrymen'. But some gang warfare did continue. 'The blackout was great fun for the teenagers not yet called up', they write. 'The temptations of bombed or derelict houses where there could be cash, the tripping up and baiting of drunks in the back streets, the thrill of escaping down moonlit alleys, the real fireworks on Clydeside with the bombs blitzing the shipyards and the world gone mad with violence, and all of this with Dad away at the wars and Mum too busy coping with rationing and no discipline anywhere except from exasperated policemen with inefficient torches stabbing through the darkness'.[44]

Girls, too, were involved in shoplifting, stealing cosmetics or cheap jewellery from chain stores, for example, but, as always, it was female morality that gave rise to the most serious concern in the juvenile courts, with a number of girls brought in as being 'in moral danger' or needing care and attention. The presence of large detachments of troops, including during the last three years of the War, American and other foreign soldiers, particularly affected adolescent girls. The incidence of venereal disease rose sharply and the newspapers reacted to the situation by producing sensational headlines like 'Camp Followers; Girls 16-18 Running Wild'.[45]

In the West country the *Bath Weekly Chronicle* in March 1943 lamented the way in which 'children of school age were becoming utterly spoilt ... Too much money and many soldiers with money to fling about were ... factors leading to their downfall'. Some girls were said to be 'suffering from sexual mania'. Bath's woman probation officer complained of females 'whose only ideas in life are men, lipstick, and showing as much of their bodies as they can ... war-time conditions ... were having [an] appalling effect ... on some girls'.[46] As Edward Smithies points out, the fact that Bath was the central point for a number of large American bases in the West of England led to 'good-time girls' and prostitutes being attracted to the city. Local teenagers soon joined in. At the end of March 1944, the Archdeacon of Bath complained of the 'grossest forms of immorality' going on every night. He added that he knew of one girl aged twelve, two of thirteen and one of fourteen who were pregnant.[47]

Among those likely to cause the Archdeacon and other members of 'respectable' Bath society concern was the fifteen-year-old who appeared before the city's juvenile court in February 1944 'as being exposed to moral danger and beyond control'. She was committed to an approved school, although she was pregnant. She admitted to having met several American soldiers whom she knew only by their first names 'and had associated with them in Victoria Park, Queen Square, and Hedgemead Park'. In all she had been 'intimate with six American airmen and soldiers ... but did not know the father of her unborn child'. For a month she had tried 'to be a good girl, but since Christmas she had been with three other men'.[48] Her exploits paled into insignificance, however, when compared to those of another fifteen-year-old, who claimed that she had repeatedly run away from home, on the fourth occasion for nearly three weeks, because she did not get on with her stepmother. During the last period away she had, by her own account, been with more than fifteen different GIs, in addition to visiting four camps and sleeping in a barn on at least two nights. She had accompanied Americans to London and to Weston-super-Mare, as well as moving between Bath and Swindon. Her saga began on Christmas Eve in 1943 when she went to a US camp party. She then travelled to Swindon, where she passed the night in a Great Western Railway cloakroom. She spent Christmas Day wandering around the town until 7 p.m. when she dined with an American soldier. She left him in the early hours of the morning and spent the night in a barn: 'Met a US soldier, went to London with him: went back to Swindon; met another soldier, went to the pictures with him; next day went to a camp to meet some friends, stayed until 2 a.m. Came back to Bath; put on a new dress given her by an American, went to a dance; went to a camp with a soldier; stayed in an empty house on the camp site all night. Got a lift to Swindon, met a sergeant; went to Weston-super-Mare, stayed at a hotel there; next morning went to Swindon; went to dance in the evening'.

And so the story continued until she was eventually picked up by the police. In view of her youth and her general conduct it is surprising to learn that her father, who was her legal guardian, told the magistrates 'that he considered the case [was] brought without justification'. She had been taken to court as 'being in moral danger'. On this occasion the magistrates postponed their decision for three weeks, presumably so that further

WITH SOLDIERS AT MIDNIGHT
Bath Girl Sent To Approved School

A 14-years-old Bath girl who, at previous Court hearings, was stated to be uncontrollable, to have been found with American soldiers at midnight and to have slept on park benches, was on Thursday sent by the magistrates of Bath City Juvenile Court to an Approved School. She was stated to be exposed to moral danger.

Her parents were ordered to contribute 10/- per week towards her keep.

The stresses of war time – a fourteen-year-old girl fraternizing with American soldiers.

investigations into her circumstances could be made, but no later account of the case appeared in the Bath newspaper.[49]

Significantly a Home Office study commissioned in 1943 attributed the 'wave of sexual delinquency' to the arrival of the GIs:

> To girls brought up on the cinema, who copied the dress, hairstyles, and manners of Hollywood stars, the sudden influx of Americans, speaking like the films, who actually lived in the magic country and who had plenty of money, at once went to the girls' heads. The American attitude to women, their proneness to spoil a girl, to build up, exaggerate ... and to act with generosity and flamboyance, helped to make them the most attractive boyfriends. In addition, they 'picked-up' girls easily, and so even a comparatively plain and unattractive girl stood a chance.[50]

This free and easy conduct resulted in a number of girls being sent to approved schools or committed to remand homes as being in need of 'care and attention' or as in 'moral danger'. That was something that many of them resented, arguing they had only been having a good time.

The general rise in juvenile offending led to more youngsters being sent to approved schools, even though the proportion of those found guilty who went to the schools actually fell a little compared to pre-war, from 10 per cent in 1938 to around 9 per cent during the War. But the total of those despatched jumped from 3,913 in 1938 to 5,973 in 1942, of whom, in the latter year, 1,043 were girls. Numbers then fell back a little in 1943 and 1944, before climbing to 5,658 in 1945, with 1,194 of these being female. [51] The numbers resident in the schools also rose from 8,764 in 1938 to 10,257 in 1942, so that accommodation rapidly became overcrowded. The problem was made worse because some existing premises had to be vacated since they were in danger zones. Gradually new schools were opened, with 145 in operation in 1946 compared to 104 in 1938, while training periods were cut to around half the pre-war level in senior schools and to about three-quarters of the pre-1939 standard in junior and intermediate establishments. Three classifying schools were also opened, the first being at Aycliffe near Darlington in 1943 and intended for boys. The following year two senior girls' schools were opened. Over a two-month period educational psychologists and teachers in these institutions 'examined the abilities, temperament, and character of each inmate', before the young person concerned was allocated to one of the approved schools. That led to the individual institutions becoming more narrowly specialist in the kind of youngsters they took.[52]

Despite the expansion, a number of young offenders had to be sent to remand homes, to await an approved school vacancy. As Victor Bailey

Science class at an Intermediate Approved School around the mid-twentieth century. The aim was reform rather than merely retribution.

puts it, these became 'mere clearing houses for the schools' in many cases. That arrangement was highly unsatisfactory in that the homes had been intended only as short-term holding venues, to which youngsters were referred to await their court appearance or to have detailed reports upon them prepared. They lacked training facilities or even provision for physical activity, and yet some young people remained in them for a considerable time while they waited for a vacancy. A further problem was that they were unable to classify their inmates, and there were complaints that in one London remand home a seven-year-old girl, taken there by the police as in need of care or protection, was allowed to associate with far older girls, with all the risk of 'contamination' that that represented. According to Bailey, by the end of 1941 there were 1,300 children in remand homes awaiting transfer to an approved school.[53]

The situation was aggravated by the practice of some magistrates of using remand homes as a way of punishing relatively trivial offenders by giving them 'a taste of detention'. To this end they repeatedly remanded them in custody. According to a critical report in the *Police Review*, the 'week's remand to "teach the youngster a lesson" [was] still popular with some Justices', even though there was 'no statutory authority for it'.[54] Children were even remanded to prison on the grounds that they were 'too unruly or depraved' to be sent to a remand home. The total so affected rose from 395 in 1940 to 674 in 1942. It was a development that aroused alarm in official circles. In these circumstances in both 1940 and 1941 the Home Office urged local authorities to fulfil their obligations to provide more remand home accommodation, though with limited success.[55]

Sentence to an approved school was supposed to be followed by a period of after care. Even in peacetime this supervision had often been rudimentary, but once the War began it seems largely to have ceased. In the case of probation, which covered around 44.5 per cent of all juveniles charged with indictable offences, there were problems, too, caused by a shortage of probation officers, and by the fact that when probationers were evacuated it was often difficult to keep track of them. Parents were reluctant for people in the reception area to know that their offspring were on probation and they even threatened to bring them home if it became known.[56] As a consequence, writes Edward Smithies, magistrates were 'forced to balance carefully the merits of fining and sentence to an institution in the light of the growing shortage of appropriate resources for probation. They tended to opt for more fines'.[57]

Some boys and girls reacted to their incarceration in an approved school by absconding. Among the girls it was noted that care and attention cases were those most likely to rebel in this way. If they became persistent absconders this might lead to their being sent to Borstal, where the stricter disciplinary and training regime was intended to bring about an improvement. In 1944, sixty-six girls were sent to Borstal on these grounds, and critics pointed out that since they had been mostly sent to the approved school for 'moral' rather than criminal reasons, that was an undesirable trend.[58] The practice was brought to an end by the 1948 Criminal Justice Act, but during a debate on that Bill the then Home Secretary, Mr Chuter Ede, pointed out that it could help rehabilitation. He cited the case of a fifteen-year-old girl who had been sent to an approved school as 'being beyond control. She had stolen money from her mother, pawned articles taken from home, and stayed out at night'. She spent eighteen months in an approved school and was then licensed out. She at once began behaving 'badly, and had to be readmitted to the school. She ran away ... and was found living in a common lodging house as a prostitute.' Ultimately she was charged with absconding and was sent to Borstal. After serving a term there she seems to have had a change of heart as well as of conduct. She contacted the approved school from which she had absconded and two years after leaving Borstal she was married. The headmistress of her approved sohool was the godmother of her first child.[59] Such a moral tale of reform and rehabilitation may have justified the practice of using Borstal in this fashion in some eyes, but in the post-war world it was no longer seen as acceptable.

During the War radical changes were also made to the Borstal system itself, with around two-thirds of the total Borstal inmates discharged at the outbreak of hostilities. Only those who had not served six months were left in the reduced number of institutions. Shortly afterwards nearly half the housemasters left the service. This led to short-term cutbacks but over the months the number of committals to Borstal again increased, reflecting the rising crime rate. Overcrowding was the result, and a policy of early licensing was adopted to ease this, with the average period of detention only gradually creeping up from ten months in 1940 to sixteen months in 1944. According to Victor Bailey,

> Borstal in wartime was ... a shadow of its former self. The institutions were understaffed, the houses overcrowded. In the workshops, production for the war effort took precedence over work training. Nor was there much need to prepare for release, or need of after-care, when three-quarters of the boys were released directly into the forces. This weakened system, however, had to cope with more intractable boys ... One sign of this was the vastly increased rate of absconding from the institutions ... The proportion avoiding reconviction in the two years from discharge fell to around 50 per cent, but the wartime training conditions and type of inmate seemed to explain the deterioration ... The end of the war ... saw an increase in the proportion found guilty sentenced to Borstal, from 7.2 per cent [in the relevant age group] in 1944 to 10.7 per cent in 1946.[60]

More constructively the Government reacted to the problem of delinquency during the Second World War much as it had done in the First, by stressing the importance of organised recreational facilities. Youth groups and similar bodies were seen as an important means of educating young people in the values of citizenship, as well as serving as a 'preventative and cure for "moral laxity".' According to Sonya Rose, 'morally recalcitrant teenagers' were described by youth workers as 'unclubbable'. In December 1941 young people aged sixteen and seventeen were required to register with local education authorities. The aim, according to a 1942 White Paper, was to allow the authorities to contact all youngsters in the appropriate age groups so as to encourage them to 'find the best way of fitting themselves to do their duty as citizens and of assisting the ... national effort'. The young registrants were invited to list the clubs and organisations to which they belonged. If they were 'non-participating' they were asked to come for an interview, at which they would be urged to join.[61]

Local youth committees were set up as well as a national youth body, and there was increased recruitment by existing organisations like the Boy Scouts and Girl Guides, as well as by new ventures, such as the Youth

Service Corps. This was started in East Suffolk in July 1940 and within about nine months was said to be running or planning to run branches in around fifty areas.[62] As well as undertaking unspecified duties 'useful to the National War Effort', they arranged various activities, such as physical training, technical and general educational courses and social recreation. It was optimistically claimed that members were 'keen to carry on with useful work in peacetime', too, and the hope was that such initiatives would counter any tendencies to juvenile wrongdoing.

In Glasgow the local authorities extended school youth clubs to all fourteen to eighteen-year-olds, while in Dundee and Glasgow play centres for nine to eleven-year-olds were provided. Four experimental Youth Centres were also opened in Glasgow in 1940 and these had increased by the War's end to seventeen senior and twenty-nine junior centres, enrolling 13,000 members and aided by three hundred adult workers. The centres provided canteens and promoted music, cooking, film and drama. Sporting facilities were supplied, too.[63]

Inevitably, large numbers of young people remained aloof from these officially promoted bodies preferring to seek their own entertainment in less 'desirable' ways, such as frequenting greyhound racing tracks and public dances. A fourteen-year-old Sussex girl remembered the attraction of American music and the contribution of American soldiers to social life:

Britain seemed so dull and corny; the Yanks gave us cigarettes and chewing gum and the music was fantastic. I loved jitterbugging. I won a contest. We used to make these dresses with short, pleated skirts and when we danced they'd flare up right around our waists ... Who wants to listen to some schmaltzy sentimental music when they're young and can dance to the 'A-Train' with the Yanks?[64]

In a post-war debate on 2 November, 1945, the MP for Stretford called for a ban on the under-eighteens attending these 'undesirable' attractions: 'it may well be that ... young people today, are improving their style in regard to "jitter-bugging," and the other features of acrobatic dancing. But I can hardly feel that it makes them likely to be good citizens in future.' He also condemned amusement arcades. 'I feel these things are closely associated with the superficial garish, harsh forms of life which have developed here to a certain degree by American influences'. Overall there was a 'cheap, shallow, superficial outlook on the part of young people – a "Piccadilly Circus atmosphere" ... almost every parent to whom I have spoken, has expressed concern about the decadence of our young people'.[65] In the years after 1945 this attitude of disapproval of the leisure activities of the young was to form the backdrop for much of the on-going debate about juvenile offending and the best means of combating it. The increase in youthful independence and affluence called forth a hostile reaction among many older people, for whom the new 'pop' culture was not only unwelcome but morally threatening.

The Post-War World: 1945-1990s

During the second half of the twentieth century youth crime and the misdoings of adolescents loomed large as a focus of public attention. In an effort to counter the trend there were many different government initiatives and a good deal of legislation introduced, designed to turn troublemakers into good citizens. The concerns manifested themselves in the immediate aftermath of the hostilities, as the effects of the social dislocations of the War years, the poor state of housing provision and the consequent overcrowding were combined with worries about the growing self-assertiveness of young people. As Paul Rock and Stanley Cohen have commented, this led 'the ... young to seek guidance from their fellow young' rather than to rely on the 'traditional wisdom' of the older generation. The strained relations between the generations were reinforced in the 1950s by the 'relative economic emancipation of working-class adolescents ... and the establishment of a commercial market ... creating specifically adolescent desires in consumer goods and services'.[66]

By no means all youngsters were affluent enough to 'take on the new glossy teenage image, by no means all were delinquent or even in slight conflict with their elders, but these differences [tended] to be ignored by the older generation'.[67] Critics condemned the 'crooners and the heart-throbs, the hairstyles and clothing, the espresso bars and milk bars which young people frequented', and which were felt to be undesirable imports from America. Particularly frowned upon was the influence of rock 'n roll music in the 1950s. The *Daily Mail* in September 1956 bluntly described it as 'a communicable disease' and 'the music of delinquents'. Even the Welfare State came under critical scrutiny because it was taking away from families the need to look after themselves by its promise of nurture 'from the cradle to the grave'. In 1951 the recorder of Bradford commented on this when he declared that: 'Parents of this time, unfortunately, do not take sufficient care in bringing up their children. They expect somebody else to be responsible'.[68]

The disillusion felt by members of the public towards the attitudes and behaviour of the young was demonstrated in some of the reports published by *Mass-Observation* in 1949. One investigator, for example, described a group of three girls and two boys aged about fourteen to sixteen, who were sitting on chains separating the pavement from the road. The females were condemned for wearing heavy make up, 'with extra thick lipstick applied carelessly'. Five girls walked by on the other side of the street and whistled to the two boys, who ignored them. They, too, were about fourteen or fifteen years old and were heavily made up, 'two with dyed blonde hair'. They marched along 'arm-in-arm, spread out across the pavement, singing "Give Me Five Minutes More".'[69] Such unrestrained behaviour, although in no way delinquent, was seen as inappropriate and unpleasant by older and staider onlookers.

It was, however, the increase in crime levels among young people that created the most worry from the late 1940s. The figures reached a temporary peak in 1951 before falling back to the mid-1950s, when they resumed their upward trend, albeit with some fluctuations, over the decades. Those found guilty of an indictable offence were, of course, throughout the period only a small minority of their age group. As the Home Secretary, Henry Brooke, commented in 1963, 'the vast majority of our boys and girls come through their childhood and youth without ever getting into trouble with the law.' Nonetheless he pointed out that whereas in 1938 only eleven boys in a thousand in the fourteen to sixteen age group had been found guilty of indictable offences, in 1962 that had climbed to twenty-six per thousand, and was 'rising yearly. In the same period the number in the 8 to 13 age-group rose from eight per thousand to fourteen per thousand.' In each case this was accompanied by an increase in the number guilty of non-indictable offences as well. Although girls were less often charged before the courts with lawbreaking, their numbers, too, had risen sharply since 1945.[70]

Particularly alarming to many was a revival of the gang culture. For example among groups like the Teddy Boys of the 1950s and the Mods and Rockers of the 1960s, of whom more will be said later. As T. R. Fyvel pointed out in 1961, the number of youths aged fourteen to seventeen convicted of violent offences more than doubled over the four-year period from 1956 to 1959 inclusive, growing from 461 at the earlier date to 985 at the later.[71] Fyvel claimed that this 'more intensified gang life' was characterised by hostility towards all forms of authority and could 'flare into violence upon a trivial cause. Coupled with it went a sort at stylized warfare between the gangs themselves ... and a fashion for carrying improvised offensive weapons ... As ... more modern schools and housing estates went up, so more boys seemed to drift into the new gang warfare and to walk about carrying flick-knives or such things as bicycle chains "for defence".'[72] In the East End of London, the Kray twins, Reginald and Ronald, began their notorious underworld career in the late 1940s. Like a number of other London gang leaders they first of all hung around the boxing ring, but by the time they were sixteen, in 1949, they had their own gang and had been barred from most of the cinemas and dance halls in the area as a result of their skirmishes with other teenage gangs. 'We used to keep choppers, machetes, knives, swords and all kinds of weapons beneath the bed', recalled Reg Kray. 'Ron and I usually always had a knife on us. We got our first gun off some criminal at that age ... Before long we had an arsenal of guns'. At the age of sixteen they were charged with inflicting grievous bodily harm on three other youths, in a fight 'involving bike chains and coshes outside a dance hall' in Hackney. On that occasion they were acquitted, but soon they were given probation for an assault on a policeman. Already their reputation in London criminal circles was growing, as they turned 'to villainy as a way of making money'.[73] Later they became racketeers on a grand scale.

In Glasgow, too, gangs were formed on the bleak, newly-constructed housing estates that were springing up from the late 1940s. In the 1950s street violence in the city erupted with a vengeance, as gangs fought one another with great 'viciousness, with ... knives and weapons allied to a ruthless disregard for life or property'. One top surgeon in Glasgow claimed that during a single summer nine hundred and fifty cases of assault had been dealt with by the casualty department of his hospital, and staff had had to deal with forty-two serious stabbings, as the knife took over from the razor as the weapon of choice among 'the hoodlums, who were mostly in their late teens or early twenties'. According to George Forbes and Paddy Meehan, Easter 1967 was labelled 'Bloody Easter' because there were twenty-two stabbings in the city on 'the Friday and Saturday nights alone'.[74] As they comment, 'a razor will disfigure before it will kill whereas once a knife has punctured a vital organ it results in death'.

But despite this growing violence, as before the War, most of the crimes committed by the young comprised theft, burglary, shoplifting and the receiving of stolen goods. According to *Mass-Observation*, four out of every five juveniles brought before the courts for criminal offences were thieves, most of them boys. That remained largely true during the succeeding decades.[75] Among those involved were youngsters like Ronald W., aged ten, who appeared before East London Juvenile Court in April 1955, charged with stealing four hundred omnibus tickets, valued at 4s, the property of the London Transport Executive. He was found guilty of this bizarre theft and was placed on probation for two years. Then there was Andrew S., aged thirteen, who appeared before the same court in February 1955 on a charge of stealing twenty-six books, valued at 2s 6d. He was remanded on two separate occasions before being committed in mid-March to the care of the London County Council.[76]

More serious were the activities of another young Londoner, Noel 'Razor' Smith. He came from a dysfunctional Irish family and commenced his criminal career in the late 1960s or early 1970s, as a young lad, by shoplifting pencils and Mars bars, as well as stealing milk from doorsteps and 'scrumping apples and pears'. In the winter he scavenged wood for the fire by breaking down garden fences, and he and his friends also learned to work

> various scams with which to prise the odd shilling or two out of unsuspecting householders. The best one was the raffle-ticket game, which involved shoplifting a couple of books of numbered cloakroom tickets from the local stationery shop. We would then take our angelic faces around the doors of the posh houses, selling ... fake raffle-tickets for ten pence each in aid of a new hut for the Boy Scouts ... Bob-a-job was another of our moves, although most times this one did actually involve doing something for our money[77].

The Government, meanwhile, began its many post-war interventions in the juvenile crime scene with the passage of the 1948 Criminal Law Amendment Act. The Home Secretary, Chuter Ede, announced in November 1947 that one of the Bill's principal aims was to reduce the number of young persons being sent to prison, and to bring about an eventual end to imprisonment as a method of punishing young offenders convicted in magistrates' courts. Under current legislation, children under fourteen who were remanded or committed for trial in custody, had to be sent to a remand home, as had those between fourteen and seventeen, unless they were certified by the court as too unruly or depraved to be kept in such an institution. In that case they could be committed to prison. The new legislation provided for the setting up of remand centres to cater for this group, as well as for young people aged from seventeen to twenty-one. The Criminal Law Amendment Act also abolished the death penalty for the under-eighteens, and ended corporal punishment for youngsters, despite the vociferous opposition this aroused at a time when juvenile crime was rising. To placate the critics, however, the Bill envisaged the setting up of special detention centres for boys between fourteen and twenty-one years who were thought to need a short period of strict discipline to effect their reform. This incarceration was initially to be for a maximum of three months, or, in exceptional circumstances, up to six months; later those periods were cut to between twenty-one days and four months. The prime purpose of the centres was 'to bring [young offenders] up with a jerk and make them realise that they cannot flout the law with impunity'.[78] They were to be sent to a centre if they had committed an offence which would have led to a term of imprisonment if carried out by an adult, and when the court considered all other modes of treatment had been tried without success.[79] The junior centres were to cater for those aged fourteen to sixteen, and both they and their senior counterparts were to be administered by the Prison Commission. In addition, the 1948 Act introduced attendance centres for lesser offenders, where they were to be sent for a maximum period of twelve hours. The aim was to instil discipline and a sense of responsibility, and to deprive them of their freedom for a short time. Other developments included amendments to the period of detention in Borstal. This was now to be for a minimum of nine months and a maximum of three years; that was later reduced to two. In 1963 the age of admission to Borstal was reduced from sixteen to fifteen, and in 1982 their name was changed to youth custody centres.

Finally the 1948 Act amended the probation system, so that the term probation was only applied where the penalty imposed included supervision by a probation officer for a minimum period of twelve months. Additionally, though, youngsters could now be granted absolute or conditional discharges by the juvenile courts. At the beginning of the 1980s that had become the single most used sentencing disposal for male offenders aged ten to fourteen. In 1990 *half* of all those sentenced in that age group were given absolute or conditional discharges, compared to around a fifth who received supervision orders and attendance centre orders, respectively. Among those aged fourteen to seventeen in 1990, nearly one in three received an absolute or conditional discharge, while fewer than one in five received supervision orders or were fined. Under one in twelve were required to attend a young offender institution, as the old-style detention centres and Borstals had become from 1988.[80] A small number of lads in this latter age group were also given care orders or were required to carry out community service, a method of punishment introduced in the early 1980s. By the summer of 2007 community service was considered more effective than incarceration in stopping re-offending among youths.[81]

The first of the detention centres was opened in 1952 and by 1965 they were providing six thousand places. The tough regime imposed was detailed in 1962 in respect of the Send centre, which was said to be

> typical in its austerity ... no concessions are made to relaxation and comfort ... Reveille is at 6.10 ... and movement is ceaseless until tea at 5 o'clock. Time is occupied by parades, drills and physical training, outside work on the centre's market garden, cleaning and general duties and by frequent changes of clothes. Lights are out by 9.30. The emphasis is on strict discipline, hard work, appearance and deportment, cleanliness and respect for staff and other inmates.[82]

Among those who experienced the 'short sharp shock' treatment at the Send juvenile detention centre was Noel Smith, who went there in October 1975, just before his fifteenth birthday. He was committed for stealing motor cycles, breaking into a tennis club, and assaulting police officers whilst being arrested, although he denied the latter charge. He was sent to the centre for three months and as he arrived he saw its high fences, razor-wire and spotlights as well as 'ranks of shaven-headed youths in blue overalls and hobnail boots ... marching, marking time, doubling and dressing-off like a bunch of demented squaddies'. He claimed that on entry to the institution he was beaten up by some of the warders and that far from reforming him, it confirmed him in a life of crime. 'The regime made us fit and mean and full of contempt for straight society ... But, most damaging of all, the short sharp shock gave us the two essentials that were needed to consolidate our lives of crime – information and contacts ... Today I can look around the yard of almost any prison in the country and see someone I did time with in the juvenile system. None of us was rehabilitated by it ... We all went on to bigger crimes'.[83]

The brevity of the sentence precluded any form of training, such as applied to Borstals, there was much bullying, and some regarded the whole business as a kind of status symbol and a recognition of their importance as 'criminals'. This was the reaction of James H., when he first went to a young offenders' institution at the age of fifteen in the mid-1990s. He confessed that initially he was 'frightened to a certain extent but after getting used to it I thought it would boost my image when I got out. It did, amongst the lads I knew, the criminal fraternity. They feared me'.[84] Nor did it stop him re-offending for soon after his release he was charged with attempted robbery, when a fight with another youth led the latter to accuse him of trying to steal his money. James began committing burglaries at the age of thirteen or fourteen, but seems, at first, to have been remarkably unsuccessful in that he and another youth stole a television set and then broke it when they were carrying it away. Later they tried to steal a car and 'hot rod' it but when confronted with the mass of wires needed to effect ignition they did not know where to begin. James came from a one-parent family and although his mother had stood by him, other relatives had shunned him: 'because I am in gaol they think I am a disgrace'. But he did not seem particularly repentant, claiming, 'What I have done everyone else has done'.[85]

Alongside the various institutional developments in the post-war period, however, another trend emerged in the early 1950s. This was a growing desire to keep young delinquents out of the courts altogether and thereby to enable them to reintegrate into 'respectable' society easily. That was to be achieved partly by a wider use of police cautions and warnings, while from 1963 the age of criminal responsibility was raised from eight years to ten. Attempts to raise this in the late 1960s proved unsuccessful. In 1969 the concept of Intermediate Treatment was also introduced. It allowed local authority social services departments to make special provision for children and young people in trouble, and could take various forms. Among them were evening clubs, literacy classes, outdoor pursuits and voluntary work. At first the initiative had very limited success but in 1983 it was revived by a government programme to set up Intermediate Treatment as a direct alternative to custody for the 'heavy end' of young offenders. The system was to work in collaboration with the police and the juvenile courts, and seems to have achieved some of its objectives. Also developed during this decade were local multi-agency diversion panels, which offered a range of educational, recreational and therapeutic 'alternatives to prosecution', to which young people in trouble could be directed as a condition of their police caution. These various policies led to a sharp reduction in the number of youngsters entering the juvenile court system, so that whereas in 1980, 71,000 boys and girls aged fourteen to sixteen had been sentenced by these courts in England and Wales, that had dropped to 37,300 by 1987.[86] The apparent effectiveness of the scheme led to a practice known as 'cautioning plus' whereby youngsters might be

> cautioned on several different occasions if they and their parents agreed to participate in particular programmes or activities. Between 1980 and 1987, the cautioning rate for girls aged 14 to 16 rose from 58% to 82%. For boys the figures were 34% and 58% respectively. Although this approach was subsequently scrapped in favour of a less flexible system of final warnings and reprimands ... research has demonstrated that cautioning plus, when backed by ... robust diversionary programmes, was remarkably effective in diverting youngsters from court and reducing their offending.[87]

At the same time it is important to remember that what actually *constituted* juvenile offending itself changed as a result of alterations in the law or of attitudes within society. Misconduct by youngsters that might be accepted in one decade was considered unacceptable in another. John Springhall has pointed out that the nature of police activity and different notions of the 'seriousness' of 'particular forms of adolescent behaviour and of how to deal with them' affected judicial decisions:

> Thus changes over time in the number of criminal damage or vandalism cases brought before the courts may well reflect certain alterations in public sensitivity and awareness of the problem, perhaps induced by

newspaper campaigns directed against particular forms of delinquency. The number of criminal damage offences increased rapidly in the 1970s ... from 17,000 offences in 1969 to 124,000 in 1977 ... The tendency for the general public to report cases of vandalism has also shown a marked increase from an exceptionally low rate of reporting of the most common types in the 1950s, such as window breaking or vandalising telephone kiosks on housing estates ... [The] growth of large self-service supermarkets in the 1960s may well have increased the opportunities for shoplifting, as the mass ownership of motor cars from the 1950s onwards has increased juvenile opportunities for car thefts ... Changes in the law ... have also affected recorded rates of delinquency. For instance, the 'sus' section of the 1824 Vagrancy Act was replaced by the Criminal Attempts Act in 1981, which considerably reduced police arrests on the charge of being a suspicious person loitering with intent to commit an Offence. Hence the juvenile crime rate can go up or down simply by changing the definition of what is a crime, or by changes in the way the police record criminal statistics, or by greater public sensitivity towards a previously disregarded misdemeanour.[88]

Among girls, shoplifting offences increased rapidly in the 1950s and 1960s, though in this regard juveniles often had a good chance of escaping prosecution for their offence. Most stores were reluctant to deal harshly with them, partly through fear of bad public relations or perhaps from a lack of confidence in the effectiveness of the juvenile courts.[89] This seems to have been the case with Jacquie, who began shop lifting with a group of friends in the 1990s, when she was fifteen. She came from a broken home, her parents having split up when she was twelve. Sarah Curtis, an experienced juvenile court magistrate, who interviewed her, considered parental discord and subsequent separation were key indicative factors for juvenile delinquency, together with low school achievement. A survey of adolescent boys in East London in the 1960s similarly concluded that 'educationally' the delinquent was 'bottom of the heap'.[90] As for Jacquie, she claimed she was just 'dragged in ... not into a bad crowd but they was doing shop-lifting for making their money'. There was also some competition to see 'who's got the most guts to go and do this', and she had little difficulty later in selling what she had stolen. The first time she was taken into custody was when she was with an older friend who had taken a bottle of wine. 'I got taken into custody for my own welfare because I was young ... it was quite late in the evening and my Mum had to come and get me ... Now I've been arrested 17 or 18 times ... When I was going to court I was getting conditional discharges, ten pound fines and fines for not attending on the right day ... Then last summer the courts ended up giving me a supervision order to last for one year'. Much of the motivation for her thefts was her need to purchase cannabis. She denied using 'hard' drugs like heroin or crack cocaine but needed to have a drawer full of cannabis, which she smoked in the evening. 'So many people do it; it's so easy to buy it; it just seems like smoking cigarettes ... Every youngster tries nearly everything there is, that's how much it's round this area'.[91]

Other young people interviewed by Sarah Curtis testified 'to the dominance of the drugs culture'. Daniel, a black boy of sixteen, who had been involved in a building society robbery with three older lads, confirmed that there was 'a big drugs scene ... I don't do it – only small weed [cannabis] and that'.

Drug taking among the young was already under way in the 1960s but increased sharply in the subsequent decades, with cannabis especially popular among teenagers. Indeed in 1972 the annual report of the north-east London probation service noted that most young clients in Barking were 'well versed in the whys and wherefores' of cannabis smoking and that it was 'the "thing to do" amongst teenagers in Redbridge'. An investigation of drug-taking in Bromley around the same time, however, found amphetamine use most common up to the age of seventeen. 'Pills were taken to energise the taker to stay awake and lose inhibition at all-night parties', despite their often unpleasant after effects.[92]

Among girls, despite concern about rising levels of shop lifting and the like, it was the morality issue which, as always, caused most anxiety, at a time when teenage prostitution and teenage pregnancy were on the increase, especially during the 1980s and 1990s. Sharon Boyle claims it was common for the country's courts and police forces to adopt a policy of cautioning teenage girls found soliciting, even though many were not legally old enough to consent to intercourse. In 1989, the Children's Society provided figures showing that 104 police cautions had been issued to schoolgirls for soliciting in England and Wales. Of these, nine of the youngsters were aged fourteen, thirty-two were fifteen and sixty were sixteen. In 1991 that total had risen to 161, with five aged thirteen, ten aged fourteen, thirty-four aged fifteen and one hundred and eleven aged sixteen. In that year, West Yorkshire alone gave thirty-three official warnings to teenagers and Greater Manchester twenty-nine.[93]

Attention was drawn to the strong links between children who had been in care and juvenile prostitution. One reason suggested for this was that many girls prior to coming into local authority care had had 'some experience of sexually satisfying a man'. If they ran away from a local authority home or left it and were on the streets without money they knew they had 'something to fall back on'.[94] Similar motives were attributed to girls who ran away from approved schools. In the early 1950s concern was expressed at the ease with which such girls got lifts from long distance lorry drivers. One absconder, who was picked up by a lorry driver in the spring of 1951, was said to have 'travelled continuously for a fortnight between Swansea, Birmingham and London, in the course of which she was transferred from lorry to lorry. She was finally picked up by the police at Cardiff in a shocking condition'.[95] Almost three years later a Home Office memorandum expressed anxiety that approved school absconders who accepted lifts from lorry drivers were exposing themselves 'to considerable risk of infection, as it is an established fact that a large percentage of long distance lorry drivers have venereal disease.' The writer welcomed a recent decision by Calne magistrates court in Wiltshire to prosecute a driver who had harboured two sixteen-year-old girls who had absconded from St Joseph's Approved School in Marshfield. He was convicted and fined £10 with £4 10s costs. The chairman of the bench warned that future penalties 'might be more severe'.[96]

A second reason why girls who had been in care might turn to prostitution related to the very mixed population of children's homes. Some came from families where the mother was a prostitute, and the children would share their experiences with one another and encourage others by telling them it was an easy way to make money. 'If a girl goes on the run for weeks or months there is going to be a great deal of discussion on her return about how she survived. To other youngsters, she is a success because she got away and she might glamorise life on the streets'. According to Sharon Boyle, of twenty-six juveniles cautioned for prostitution in Bradford in 1991, a third were in care. 'A girl becomes embroiled in a very short time. She gets a buzz out of life if someone comes along, says he loves her and takes her to pubs and clubs ... She believes some attention is better than none and prostitution is the only way she sees to keep or attract a boyfriend.'[97]

For other girls, who were not in care, going on the streets was often a commercial decision. Jackie, who was born in the South of England in 1961, became a prostitute in the mid-1970s. She first went out with a friend, wearing school uniform: 'we did a double for £10', that is £5 each. She carried on with this, earning about £10 a night, until she was taken up by two Chinese men. who paid her and her friend £50 each. When she went home, her mother 'looked at her and said she could not stop her'. She was just fourteen but told the 'punters' she was sixteen. She then began bringing clients to her home – two a night – and had sexual intercourse with them on her mother's bed. She was earning £20 a night, of which she gave her mother £10. With her own £10 she purchased cigarettes, cosmetics and clothes, as well as keeping some cash 'for clubbing ... [I] felt elated – I had money'. She 'never had any trouble from the older girls. They knew how old I was'. However, they warned her to be careful when she got into a car, and she always took contraceptives with her. She claimed that part of her motivation was to give cash to her mother. 'I think I did it to get her love'. Later she tried to break away from the life, becoming a student for a time, but in the end it was 'easy money ... you always come back'.⁹⁸ When she was interviewed in the late 1990s she was still working as a prostitute.

Alongside these individual developments in the post-war years, however, there was emerging a generation of fashion-conscious working-class youngsters, anxious to make their mark by the way they dressed and behaved. During the 1950s this meant, among youths, the emergence of the 'Teddy Boys', dressed in long drape jackets, thick-sole 'brothel creeper' shoes, bootlace ties, narrow, drain-pipe trousers, and 'greased, duck-tail haircuts'.⁹⁹ The vogue for so-called Edwardian dress started among the well-to-do as a reaction to war-time austerity, but by 1953 it had penetrated working-class districts, first in London and then in the provinces. It seems to have been taken up first in the Elephant and Castle area of South London, among market porters, van boys, roadworkers, general labourers, and the like. They had drifted into dull, undemanding jobs offering little hope of promotion, and so their leisure pursuits became a means by which they could enjoy the 'excitement, self-respect and autonomy ... so conspicuously absent from work'.¹⁰⁰

The emergence of the Teddy boys, who went about in large groups and became involved in gang fights with rivals from other districts, was regarded with suspicion and alarm by the older generation. This was especially so when they became involved in acts of vandalism, street robberies, cinema riots, attacks on the owners of cafes and stalls, and on late-night bus crews. Their aggressive, anti-social stance was incomprehensible to much of the general public, and many gang members also displayed racist attitudes. A London lad interviewed by T. R. Fyvel in the late 1950s, when the Teddy boy cult was already waning, claimed that he and his friends did not

> have so many fights any more. We used to have them, with knives too ... [It] was the excitement!... I remember one time six of us went to get one of the Blacks; I didn't know what he'd done but anyway he was a Spade, but then the coppers chased us but we all chucked our knives away as we run and when they searched us they found nothing. When they finished we all got into a taxi and went down west. We just didn't care: it was the excitement, different from going every night to the pictures where nothing ever [happened]. One time we used to go regularly to the Angel where there's a lot of cafés and we aimed to start trouble with the Greeks and Turks, start a punch-up. They're Cypriots ... grease monkeys we used to call them – our chaps all hated them. ¹⁰¹

Public feelings of hostility towards Teddy boys intensified during 1954, fanned by reports in the popular press highlighting their lawless activities, real or exaggerated, and the acts of violence that they undoubtedly committed. To many their existence seemed aimless, sitting in milk bars and cafés where they listened to the music of juke boxes, visiting dance halls and cinemas, and taking little interest in the 'respectable' organised recreation offered by youth clubs and sporting bodies. James Patrick, who got to know a Glasgow gang in the 1970s, noted that although they visited the local youth club from time to time 'to relieve their boredom', that was the limit of their commitment. Its traditional diet of 'ping-pong, Coca-Cola and five-a-side football' failed to meet the 'thirst for thrills' of the teenagers he had met. 'Society must provide socially acceptable outlets for aggression, adventure and excitement' was his conclusion.[102] But many critics saw firm discipline and appropriate punishment as what was needed, rather than any pandering to social needs. It was in these circumstances that in 1958 the Conservative party annual conference called for a return of the birch, and complained of the 'leniency shown in the past by the courts of this country'.[103] Magistrates, for their part, demanded more detention centres, with their 'short, sharp, shock' approach, and it was in response to these demands and in an attempt to 'De-Teddyfy' the Teddy boys' that the then Home Secretary increased the number of detention centres.[104]

It was in 1954 that dance hall managers, café proprietors, publicans and cinema managers began banning Teddy boys because of fears of gang violence and rowdy conduct. Newspapers fed the mood with their stories of 'mixed-up teenagers' and 'rebels without a cause'.[105]

Some sympathetic observers like the Revd. Douglas Griffiths, a prominent Methodist minister and youth worker, described much of the youngsters' 'swagger' as 'bogus. Deep down they are in a bit of a funk about H-bombs and insecurity. Limelight and police action continue to make thuggery seem exciting and important'.[106] He succeeded in enticing a number of Teddy boys to join the youth club he ran.

Some of the youngsters who were being so fiercely condemned in the media answered back in the columns of the newspapers. In an interview in the *Daily Sketch* early in May 1954, Owen Summers, an unemployed eighteen-year-old living with his family in Battersea Park Road in London, expressed his frustration. He had had eight jobs since leaving school three years before, but complained of the prejudice he had faced because of his Teddy boy appearance:

> I go after jobs and don't get them. I go to dance halls and I'm told to leave. I go to cinemas and they won't admit me. I talk on street corners and the police move me on. Why? Because I am a Teddy boy. A boy

WE read Owen Summers's article in the Daily Sketch concerning the Teddy Boys. The only bundle (fight) that we've had in Kingston between rival gangs was when the Elephant and Castle boys came down from London.

The Teddy Boys are polite, never swear in front of a girl; sometimes they might let slip a word, but they always apologise. They treat girls with respect.—**FROM 12 FEMALE ENTHUSIASTS OF THE "EDWARDIAN SET," Kingston, Surrey.**

YOU have bestowed a far too clean and generous title in Teddy Boys, which likens them to our "Edward the Peacemaker" days.

I would like to see you call them "drainpipe slugs" or "loutish loonies."

Why not ask Pungent Post readers to suggest suitable names? Even the dress for the gentleman has been killed by the gang thugs.—**D. M., Tunbridge Wells (name and address supplied).**

Daily Sketch, 8 May 1954. Divided views on the 'Teddy Boy' phenomenon as expressed in readers' letters.

who wears a suit which labels me as a trouble-maker, a hooligan ... I am classed with troublemakers who dress like me ... We get insulted in the street – that's why we go around in crowds, seven or eight-handed.[107]

Another lad from New Malden in Surrey also complained about the prejudice he faced because of the way he dressed. He claimed to attend church three times a week and to take a Sunday school class, as well as digging someone's garden free of charge on Saturdays. He belonged to a youth club, too: 'a lot more boys and young men are very much like myself. We pay for our suits with money we have worked for hard ... I don't want to be tough. I want to wear ... good suits'.[108]

By the late 1950s the Teddy boy era was passing away, only to be replaced by new adolescent 'folk devils', as Stanley Cohen has labelled them. These were the Mods and the Rockers, who came to public notice when they descended upon seaside towns on Bank holidays during the 1960s and created disturbances. The Mods wore fashionable clothes and many of them rode on scooters. Music was also an important facet of the 'Mod' scene. On the whole they came from a semi-skilled manual background. The Rockers, their rivals, were rougher and more macho. Typically they wore black leather and rode on motor-cycles. Their world, writes Stanley Cohen, was that of 'the motorway and the transport cafes'. In practice, many young people were attracted to one or other of the groups without possessing these distinguishing characteristics.[109]

It was in 1964 that they first made headlines with their invasion of seaside towns at the Easter, Whitsun and August bank holidays. They began with Clacton, a small, not very affluent, east coast resort. According to Stanley Cohen, who has researched the 'Mods and Rockers' phenomenon, Easter 1964 was cold and bleak and Clacton offered few amenities to entertain the young people who had arrived for the holiday weekend. Their boredom and feelings of frustration were aggravated by rumours that café proprietors and barmen were refusing to serve some of them. Trouble began when a few youths started scuffling on the pavement and throwing stones at one another. Those with motor-cycles and scooters then began riding up and down, windows were broken and some beach huts were wrecked. The fact that the police were initially unable to deal with the disturbances added to public alarm.[110] Although the damage done was relatively minor, the press seized on the event at a time when there was little other news of interest. Lurid headlines appeared, such as 'Day of Terror by Scooter Groups' in the *Daily Telegraph* and 'Wild Ones Invade Seaside – 97 Arrested' in the *Daily Mirror*. The youngsters were said to be 'drunk with notoriety' and 'hell-bent for destruction'. It is perhaps indicative of the exaggerated reporting associated with this event that a few days after the Clacton disturbances the assistant editor of the *Daily Mirror* admitted in conversation that the matter had been 'a little over-reported'.[111]

Further 'invasions' took place at Whitsuntide and in August, with Brighton, Margate and Bournemouth making the headlines at Whitsun and Hastings at the August bank holidays. On 19 May 1964, *The Times*, for example, carried a headline '1,000 Youths fight at Brighton', over a report that the 'battles' on the previous day had led to the arrest of seventy-five young people. According to *The Times*, in one incident alone a thousand youngsters had 'waged a running scrimmage near the aquarium. Deck chairs and rubbish were thrown as the gangs moved to the east end of the seafront'. An investigation by the newspaper revealed that many of those taking part came from 'respectable' homes and that, as at Clacton, it was an over simplification to divide them into Mods and Rockers. Many had simply come for a day out and had then been 'caught up in the excitement'. Among the facts highlighted by the newspaper was that parents often had little knowledge of their offspring's whereabouts during the evenings and at weekends, let alone over a bank holiday. 'A father of a 15-year-old boy was asked "where did your boy sleep on Sunday?" "I have no idea", he said. "I think he was camping"'.[112] In reality, according to the reporter, the boy had been sleeping under the pier. He also commented, much as his predecessors had done in the previous decade about the Teddy boys, that the sterile daily existence of many young people was a factor in the way they chose to spend their leisure.

> The general impression is that after spending evenings on end sitting in coffee bars listening to juke boxes, they get bored and seize on any new excitement. The 'Mods' and 'Rockers' cult is a way of showing their independence and a need to be different.
>
> But it is an error to associate the troubles of Brighton and Margate purely with scooters and motorcycles. Large numbers of young people, from London in particular, went by train or car with one or two friends, wearing ordinary casual holiday clothes.[113]

An analysis of some of those arrested at Margate came to much the same conclusion. Of forty-four youngsters appearing in court the day after the disturbances, thirty-seven were charged with threatening behaviour and three of those also with possessing an offensive weapon. Five were solely on an offensive weapon charge and one, it was alleged, had caused actual bodily harm as well as carrying a weapon. One was charged with inciting a breach of the peace. All were found guilty and received punishments ranging from conditional discharges, fines and a spell in a detention centre to three months' in prison for two defendants aged over twenty-one.

According to researchers into the Margate troubles, whatever those found guilty thought of their punishment, their friends regarded it as 'a great joke' or 'they looked up to me after that'. The chairman of the Margate bench, for his part, labelled them 'petty sawdust Caesars'.[114]

The Brighton survey also revealed what was to be a growing trend among young people, namely the taking of drugs. Of a hundred Brighton 'Mods' questioned, sixty-two said they took drugs; among a hundred Rockers, forty-two admitted to doing so.[115]

It was in these circumstances that the Home Secretary, Henry Brooke, appealed to parents to take more interest in their children's activities. He also announced the introduction of a Bill requiring an offender to pay 'reasonable compensation' for damage done, as well as facing a fine and possible imprisonment for offences committed in these kinds of incidents.[116]

The 'Mods' and 'Rockers' era eventually faded away to be followed by other youth cults and fashions, such as the hippies, Hells Angels and punks. Football hooliganism, too, became a cause for concern, with the 1978 annual Conservative party conference again demanding a return of the birch and the introduction of 'Saturday night floggings' for football hooligans.[117]

In the 1970s and 1980s drugs became increasingly important as causes of juvenile offending, and in teenage gang culture. They were also common within young offender institutions. Paul V., interviewed in the late 1990s in one such institution, claimed to have taken heroin and cocaine while he was inside, but he had not enjoyed them. 'Cannabis is the main one. It is all over'. There were also fights among the inmates over drugs.[118]

This development had its effect on juvenile crime figures so that by 2005, 22 per cent of all male offenders aged from ten to seventeen had been convicted of selling drugs, compared to 31 per cent found guilty of property offences and 47 per cent of violence. Among girls in that age group, by contrast, only 7 per cent were found guilty of selling drugs, compared to 43 per cent convicted of property offences and 49 per cent of violence. Much of the violence involved assaults on other young people. Most of the assaults took place at or near school and involved perpetrators of approximately the same age. Many assaults were 'deeply disturbing incidents of Bullying', and in recent times sometimes involved the use of knives.

A report in February 2008 claimed that a 'fear factor' led teenagers to carry weapons to protect themselves in the streets, however false a security that might prove in practice. There was rising alarm, too, at the number of juveniles murdered by other young people. In 2007, 26 teenagers were killed in London, 16 of them after knife attacks. Already by late May,

14 had been killed in 2008, most of them as a result of being stabbed. Sometimes the fatalities arose out of gang conflicts involving drugs or as a result of 'binge' drinking by the perpetrators. But there were cases, too, like that of Paul Erhahon, aged fourteen, who was stabbed with a sword after 'straying into the path' of young thugs, members of the Cathall Boys gang, who had been told 'to prove themselves' by older members of their Leytonstone East London gang. Two of the three youngsters convicted of Paul's murder at the Old Bailey were aged fifteen and a third was aged sixteen. Two others, aged sixteen and nineteen, respectively, were found guilty of manslaughter. A sustained press campaign on the issue of knife crime in the spring of 2008 was followed by a proliferation of Government initiatives on the subject and by measures to curb under-age drinking. By early June the Prime Minister himself had become involved in the debate, when he confirmed that anyone aged sixteen or seventeen caught in possession of a knife for the first time could expect to be taken to court and prosecuted rather than merely cautioned, as had been the case previously. Children under sixteen found carrying a blade in public were to be sent on day-long courses to educate them about the injuries caused by stabbing. Parents could also become involved and might receive parenting orders.[119]

During the final decades of the twentieth century race, too, emerged as a major point of friction. That applied to the 'sus' law which black teenagers felt unfairly targeted them, before its repeal in 1981. But the problems of high unemployment in the 1980s, which disproportionately affected African-Caribbean youngsters and the fact that many were living in deprived inner city areas added to the difficulties. It was in the late 1970s that the issue of black involvement in street crime came to the fore, with the media and political commentators 'linking "mugging" with the problems of inner city decay in general and "black youth" in particular ... The mugging panics of the late 1970s spawned a strategy of high profile policing black localities ... This strategy was prosecuted via the extensive use of police "stop-and-search" procedures and a sharp rise in the numbers of black defendants attracting prison sentences', declares Anita Kalunta-Crumpton.[120]

The policy applied particularly to London but was also put into operation elsewhere, such as in black inner city neighbourhoods in Liverpool, Greater Manchester and the West Midlands. In 1984-85 a higher proportion of young black people aged fourteen to twenty were sentenced to immediate custody in the Metropolitan Police District than any other ethnic group. The level of custodial remand for these youngsters was also disproportionately high.[121] Not surprisingly a survey conducted among young black men in the capital in 1980-81 presented an unfavourable picture of police officers as 'racially prejudiced in their attitudes, and discriminatory in their actions'. One youth claimed that he had been stopped by the police on his way to work and had been told that there had been a burglary in the neighbourhood and they wanted to search him. They went through his holdall, his jacket trouser pockets, and even his hair and woollen hat. What annoyed him most was when they opened his lunchbox and looked through the contents before throwing them on the ground. They then left him.[122]

It was against this background and at a time of rising unemployment that the Brixton riots took place in April 1981, as young black men vented their anger and frustration at the conditions under which they were living. The disturbances began in the Railton Road area and led to the looting of shops, the destruction of vehicles, and attacks on private property. After four days of rioting almost two hundred arrests had been made and twenty-six buildings had been damaged by fire, including three public houses, five houses, and two boutiques. A total of seventy-six shops and houses were badly damaged.[123] Significantly, however, in a debate on the disturbances in the Commons on 13 April, 1981, one MP pointed out that during the previous year unemployment among young blacks had quadrupled, while another MP referred to a 'Niagara of discontent' existing among young black men who were 'discriminated against over jobs, housing' and other things.[124]

The disturbances led to the appointment of a public inquiry under Lord Scarman to investigate the causes of this upsurge in violence. According to the *Annual Register*, the immediate 'trigger had been an incident on 10 April when a crowd of some hundred black youths attacked police officers who were questioning a black boy found with stab wounds.' Police reinforcements were called in and this added to the tension, before the mob was dispersed. However, it was on the following day, 11 April, that serious rioting began.[125] As a result of the Scarman inquiry, changes were made to policing. Significantly Lord Scarman also highlighted the unemployment, poor housing and inadequate educational provision which characterised inner city areas like Brixton.[126]

During early July in the same year the rioting spread to Toxteth, a depressed district in Liverpool. Here the trouble started when policemen investigating a stolen car were attacked by a gang of youths, black and white, who were estimated to number around one hundred and fifty. They took over the district's main thoroughfare, wrecking cars, looting and burning shops, and attacking police with an array of missiles. The violence was resumed on the following Monday, when a hospital was looted and medical staff attacked. After three days, the main thoroughfare itself was left in ruins. Soon after, the trouble spread to the Moss Side district of Manchester, with hundreds of young men and boys, most of them black, rampaging through the streets, 'smashing windows, looting shops and attacking the police'.[127] Significantly one of the Liverpool MPs pointed out that there was a 40 per cent unemployment rate in the area, with 'youngsters doing absolutely nothing'.[128] In the following days more rioting followed in Brixton, Southall and other areas of London, as well as in Reading, Liverpool, Hull and Preston. As the *Annual Register* pointed out, all of it was of much the same kind – 'young people defying police and opening the way to destruction and looting in which some older people took part'.[129] The government, meanwhile, gave its backing to the forces of law and order but it also appointed a special task force after the Toxteth disturbances, to investigate the conditions which had provoked them. Recommendations were made to bring about redevelopment on Merseyside, and various administrative changes were proposed to alter the method of disbursement of public expenditure in inner-city areas.[130]

The riots of 1981 were signs of the simmering discontent among some teenagers at their unsatisfactory daily lives and their inability to find work. Several other relatively minor disturbances occurred during the early 1980s, followed in 1985 by more serious unrest leading to riots in Brixton, the Handsworth area of Birmingham and on the Broadwater Farm estate at Tottenham, in north London. All led to extensive damage to property, arson, looting and bitter conflicts between the police and the rioters. Two years later in the Chapeltown area of Leeds, as Bill Osgerby notes, 'developing tensions between the police and black youngsters climaxed in two days of disorder in which shops, cars and police vehicles were petrol-bombed.' By the beginning of the 1990s trouble had spread to Oxford's Blackbird Leys housing estate, with gangs of local youths fighting running battles with riot police. They were attempting to end the practice of 'hotting', or the execution of 'high-speed stunts in stolen high-performance cars.' On run-down housing estates in Yorkshire, Humberside and the East Midlands, boredom, lack of leisure facilities and high unemployment encouraged some youngsters to seek 'status and excitement in car theft and high-speed chases', with 'joy riding' becoming a serious problem. In 1991 the government recognised the danger of this by introducing a new offence of Aggravated Vehicle Taking, 'to cover car thefts that had been compounded by dangerous driving'. In these circumstances Bill Osgerby has concluded that the 1980s and early 1990s 'witnessed a steady polarisation within British youth. While the course of economic change saw some people prosper, many others faced a bleak future'.[131]

A minority of young people, faced with high unemployment and living in deprived areas, reacted by turning to crime, as a way of seeking an 'alternative' livelihood. This ranged from drug dealing, illicit street trading, benefit frauds, organised shop lifting and burglary to straightforward theft. In the case of one run-down council estate in Manchester during the 1980s, many of these illegitimate careers were controlled by two notorious 'hard families' who lived on the estate and operated various rackets from organised prostitution and drug dealing to commissioning large-scale shop lifting, burglaries and robberies.[132] Similar gang-controlled criminals operated in deprived areas elsewhere.

But if this was bleak side of life for sections of the teenage population during the 1980s, by the end of the decade some efforts were again being made to reduce the number of youngsters coming before the courts through the 1991 Criminal Justice Act. This envisaged an end to custody for children under fifteen, while the juvenile courts themselves were re-named youth courts.

The change proved short-lived, however, with continuing high crime figures among a hard core of young people, in March 1993 the then Home Secretary, Kenneth Clarke, announced a new strategy designed to deal with the 'comparatively small number of school-age children … responsible for a high proportion of crime, particularly burglary and car crime, in many parts of the country'. Under current legislation the courts were unable to impose a custodial sentence on them. 'I believe that it is not in the interests of school-age children that they should be left at large in the community if they are out of control, playing truant … and repeatedly committing criminal acts against the general public', he declared. As a consequence it was proposed to introduce secure training centres to deal with persistent offenders aged from twelve to fourteen. The centres were to be established by private organisations, voluntary bodies and the public sector, with the central government purchasing their facilities. The aim was so to change the behaviour of young offenders that they were 'no longer a threat to society'.[133] The 1994 Criminal Justice and Public Order Act therefore created a new custodial sentence, a Secure Training Order, for children aged from twelve to fourteen. Just how effective a deterrent it was, however, remains open to question. Certainly James H., who was sent to a secure unit when he was fourteen, thought it was 'like a holiday home'. He found a young offender institution very different: 'there is no freedom here', he stated when interviewed in one such institution. By the early twenty-first century young offender institutions were being described as 'beset with brutality, suicide, self-harm and barbaric conditions' and yet unable to prevent re-offending.[134]

The 1994 legislation marked the start of a more punitive approach by both government and society at large towards the misdoings of children and adolescents. 'Childhood', it has been said, became 'the most intensively governed sector of personal existence'. The preoccupation with crime prevention and community safety led to a growing intolerance of acts of petty vandalism and anti-social behaviour among the young. In 1998 the Crime and Disorder Act provided, among other things, for the introduction of anti-social behaviour orders (ASBOS), designed to show zero tolerance towards minor offences and general bad behaviour. ASBOS prohibited the defendant from doing anything mentioned in the order for a minimum period of two years, and non-compliance was to be regarded as a criminal matter.[135] Although the new orders proved effective in some communities, in others they were criticised for failing to bring about improvements and for being regarded by offending teenagers as a badge of honour. Overall the number of ASBOS issued dropped from 4,123 in 2005 to 2,706 in 2006 and Home Office figures showed that breach rates among teenagers in the latter year had risen to 61 per cent. In these circumstances, according to *The Guardian* of 8 May, 2008, fresh initiatives were being tried, such as Acceptable Behaviour Contracts. These were written agreements between a young person, the local housing office or registered social landlord, and the local police by which the youngsters agreed not to carry out a series of identifiable behavioural acts which were defined as anti-social. The contracts were aimed primarily at youngsters aged between ten and eighteen.

CONCLUSION

In the early twenty-first century, therefore, youth crime became a matter of concern to the general public, the media and the central government, with a plethora of differing policies and nostrums brought forward to tackle the problem. These could include, as in Essex in 2007-8, the harassing of a small number of badly behaved youths by the police, by filming them and visiting them at home. Although the mass unemployment which helped to fuel adolescent crime in the 1980s had disappeared, areas of deprivation and limited work opportunities remained, as did other factors likely to encourage young people to resort to criminal activities. These included drug taking and dealing, with territorial gang rivalries associated with the vending of drugs. Knife crime, too, as we have seen, gave rise to increasing concern in regard to young people. A report commissioned in 2004 by the Bridge House Trust found that: 'Fear and victimisation [played] the most significant role in a young person's decision to carry a knife or weapon', although for some it was also 'a means of acquiring status'.[136] This was especially true of children who had failed at school or experienced other forms of social exclusion. Peer pressure, too, could encourage violence among some young people, as applied in the murder of Paul Erhahon in London. Lack of discipline in the home was also blamed, particularly in the case of one-parent families. In 2008 it was suggested that as many as 70 per cent of teenage offenders came from homes with only one resident parent.

Yet, despite these problems it is important to remember that juvenile delinquency in this century, as in earlier ones, affects a small minority of young people only and that, at least in recent years, press campaigns highlighting particular offences committed by children have helped to fuel what have frequently been spurious 'moral panics'. Politicians, too, have added to the unease by identifying youth offending as a sign of a wider breakdown in society or a symbol of its moral bankruptcy. It is no such thing. As Alan Marlow has written, 'each generation of young people tends to stimulate fears and anxieties among its parents' generation', even though research confirms that for most youngsters, offending proved to be merely a 'rite of passage' to a settled adulthood. Significantly in June 2008 the four children's commissioners for England, Scotland, Wales and Northern Ireland drew attention to public attitudes that demonised teenagers. They also commented on the large number of youngsters incarcerated each year in secure training centres and young offender institutions. In these between January 2004 and September 2005 forcible physical restraint was used on inmates on more than seven thousand occasions. This involved painful nose, rib and thumb holds, described by the authorities as 'distraction techniques'. According to the commissioners on 'many occasions' these techniques had caused injury to the children.[137]

As preceding chapters have shown, children and young people have transgressed against the norms and laws of adult society for centuries. There has never been a 'golden age' of order and security of the kind some nostalgic commentators suggest. 'Historical myth proposed that our contemporary problems are a break with the past', declared Geoffrey Pearson. 'Historical realism shows that they are not'.[138]

But perhaps the last word should be left to Professor Rod Morgan, a former chairman of the Youth Justice Board for England and Wales. In 2005 he expressed concern that in Britain the 'discourse of control rather than care too often predominates in discussions about young people and their occasionally disturbing behaviour'. Even the advocates of restorative justice, designed to bring about a degree of conciliation between offender and victim, in practice seemed more interested in ensuring that the transgressors faced up to the consequences of their actions rather than in taking part in a process designed to heal rifts.[139] In February 2010 *The Times* noted that England and Wales were 'the only countries in Western Europe' habitually to imprison children under the age of 14.[140]

ENDNOTES

Abbreviations

Brit. Lib. = British Library
HMSO = Her Majesty's Stationery Office
NA = The National Archives at Kew.
P.P. = Parliamentary Papers

Chapter 1

1. *Oxford Times*, 2 March, 2007. *The Guardian*, 16 February, 2007 for two examples of the growing concern about the criminal young. *Glasgow Evening Times*, 7, 8, 10 and 13 February, 2006 for details of gang fights and the gang culture in Glasgow.
2. Roy Porter, *English Society in the Eighteenth Century* (Harmondsworth, 1994 edn) pp. 54 and 357.
3. Peter King, *Crime, Justice and Discretion in England 1740-1820* (Oxford, 2000), pp. 173-174. Leon Radzinowicz, *A History of English Criminal Law and its Administration from 1750* (London, 1948), Vol. 1, p. 11. See also *The Times*, 20 September, 1785.
4. Wiley B. Sanders ed., *Juvenile Offenders for a Thousand Years* (Chapel Hill: University of North Carolina, 1970), p. 35.
5. Michael Ignatieff, *A Just Measure of Pain. The Penitentiary in the Industrial Revolution, 1750-1850* (London and Basingstoke, 1978), p. 16.
6. J. M. Beattie, 'The Pattern of Crime in England 1660-1800' in *Past and Present*, No. 62 (February 1974), p. 79. On one occasion around the middle of the eighteenth century a Wiltshire widow who sent her two young sons out to collect fuel was fined for 'receiving stolen wood'.
7. 17 Geo. II c.5. *An Act to amend and make more effectual the laws relating to Rogues and Vagabonds, 1744.*
8. Calendar of Prisoners at Quarter Sessions and in the New Prison or County Bridewell, Winchester, Midsummer and Michaelmas Sessions, 1806, at Hampshire Record Office. All the other Calendars for the county's quarter sessions subsequently cited are in the Record Office.
9. Elizabeth Crittall ed., *The Justicing Notebook of William Hunt 1744-1749* (Wiltshire Record Society, Vol. 37 for 1981), pp. 14, 30 and 76 (nos. 128, 130 and 515).

10. Peter King and Joan Noel, 'The Origins of "The Problem of Juvenile Delinquency"; The Growth of Juvenile Prosecutions in London in the Late Eighteenth and Early Nineteenth Centuries' in *Criminal Justice History*, Vol. IV (1993), p. 28.

11. Alan F. Cirket ed., *Samuel Whitbread's Notebooks 1810-11, 1813-14* (Bedfordshire Historical Record Society, Vol. 50, 1971), pp. 22 and 68.

12. Calendar of the Prisoners at Quarter Sessions and in the New Prison or County Bridewell, Winchester, Midsummer Sessions, 1802.

13. Calendar of Prisoners at Quarter Sessions and in the New Prison or County Bridewell, Winchester, Epiphany 1792 and Q9/1/448; Calendars of Prisoners for Quarter Sessions. Epiphany 1793 and Midsummer 1793.

14. Calendar of Prisoners at the Quarter Sessions and in the New Prison or County Bridewell, Winchester, Easter 1791 and Q9/1/445.

15. King, *Crime, Justice and Discretion*, p. 105. J. J. Tobias, *Crime and Industrial Society in the 19th Century* London, 1967), pp. 57-58. David Philips, *Crime and Authority in Victorian England. The Black Country 1835-860* (London, 1977), p. 42.

16. Quoted in Philips, *Crime and Authority*, p. 42.

17. Dorothy George, *London Life in the Eighteenth Century* (Harmondsworth, 1965 edn) p. 47. Porter, *English Society*, pp. 54, 381 and 384.

18. Quoted in Tobias, *Crime and Industrial Society*, pp. 22-23.

19. Tobias, *Crime and Industrial Society*, pp. 33, 38 and 39.

20. Roy Porter, *London. A Social History* (London, 2000 edn), p. 185.

21. J. M. Beattie, *Policing and Punishment in London, 1660-1750* (Oxford, 2002 edn), p. 29. Sanders, *Juvenile Offenders*, p. 41.

22. Sanders, *Juvenile Offenders*, p. 51.

23. Sanders, *Juvenile Offenders*, pp. 54, and 62-63.

24. Peter King, 'Decision-makers and Decision-making in the English Criminal Law, 1750-1800' in *The Historical Journal*, Vol. 27, No. 1 (1984), p. 40.

25. Sanders, *Juvenile Offenders*, p. 68.

26. Sanders, *Juvenile Offenders*, p. 68.

27. George, *London Life*, p. 387.

28. Notebook of Sir John Silvester, Bart., 1816 at the Brit. Lib., MS. Egerton 3710, ff. 11 and 13-13b. Another fence, John Godbier of St Giles kept a chandler's shop and fenced from about twenty young boys, 'chiefly Cheese, Butter &c. as also watches'.

29. *Report from the Select Committee on the Police of the Metropolis*, P.P. 1828 , Vol. VI, Evidence of Sir Richard Birnie, p. 34.

30. *Report from the Committee on the State of the Police of the Metropolis*, P.P. 1816, Vol. V, Evidence of Philip Holdsworth, p. 262.

31. William Augustus Miles, *A Letter to Lord John Russell concerning Juvenile Delinquency together with Suggestions concerning a Reformatory Establishment* (Shrewsbury, 1837) p. 8. This pamphlet is in the Brit. Lib. 8289.bb.37(4).

32. Miles, *A Letter to Lord John Russell*, p. 9.

33. Robert Hughes, *The Fatal Shore. A History of Transportation of Convicts to Australia 1787-1868* (London, 2003 edn), p. 72.

34. Calendar of Prisoners in Reading Bridewell, Midsummer 1791, Q/SR/230 at Berkshire Record Office and Examination of William Wheeler, Francis Bury and John Warren before the Revd George Watts, at the same reference.

35. Peter King, 'The Rise of Juvenile Delinquency in England 1780-1840: Changing Patterns of Perception and Prosecution' in *Past and Present*, No. 160 (August, 1998), pp. 123 and 151.

36. King. 'The Rise of Juvenile Delinquency'. pp. 157-158.
37. *Report from the Committee on the State of the Police of the Metropolis, 1816*, p. 222. Other factors, according to Sir John, included the increase in the system of outdoor apprenticeships and the growing number of offspring of convicts and of soldiers who had been killed in the recent war and who were 'let loose on the public'. (p. 223). King, 'The Rise of Juvenile Delinquency', p. 138. In 1670, the proportion of children under fourteen in the total population had been estimated at 29 per cent.
38. King, 'The Rise of Juvenile Delinquency', p. 142.
39. Ignatieff, *A Just Measure of Pain*, p. 156.
40. Mary Thale ed., *The Autobiography of Francis Place (1771-1854)* (Cambridge, 1972), pp. 76 and 78.
41. Joan Lane, *Apprenticeship in England 1600-1914* (London, 1996), p. 205.
42. *Salisbury and Winchester Journal*, 8 March, 1779.
43. Lane, *Apprenticeship in England*, p. 201.
44. George, *London Life*, p. 277. A calenderer was a specialist clothworker engaged in the smoothing and glazing of cloth among other things.
45. 18 Geo. III c.19. *An Act for the Payment of Costs to Parties ... and for the more effective Payment of Charges to Witnesses and Prosecutors of any Larceny or other Felony, 1778*.
46. King, 'The Rise of Juvenile Delinquency', pp. 151, 161 and 162. Tobias, *Crime and Industrial Society*, p. 37.
47. *First Report of the Philanthropic Society Instituted in London, September 1788, for the Prevention of Crimes* (1789) pp. 22 and 23 in the Brit. Lib., T.165(3).
48. Donna T. Andrew, *Philanthropy and Police. London Charity in the Eighteenth Century* (Princeton, New Jersey, 1989), pp. 117 and 119.
49. Sir Leon Radzinowicz and Roger Hood, A *History of English Criminal Law*, Vol. 5 (London,1986), pp. 133-134.
50. Sanders, *Juvenile Offenders*, pp. 52-53
51. Radzinowicz and Hood, *A History of English Criminal Law*, Vol. 5, p. 134.
52. Sanders, *Juvenile Offenders*, pp. 53-54.
53. *Notice to the Philanthropic Society Instituted September 1788*, Brit. Lib T.165(3).
54. Julius Carlebach, *Caring for Children in Trouble* (London, 1998 edn) pp. 6, 8 and 11.
55. Old Bailey Sessions Papers, 1791-92. December 1791. p. 22, No. 22 and Newgate Criminal Register HO.26/1, December 1791 at the NA.
56. Sanders, *Juvenile Offenders*, pp. 80-81.
57. *An Account of the Nature and Views of the Philanthropic Society* (1799), p. 15, at the Brit. Lib 1129.b.52.
58. *Annual Report of the Philanthropic Society for 1816*, pp. 9-10 at the Brit. Lib. 8285.d.1(1).
59. *An Account of the Nature and Present State of the Philanthropic Society* (1821), p. 9 at the Brit. Lib. 8285.d.1(1). Carlebach, *Caring for Children in Trouble*, p. 11.
60. Carlebach, *Caring for Children in Trouble*, p. 9.
61. Carlebach, *Caring for Children in Trouble*, p. 14.
62. Carlebach, *Caring for Children in Trouble*, p. 15.
63. *Annual Report of the Society for the Philanthropic Reformation of Juvenile Offenders, 1848*, pp. 11, 12 and 15-17 at the Brit. Lib. 8277.ee.6.
64. *Annual Report of the Refuge for the Destitute for the year 1832* (London, 1833), p. 5 at the Brit. Lib. C.T.62(5).

65. *Annual Report of the Refuge for the Destitute for 1818*, at the Brit. Lib 08275. df.20. The accounts related to1817. Minute Book of the Refuge for the Destitute D/S/4/1 at Hackney Archives, entry for 27 July, 1820.

66. *Report from the Select Committee on the Police of the Metropolis for 1828*, evidence of James Ross, superintendent of the male establishment of the Refuge for the Destitute, pp. 181-182.

67. Minute Book of the Refuge for the Destitute D/S/4/l, entry for 29 January. 1819 and entry for 27 July, 1820. Evidence of James Ross, p. 184 in *Report from the Select Committee on the Police.*

68. Sanders, *Juvenile Offenders*, p. 97.

69. Sanders, *Juvenile Offenders*, p. 97.

70. Refuge for the Destitute: Petitions for Admission in 1812 D/S/1/5 at Hackney Archives, entries for 15 April and 12 August, 1812.

71. Refuge for the Destitute: Petitions for Admission in 1812, entry for 19 August, 1812.

72. Minute Book of the Refuge for the Destitute D/S/4/1, meeting of the General Court, 27 July, 1820 and Annual Meeting of the General Court, January 1827.

73. Annual Meeting of the General Court of the Refuge for the Destitute. 28 January, 1836, D/S/4/1 at Hackney Archives. It was noted that ten out of 62 youths discharged in 1835 had been sent as emigrants to Upper Canada and New York. By 1841 that total had increased to nineteen sent as emigrants to Upper Canada. See meeting of the General Court, 27 January, 1842 D/S/4/2 at Hackney Archives.

74. *Minutes of Evidence before the Select Committee on Gaols and Houses of Correction*, P.P. 1835, Vol. XII, Evidence of the Revd Thomas Ross Bromfield, honorary secretary of the Warwick County Asylum, pp. 427 and 435. Sanders, *Juvenile Offenders*, p. 120. Radzinowicz and Hood, *History of English Criminal Law*, Vol. 5, pp. 135-136.

75. *Minutes of Evidence before the Select Committee on Gaols*, evidence of the Revd Thomas Ross Bromfield, p. 428.

76. *Minutes of Evidence before the Select Committee on Gaols*, evidence of the Revd Thomas Ross Bromfield, p. 430.

77. *Minutes of Evidence before the Select Committee on Goals*, evidence of the Revd Thomas Ross Bromfield, p. 432.

78. Radzinowicz and Hood, *History of English Criminal Law*, Vol. 5, p. 136.

79. Calculated from Appendix in the *Second Report on the Execution of the Criminal Law*, P.P. 1847, Vol. VII, on the Warwick County Asylum, pp. 213-216.

80. Ignatieff, *A Just Measure of Pain*, p. 157.

81. Heather Shore, *Artful Dodgers. Youth Crime in Early Nineteenth Century London* (Woodbridge, 1999), p. 14.

82. Shore, *Artful Dodsers*, p. 2.

83. *Minutes of Evidence before the Select Committee on Gaols and Houses of Correction*, p. 435.

84. Quoted in Shore, *Artful Dodgers*, p. 1.

85. Quoted in Porter, *London*, p. 183.

86. See a copy of this *Report* at the Guildhall Library, London, A.18.6 no. 29.

87. *Report of the Committee for Investigating the Causes of the Alarming Increase of Juvenile Delinquency in the Metropolis.* (1816), pp. 10-11.

88. *Report of the Committee for Investigating ... Juvenile Delinquency*, p. 25.

89. *Annual Report of the Committee of the Society for the Improvement of Prison Discipline and for the Reformation of Juvenile Offenders* (1818), pp. 5, 8, 10-

11 and 13-18. *Annual Report of the Society for 1823*, p. 70. These *Reports* are both at the Brit. Lib. B.740(9) and 1127.c.12, respectively

90. *Minutes of Evidence before the Select Committee on Gaols and Houses of Correction*, pp. 512-513.
91. Miles, *A Letter to Lord John Russell*, p. 2.
92. Shore, *Artful Dodgers*, p. 49.
93. Evidence of Thieves Collected by William Augustus Miles, Notebook No. 1 in HO.73/16 at the NA.
94. Evidence of Thieves, Notebook No. 1 in HO.73/16.
95. Miles, *A Letter to Lord John Russell*, p. 10.
96. *Select Committee on the Causes of the Increase in the Number of Criminal Commitments*, P.P. 1828, Vol. VI, p. 10, evidence of Sir Thomas Baring, Bart.

Chapter 2

1. Michael Ignatieff, *A Just Measure of Pain. The Penitentiary in the Industrial Revolution, 1750-1850* (London and Basingstoke, 1978), pp. 16 and 24-25.
2. Calendar of Prisoners at Hampshire quarter sessions, 1789-1795 at Hampshire Record Office.
3. V. A. C. Gatrell, *The Hanging Tree. Execution and the English People 1770-1868* (Oxford, 1996 edn), p. 589.
4. S. E. F. Knell, 'Capital Punishment: Its Administration in Relation to Juvenile Offenders in the Nineteenth Century and its Possible Administration in the Eighteenth' in *British Journal of Criminology.* Vol. 5 (1965), p. 202.
5. Heather Shore, *Artful Dodgers. Youth and Crime in Early Nineteenth-Century London* (Woodbridge, 1999), pp. 106-107.
6. *Minutes of Evidence before the Committee on the State of the Police of the Metropolis*, P.P. 1817, Vol. VII, evidence of Samuel Hoare, 19 June, 1817 p. 529.
7. *Report from the Committee on the State of the Police of the Metropolis*, P.P. 1816, Vol. V, evidence of Philip Holdsworth, p. 262.
8. Calculated from Appendix No. 5 in *Select Committee on the Causes of the Increase in the Number of Criminal Commitments*, P.P. 1828, Vol. VI, p. 105 and Shore, *Artful Dodgers*, pp. 103 and 122.
9. Shore, *Artful Dodgers*, p. 103.
10. Calendar of Prisoners at the Hampshire Epiphany quarter sessions, 1819.
11. Peter King, 'War as a judicial resource. Press gangs and prosecution rates, 1740-1830' in Norma Landau ed., *Law, Crime and English Society, 1660-1830* (Cambridge, 2002), p. 108.
12. Alan F. Cirket ed., *Samuel Whitbread's Notebooks 1810-11, 1813-14* (Bedfordshire Historical Record Society, Vol. 50, 1971), pp. 23 and 83. Nos. 517 and 519.
13. King, 'War as a judicial resource', pp. 106-107.
14. King, 'War as a judicial resource', p. 112.
15. Elizabeth Silverthorne ed., *Deposition book of Richard Wyatt JP 1767-1776* (Guildford: Surrey Record Society, Vol. 30, 1978), p. 28, Nos. 150 and 151.
16. Jack Ayres, *Paupers and Pig Killers. The Diary of William Holland. A Somerset Parson, 1799-1818* (Stroud 2000 edn), p. 45.
17. Peter King, *Crime, Justice and Discretion in England 1740-1820* (Oxford, 2000), p. 27.

18. J. M. Beattie, *Crime and the Courts in England 1660-1800* (Oxford, 1986), p. 317.

19. Calendar of Prisoners for the Lent Assizes, Dorchester, Dorset, 12 March, 1801 at Dorset Record Office D1/10951A.

20. Calendar of Prisoners for the Summer Assizes, Dorchester, Dorset, 23 July, 1801 at Dorset Record Office D1/10951A

21. I. Wyatt, 'Some Transportees from Gloucestershire 1815-1818' in *Gloucestershire Historical Studies*, Vol. 11 (1969), p. 18.

22. Beattie, *Crime and the Courts*, p. 399.

23. *The Times*, 20 September, 1785.

24. *The Times*, 9 May, 1788.

25. Wiley B. Sanders ed., *Juvenile Offenders for a Thousand Years. Selected Readings from Anglo-Saxon Times to 1900* (Chapel Hill: University of North Carolina Press, 1970), pp. 37-38.

26. Knell, 'Capital Punishment', p. 200.

27. Knell, 'Capital Punishment', p. 200.

28. Knell, 'Capital Punishment', pp. 204-205.

29. Gatrell, *The Hanging Tree* p. 512.

30. Knell, 'Capital Punishment', pp. 199 and 102.

31. William Augustus Miles, *A Letter to Lord John Russell concerning Juvenile Delinquency together with Suggestions concerning a Reformatory Establishment* (Shrewsbury, 1837 pamphlet), p. 11.

32. Miles, *A Letter to Lord John Russell*, p. 11.

33. Calendars of Prisoners at the Lent Assizes at Dorchester, 11 March, 1812 and 12 March, 1813 at Dorset Record Office, D1/10951A.

34. Leon Radzinowicz, *A History of English Criminal Law and its Administration from 1750*, Vol. 1 (London, 1948), p. 14.

35. *Annual Register for 1831* (London, 1832), pp. 112-116. *Gentleman's Magazine*, Vol. 101, Pt.2 (1831), p. 169. Gatrell, *The Hanging Tree*, pp. 3-4.

36. Gatrell, *The Hanging Tree*, pp. 59-60.

37. Gatrell, *The Hanging Tree*, p. 58.

38. *Minutes of Evidence before the Select Committee on Metropolitan Police Offices,* P.P. 1837, Vol. XII, evidence of Edward Gibbon Wakefield, 1 June, 1837, pp. 124-125. Qu. 1200-1204.

39. *Report from the Select Committee on Criminal Laws &c.*, P.P. 1819, Vol. VIII, evidence of Mr James Jennings, 18 May, 1819, p. 104.

40. *Report from the Select Committee on Criminal Laws*, p. 10.

41. King, *Crime, Justice and Discretion*, p. 174.

42. King, *Crime, Justice and Discretion*, p. 301.

43. Petitions for Pardon, letter from Mr Serjeant Kirby, 8 April, 1788 in HO.47/7, f.56 in the NA.

44. Petitions for Pardon, Petition to the Rt. Hon. Lord Sidney in HO/47/7 ff.66 and 68 and 70 in the NA. King, *Crime, Justice and Discretion*, p. 322.

45. Elizabeth Melling ed., *Kentish Sources. VI. Crime and Punishment* (Maidstone: Kent County Council, 1969), p. 18.

46. Melling ed., *Kentish Sources*, pp. 80-81.

47. Post-trial Calendars of Prisoners at Assizes and Quarter Sessions in Dorset, 1801-1819 at Dorset Record Office, Dl/10951A.

48. Notes by William Augustus Miles in HO.73/16, f.17 in the NA.

49. *Minutes of Evidence before the Select Committee on Metropolitan Police Offices*, evidence of James Traill, 4 May, 1837, pp. 43-44.

50. William Smith, MD *State of the Gaols in London, Westminster and the Borough of Southwark* (London, 1776), pp. 62-63.

51. John Howard, *The State of the Prisons* (London, 1929 edn), pp. 1-6 and 164.

52. Howard, *The State of the Prisons*, p. 1.

53. Sanders ed., *Juvenile Offenders*, pp. 100-101.

54. Sanders ed., *Juvenile Offenders*, p. 101.

55. Sanders ed., *Juvenile Offenders*, pp. 155-159.

56. Ignatieff, *A Just Measure of Pain*, p. 30.

57. Henry Mayhew and John Binny, *The Criminal Prisons of London* (New York, 1968 edn), p. 592. The book was first published in 1862.

58. W. J. Sheehan, 'Finding Solace in Eighteenth-Century Newgate' in J. S. Cockburn ed., *Crime in England 1550-1800* (London, 1977), p. 229.

59. Mayhew and Binny, *The Criminal Prisons of London*, p. 592.

60. Ignatieff, *A Just Measure of Pain*, p. 39.

61. *First Report of the Inspectors of Prisons of Great Britain*, P.P. 1835, Vol. XXV, p. 85 and appendix 13, p. 145. Newgate Visitors book, 1823-1825, comments by the Newgate ordinary, or chaplain, the Revd H. S. Cotton, e.g. 28 May, 1824: 'Visited the untried women – in one ward I found six little girls of very tender age ... it is really grievous to see the wretched associations they must here submit to'. The book is at the London Metropolitan Archives, CLA/035/02/053. *Report from the Committee on the State of the Police of the Metropolis*, P.P. 1816, Vol. V, evidence of the Revd H. S. Cotton, 20 June, 1816, pp. 231-232.

62. *First Report of the Inspectors of Prisons*, p. 86.

63. Newgate Visitors Book, entries for 8 and 10 November, 1823.

64. Newgate Visitors Book, entry for 18 December, 1824. On 30 December, he visited the 'condemned women, the two little girls under sentence of death do great credit to the care & attention of Margaret Stewart the wardswoman'. Not until 9 February. 1825 was he able to report, with evident satisfaction, that all the women were respited. They were 'much agitated – particularly the two little girls who attempted as well as their tears would permit, to return their thanks'.

65. Mayhew and Binny, *The Criminal Prisons of London*, p. 593.

66. Rules for the Government of the Bridewell at Reading, 24 January, 1792 Q/AG/3/1 at Berkshire Record Office.

67. Rules for the Government of the Bridewell at Reading, 24 January, 1792. There were also strict dietary regulations: 'convicted Prisoners shall have only bread and water, with vegetables occasionally from the Garden, on Week Days, and some Meat and Broth on Sundays if they have behaved well in the course of the Week.'

68. Clean linen was allowed once a week. Rules for the Government of the Bridewell at Reading.

69. Margaret de Lacey, *Prison reform in Lancashire, 1700-1850. A study in local administration* (Manchester for the Chetham Society, 1986) pp. 102 and 198-199.

70. Randall McGowen, 'The Well-Ordered Prison. England, 1780-1865' in Norval Morris and David J. Rothman ed., *The Oxford History of the Prison. The Practice of Punishment in Western Society* (New York and Oxford, 1995), p. 86.

71. Randall McGowen. 'The Well-Ordered Prison', p. 86.

72. *Report of the Select Committee on Criminal Commitments and Convictions*, P.P. 1828, Vol. VI, evidence of Thomas Cunningham, p. 93. Ignatieff, *A Just Measure of Pain*, p. 124.

73. Ignatieff, *A Just Measure of Pain*, pp. 127-128.

74. *An Act to explain and amend the Laws relating to the Transportation, Imprisonment, and other Punishments of certain Offenders*, 19 Geo. III c.74, 1779.

75. Francis Sheppard, *London 1808-1870. The Infernal Wen* (London, 1971), pp. 374-376. In 1840 *The Fifth Report of the Inspectors of Prisons*, P.P. 1840, Vol. XXV, noted that the juvenile prisoners were 'subjected to the ordinary discipline of the Penitentiary, and are distributed through the several wards of the prison. At the time of recent inspection there were 27 boys and 17 girls of 15 years of age and under in confinement' (p. 195).

76. Randall McGowen, 'The Well-Ordered Prison', p. 88.

77. Jeannie Duckworth, *Fagin's Children. Criminal Children in Victorian England* (London and New York, 2002), pp. 69-70.

78. Ignatieff, *A Just Measure of Pain*, pp. 207-208.

79. Calendar of Prisoners for the Epiphany Quarter Sessions, January 1819 at Hampshire Record Office.

80. Calendar of Prisoners for the Midsummer Sessions for Berkshire, 14 July, 1829, D/EPb/015, at Berkshire Record Office.

81. Shore, *Artful Dodgers*, p. 106.

82. *Report of the Select Committee on Criminal Commitments and Convictions*, evidence of Samuel Hoare, p. 85.

83. *Third Report of the Inspectors of Prisons: England and Wales*, P.P. 1837-38, Vol. XXX, p. 108.

84. *Third Report of the Inspectors of Prisons*, p. 108 and *First Report of the Inspectors of Prisons*, report on Coldbath Fields House of Correction, p. 88.

85. Evidence of thieves collected by William Augustus Miles, HO.73/16, Notebook No. 1, in the NA.

86. Evidence of thieves collected by William Augustus Miles, Notebook No. 1.

87. Evidence of thieves collected by William Augustus Miles, Notebook No. 2, evidence of Thompson alias Wade.

88. *An act for consolidating and amending the laws relating to the building, repairing and regulating of certain Gaols and Houses of Correction in England and Wales, 1823*, 4 Geo. IV c.64.

89. *Second Report of the Inspectors of Prisons of Great Britain*, P.P. 1837, Vol. XXXII, p. 67.

90. *Third Report of the Inspectors of Prisons*, pp. 108-109.

91. *Fourth Report of the Inspectors of Prisons of Great Britain*, P.P. 1839, Vol. XXII, Report on Parkhurst, p. 1.

92. Parkhurst Prison Register H.O.24/15 at the NA.

93. Julius Carlebach, *Caring for Children in Trouble* (London, 1998 edn), p. 27.

94. Carlebach, *Caring for Children.* p. 28.

95. Parkhurst Prison Register HO.24/15.

96. Carlebach, *Caring for Children.* pp. 30-31.

97. Carlebach, *Caring for Children*, pp. 35-36 and 40-41.

98. W. Branch Johnson, *The English Prison Hulks* (Chichester, 1970 edn), pp. 198-199. Leon Radzinowicz and Roger Hood, *The Emergence of the Penal Policy In Victorian and Edwardian England* (Oxford,1990), p. 142.

99. Howard, *The State of the Prisons*, pp. 252-253

100. Quoted in Duckworth, *Fagin's Children*, p. 81.

101. Alan Brooke and David Brandon, *Bound for Botany Bay. British Convict Voyages to Australia* (London, 2005), p. 26.

102. Branch Johnson, *The English Prison Hulks* p. 89.

103. *Papers Relating to the Convict Hulks in the Rivers Thames and Medway, and in Portsmouth and Langston Harbours &c.* 19 May, 1815, submitted by John Henry Capper, Inspector, in P.P. 1814-15, Vol. XI. Howard, *The State of the Prisons*, p. 255

104. Radzinowicz and Hood, *The Emergence of Penal Policy*, p. 142.

105. *Select Committee on Secondary Punishments*, P.P. 1831-32, Vol. VII, interview with A. B., a discharged convict, on 23 February, 1832. p. 51, Qu.418 and p. 58, Qu.544-547 and Qu. 644-654.

106. *Instructions to John Henry Capper*, P.P. 1816. Vol. XVIII. p. 16.

107. Old Bailey Sessional papers, December 1785-April 1786, p. 9, No. 3 and December 1787-October 1788, pp. 476-477, No. 373. Michael Flynn ed., *The Second Fleet. Britain's Grim Convict Armada of 1790* (Sydney, 1993), pp. 254-255.

108. The Hon. Henry Grey Bennet MP, *Letter to Viscount Sidmouth, Secretary of State for the Home Department on the Transportation Laws, The State of the Hulks and of the Colonies in New South Wales* (London, 1819), p. 23, pamphlet in the Brit. Lib., RB.23.a.28462.

109. Bennet, *Letter to Viscount Sidmouth*. pp. 28 and 31.

110. *Minutes of Evidence Taken Before the Committee on the State of the Police of the Metropolis*, P.P. 1816, Vol. V. evidence of John Henry Capper, 18 June, 1816, p. 218.

111. Quoted in Irene Wyatt, 'Juveniles Transported to Australia and Tasmania 1815-1835' in *Gloucestershire Historical Studies*, Vol. X (1979), p. 60.

112. Bennet, *Letter to Viscount Sidmouth*, pp. 33 and 35.

113. *Report of John Henry Capper, Superintendent of Ships and Vessels*, No. 1, 15 July, 1824 in P.P. 1825, Vol. XXIII, p. 1 and Report of the Chaplain, the Revd E. Edwards on the *Bellerophon*, 1 July 1824, pp. 2 and 4. Charles Campbell, *The Intolerable Hulks* (Maryland, 1994), pp. 130-131. A copy is available in the library of the London Metropolitan Archives.

114. *Report of John Henry Capper*, No. 2, 27 January, 1827 in P.P. 1826-27, Vol. XIX, p. 6. For Thomas Price's comment, made on 30 June, 1826, see P.P. 1826-27, Vol. XIX, p. 3.

115. See evidence of Mr Steadman and John Henry Capper to the *Select Committee on Gaols and Houses of Correction*. P.P. 1835, Vol. XI, Appendix 21, pp. 259. Interview with William Johnson alias Harris in William Augustus Miles, interviews with young thieves, rough notebook No. IV in HO.73/16 in the NA.

116. Evidence of Mr Steadman and John Henry Capper, Appendix 21, pp. 258-259 Brooke and Brandon, *Bound for Botany Bay*, p. 124.

117. Evidence of Mr Steadman and John Henry Capper, Appendix 21. p. 259.

118. *Select Committee on Gaols and Houses of Correction*, evidence of Thomas Dexter, p. 321.

119. *Select Committee on Gaols and Houses, of Correction*, evidence of Thomas Dexter, p. 323.

120. Evidence of William Johnson alias Harris in Rough Notebook No. IV in HO.73/16 in the NA, and Register of Prisoners on the *Euryalus*, HO.9/2 in the NA.

121. Shore, *Artful Dodgers*, p. 130.

122. Register of Prisoners on the *Euryalus*, HO.9/2 and Shore, *Artful Dodgers*, p. 130.

123. Register of Prisoners on the *Euryalus*, HO.9/2 and Shore, *Artful Dodgers*, p. 130.

124. Shore, *Artful Dodgers*, pp. 130-131.

125. Register of Prisoners on the *Euryalus*, HO.9/2.

126. Register of Prisoners on the *Euryalus*, HO.9/2. The two Ogilby boys were received from Newgate in October 1833, following their trial at the Old Bailey. *Select Committee on Gaols and Houses of Correction*, Appendix 21, pp. 260-261. 1837 Muster: New South Wales HO.10/34 at the NA.

127. Register of Prisoners on the *Euryalus*, HO.9/2. Evidence of thieves collected by William Augustus Miles, Notebook No. 2 in HO.73/16 and Shore, *Artful Dodgers*, p. 136.

128. Radzinowicz and Hood, *The Emergence of Penal Policy*, p. 144.

129. Duckworth, *Fagin's Children*, pp. 89-90.

130. See Parkhurst Prison Register, HO.24/15 at the NA.

131. Duckworth, *Fagin's Children*, p. 90.

132. Mayhew and Binny, *The Criminal Prisons of London*, p. 379.

133. Branch Johnson, *The English Prison Hulks*, pp. 198-199.

Chapter 3

1. Alan Brooke and David Brandon, *Bound for Botany Bay. British Convict Voyages to Australia* (London, 2005), p. 22. Robert Hughes, *The Fatal Shore. A History of the Transportation of Convicts to Australia 1787-1868* (London, 2003 edn), p. 40.

2. Geoff Blackburn, *The Children's Friend Society. Juvenile Emigrants to Western Australia, South Africa and Canada 1834-1842* (Northbridge, Western Australia, 1993), p. ix. Philip Bean and Joy Melville, *Lost Children of the Empire* (London, 1989), p. 1.

3. Roger Ekirch, *Bound for America. The Transportation of British Convicts to the Colonies, 1718-1775*, (Oxford, 1987), pp. 17-21

4. 4 Geo. I c.11, *An Act for the further preventing Robbery, Burglary and other Felonies, 1718.*

5. J. W. Wyatt, 'The Transportation of Criminals from Gloucestershire 1718-1773' in *Gloucestershire Historical Studies*, Vol III (1969), pp. 2-8.

6. Ekirch, *Bound for America*, pp. 19 and 225.

7. Brooke and Brandon, *Bound for Botany Bay*, p. 33.

8. Ekirch, *Bound for America*, pp. 1 and 23.

9. Brooke and Brandon, *Bound for Botany Bay*, p. 22. According to Hughes, *The Fatal Shore*, p. 41, on the eve of the American Revolution around 47,000 African slaves were entering America each year. He also notes that a wide range of colonies accepted British felons, ranging from 'Puritan Massachusetts ... to the tidewater settlements of the South'.

10. Ekirch, *Bound for America*, p. 51. Of those who absconded from their masters in Maryland and Virginia, few were children. Out of a total of 976 mentioned by Ekirch, only two were aged from ten to fourteen years; a further fifty-seven were in the age range fifteen to nineteen inclusive (p. 24).

11. Gwenda Morgan and Peter Rushton, *Eighteenth-Century Criminal Transportation: The Formation of the Criminal Atlantic* (Basingstoke, 2004), p. 45.

12. Morgan and Rushton, *Eighteenth-Century Criminal Transportation*, pp. 38 and 46.

13. Morgan and Rushton, *Eighteenth-Century Criminal Transportation*, p. 46.

14. Ekirch, *Bound for America*, p. 225.

15. Brooke and Brandon, *Bound for Botany Bay*, p. 32. Hughes, *The Fatal Shore*, p. 64.

16. This newspaper later changed its title to *The Times*.

17. John Cobley, *The Crimes of the First Fleet Convicts* (Sydney, 1970), p. 35. Mollie Gillen, *The Founders of Australia: A Biographical Dictionary of the First Fleet* (Sydney, 1989), p. 47.

18. Hughes, *The Fatal Shore*, p. 66.

19. Hughes, *The Fatal Shore*, p. 71. Brooke and Brandon, *Bound for Botany Bay* p. 44.

20. Cobley, *The Crimes of the First Fleet Convicts*, p. 138. Gillen, *The Founders of Australia*, p. 181.

21. Cobley, *The Crimes of the First Fleet Convicts*, p. 127. Gillen, *The Founders of Australia*, p. 169.

22. Hughes, *The Fatal Shore*, p. 71.

23. Journal of Arthur Bowes, surgeon of the convict transport *Lady Penrhyn*, Add. MSS.47966, ff.25 and 31 in the Brit. Lib.

24. Journal of Arthur Bowes, f.33.

25. Hughes, *The Fatal Shore*, pp. 2, 142 and 145. There were apparently 825 shiploads despatched, averaging two hundred convicts apiece.

26. John Cobley, *The Crimes of the Lady Juliana Convicts: 1790*, (Sydney, 1989), p. 87.

27. Cobley, *The Crimes of the Lady Juliana Convicts*, p. 49. Siân Rees, *The Floating Brothel* (London, 2002 edn), pp. 108-109 and *The Life and Adventures of John Nicol, Mariner* (London, 1937 edn), p. 134. The book was first published in 1822.

28. Rees, *The Floating Brothel*, p. 215. Michael Flynn, *The Second Fleet: Britain's Grim Convict Armada of 1790* (Sydney, 1993), p. 278.

29. Cobley, *The Crimes of the Lady Juliana Convicts*, pp. 30 and 34. Rees, *The Floating Brothel* pp. 108 and 215.

30. Margaret Spence, *Hampshire and Australia, 1783-1791. Crime and Transportation*, Hampshire Papers No. 2 (Hampshire County Council, 1992), pp. 17-19. Flynn, *The Second Fleet*, pp. 49-50.

31. John Hirst, 'The Australian Experience: The Convict Colony' in Norval Morris and David J. Rothman ed., *The Oxford History of the Prison. The Practice of Punishment in Western Society* (Oxford and New York, 1998 edn), p. 238.

32. Flynn, *The Second Fleet*, p. 728.

33. Flynn, *The Second Fleet*, p. 254. Spence, *Hampshire and Australia*, p. 24 notes that the conditions of the Second Fleet were atypical. 'On other ships there seems to have been unnecessary harshness or even brutality but not sufficient to result in actual deaths of convicts'.

34. The Hon. Henry Grey Bennet MP, *Letter to Viscount Sidmouth Secretary of State for the Home Department on the Transportation Laws, the State of the Hulks and Of the Colonies in New South Wales* (London, 1819), p. 10. During the period January 1812 to January 1817, 4,659 prisoners were transported in total.

35. A. G. L. Shaw, *Convicts and the Colonies. A Study of Penal Transportation from Great Britain and Ireland to Australia and other parts of the British Empire* (London 1966), p. 124. Jeannie Duckworth, *Fagin's Children. Criminal Children in Victorian England* (London, 2002), p. 118.

36. Bennet, *Letter to Viscount Sidmouth*, pp. 60-63.

37. *Report from the Select Committee on Transportation* P.P. 1837 Vol. XIX, evidence of Thomas Galloway, p. 183, Qu.2794-2799.

38. William Augustus Miles, Interviews with Young Thieves, Rough Notebook No. V in HO.73/16 at the NA. All the notebooks are at this reference.

39. William Augustus Miles, Interviews with Young Thieves, Notebook No. 3.

40. William Augustus Miles, Interviews with Young Thieves, Notebook No. 2.

41. William Augustus Miles, Interviews with Young Thieves, Notebook No. 2.

42. Petitions of Peter Daniels concerning David Daniels, 1829 in HO.17/108 at the NA.

43. Petition of Michael Hallman and Margaret Hallman in respect of Margaret Allen (*sic*), aged 15, 1833. HO.17/104 at the NA.

44. Heather Shore, *Artful Dodgers. Youth and Crime in Early Nineteenth-Century London* (Woodbridge, 1999), p. 53.

45. *Appendix to the Report from the Select Committee on Transportation*, P.P. 1837-38, Vol. XXII, Appendix B, No. 38, pp. 216-218.

46. *Appendix to the Report from the Select Committee on Transportation*, p. 217.

47. Duckworth, *Fagin's Children*, p. 119.

48. *Appendix to the Report from the Select Committee on Transportation*, pp. 217-218.

49. Kim Humphery, 'Objects of Compassion: Young Male Convicts in Van Diemen's Land 1834-1850' in *Australian Historical Studies*, Vol. 25 (April 1992), p. 13. Humphery's list omits the *Elphinstone* which sailed in 1842.

50. Humphery, 'Objects of Compassion', p. 29.

51. Journal of the *Elphinstone* Convict Ship, W. H. B. Jones, Surgeon, in ADM.101.24/11 at the NA, entries for 19 March to 28 July, 1842.

52. Journal of the *Elphinstone* Convict Ship, entry for 22 June, 1842.

53. Brooke and Brandon, *Bound for Botany Bay*, pp. 223 and 253. Hughes, *The Fatal Shore*, pp. 572 and 578. The formal end of transportation to Van Diemen's Land came with the colony's Jubilee in August 1853. The following year, in an effort to divest itself of its unsavoury past, it changed its name to Tasmania.

54. Hughes, *The Fatal Shore*, p. 126.

55. Wilfrid Oldham, *Britain's Convicts to the Colonies* (Sydney, 1990), pp. 175-181.

56. Hirst, 'The Australian Experience', p. 236.

57. Gillen, *The Founders of Australia*, p. 169.

58. Gillen, *The Founders of Australia*, p. 181.

59. *Appendix to the Report from the Select Committee on Transportation*, P.P. 1837 Vol. XIX, Appendix No. 9, p. 241.

60. *Appendix to the Report from the Select Committee on Transportation*, Appendix No. 9, p. 242.

61. Brooke and Brandon, *Bound for Botany Bay*. p. 238. Hughes, *The Fatal Shore*, p. 255. Hirst, 'The Australian Experience', pp. 244-245;. The first factory was opened in a room above the gaol at Parramatta. A new factory was opened at Parramatta in 1821 and was sometimes also known as the Female Penitentiary.

62. Duckworth, *Fagin's Children*, p. 116.

63. Brooke and Brandon, *Bound for Botany Bay*, p. 131.

64. Brooke and Brandon, *Bound for Botany Bay*, pp. 235-236 Duckworth, *Fagin's Children*, p. 121.

65. *Report of the Commission of Inquiry into the State of the Colony of New South Wales*, P.P. 1822, Vol. XX, pp. 23, 27, 33. Shaw, *Convicts and the Colonies* pp. 81 and 243.

66. *Report ... into the State of the Colony of New South Wales*, p. 23.

67. Shaw, *Convicts and the Colonies*, p. 243.

68. *Select Committee on Transportation, 1837*, evidence of James Mudie, 21 April, 1837, p. 44, Qu.721-724.

69. *Select Committee on Transportation*, evidence of Ernest A. Slade, 25 April, 1837, p. 66, Qu.1032 and 1040.

70. *Select committee on Transportation*, P.P. 1837-38, Vol. XXII, evidence of the Very Revd W. Ullathorne, 8 February, 1838, pp. 15-16. Qu.163.

71. Humphery, 'Objects of Compassion', p. 17.

72. F. C. Hooper, *Prison Boys of Port Arthur. A Study of the Point Puer Boys' Establishment in Van Diemen's Land, 1834 to 1850*, (Melbourne, 1967), p. 1.

73. Humphery, 'Objects of Compassion', pp. 19-20.

74. Hooper, *Prison Boys of Port Arthur* p. 3.

75. *Correspondence Relative to Convict Discipline in Van Diemen's Land*, P.P. 1846, Vol. XXIX, W. Champ to the Controller-general, 29 July, 1844, p. 36.

76. *Select Committee on Transportation, 1837-38*, Enclosure No. 2 in No. 38, 'Report on the Juvenile Establishment at Point Puer by Charles O'Hara Booth', pp. 218-219.

77. Hooper, *Prison Boys of Port Arthur*, p. 11.

78. *Select Committee on Transportation, 1837-38*. 'Report on the Juvenile Establishment at Point Puer', p. 220.

79. Calculated from Synopsis of Offences Tried, with the Punishments Awarded at the Police Office, Point Puer, for the half-year ending 30 June, 1837, provided by Charles O'Hara Booth in *Select Committee on Transportation, 1837-38*, p. 223.

80. Hooper, *Prison Boys of Port Arthur*, p. 12.

81. Quoted in Hughes, *The Fatal Shore*, p. 403.

82. Duckworth, *Fagin's Children*, p. 130.

83. Appropriation Listings and Conduct Records of Samuel Holmes in the Archives Office of Tasmania. I am indebted to the staff for their help in providing this information.

84. Appropriation Listings and Conduct Records of George Hickman in the Archives Office of Tasmania. Shore, *Artful Dodgers*, p. 137.

85. Pardons, &c granted, 1846 in Australia, HO.10/38 at the NA. This noted that George Hickman, who had travelled to Australia on the *Elphinstone*, had been granted a free certificate.

86. Hooper, *Prison Boys of Port Arthur*, p. 14.

87. Hooper, *Prison Boys of Port Arthur*, p. 15.

88. Hooper, *Prison Boys of Port Arthur*, p. 15.

89. Hooper, *Prison Boys of Port Arthur*, pp. 26-27.

90. *Correspondence Relative to Convict Discipline in Van Diemen's Land*, 1846, Despatch from Lieutenant-governor Sir Eardley Wilmot, Bart to Lord Stanley, 25 October, 1845, p. 33.

91. Humphery, 'Objects of Compassion', p. 25. After 1843, according to Hooper, only the younger boys were sent to Point Puer; all boys over 15 years were sent to other stations. Hooper, *Prison Boys of Port Arthur*, p. 26.

92. Hooper, *Prison Boys of Port Arthur*, pp. 25-26.

93. *Report ... into the State of the Colony of New South Wales*, 1822, pp. 80-83.

94. Petition of William Wilkes in HO.17/104, Tr., at the NA.

95. Endorsement by Sir George Grey on 27 July, 1856, in HO.17/104, Tr.

96. Carol Richmond *Banished! Sentences of Transportation from Oxfordshire Courts 1787-1867*, Vol. 2 (Witney, 2007), p. 39 and information provided in 'Banished Beyond the Seas: An Exhibition at Oxfordshire Record Office,' September to November, 2007.

97. Hirst, 'The Australian Experience', pp. 252 and 258.

98. Flynn, *The Second Fleet*, p. 278.

99. Gillen, *The Founders of Australia*, p. 147.

100. *Report from the Select Committee on Transportation, 1837-38*, p. xxii.

101. *Report from the Select Committee on Transportation, 1837-38*, p. xlvi.

102. *Minutes of Evidence before the Select Committee on the Police of the Metropolis*, P.P. 1828, Vol. VI, evidence of Henry M. Dyer, 28 March, 1828, p. 172.

103. Jo Manton, *Mary Carpenter and the Children of the Streets* (London, 1976), p. 4.

104. *Minutes of Evidence before the Committee on the State of Police in the Metropolis*, P.P. 1816, Vol. V, p. 127.

105. *Select Committee on Emigration from the United Kingdom*, P.P. 1826, Vol. IV, p. 83, Qu. 773 and 776-777.

106. *Statement of the Views and Reports of the Society for the Suppression of Juvenile Vagrancy* (London, 1830), pp. 5 and 8. This pamphlet is in the Bodleian Library, Oxford. Vet.A6.d.772. Elaine Hadley, 'Natives in a Strange land: The Philanthropic Discourse of Juvenile Emigration in Mid-Nineteenth Century England' in *Victorian Studies*, Vol. 33, No. 3 (Spring 1990), p. 411.

107. Blackburn, *The Children's Friend Society*, p. 15. Gillian Wagner, *Children of the Empire* (London, 1982), p. 13. Duckworth, *Fagin's Children*, p. 148.

108. Blackburn, *The Children's Friend Society*, pp. 4 and 9-10.

109. Blackburn, *The Children's Friend Society*, pp. 1, 61 and 239.

110. Minute Book of the Refuge for the Destitute at Hackney Archives, D/S/4/1, meeting of the general court, 27 January 1820 and Minute Book of the Refuge for the Destitute. D/S/4/2, meeting of the general court, 27 January, 1842.

111. *First Report of the Inspectors of Prisons in Great Britain*, P.P. 1836, Vol. XXXV, p. 96.

112. *Report on the Children's Friend Society (Cape of Good Hope)*, P.P. 1840, Vol. XXXIII, p. 28.

113. *Report on the Children's Friend Society*, p. 14.

114. *Report on the Children's Friend Society*, p. 4.

115. Quoted in Barry Coldrey, *Good British Stock. Child and Youth Migration to Australia* (Canberra, 1999), p. 16. Blackburn, *The Children's Friend Society*, p. 6.

116. Blackburn, *The Children's Friend Society*, p. 11.

117. *Report on the Children's Friend Society*, p. 14.

118. *Report on the Children's Friend Society*, p. 10. Blackburn, *The Children's Friend Society*, p. 4. Shore, *Artful Dodgers*, p. 141.

119. Edna Bradlow, 'The Children's Friend Society at the Cape of Good Hope' in *Victorian Studies*, Vol. 27, No. 2 (Winter 1984), p. 169.

120. *The Times*, 9 April, 1839 and Blackburn, *The Children's Friend Society*, p. 62.

121. *Report on the Children's Friend Society*, pp. 1-3 and 4.

122. *Report on the Children's Friend Society*, p. 11.

123. *Report on the Children's Friend Society*, p. 1.

124. Bradlow, 'The Children's Friend Society', p. 174. Blackburn, *The Children's Friend Society*, p. 61.

125. *Minutes of Evidence from the Select Committee on Criminal and Destitute Juveniles*, P.P. 1852, Vol. VII, evidence of the Revd S. Turner, Resident Chaplain of the Philanthropic Society's Farm School at Red Hill, p. 23, Qu.247-255.

126. *Hansard*, 3rd Series, Vol. XCIX, 6 June, 1848, cols. 449-450 and 454. *Hansard*, 3rd Series, Vol. CVII, col. 909.

127. *Hansard*, 3rd Series, Vol. CXI, cols. 438-439.

128. Wagner, *Children of the Empire*, pp. 26-28 and 32-33.

129. Wagner, *Children of the Empire*, pp. 20-21. Parkhurst Prison Register HO.24/15 in the NA and *Fourth Report of the Inspectors of Prisons in Great Britain*, P.P. 1839, Vol. XXII, Report on Parkhurst Prison, pp. 6-13.

130. Wagner, *Children of the Empire*, p. 21 and information provided in 'Banished beyond the Seas. Exhibition at Oxfordshire Record Office, September to November. 2007'.

131. Hadley, 'Natives in a Strange Land', p. 423.

132. Julius Carlebach, *Caring for Children in Trouble* (London, 1998 edn), pp. 28-29. Ivy Pinchbeck and Margaret Hewitt, *Children in English Society*, Vol. II.

From the Eighteenth Century to the Children Act 1948 (London, 1973), pp.
547-548.

133. Wagner, *Children of the Empire*, p. 23.
134. *Minutes of Evidence Before the Select Committee on Transportation*, P.P. 1861,
   Vol. XIII, evidence of W. Burgess, p. 67, Qu.1695-1696.
135. Wagner, *Children of the Empire*, p. 21.
136. Wagner, *Children of the Empire*, pp. 21-22 and Parkhurst Prison Register.
137. Pinchbeck and Hewitt, *Children in English Society*, p. 548.
138. Carlebach, *Caring for Children in Trouble*, p. 34.
139. Bean and Melville, *Lost Children of the Empire*, pp. 35-36. Pinchbeck and
   Hewitt, *Children in English Society*, pp. 554-555. Pamela Horn, *The Victorian
   Town Child* (Stroud,1997 edn), pp. 197-200.

Chapter 4

1. Mary Carpenter, *Reformatory Schools for the Children of the Perishing and
   Dangerous Classes and for Juvenile Offenders* (London, 1851), p. v. David
   Philips, *Crime and Authority in Victorian England. The Black Country 1835-
   1860* (London,1977), p. 161.
2. Susan Magarey, 'The Invention of Juvenile Delinquency in Early Nineteenth
   Century England' in *Labour History* (Canberra), No. 34 (May 1978), p. 11.
3. Sir Leon Radzinowicz and Roger Hood, *A History of English Criminal Law
   and its Administration from 1750. Vol. 5, The Emergence of Penal Policy*
   (London, 1986), p. 172.
4. *Hansard*, 3rd Series. Vol. XCIII (2 June-6 July 1847), col. 699.
5. *Select Committee on Prison Discipline*, P.P. 1850, Vol. XVII, p. 505. Calculated from
   the tables of the 'Ages of Prisoners Tried at Assizes and Sessions and Summarily
   Convicted' in England and Wales, 1839-47.
6. *An Act for the More Speedy Trial and Punishment of Juvenile Offenders*, 1847,
   10 & 11 Victoria c.82. Philips, *Crime and Authority* pp. 132 and 173.
7. Margaret May, 'Innocence and Experience: The Evolution of the Concept of
   Juvenile Delinquency in the Mid-Nineteenth Century' in *Victorian Studies*, Vol.
   18, No. 1 (September 1973). p. 7 *An Act for the Further Extension of Summary
   Jurisdiction in Cases of Larceny*, 1850, 13 &14 Victoria c.37.
8. Radzinowicz and Hood, *A History of English Criminal Law*, p. 622.
9. *Hansard*, 3rd Series, 27 April-1 June, 1847. Vol. XCII, col. 35.
10. Philips, *Crime and Authority*, p. 131.
11. Philips, *Crime and Authority*, p. 132.
12. *Abstract of Returns Relating to Juvenile Offenders 1850-52*, P.P. 1852-53, Vol.
   LXXXI.
13. Philips, *Crime and Authority*, p. 133.
14. Carpenter, *Reformatory Schools*, pp. 301-302. Radzinowicz and Hood, *A
   History of English Criminal Law*, p. 624. *Report of the Hardwicke Reformatory
   1860-62*, (1862), p. 7 at Gloucestershire Archives, D.3549/25/2/3.
15. Carpenter, *Reformatory Schools*, p. 302. She also quoted Adams's comment that
   he believed prison discipline to be 'incompatible' with the reform of children.
   'I have not the slightest doubt, that with children it would be better to apply
   ourselves to a reformatory than to a deterring process'. Jeannie Duckworth,
   Fagin's Children. Criminal Children in Victorian England (London, 2002), p.
   176.

16. Cases under the Juvenile Offenders Act, 13 September, 1847 to 26 February, 1848 at the London Metropolitan Archives, MSJ/CY/01/001.

17. Case Records of Edward Toghill, 13 September, 1847 and 31 December, 1847 in MSJ/CY/01/001.

18. Calculated from Cases under the Juvenile Offenders Acts of 1847 and 1850, 24 June to 16 December, 1853 at the London Metropolitan Archives, MSJ/CY/01/006.

19. Case Record of Robert Allcock, 22 November, 1853 and Case Records of William Williams, 16 November, 1853 and 25 November. 1853, both in MSJ/CY/01/006.

20. Radzinowicz and Hood. *A History of English Criminal Law*, p. 624.

21. Gertrude M. Tuckwell, *The State and its Children* (London, 1894), p. 3.

22. Radzinowioz and Hood, *A History of English Criminal Law*, pp. 165-167.

23. Carpenter, *Reformatory Schools*, pp. 2-3 and 347-349.

24. *Hansard*, 3rd Series, Vol. XCIII, 2 June-6 July, 1847, col. 700.

25. Radzinowicz and Hood, *A History of English Criminal Law*, pp. 155-157.

26. Julius Carlebach, *Caring for Children in Trouble* (London, 1998 edn), p. 70. *Annual Report of the Philanthropic Farm School, Redhill 1856*. p. 25 at the Brit. Lib. 6059.a.5.

27. T. Barwick Lloyd Baker. *War with Crime* (London, 1889). pp. 232-233. John A. Stack, 'Interests and Ideas in Nineteenth-Century Social Policy: The Mid-Victorian Reformatory School' in *Journal of Educational Administration and History*, Vol. XIV, No. 1 (January, 1982), p. 39.

28. Radzinowicz and Hood, *A History of English Criminal Law*, p. 205. Stack, 'Interests and Ideas in Nineteenth-Century Social Policy', p. 39.

29. Quoted in Carlebach, *Caring for Children*, p. 26.

30. Carpenter. *Reformatory Schools*, p. 322. She later referred to Parkhurst's 'bolts and keys – its sentinels with loaded guns – and officers regarded by the boys with profound suspicion', p. 337.

31. Carlebach, *Caring for Children*, p. 34.

32. Carlebach, *Caring for Children*, p. 21.

33. *Annual Report of the Philanthropic Farm School, Redhill, 1856*. p. 27 at the British Library 6059.a.5. All the Farm School reports quoted are in the Brit. Lib.

34. *Annual Report of the Philanthropic Farm School 1863*, pp. 15 and 20.

35. *Annual Report of the Philanthropic Farm School, 1863*, p. 14.

36. John Springhall. *Coming of Age: Adolescence in Britain 1860-1960* (Dublin, 1986). p. 172.

37. See correspondence between the Earl of Radnor and Sydney Turner at Berkshire Record Office, D/EPb/C.49.

38. Sydney Turner to the Earl of Radnor, 29 December, 1849 in D/EPb/C.49.

39. Letter from Redhill Farm School to the Earl of Radnor, 11 April, 1850, in D/EPb/C.49.

40. Sydney Turner to the Earl of Radnor, 25 July, 1850, in D/EPb/C.49.

41. Sydney Turner to the Earl of Radnor, 28 December, 1850, in D/EPb/C.49.

42. Carlebach, *Caring for Children*, pp. 62-63.

43. Carlebach, *Caring for Children*, p. 61.

44. *Report of the Children's Friend Reformatory School. Hardwicke*, January 1854, p. 13. in D.3549/25/2/3 at Gloucestershire Archives. *Hardwicke Reformatory Closed*, reprinted from *Gloucester Journal*, 25 March, 1922, in D.3549/25/3/20 at Gloucestershire Archives.

45. *Report of the Children's Friend Reformatory School, Hardwicke*, January 1854.

46. *Annual Report of Hardwicke Reformatory for 1884*, Diet table in D.3549/25/2/3.

47. *Report of the Children's Friend Reformatory School, Hardwicke*, January 1854.

48. *Report of the Children's Friend Reformatory School, Hardwicke*, January 1854.

49. *Third Report of the Inspector of Reformatory Schools in Great Britain*, P.P. 1860, vol. XXXV, p. 32. Duckworth, *Fagin's Children*, p. 175.

50. Jo Manton, *Mary Carpenter and the Children of the Streets* (London, 1976), p. 114.

51. *Thirteenth Report of the Inspector of Reformatory and Industrial Schools in Great Britain*, P.P. 1870, Vol. XXXVI, p. 50. Manton, *Mary Carpenter*, p.115. In 1882 the Inspector of Reformatory and Industrial Schools condemned the brickmaking at Kingswood as having 'a rough and degrading tendency on Reformatory boys, and is open to great objections'. *Twenty-fifth Report of the Inspector of Reformatory and Industrial Schools in Great Britain*, P.P. 1882, Vol. XXXV, p. 59.

52. J. Estlin Carpenter, *The Life and Work of Mary Carpenter* (London, 1870), pp. 188-189.

53. Carpenter, *The Life and Work of Mary Carpenter*, pp. 189-190.

54. Carpenter, *The Life and Work of Mary Carpenter*, pp. 207 and 209. Manton, *Mary Carpenter*, p. 121.

55. [Mary Carpenter], *Red Lodge Girls' Reformatory School, Bristol* (Bristol, 1875), p. 3.

56. *An Act for the Better Care and Reformation of Youthful Offenders in Great Britain*. 17 & 18 Victoria c.86.

57. May, 'Innocence and Experience', p. 26.

58. May, 'Innocence and Experience', p. 28.

59. *Thirteenth Report of the Inspector of Reformatory and Industrial Schools*, p. 27. Stack, 'Interests and Ideas in Nineteenth-Century Social Policy' also points out that there were relatively few agents appointed to collect the contributions and that, in any case, magistrates resented central government interference in the matter and feared that impositions on poor parents would necessitate them applying for parish relief out of the rates. (pp. 42-43).

60. Minutes of the Reformatory General Committee of Hardwicke Reformatory, entries for 5 July and 12 August, 1885 in D.3549/25/2/8 at Gloucestershire Archives.

61. *Report of the Royal Commission on Reformatories and Industrial Schools*, P.P. 1884. Vol. XLV. p. xliv.

62. *Fourth Report of the Inspector of Reformatory Schools in Great Britain*, P.P. 1861, Vol. XXX. p. 9. A year earlier the total had been 3,222.

63. *Fourth Report of the Inspector of Reformatory Schools*, pp. 9 and 17.

64. *Thirteenth Report of the Inspector of Reformatory and Industrial Schools*, p. 5.

65. Duckworth, *Fagin's Children*. p. 177.

66. *Thirteenth Report of the Inspector of Reformatory and Industrial Schools*, p. 6.

67. Joan Rimmer. *Yesterday's Naughty Children. Training Ship, Girls' Reformatory and Farm School. A History of the Liverpool Reformatory Association* (Manchester. 1986), pp. 6-10.

68. Rimmer, *Yesterday's Naughty Children*, pp. 12-14.

69. Rimmer, *Yesterday's Naughty Children*, pp. 14-15. Duckworth, *Fagin's Children*, p.178.

70. Rimmer, *Yesterday's Naughty Children*, pp. 23-24

71. Rimmer, *Yesterday's Naughty Children*, pp. 24-25.

72. Rimmer, *Yesterday's Naughty Children*, pp. 28-31.

73. Rimmer, *Yesterday's Naughty Children*, pp. 41-43.

74. Linda Mahood, *Policing , gender, class and family* (London, 1995), p. 149.

75. Mahood, *Policing gender*, p. 149.

76. Mahood, *Policing gender*. p. 149.

77. Duckworth. *Fagin's Children*, p. 182.

78. Duckworth, *Fagin's Children*, p. 174.

79. Mahood, *Policing gender*, p. 46. E. A. G. Clark, 'Sir Stafford Northcote's "Omnibus": The Genesis of the Industrial Schools Act, 1857' in *Journal of Educational Administration and History*, Vol. XIV, No. 1 (January 1982), p. 28.

80. John Springhall, *Coming of Age: Adolescence in Britain 1860-1960* (Dublin, 1986), pp. 166-167.

81. *Ninth annual report of the Superintendent of the Middlesex Industrial School*, MA/GS/8/2 at the London Metropolitan Archives.

82. Feltham Industrial School: Individual Account of Boys Discharged in 1864-66, MA/GS/8/18 at the London Metropolitan Archives.

83. Feltham Industrial School: Individual Account of Boys Discharged.

84. *An Act to Make Better Provision for the Care and Education of Vagrant, Destitute and Disorderly Children, and for the Extension of Industrial Schools, 1857*. 20 & 21 Victoria, c.48.

85. *An Act for Amending and Consolidating the Law relating to Industrial Schools*, 1861, 24 & 25 Victoria, c.113.

86. Springhall, *Coming of Age*, p. 167. *Industrial Schools Act, 1866*, 29 &30 Victoria, c.118.

87. Mahood, *Policing gender*, pp. 52-53.

88. Stephen Humphries, *Hooligans or Rebels? An Oral History of Working Class Childhood and Youth 1882-1932* (Oxford, 1984 edn), p. 212.

89. *Report of the Departmental Committee on Reformatory and Industrial Schools*, P.P. 1896 , Vol. XLV, p. 15.

90. *Thirteenth Report of the Inspector of Reformatory and Industrial Schools*, pp. 15-16.

91. *Report of the Departmental Committee on Reformatory and Industrial Schools*, p. 15.

92. Humphries, *Hooligans or Rebels?* p. 220.

93. Humphries, *Hooligans or Rebels?* p. 220.

94. Mark Benney, *Low Company* (London, 1936). pp. 142-143 and 144-145.

95. Reminiscences of Daisy Wintle (b. 1897) at Bristol Local History Library, R.011.

96. *Report of the Departmental Committee on Reformatory and Industrial Schools*, pp. 44-46

97. Rimmer, *Yesterday's Naughty Children*, pp. 52-53.

98. Rimmer, *Yesterday's Naughty Children*, p. 52.

99. *The Reformatory and Refuge Journal*, November, 1890, p. 455. *The Twenty-second Annual Report of Feltham Industrial School, 1880-81*, noted that of 48 boys placed out in employment in the trade and farming sector of the school's operations, 37 were provided with situations in Wales, 'chiefly through the kind assistance of the Revd Roger Williams, Rector of Llanedy'. *Twenty-fifth Report of the Inspector of Reformatory and Industrial Schools*, pp. 59 and 159.

100. *The Reformatory and Refuge Journal*, October 1890, advertisement on the cover of the journal.

101. *The Reformatory and Refuge Journal*, October 1890, advertisements.

102. Springhall, *Coming of Age*, p. 171.

103. *Report of the Departmental Committee on Reformatory and Industrial Schools*, p. 24.

104. *Report of the Departmental Committee on Reformatory and Industrial Schools*, p. 26.

105. *Annual Report of Kingswood Reformatory School*, 1902, pp. 9-11 and 16, at Bristol Local History Library.

106. Quoted in *Seeking and Saving*, January 1900. p. 10. P.P. 1106D at the Brit. Lib.

107. Reminiscences of an anonymous man (b. 1885) interviewed by Stephen Humphries. He was aged 11 at the time of the offence. At Bristol Local History Library, R.003.

108. Gordon Rose, *Schools for Young Offenders* (London, 1967), pp. 10-11.

109. For a detailed examination of the implications of the 1870 Education Act see, for example, Eric E. Rich, *The Education Act 1870. A study of Public Opinion* (London, 1970), pp. 89-103.

110. *An Act to make further Provision for Elementary Education*, 1876, 39 & 40 Victoria c.79, ss.14-17.

111. Wendy Prahms. *Newcastle Ragged and Industrial School* (Stroud, 2006), p. 16.

112. Humphries, *Hooligans or Rebels?* p. 220.

113. Manton, *Mary Carpenter*, p. 231.

114. Manton, *Mary Carpenter*, p. 231.

115. *Thirty-second Annual Report of the Inspector of Reformatory and Industrial Schools*, P.P. 1889, Vol. XLII, p. 35.

116. *Reformatory and Refuge Journal*, October 1889, p. 301. It also noted that some children had later to be sent to reformatory or certified industrial schools. These ranged from 3 per cent of boys from the Oxford Day Industrial School being so despatched because of their unsatisfactory record to 26 per cent in respect of the Bristol Day Industrial School. *Thirty-ninth Annual Report of the Inspector of Reformatory and Industrial Schools in Great Britain*, P.P. 1896, Vol. XLV, pp. 31-32.

117. *Forty-second Annual Report of the Inspector of Reformatory and Industrial Schools of Great Britain*, P.P. 1899, Vol. XLIV, pp. 31 and 32.

118. *Report and Minutes of Evidence of the Royal Commission on Reformatories and Industrial Schools*, P.P. 1884, Vol. XLV, p. xxxvi.

119. *Report of the Departmental Committee on Reformatory and Industrial Schools*, p. 122.

120. *Report of the Departmental Committee on Reformatory and Industrial Schools*, p. 122.

121. *Report of the Departmental Committee on Reformatory and Industrial Schools*, p. 122.

122. *Report of the Departmental Committee on Reformatory and Industrial Schools*, pp. 122-123.

123. *Report of the Departmental Committee on Reformatory and Industrial Schools*, p. 123.

124. *Report of the Departmental Committee on Reformatory and Industrial Schools*, pp. 123-124.

125. Quoted in the *Report of the Departmental Committee on Reformatory and Industrial Schools*, p. 124.

126. *Thirty-second Annual Report of the Inspector of Reformatory and Industrial Schools*, p. 311.

127. *Admission Register of Highbury Truant School*, SBL.1832 at the London Metropolitan Archives.

128. Admission Register of Highbury Truant School.

129. Malcolm Mercer, *Schooling the Poorer Child. Elementary Education in Sheffield 1560-1902* (Sheffield, 1996), p. 201.

130. Mercer, *Schooling the Poorer Child*, p. 201. *Fifty Years Record of Child saving and Reformatory Work (1856-1906) being the Jubilee Report of the Reformatory and Refuge Union* (London, 1906), p. 25. 08275.b.34 at the Brit. Lib.

131. Drury Lane Day Industrial School Minute Book No. 1, SBL.337 at the London Metropolitan Archives, meetings on 12 November, 1895, f.162 and 10 December, 1895, f.181.

132. Brunswick Road Day Industrial School Sub Committee of Managers Minute Book, SBL.333 at the London Metropolitan Archives, meeting on 11 November, 1901, f.21.

133. Evidence of Thomas Humphreys on 27 April, 1896, to the *Departmental Committee on Reformatory and Industrial Schools*, Vol. II, P.P. 1897, Vol. XLII, p. 941, Qu.31,093 and 31,104.

134. Evidence of Thomas Humphreys on 27 April, 1896, Qu.31,233-31,234.

135. Admission and Discharge Book for Brunswick Road Day Industrial School, entry no. 5 in SSL.1823 at the London Metropolitan Archives and Brunswick Road Sub Committee of Managers Minute Book, entry for 11 November, 1901, SBL.333.

136. Admission and Discharge Book for Brunswick Road Day Industrial School, entry no. 10 for Frederick Miles and Brunswick Road Sub Committee of Managers Minute Book, entries for 9 December, 1901, f. 27 and 5 May, 1902, f.50.

137. Mahood, *Policing gender*, p. 54.

138. *Twenty-fifth Report of the Inspector of Reformatory and Industrial Schools*, p. 10.

Chapter 5

1. John R. Gillis, 'The Evolution of Juvenile Delinquency in England 1890-1914' in *Past and Present*, No. 67 (May, 1975), pp. 96-97.

2. Rob Sindall, *Street Violence in the Nineteenth Century: Media Panic or Real Danger?* (Leicester, London and New York, 1990), p. 5.

3. *The County Telephone and Salford District Review*, 16 January, 1892.

4. Fred Bickerton, *Fred of Oxford* (London, 1953), pp. 3-4.

5. *Home Office: First Report of the Work of the Children's Branch, April 1923* (London: HMSO, 1923), p. 110.

6. Walter Southgate, *That's The Way it Was. A Working Class Autobiography 1890-1950* (Oxted, 1982), pp. 83-84.

7. *The County Telephone and Salford District Review*, 24 December, 1892.

8. Raphael Samuel, *East End Underworld. Chapters in the Life of Arthur Harding* (London, 1981), pp. 46 and 37.

9. Geoffrey Pearson. *Hooligan. A history of respectable fears* (London and Basingstoke, 1983), p. 55.

10. Pearson, *Hooligan*, p. 55.
11. Harry Hendrick, *Images of Youth. Age, Class, and the Male Youth Problem* (Oxford, 1990), p. 139.
12. *The Times*, 16 August, 1899. Loveland was particularly disturbed by one case he was trying, in which a gang of youths had 'gone about armed with bread knives and other weapons, attacking people in the neighbourhood of Clerkenwell. For the last year this Court has been endeavouring to put a stop to practices of this kind by passing exemplary sentences.'
13. Pearson, *Hooligan*, p. 57.
14. Pearson, *Hooligan*, p. 63. See also p. 66 for an example of newspaper condemnation of 'The Cyclist Terror'.
15. Pearson, *Hooligan*, p. 101.
16. Stephen Humphries, *Hooligans or Rebels? An Oral History of Working-Class Childhood and Youth 1889-1939* (Oxford, 1984 edn), p. 174.
17. Pearson, *Hooligan*, p. 76.
18. Pearson, *Hooligan*, pp. 93-94.
19. Hendrick, *Images of Youth*, p. 140.
20. Pearson. *Hooligan*, p. 77.
21. Michael Childs, *Labour's Apprentices. Working-Class Lads in Late Victorian and Edwardian England* (London, 1992), pp. 97-98.
22. Humphries, *Hooligans or Rebels?* p. 178.
23. Childs, *Labour's Apprentices*, p. 99.
24. Clarence Rook, *The Hooligan Nights* (Oxford, 1979 edn), p. 16. The book was first published in 1899.
25. Reminiscences of Charles Holbrooke (b.1901), R.032 at Bristol Reference Library.
26. Rook, *The Hooligan Nights*, p. 16.
27. Humphries, *Hooligans or Rebels?* p. 174. Sindall, *Street Violence*, p. 66.
28. Charles E. B. Russell, *Manchester Boys. Sketches of Manchester Lads at Work and Play* (Manchester, 1905), pp. 52-53.
29. James Bent, *Criminal Life. Reminiscences of Forty-two years as a Police Officer* (London, 1891), p. 225.
30. Jon Savage, *Teenage. The creation of Youth 1875-1945* (London, 2007), pp. 42-43.
31. *The Times*, 8 April, 1897.
32. Robert Roberts, *A Ragged Schooling* (Manchester, 1976), p. 33.
33. Robert Roberts, *The Classic Slum. Salford life in the first quarter of the century* (Manchester, 1971), p. 123.
34. Andrew Davies, '"These Viragoes are no less Cruel than the Lads". Young Women, Gangs and Violence in Late Victorian Manchester and Salford' in *British Journal of Criminology*, Vol. 39, No.1 (1999), p. 84.
35. Davies, '"These Viragoes"', p. 85.
36. Davies, '"These Viragoes"', pp. 85-86.
37. Davies, '"These Viragoes"', p. 86. For a general account of youth gangs during the period see also Andrew Davies, 'Youth Gangs, Masculinity and Violence in Late Victorian Manchester and Salford' in *Journal of Social History*, Vol. 32, No. 2 (Winter 1998), pp .349-364.
38. Roberts, *The Classic Slum*, p. 123.
39. Russell, *Manchester Boys*, p. 53.
40. Quoted in Savage, *Teenage*, p. 41.
41. *The Times*, 6 February, 1899.
42. Paul Thompson, 'The War with Adults' in *Oral History*, Vol. 3, No. 2 (Autumn 1975), p. 31.

43. Oxford Police Court Minute Book 1880-82, 16 March, 1880, in PST/Al/16 at Oxfordshire Record Office.

44. Humphries, *Hooligans or Rebels?* p. 204.

45. Gillis, 'The Evolution of Juvenile Delinquency', p. 122.

46. Gillis, 'The Evolution of Juvenile Delinquency', p. 122.

47. Gillis, 'The Evolution of Juvenile Delinquency', p. 121. But Gillis considers that youth workers, sensitive 'to rejection of the new norms of organised adolescence ... were prone to exaggerate delinquent tendencies among the younger generation'.

48. Frank Dawson. *A Cry from the Streets* (Hove. 1975). p. 37.

49. *Report of the Select Committee on the Law Relating to the Protection of Young Girls,* P.P. 1882, Vol. XIII, evidence of the Revd James Nugent, 16 June. 1882, p. 17. Qu.112-113.

50. Pamela Horn, 'Aspects of Child Employment. 1890-1914: Continuity and Change' in C. Alan McClelland ed., *Children at Risk* (Hull, 1994), pp. 132-134.

51. Horn, 'Aspects of Child Employment', p. 133.

52. *Royal Commission Report on Reformatory and Industrial Schools,* P.P. 1884, Vol. XLV. p. xxxix.

53. *Annual Report of the Chief Constable of Oxford for 1908* (1909), pp. 6-7. At the Centre for Oxfordshire Studies, as are the other *Reports* quoted.

54. *Annual Report of the Chief Constable of Oxford for 1911* (1912), p. 6.

55. *Annual Report of the Chief Constable of Oxford for 1913* (1914), p. 7.

56. *The County Telephone, and Salford District Review.* 9 April. 1892.

57. *The County Telephone and Salford District Review,* 27 February, 1892, recounted the case of a sixteen-year-old Salford lad who had stolen a pair of his father's trousers and had pawned them, spending the proceeds on 'cakes and cigarettes'. He was sent to a 'home'.

58. Pamela Horn, *The Rise and Fall of the Victorian Servant* (Stroud, 2004 edn), p. 72. Humphries, *Hooligans or Rebels?* p. 170.

59. *Forty-second Report of the Inspector of Reformatory and Industrial Schools of Great Britain,* P.P. 1899, Vol. XLIV, p. 22 for details of juvenile offenders under 16 committed to prison in England and Wales.

60. Quoted in Jeannie Duckworth, *Fagin's Children. Criminal Children in Victorian England* (London, 2002), p. 191.

61. Royal Commission Report on Reformatory and Industrial Schools, p. xxvi.

62. Joan Rimmer, *Yesterday's Naughty Children. Training Ship, Girls' Reformatory and Farm School. A History of the Liverpool Reformatory Association founded in 1855* (Manchester, 1986), pp. 49-50.

63. For the cases of Annie Lloyd and Martha Pendle see Brunswick Road Admission and Discharge Register, SBL,1823, ff. 19 and 61 and Managers' Minute Book for Brunswick Road Day Industrial School SBL.350, f.89, entry for 22 October, 1902, at the London Metropolitan Archives.

64. Kellow Chesney, *The Victorian Underworld* (London, 1970), p. 325.

65. Judith R. Walkowitz, *City of Dreadful Delight* (London, 1992), p. 123.

66. *Minutes of Evidence taken before the Select Committee on the Law Relating to the Protection of Young Girls* P.P. 1881, Vol. IX, p. 63, Qu.579 and p. 64, Qu.584 and 594.

67. *Report of the Select Committee on the Protection of Young Girls, 1882,* evidence of Commander Alfred Eaton and the Revd James Nugent on 16 June, 1882, p. 24, Qu. 203 and p. 26, Qu. 207. See also pp. 15-16, Qu. 102.

68. *Minutes of the Select Committee on the Protection of Young Girls, 1881,* p. 78, Qu.746.

69. *Report of the Select Committee on the Protection of Young Girls, 1882*, p. 52, Appendix B.

70. Case Study of Alice Diver at the Exhibition at the Women's Library on 'Prostitution: What's Going On?', Autumn 2006. Entry from Salvation Army Girl's Statement Book, 1886-1888.

71. Jane Jordan and Ingrid Sharp ed., *Child Prostitution and the Age of Consent* (London, 2003), p. 173.

72. R. C. Riley and Philip Eley, *Public Houses and Beerhouses in Nineteenth Century Portsmouth* (Portsmouth Papers, No. 38, 1983), p. 13.

73. *Minutes of the Select Committee on the Protection of Young Girls. 1881*, pp. 76-77, Qu.718.

74. Edward J. Bristow, *Vice and Vigilance. Purity Movements in Britain since 1700* (Dublin, 1977), p. 82. For the *Contagious Diseases Act, 1869*. See 32 & 33 Vict. c.96.

75. *Report of the Royal Commission on the Contagious Diseases Acts*, P.P. 1871, Vol. XIX, evidence of Mr C. Bulteel, Qu.6236. Judith R. Walkowitz, *Prostitution and Victorian Society. Women, Class and the State* (Cambridge, 1980), p. 17 suggests that sixteen 'seems to have been the most common age when, as the prostitutes interviewed described it, they "first went wrong."'

76. *Royal Commission on the Contagious Diseases Acts*, evidence of Mr P. D. Hopgood, Qu.11,575.

77. Bristow, *Vice and Vigilance*, p. 79. *The Contagious Diseases Act, 1869*, sect. 7.

78. 'Prostitutes'. Information on Elizabeth Evans from cards kept at Portsmouth Record Office, quoting from the *Hampshire Telegraph*.

79. Bristow, *Vice and Vigilance*, pp. 81 and 84.

80. *Report of the Select Committee on the Protection of Young Girls, 1882*, p. iv.

81. *Hansard*, 3rd Series, Vol. CCLIV, cols. 995-996, comments by Colonel Alexander. *Industrial Schools Acts Amendment Act, 1880*, 43 & 44 Victoria c.15.

82. *Hansard*, 3rd Series, Vol. CCLIV, col.1458.

83. *Royal Commission Report on Reformatories and Industrial Schools*, p. xxvi. See also evidence of Francis Headlam, stipendiary magistrate of Manchester, p. 650, QU.15,190-15,192. He noted that the only cases he had had brought before him were when parents had been convicted as brothel keepers and sent to prison. T. S. Raffles, stipendiary magistrate of Liverpool, similarly gave evidence, p. 655, Qu.15,297 that he had applied the 1880 Act in respect of children living in houses of ill-fame in Liverpool.

84. Portsmouth School Board Minute Book. G/SB.1/8 1st February, 1883, ff. 45-46 at Portsmouth Record Office.

85. *Twenty-fifth Report of the Inspector of Reformatory and Industrial Schools in Great Britain*, P.P. 1882, Vol. XXXV, p. 147. By 1884 there were thirty-one children in residence. P.P. 1884-85, Vol. XXXIX, p. 164.

86. Ellice Hopkins, *Drawn Unto Death. A Plea for the Children Coming Under the Industrial Schools Amendment Act. 1880* (London, 1884), pp. 1 and 3-4.

87. Portsmouth School Board Minute Book, G/SB.1/7, entry for 18 July, 1882, f.628 at Portsmouth Record Office.

88. *Report of the Select Committee on the Protection of Young Girls, 1882*, Appendix, p. 48. Portsmouth School Board Minute Book, entry for 28 February, 1882. 1881 Census of Population for Portsmouth, RG.11.1155, f.71, p.31 shows Elizabeth Perryman as a labourer's widow, aged 34, and living with her sister, a male lodger and another widow, who declared herself to be a sempstress.

89. *Report of the Select Committee on the Protection of Young Girls, 1882*, Appendix, p. 48.

90. *Hansard*, 3rd Series, Vol. CCC, 3 August, 1885, comment by Mr Hopwood, cols. 855-856. Sheila Jeffreys, *The Spinster and her Enemies* (London, 1985), p. 17.

91. *Report of the Departmental Committee on Reformatory and Industrial Schools*, P.P. 1896, Vol. XLV, pp. 91-92.

92. Bristow, *Vice and Vigilance*, p. 91.

93. Charles Terrot, *The Maiden Tribute. A Study of the White Slave Traffic of the Nineteenth Century* (London 1959), pp. 166-167

94. Quoted in Jordan and Sharp ed., *Child Prostitution*, p. 170.

95. Deborah Gorham, 'The "Maiden Tribute of Modern Babylon" Re-examined: Child Prostitution and the Idea of Childhood in Later Victorian England' in *Victorian Studies*, Vol. 21, No. 3 (Spring 1978), pp. 353 and 361. Terrot, *The Maiden Tribute*, p. 219. Stead described his spell in Holloway in enthusiastic terms: 'Never had I a pleasanter holiday, a more charming season of repose.'

96. Terrot, *The Maiden Tribute*, pp. 149-153

97. *Hansard*, 3rd Series, Vol. CCC, 30 July, 1885, col.582.

98. Walkowitz, *City of Dreadful Delight*, p. 104., and Terrot, *The Maiden Tribute* p. 187.

99. *Criminal Law Amendment Act. 1885* 48 &49 Victoria, c.69.

100. Chesney, *Victorian Underworld*, p. 364.

101. Walkowitz, *City of Dreadful Delight*, p. 82.

102. Chesney, *Victorian Underworld*, p. 364.

103. John Muncie, *Youth and Crime*, 2nd edn(London, 2005), pp. 67-68.

104. Sir Leon Radzinowicz and Roger Hood, *A History of English Criminal Law and its Administration from 1750: Vol V. The Emergence of Penal Policy in Victorian and Edwardian England* (Oxford, 1990), p. 633.

105. Ivy Pinchbeck and Margaret Hewitt, *Children in English Society* Vol. II *From the Eighteenth Century to the Children Act 1948* (London, 1973), pp. 489-490.

106. John A. F. Watson, *The Child and the Magistrate* (London, 1965 edn), pp. 44-45.

107. *Report of the Departmental Committee on the Probation of Offenders Act, 1907*, P.P. 1910, Vol. XLV, p. 9, Qu.154.

108. Radzinowicz and Hood, *A History of English Criminal Law*, p. 628.

109. *The County Telephone and Salford District Review*, 9 April to 18 June, 1892.

110. *Probation of First Offenders Act, 1887*, 50 & 51 Victoria c.25.

111. Philip Whitehead and Roger Statham, *The History of Probation. Politics, Power and Cultural Change 1876-2005* (Crayford, Kent, 2006), p .28. Radzinowicz and Hood, *A History of English Criminal Law*, p. 641.

112. Radzinowicz and Hood, *A History of English Criminal Law*, pp. 641-642.

113. *Report of the Departmental Committee on the Probation of Offenders*, p.97, Qu.2688-2689 and 2693.

114. Radzinowicz and Hood, *A History of English Criminal Law*, p. 642.

115. *Report of the Departmental Committee on the Probation of Offenders*, p. 42, Qu.1054. *Probation of Offenders Act, 1907*, 7 Edward 7 c.17.

116. *Probation of Offenders Act, 1907* sect. 4(d).

117. *Report of the Departmental Committee on the Probation of Offenders*, p. 43, Qu.1077-1078.

118. *Report of the Departmental Committee on the Probation of Offenders*, p. 43, Qu.1079-1080.

119. *Report of the Departmental Committee on the Probation of Offenders* p. 97 Qu.2693-2694.

120. *Report of the Departmental Committee on the Probation of Offenders*, p. 22, Qu.476.

121. *Report of the Departmental Committee on the Probation of Offenders*, pp. 120-121, Appendix IV. In that year there were 7,671 persons in England and 235 in Wales against whom probation orders were made in 1908; of these, 2,574 in England and 110 in Wales were under sixteen years if age.

122. Radzinowicz and Hood, *A History of English Criminal Law*, p. 647.

123. John Muncie, Gordon Hughes, Eugene McLaughlin ed., *Youth Justice, Critical Readings* (London, 2006 edn), p. 203.

124. Muncie, Hughes, McLaughlin ed., *Youth Justice,* p. 204.

125. *The Children Act, 1908* 8 Edward 7 c.67, sects. 102-103.

126. *Fourth Annual Report of the Oxford Police Court and Prison Gate Mission* (1910), p. 7 at the Centre for Oxfordshire Studies.

127. Watson, *The Child and the Magistrate*, p. 45.

128. Radzinowicz and Hood, *A History of English Criminal Law*, pp. 630-631.

129. *The Children Act, 1908*. sect. 111. From the start the jurisdiction of juvenile courts was extended beyond criminal offences to include cases where children were considered to be in need of care or protection.

130. Cecil Leeson, *The Probation System* (London, 1914), pp. 14-16.

131. Radzinowicz and Hood, *A History of English Criminal Law*, pp. 632-633.

132. *Home Office. First Report of the Work of the Children's Branch* (London: HMSO, 1923), p. 11.

133. Quoted in Roger Hood, *Borstal Re-assessed* (London, 1965) p. 1.

134. Hood, *Borstal Re-assessed*, p. 14.

135. Hood, *Borstal Re-assessed*, pp. 14-16.

136. *An Act to make better provision for the prevention of Crime, and for that purpose to provide for the reformation of Young Offenders and the prolonged detention of Habitual Criminals*, 8 Edward 7 c.59, sects 1-9.

137. Hood, *Borstal Re-Assessed*, pp. 23-24.

138. Radzinowicz and Hood, *A History of English Criminal Law*, p. 396.

139. Hood, *Borstal Re-assessed*, p. 32.

140. Samuel, *East End Underworld*, p. 74.

141. Louis Edward, *Borstal Lives* (London, 1939), p. 13.

142. Edward, *Borstal Lives*, p. 31.

Chapter 6

1. Victor Bailey, *Delinquency and Citizenship. Reclaiming the Young Offender, 1914-1948* (Oxford, 1987), p. 311. A similar trend was apparent in Scotland. See David Smith, 'Official Responses to Juvenile Delinquency in Scotland during the Second World War' in *Twentieth Century British History*, Vol. 18, No. 1 (2007), p. 79. John Muncie, *Youth and Crime*, 2nd edn (London, 2005), p. 77.

2. The Home Office circular, dated 11 May, 1916 was reprinted in the *Justice of the Peace*, 20 May, 1916, p. 225.

3. Home Office circular, 11 May, 1916 and Cecil Leeson, *The Child and the War. Being Notes on Juvenile Delinquency* (London, 1917), pp. 22-27. *Annual Report of the Board of Education for the Year 1915-16*, P.P. 1917-18, Vol. XI, p. 4.

4. Barbara Weinberger, 'Policing Juveniles: Delinquency in the Late Nineteenth and Early Twentieth Century Manchester' in *Criminal Justice History* Vol. 14 (1993), p. 51.

5. Weinberger, 'Policing Juveniles', pp. 49-51.

6. *Salford Chronicle*, 29 January, 1916.

7. Home Office circular, 11 May, 1916.

8. Quoted in John Springhall, *Coming of Age: Adolescence in Britain 1860-1960* (Dublin, 1986), p. 179.

9. Leeson, *The Child and the War*, p. 9.

10. Leeson, *The Child and the War*, p. 9.

11. Leeson, *The Child and the War*, p. 9. *The Justice of the Peace*, 16 December, 1916, p. 492 for an account of the appointment of the Committee and its aims. *Board of Education. Educational Pamphlets No.8. The Work of Juvenile Organisations Committees* (London, HMSO, 1933), p. 5.

12. Leeson, *The Child and the War*, p. 38.

13. *The Staffordshire Sentinel*, 29 January, 1915.

14. *Salford Chronicle*, 6 February, 1915.

15. *The Staffordshire Sentinel*, 7 January, 1915.

16. A. S. Jasper, *A Hoxton Childhood* (London, 1969), pp. 61-63.

17. Leeson, *The Child and the War*, p. 19.

18. Springhall, *Coming of Age*, p. 179.

19. Quoted in Leeson, *The Child and the War*, p. 38. See also *First Report of the Work of the Children's Branch. Home Office, April 1923* (London: HMSO,1923), p. 10, which attributed the upsurge in juvenile crime to the 'restlessness and excitement and the martial spirit' of the times, and the fact that lads' clubs had been closed and playing-fields ploughed up for allotments: 'the boys sought in vain for some means of satisfying their desire for excitement. Naturally a neglected baker's cart became a German convoy, the little gang a British patrol, and the loaves trophies of the raid. Much of the so-called crime was not in itself serious, but persistent mischief and misguided adventure'.

20. Leeson, *The Child and the War*, pp. 38-39.

21. Quoted in Jon Savage. *Teenage. The Creation of Youth 1875-1945* (London, 2007), p. 163.

22. Stephen Humphries, *Hooligans or Rebels? An Oral History of Working-class Childhood and Youth 1889-1939* (Oxford, 1984 edn), p. 175.

23. Bailey, *Delinquency and Citizenship*, p. 317.

24. Leeson. *The Child and the War*, pp. 49-50. *The Justice of the Peace*, 6 January, 1917. p. 6.

25. *The Justice of the Peace*, 6 January, 1917. p. 6.

26. Quoted in Geoffrey Pearson, *Hooligan, A history of respectable fears* (London & Basingstoke, 1983), p. 31. *The Justice of the Peace*, 20 May. 1916, p. 225.

27. *Glasgow Weekly Herald*, 18 March 1916.

28. *The Sunday Chronicle*, 21 May, 1916.

29. Arthur Marwick, *The Deluge. British Society and the First World War* (London, 1965), p. 118. Pearson, *Hooligan*, p.32.

30. Humphries, *Hooligans or Rebels?* p. 176.

31. *Glasgow Weekly Herald*, 22 April, 29 April, 27 May and 3 June, 1916, for example.

32. *Glasgow Evening Times*, 19 January, 1920. The newspaper complacently concluded that 'the time was past' when such actions could take place with impunity. But see, for example, Andrew Davies. 'Street gangs, crime and policing in Glasgow during the 1930s: the case of the Beehive Boys' in *Social History*,

Vol. 23. No. 3 (October. 1998). pp. 251-267 for later examples of gang warfare in the city.

33. Humphries, *Hooligans or Rebels?* p. 191.
34. Humphries, *Hooligans or Rebels?* pp. 191-192.
35. Humphries, *Hooligans or Rebels?* p. 192.
36. *The Times*, 13 May, 1915.
37. *Salford Chronicle.* 15 May and 29 May, 1915.
38. Robert Roberts, *The Classic Slum. Salford life in the first quarter of the century* (Manchester, 1971). pp. 155-156 and *Salford Chronicle.* 29 May, 1915.
39. *Yorkshire Evening Post*, 2 June, 1917.
40. *Yorkshire Evening Post*, 2 June, 1917.
41. *Yorkshire Evening Post*, 6 June, 1917. See also *Yorkshire Evening Post*, 5 June, 1917.
42. *Yorkshire Evening Post.* 6 June. 1917.
43. Savage, *Teenage*, p. 164. Roberts. *The Classic Slum*, pp.166-167. Roberts notes that in the country as a whole the number of girls under the age of twenty-one committed to gaol for prostitution rose by 54 per cent.
44. Joan Rimmer, *Yesterday's Naughty Children. Training Ship, Girls' Reformatory and Farm School. A History of the Liverpool Reformatory Association founded in 1855* (Manchester, 1986) p. 113.
45. *Fifty-Ninth Report of the Chief Inspector of Reformatory and Industrial Schools in Great Britain*, P.P. 1916, Vol. XV, p. 6.
46. *Fifty-Eighth Report of the Chief Inspector of Reformatory and Industrial Schools in Great Britain*, P.P. 1914-16. Vol. XXXIV, pp. 8-9.
47. *Fifty-Ninth Report of the Chief Inspector of Reformatory and Industrial Schools*, p .6.
48. *Fifty-Ninth Report of the Chief Inspector of Reformatory and Industrial Schools*, pp. 37-39. David Smith, 'Official Responses to Juvenile Delinquency', p. 80.
49. Weinberger, 'Policing Juveniles', p. 51.
50. Bailey, *Delinquency and Citizenship*, p. 17.
51. *Children and Young Persons Act, 1933*, 23 Geo. 5 c.12.
52. Maurice Bruce, *The Coming of the Welfare State* (London, 1966 edn), pp. 251 and 253.
53. John Lawson and Harold Silver, *History of Education in England* (London, 1973), pp. 384-385.
54. Lawson and Silver, *History of Education*, p. 384.
55. Basil L. Q. Henriques, *The Indiscretions of a Warden* (London, 1937), p. 240. S. F. Hatton, *London's Bad Boys* (London, 1931), p. 29.
56. Henriques, *The Indiscretions of a Warden*, p. 241.
57. James Butterworth, *Clubland* (London, 1932), pp. 37-38.
58. Hatton, *London's Bad Boys*, p. 140.
59. Cyril Burt, *The Young Delinquent* (Beckley, Kent, 1944 edn), p. 5. The book was first published in 1925.
60. Bailey, *Delinquency and Citizenship*, p. 17.
61. Burt, *The Young Delinquent*, pp. 79-82.
62. Burt, *The Young Delinquent*, pp. 84-87.
63. Burt, *The Young Delinquent*, pp. 150-151.
64. Burt, *The Young Delinquent*, p. 150.
65. Burt, *The Young Delinquent*, p. 153.
66. Henriques, *The Indiscretions of a Warden*, pp. 241-242.
67. Toynbee Hall Juvenile Court Register, PS/IJ/o/19, 11 March, 1930, at the London Metropolitan Archives.

68. *Annual Reports of the Philanthropic Society's Farm School, Redhill for 1924*, p. 7 and *for 1934*, p. 34, at the Brit. Lib. 6059.a.5.

69. Bailey, *Delinquency and Citizenship*. p. 326.

70. *Third Report of the Children's Branch of the Home Office* (London: HMSO, 1925), p. 64.

71. Bailey, *Delinquency and Citizenship*, p. 326.

72. Bailey, *Delinquency and Citizenship*. p. 61.

73. *Report of the Departmental Committee on the Treatment of Young Offenders* (London: HMSO, 1927), p. 124.

74. *Justice of the Peace and Local Government Review*, 20 April, 1935, p. 255. Memorandum on Juvenile Offences, 1941, p. 11 in HO.45/20250 at the NA.

75. *Justice of the Peace and Local Government Review*. 27 June. 1936. p. 420.

76. Toynbee Hall Juvenile Court Register. 31 December, 1929. PS/IJ/o/19 at the London Metropolitan Archives.

77. Toynbee Hall Juvenile Court Register. 26 November, 1935. PS/IJ/o/30 at the London Metropolitan Archives.

78. Toynbee Hall Juvenile Court Register, 14 January, 1936, PS/IJ/o/30.

79. Bailey, *Delinquency and Citizenship*, pp. 311 and 314.

80. *Fourth Report of the Children's Branch of the Home Office* (London: HMSO, 1928). pp. 2-3.

81. Bailey, *Delinquency and Citizenship*, pp. 317-318.

82. Bailey, *Delinquency and Citizenship*, pp. 51-53.

83. Bailey, *Delinquency and Citizenship*, p. 53.

84. *Gloucester Journal*, 25 March, 1922.

85. *Annual Report of the Philanthropic Society's Farm School, Redhill, for 1924*, pp. 7 and 12.

86. *Annual Report of the Philanthropic Society's Farm School, Redhill, for 1934* pp. 8-9.

87. *Annual Report of the Philanthropic Society's Farm School for 1938*, p. 6.

88. *Annual Report of the Philanthropic Society' s Farm School for 1938*, p. 5.

89. Stephen Humphries, 'Steal to Survive: The Social Crime of Working Class Children 1890-1940' in *Oral History Journal*, Vol. 9, No. 1 (Spring 1981), pp. 25-26.

90. Stephen Humphries, 'Steal to Survive', p. 27.

91. Stephen Humphries, 'Steal to Survive', p. 26.

92. *Justice of the Peace and Local Government Review*, 27 June, 1936, p. 419.

93. Windsor Juvenile Court Register, entries for 3 April, 19 April and 7 May, 1934 at Berkshire Record Office, PS/WI/4/1.

94. *Liverpool Weekly Post*, 9 January, 1937.

95. Humphries, *Hooligans or Rebels?* pp. 234-235.

96. Savage, *Teenage*, p. 302.

97. Pearson, *Hooligan*, p. 30.

98. Andrew Davies, 'The Scottish Chicago? From "Hooligans" to "Gangsters" in Inter-War Glasgow' in *Cultural and Social History*, Vol. 4, No. 4, (December 2007) p. 512.

99. Davies, 'The Scottish Chicago?', pp. 512 and 516.

100. *Glasgow Weekly Herald*, 11 July, 1936.

101. James Patrick, *A Glasgow Gang Observed* (London. 1973), p. 170.

102. Sir Percy Sillitoe, *Cloak Without Dagger* (London, 1955). pp. 123-124. Andrew Davies, 'Street gangs, crime and policing in Glasgow during the 1930s: the case of the Beehive Boys' in *Social History*, Vol. 23, No. 3 (October 1998), p. 252.

103. George Forbes and Paddy Meehan. *Such Bad Company. The Story of Glasgow Criminality* (Edinburgh, 1982), pp. 71-73 *Glasgow Weekly Herald*, 18 April, 1936. Davies, 'Street gangs, crime and policing', p. 267.
104. *Report of the Departmental Committee on the Treatment of Young Offenders,* pp. 121-122.
105. Bailey, *Delinquency and Citizenship*, p. 117.
106. Bailey, *Delinquency and Citizenship*, p. 119.
107. Bailey, *Delinquency and Citizenship*, p. 314. *Liverpool Weekly Post*, 9 January, 1937, reporting the comments of Mr J. F. Henderson, head of the Children's Branch of the Home Office: 'Those who in recent months have been glibly talking of "waves" of juvenile crime or delinquency have been doing a disservice. There is no such wave ... There is also a subtle danger in the use of the word "delinquent". It makes people suppose that there is a large number of boys and girls wholly given over to delinquency. This is quite untrue'. *Fifth Report of the Children's Branch: Home Office* (London: HMSO, 1938), p. 8. In 1938, 26,369 males and 1,747 females under 17 years of age were convicted of indictable offences. See HO.45/21951 at NA.
108. *Justice of the Peace and Local Government Review*, 10 April, 1937, p. 234 quoting a Report by the Education Officer of the London County Council and *Fifth Report of the Children's Branch*, pp. 9-10. *The Times*, 9 January, 1937, article headed: 'Learning to be Honest. Treatment of Child Offenders'. Bailey, *Delinquency and Citizenship*, pp. 124 and 127.
109. *Fifth Report of the Children's Branch*, p. 9. *The Times*, 9 January, 1937.
110. *The Times*, 25 October, 1937, article headed '"Dull" Children and Crime'.
111. *First Report of the Children's Branch of the Home Office* (London: HMSO, 1923), pp. 17-19.
112. Bailey, *Delinquency and Citizenship*, p. 318.
113. *Fifth Report of the Children's Branch*, p. 53.
114. *The Times*, 4 January, 1937, article headed 'The Bench and the Boy. A Myth Analysed'.
115. *The Times*, 7 January, 1937, letter headed 'The Bench and the Boy'.
116. Bailey, *Delinquency and Citizenship*, p. 117.

Chapter 7

1. *Memorandum on Juvenile Offences,* issued jointly by the Home Office and the Board of Education (London: HMSO, June 1941), p. 3 in Ho.45/20250 at the NA.
2. Hermann Mannheim, *Juvenile Delinquency in an English Middletown* (London, 1948), p. 13.
3. *Annual Report of the Chief Constable for the City of Oxford for 1940*, p. 11. at the Centre for Oxfordshire Studies, Oxford.
4. *Justice of the Peace and Local Government Review*, 22 February, 1941, p. 104.
5. *Memorandum on Juvenile Offences*, pp. 3-4.
6. *Justice of the Peace and Local Government Review*, 4 October, 1941, p. 539.
7. Minutes of a Conference on Juvenile Delinquency held at the Home Office, 3 April, 1941, comment by Mr S. Laskey, Board of Education, p. 6 and *Yorkshire Observer*, 21 March, 1941, article on 'Youth Astray' in HO.45/20250 at the NA.
8. Maureen Waller, *London 1945. Life in the Debris of War* (London, 2004), p. 363.

9. Jon Savage, *Teenage. The Creation of Youth 1875-1945* (London, 2007), pp. 350-351.

10. Mannheim, *Juvenile Delinquency*, p. 64. Mannheim also quotes the cases of children moved around from billet to billet, including a boy of eight who had been sent to eight or nine different billets, and a girl of eleven who had been in at least nine billets, as well as in the Evacuation Hostel, before being referred to the Child Guidance Clinic 'for lying and stealing from her foster-mother'. Savage, *Teenage*, p. 351.

11. Waller, *London 1945*, p. 255.

12. Sonya O. Rose, *Which People's War? National Identity and Citizenship in Britain 1939-1945* (Oxford, 2003), p. 59.

13. Mannheim, *Juvenile Delinquency*, p. 64.

14. Edward Smithies, *Crime in Wartime. A Social History of Crime in World War II* (London, 1982), p. 176.

15. Victor Bailey, *Delinquency and Citizenship. Reclaiming the Young Offender 1914-1948* (Oxford, 1987), pp. 277-278.

16. Bailey, *Delinquency and Citizenship*, pp. 277-278. *Hereford Juvenile Court Inquiry, November 1943* in P.P. 1942-43, Vol. IV, pp. 3-18.

17. David Smith, 'Official Responses to Juvenile Delinquency in Scotland During the Second World War' in *Twentieth Century British History*, Vol. 18, No. 1 (2007), pp. 82-83.

18. Minute dated 11 March, 1941 on Juvenile Crime in HO.45/20250 at the NA and referring to a Memorandum written by Mr C. P. Hill of the Children's Branch of the Home Office.

19. Smithies, *Crime in Wartime*, p. 176. Waller, *London 1945*, pp. 355 and 362-363.

20. Waller, *London 1945*, pp. 359-360.

21. Savage, *Teenage*, p. 351 and Bailey, *Delinquency and Citizenship*, p. 271.

22. *Bath Weekly Chronicle*, 22 April, 1944.

23. Smith, 'Official Responses to Juvenile Delinquency', p. 88.

24. Donald Thomas, *An Underworld at War. Spivs, Deserters, Racketeers and Civilians in the Second World War* (London, 2003), p. 82.

25. Basil L. Q. Henriques, *The Indiscretions of a Magistrate. Thoughts on the Work of the Juvenile Court*, (London, 1950), p. 130.

26. East London Juvenile Court Register, PS/1J/0/59, entry for 14 May, 1945, at the London Metropolitan Archives.

27. Smithies, *Crime in Wartime*, p. 181.

28. Quoted in Smithies, *Crime in Wartime*, p. 182.

29. Smith, 'Official Responses to Juvenile Delinquency', p. 98.

30. *Bath Weekly Chronicle*, 29 January, 1944. Smithies, *Crime in Wartime*, pp. 180-181.

31. *The Police Review*, 12 March, 1943. p. 122.

32. *The Police Review*, 30 April, 1943, p. 205.

33. Waller, *London 1945* p. 353.

34. Smith, 'Official Responses to Juvenile Delinquency', p. 89.

35. Commons Debate on Juvenile Delinquency, 2 November, 1945, col.815 in HO.45/20250 at the NA.

36. Memorandum sent to Mr Oliver, the under-secretary of state for the Home Department on 11 October, 1945 by CMG in HO.45/20250 at the NA.

37. John Muncie, Gordon Hughes and Eugene McLaughlin ed., *Youth Justice. Critical Readings* (London, 2006 edn), p. 90.

38. East London Juvenile Court Register PS/IJ/O/59 at the London Metropolitan Archives, entry for 7 May, 1945. In all, 21 cases involving 37 children were heard on

this date, and of those twelve children were aged twelve or less. The youngest was Joan P., aged 8, for whom a third non-compliance with a school attendance order meant that she was to be put under the supervision of the probation officer for two years.

39. A. M. Struthers, 'Juvenile Delinquency in Scotland' in *American Sociological Review*, Vol. 10 (1945), p. 659.

40. *Norfolk News*, 8 January, 1944.

41. Smithies, *Crime in Wartime*, p. 179.

42. Waller, *London 1945*, pp. 360-361.

43. Lyn Smith, *Young Voices. British Children Remember the Second World War* (London, 2007), p. 248.

44. George Forbes and Paddy Meehan, *Such Bad Company. The Story of Glasgow Criminality* (Edinburgh, 1982), pp. 73-74.

45. Savage, *Teenage*, p. 354.

46. Smithies, *Crime in Wartime*, p. 183.

47. *Bath Weekly Chronicle*, 1 April, 1944. Smithies, *Crime in Wartime*, p. 183.

48. *Bath Weekly Chronicle*, 5 February, 1944.

49. *Bath Weekly Chronicle*, 5 February, 1944.

50. Quoted in John Costello, *Love, Sex and War: Changing Values 1939-45* (London, 1985), pp. 280-281.

51. Bailey, *Delinquency and Citizenship*. pp. 280-281. List of Admissions to Approved Schools 1942-1946 inclusive in discussions on the Criminal Justice Bill, 1948 in HO.45/21988 at the NA.

52. Bailey, *Delinquency and Citizenship*, pp. 280-281.

53. Bailey, *Delinquency and Citizenship*, pp. 271 and 275-277. Smithies, *Crime in Wartime*, p. 179.

54. *The Police Review*, 22 January, 1943, p. 40.

55. Bailey, *Delinquency and Citizenship*, pp. 271-273

56. Bailey, *Delinquency and Citizenship*, p. 279.

57. Smithies, *Crime in Wartime*, p. 185.

58. Memorandum by Mr C. P. Hill on a proposed clause, put forward by Mr Benson, in a debate on the 1948 Criminal Justice Bill, dated 24 March, 1948, in HO.45/21988 at the NA.

59. Criminal Justice Bill Standing Committee, Official Report on 4 March, 1948 on a new Clause concerning liability to sentence to a Borstal Institution, cols. 581-582 in HO.45/21988, at the NA.

60. Bailey, *Delinquency and Citizenship*. pp. 283-284. Smithies, *Crime in Wartime*, p. 179.

61. Rose, *Which People's War?* pp. 89-90.

62. Minutes of a Conference on Juvenile Delinquency held at the Home Office, 3 April, 1941 in HO.45/20250, p. 5, comments by Miss Missen and Mr Valentine Bell, at the NA. *Memorandum on Juvenile Offences* pp. 7-8.

63. Smith, 'Official Responses to Juvenile Delinquency', p. 103.

64. Quoted in Savage, *Teenage*, pp. 416-417.

65. Commons Debate on Juvenile Delinquency, 2 November, 1945. cols. 814-815, in HO.45/20250 at the NA.

66. Paul Rock and Stanley Cohen, 'The Teddy Boy' in *The Age of Affluence 1951-1964*, ed. Vernon Bogdanor and Robert Skidelsky (London and Basingstoke, 1970), p. 288.

67. Rock and Cohen, 'The Teddy Boy', p. 288.

68. Geoffrey Pearson, *Hooligan. A history of respectable fears* (London and Basingstoke, 1983), pp. 21 and 24.

69. H. D. Willcock, *Mass-Observation Report on Juvenile Delinquency* (London, 1949), p. 40.
70. *Report of the Work of the Children's Department 1961-63* (London: HMSO,1964) p. iii.
71. T. R. Fyvel, *The Insecure Offenders. Rebellious Youth and the Welfare State* (London 1961), p. 19.
72. Fyvel, *The Insecure Offenders*, p. 19.
73. Reg Kray, *Born Fighter* (London, 1990), pp. 22-27.
74. Forbes and Meehan, *Such Bad Company*, pp. 77-78.
75. Willcock, *Mass-Observation*, p. 27. See, for example, *Criminal Statistics: England and Wales, 1973* (London: HMSO, 1974), where out of 19,839 boys aged under 14 found guilty in magistrates courts, 8,302 were guilty of theft and handling stolen goods and a further 7,547 of burglary; among boys aged 14 and under 17, the total of 50,871 offences included 23,953 of theft and handling stolen goods and 14,583 of burglary (p. 210).
76. East London Juvenile Court Register for 1954-55, PS/IJ/o/82, entries for 21 February and 11 April, 1955 at the London Metropolitan Archives.
77. Razor Smith, *A few Kind Words and a Loaded Gun. The Autobiography of a career criminal* (London, 2004), pp. 34-35.
78. Bailey, *Delinquency and Citizenship*, pp. 291-296.
79. Muncie, Hughes and McLaughlin ed., *Youth Justice*, p. 334.
80. *Criminal Statistics. England and Wales 1990* (London: HMSO, 1992), pp. 146-148. Bailey, *Delinquency and Citizenship*, pp. 298-301.
81. *The Guardian*, 17 August, 2007.
82. Muncie, Hughes and McLaughlin ed., *Youth Justice*, p. 336.
83. Smith. *A few Kind Words*, pp. 50-51.
84. Interview with James H. at the end of the 1990s in the Brit. Lib. Sound Archives, C0900X09095X.
85. Interview with James H. at the end of the 1990s in the Brit. Lib. Sound Archives.
86. Tim Bateman and John Pitts ed., *The RHP Companion to Youth Justice* (Lyme Regis, 2005), pp. 3-.5.
87. Bateman and Pitts ed., *The RHP Companion to Youth Justice*, p. 6.
88. John Springhall, *Coming of Age; Adolescence in Britain 1860-1960* (Dublin, 1986), pp. 197-199.
89. Anne Campbell, *Girl Delinquents* (Oxford, 1981), pp. 95 and 98.
90. Sarah Curtis, *Children Who Break the Law or Everybody Does It* (Winchester, 1999), pp. 38, 40 and 91. Peter Willmott, *Adolescent Boys of East London* (London, 1966), p. 157.
91. Curtis, *Children Who Break the Law*, pp. 38-42.
92. John Davis, 'The London Drug Scene and the Making of Drug Policy, 1965-1973' in *Twentieth Century History*, Vol. 17, No. 1 (2006), pp. 26 and 35-47. Curtis, *Children Who Break the Law*, p. 51.
93. Sharon Boyle, *Working Girls and their Men* (London, 1994), p. 120.
94. Boyle, *Working Girls*, pp. 121-122.
95. Draft letter to be sent to *The Times* from William C. May, Correspondent of Coed-y-Mwstwr Approved School for Senior Girls, Bridgend, dated 31 May, 1951. In the end it was not sent as the Home Office advised against it. See correspondence about the 'Menace of the "Lorry Girl"' in HO.45/24986 at the NA.
96. Memorandum dated 6 January 1954 and letter from J. Ross at the Home Office, dated 18 January, 1954 to W. L. Dacey of the County Council Association in HO.45/24986 at the NA.

97. Boyle, *Working Girls*, p. 122. A Leeds prostitute quoted by Boyle (p. 125) branded the city's council-run children's homes as 'schools for sex'.
98. Recording of a young prostitute at the Women's Library, in the Exhibition run in the autumn of 2006 on 'Prostitution: What's Going On?' The interview was conducted at the end of the 1990s.
99. Pearson. *Hooligan*. p. 18.
100. Pearson, *Hooligan*. p. 17 Rock and Cohen, 'The Teddy Boy'. p. 316.
101. Fyvel, *The Insecure Offenders*, pp. 16-17.
102. James Patrick, *A Glasgow Gang Observed* (London, 1973). p. 227. See also Ross Deuchar, 'The Outsiders' in *RSA Journal*, (Autumn 2009), pp. 28-31.
103. Pearson, *Hooligan*, p. 13. Muncie, Hughes and McLaughlin ed., *Youth Justice*, pp. 335-336.
104. Muncie. Hughes and McLaughlin ed., *Youth Justice*. pp. 335-336. Pearson, *Hooligan*. p. 18.
105. *News Chronicle*, 3 May, 1954. Pearson *Hooligan*, p. 15.
106. *News Chronicle*, 5 May, 1954.
107. *Daily Sketch*, 7 May, 1954.
108. *Daily Sketch*, 8 May 1954.
109. Stanley Cohen, *Folk Devils and Moral Panics*, 3rd edn (London and New York, 2002), pp. 155-156.
110. Cohen, *Folk Devils*, pp. 17-18.
111. Cohen, *Folk Devils*, pp. 18-19.
112. *The Times*, 19 and 22 May, 1964.
113. *The Times*, 22 May, 1964.
114. Paul Barker with Alan Little, 'The Margate Offenders: A Survey' in *New Society*, 30 July, 1964, pp. 6-7.
115. *The Times*, 22 May, 1964.
116. *Hansard*, 5th Series, Vol. 697 (22 June-3 July. 1964), 23 June, 1964, cols. 239-242 in a debate on the Malicious Damages Bill.
117. Pearson, *Hooligan*, p. 12.
118. Interview with Paul V. at the end of the 1990s in the British Library Sound Archives, C0900X09095X.
119. Debbie Wilson, Clare Sharp and Alison Patterson, *Young People and Crime: Findings from the 2005 Offending, Crime and Justice Survey* (Home Office Paper No. 17, 2006), p. 24. Bateman and Pitts ed., *The RHP Companion to Youth Justice*, p. 70. *The Guardian*, 14 February, 2008. *The Times*, 10 May 2008. *The Guardian*, 27 May 2008 and 6 June, 2008
120. Bateman and Pitts ed., *The RHP Companion to Youth Justice*, p. 231.
121. Bateman and Pitts ed., *The RHP Companion to Youth Justice*, p. 231. Bill Osgerby, *Youth in Britain since 1945* (Oxford, 1998), p. 149.
122. Stephen Small, *Police and People in London. A group of young black people* (London: Policy Studies Institute, No. 619, November 1983), pp. 104-105. This lad did admit, however, that on another occasion when he was stopped he did have a quantity of cannabis upon him, which, fortunately for him, the police did not find.
123. *The Times*, 13 and 14 April, 1981.
124. *Hansard*, 6th Series, Vol. 3 (13 April-l May, 1981), cols. 21, 24 and 27.
125. *The Annual Register for 1981* (London, 1982), p. 9. White youths also joined in to some extent and although the police were the prime targets, some black-owned shops were severely damaged, too.
126. *The Annual Register for 1981*, p. 12.
127. *The Annual Register for 1981*, p. 10.

128. *Hansard*, 6th Series, Vol. 8, debate on 6 July, 1981, col. 29.
129. *The Annual Register for 1981*, p. 10.
130. *The Annual Register for 1981*, p. 12.
131. Osgerby, *Youth in Britain*, pp. 163-167.
132. Steve Craine and Bob Coles, 'Alternative Careers: Youth Transitions and Young People's Involvement in Crime' in *Youth and Policy*, No. 48 (Spring 1995).
133. Muncie, Hughes and McLaughlin ed., *Youth Justice*, pp. 389, 391 and 394. *Hansard*, 6th Series, Vol. 220 (1-12 March, 1991), debate on 2 March, 1991.
134. Interview with James H. in the Brit. Lib. Sound Archives, Co9ooXo9o95X. Muncie, Hughes and McLaughlin ed., *Youth Justice*, p. 11.
135. Muncie, Hughes and McLaughlin ed., *Youth Justice*, pp. 2, 9, 13, 455-456.
136. '"Knife Crime": Ineffective reactions to a distracting problem? A Review of Evidence and Policy', Research paper issued by *The Centre for Crime and Justice Studies*, August, 2006, p. 21. *The Guardian*, 8 May, 2008.
137. Bateman and Pitts ed., *The RHP Companion to Youth Justice*, p. 66. *The Guardian*, 9 June, 2008.
138. Pearson, *Hooligan*, pp. 7 and 237.
139. Bateman and Pitts ed., *The RHP Companion to Youth Justice*, pp. vi-vii. Prior to chairing the Youth Justice Board from April 2004, Rod Morgan had been HM Inspector of Probation and a professor of criminal justice at Bristol University. In August 2006 he expressed concern that there were 'almost 3,000 children in penal custody in England and Wales.' The biggest increase in these young prisoners was among those aged fifteen to seventeen. *The Guardian*, 16 August, 2006. Morgan has now resigned his post at the Youth Justice Board. Muncie, Hughes and McLaughlin ed., *Youth Justice*, p. 4.
140. *The Times*, 9 February, 2010.

BIBLIOGRAPHY

N.B. Only printed sources are given here. All manuscripts, court records and oral history material used are detailed in the Notes.

P.P. = Parliamentary Papers.
HMSO = Her Majesty's Stationery Office.

Official Papers

Capper, John Henry, Superintendent of Ships and Vessels, Annual Reports of

Causes of the Increase in the Number of Criminal Commitments, Select Committee on, P.P. 1828, Vol. VI

Children's Friend Society (Cape of Good Hope), Report on the, P.P. 1840, Vol. XXXIII

Contagious Diseases Acts, Royal Commission on, P.P. 1871, Vol. XIX

Convict Discipline in Van Diemen's Land, Correspondence Relative to, P.P. 1846, Vol. XXIX

Convict Hulks in the Rivers Thames and Medway, and in Portsmouth and Langston Harbours &c., Papers Relating to, P.P. 1814-15, Vol. XI

Criminal Commitments and Convictions, Report of the Select Committee on, P.P. 1828, Vol. VI

Criminal and Destitute Juveniles, Select Committee on, P.P. 1852, Vol. VII

Criminal Statistics, Annual

Emigration from the United Kingdom, Select Committee on, P.P. 1826, Vol. IV

Execution of the Criminal Law, Report on, P.P. 1847. Vol. VII

Gaols and Houses of Correction, Select Committee on, P.P. 1835, Vol. XI

Hereford Juvenile Court Inquiry, November 1943, P.P. 1942-43, Vol. IV

Home Office: Reports of the Work of the Children's Branch (later the Children's Department) (HMSO, 1923; 1928; 1938; 1964)

Inspectors of Prisons of Great Britain, Annual Reports of

Law Relating to the Protection of Young Girls, Report of the Select Committee on, P.P. 1881, Vol. IX and 1882, Vol. XIII

Metropolitan Police Offices, Select Committee on, P.P. 1837, Vol. XII

New South Wales, Report of the Commission of Inquiry into the State of the Colony of, P.P. 1822. Vol. XX

Police of the Metropolis, Report from the Select Committee on, P.P. 1828, Vol. VI

Prison Discipline, Select Committee on, P.P. 1850, Vol. XVII

Young Offenders

Probation of Offenders Act, Report of the Departmental Committee on, P.P. 1910, Vol. XLV
Reformatory and Industrial Schools, Annual Reports of the Inspector of
Reformatories and Industrial Schools, Report of the Royal Commission on, P.P. 1884, Vol. XLV
Reformatory and Industrial Schools, Report of Departmental Committee on, P.P. 1896, Vol. XLV
State of the Police of the Metropolis, Reports from the Committee on the, P.P. 1816, Vol. V and P.P. 1817, Vol. VII
Secondary Punishments, Select Committee on, P.P. 1831-32, Vol. VII
Transportation, Select Committee on, P.P. 1837, Vol. XIX and 1837-38, Vol. XXII
Transportation, Select Committee on, P.P. 1861, Vol. XIII
Young Offenders, Report of the Departmental Committee on the Treatment of (HMSO, 1927)
Hansard

Newspapers and Journals

Bath Weekly Chronicle
County Telephone and Salford District Review
Daily Sketch
Gentleman's Magazine
Glasgow Evening Times
Glasgow Weekly Herald
Guardian, The
Justice of the Peace and Local Government Review
Liverpool Weekly Post
News Chronicle
Norfolk News
Oxford Times
Police Review, The
Reformatory and Refuge Journal
Salford Chronicle
Salisbury and Winchester Journal
Seeking and Saving
Staffordshire Sentinel, The
Times, The
Yorkshire Evening Post

Books and Articles

Andrew, Donna T., *Philanthropy and Police. London Charity in the Eighteenth Century* (Princeton, New Jersey, 1989)
Annual Register (London, 1832) and (London, 1982)
Ayres, Jack. *Paupers and Pig Killers. The Diary of William Holland. A Somerset Parson, 1799-1818* (Stroud 2000 edn)
Bailey, Victor. *Delinquency and Citizenship. Reclaiming the Young Offender, 1914-1948* (Oxford, 1987)
Baker, T. Barwick Lloyd, *War with Crime* (London, 1889)

Barker, Paul with Little, Alan, 'The Margate Offenders: A Survey' in *New Society* 30 July 1964

Bateman, Tim and Pitts, John. ed., *The RHP Companion to Youth Justice* (Lyme Regis, 2005)

Bean, Philip and Melville, Joy, *Lost Children of the Empire* (London, 1989)

Beattie, J. M., *Crime and the Courts in England 1660-1800* (Oxford, 1986)

Beattie, J. M., *Policing and Punishment in London, 1660-1750* (Oxford, 2002 edn)

Beattie, J. M. 'The Pattern of Crime in England 1660-1800' in *Past and Present*, No. 62 (February 1974)

Bennet, The Hon. Henry Grey, *Letter to Viscount Sidmouth, Secretary of State for the Home Department on the Transportation Laws, The State of the Hulks and of the Colonies in New South Wales* (London, 1819)

Benney, Mark, *Low Company* (London, 1936)

Bent, James, *Criminal Life. Reminiscences of Forty-Two Years as a Police Officer* (London, 1891)

Bickerton, Fred, *Fred of Oxford* (London, 1953)

Blackburn, Geoff, *The Children's Friend Society. Juvenile Emigrants to Western Australia, South Africa and Canada 1834-1842* (Northbridge, Western Australia, 1993)

Boyle, Sharon, *Working Girls and their Men* (London, 1994)

Bradlow, Edna, 'The Children's Friend Society at the Cape of Good Hope' in *Victorian Studies*, Vol. 27, No. 2 (Winter 1984)

Bristow, Edward J., *Vice and Vigilance. Purity Movements in Britain since 1700* (Dublin, 1977)

Brooke, Alan and Brandon, David, *Bound for Botany Bay. British Convict Voyages to Australia* (London, 2005)

Bruce, Maurice, *The Coming of the Welfare State* (London, 1966 edn)

Burt, Cyril, *The Young Delinquent* (Beckley, Kent, 1944 edn)

Butterworth, James, *Clubland* (London, 1932)

Campbell, Anne, *Girl Delinquents* (Oxford, 1981)

Campbell, Charles, *The Intolerable Hulks* (Maryland, 1994)

Carlebach, Julius, *Caring for Children in Trouble* (London, 1998 edn)

Carpenter, J. Estlin, *The Life and Work of Mary Carpenter* (London, 1870)

[Carpenter, Mary], *Red Lodge Girls' Reformatory School, Bristol* (Bristol, 1875)

Carpenter, Mary, *Reformatory Schools For the Children of the Perishing and Dangerous Classes and for Juvenile Offenders* (London, 1851)

Chesney, Kellow, *The Victorian Underworld* (London, 1970)

Childs, Michael, *Labour's Apprentices. Working-Class Lads in Late Victorian and Edwardian England* (London, 1992)

Cirket, Alan F. ed., *Samuel Whitbread's Notebooks 1810-11 1813-14* (Bedfordshire Historical Record Society, Vol. 50, 1971)

Cobley, John, *The Crimes of the First Fleet Convicts* (Sydney, 1970)

Cobley, John, *The Crimes of the Lady Juliana Convicts: 1790* (Sydney, 1989)

Cockburn J. S., ed., *Crime in England 1550-1800* (London 1977)

Cohen, Stanley, *Folk Devils and Moral Panics*, 3rd edn (London and New York, 2002)

Coldrey, Barry, *Good British Stock. Child and Youth Migration to Australia* (Canberra, 1999)

Costello, John, *Love, Sex and War: Changing Values 1939-45* (London, 1985)

Craine, Steve and Coles, Bob, 'Alternative Careers: Youth Transitions and Young People's Involvement in Crime' in *Youth and Policy*, No. 48 (Spring 1995)

Crittall, Elizabeth ed., *The Justicing Notebook of William Hunt 1744-1749* (Wiltshire Record Society, Vol. 37, 1981)

Curtis, Sarah, *Children Who Break the Law or Everybody Does It* (Winchester, 1999)

Davies, Andrew, 'Street gangs, Crime and Policing in Glasgow during the 1930s: the case of the Beehive Boys' in *Social History*, Vol. 23, No. 3 (October, 1998)

Davies, Andrew, 'The Scottish Chicago? From "Hooligans" to "Gangsters" in Inter-War Glasgow' in *Cultural and Social History*, Vol. 4, No. 4 (December 2007).

Davies, Andrew, '"These Viragoes are no less Cruel than the Lads". Young Women, Gangs and Violence in Late Victorian Manchester and Salford' in *British Journal of Criminology*, Vol. 39, No. 1 (1999)

Davies, Andrew, 'Youth Gangs, Masculinity and Violence in Late Victorian Manchester and Salford' in *Journal of Social History*, Vol. 32, No. 2 (Winter 1998)

Davis, John, 'The London Drug Scene and the Making of Drug Policy, 1965-1973' in *Twentieth Century History*, Vol. 17, No. 1 (2006)

Dawson, Frank, *A Cry from the Streets* (Hove, 1975)

de Lacey, Margaret, Prison reform in Lancashire, 1700-1850. A study of local administration (Manchester for the Chetham Society, 1986)

Deuchar, Ross 'The Outsiders' in *RSA Journal*, Autumn 2009

Duckworth, Jeannie, *Fagin's Children. Criminal Children in Victorian England* (London and New York, 2002)

Edward, Louis, *Borstal Lives* (London, 1939)

Ekrich, Roger, *Bound for America, The Transportation of British Convicts to the Colonies, 1718-1775* (Oxford, 1987)

Flynn, Michael, *The Second Fleet. Britain's Grim Convict Armada of 1790* (Sydney, 1993)

Forbes, George and Meehan, Paddy, *Such Bad Company. The story of Glasgow Criminality* (Edinburgh, 1982)

Fyvel, T. R., *The Insecure Offenders. Rebellious Youth in the Welfare State* (London, 1961)

Gatrell, V. A. C., *The Hanging Tree. Execution and the English People 1770-1868* (Oxford, 1996 edn)

George, Dorothy, *London Life in the Eighteenth Century* (Harmondsworth, 1965 edn)

Gillen, Mollie, *The Founders of Australia: A Biographical Dictionary of the First Fleet* (Sydney, 1989)

Gillis, John R., 'The Evolution of Juvenile Delinquency in England 1890-1914' in *Past and Present*, No. 67 (May, 1975)

Gorham, Deborah. 'The "Maiden Tribute of Modern Babylon" Re-examined: Child Prostitution and the Idea of Childhood in Later Victorian England' in *Victorian Studies*, Vol. 21, No. 3 (Spring 1978)

Hadley, Elaine, 'Natives in a Strange Land: The Philanthropic Discourse of Juvenile Emigration in Mid-Nineteenth Century England' in *Victorian Studies*, Vol. 33, No. 3 (Spring 1990)

Hatton, S. F., *London's Bad Boys* (London, 1931)

Hendrick, Harry, *Images of Youth. Age, Class, and the Male Youth Problem* (Oxford, 1990)

Henriques, Basil L. Q., *The Indiscretions of a Magistrate. Thoughts on the Work of the Juvenile Court* (London, 1950)

Henriques, Basil L. G., *The Indiscretions of a Warden* (London, 1937)

Hood, Roger, *Borstal Re-Assessed* (London, 1965)

Hooper, F. C., *Prison Boys of Port Arthur. A study of the Point Puer Boys' Establishment, Van Diemen's Land, 1834 to 1850* (Melbourne, 1967)

Hopkins, Ellice, *Drawn Unto Death. A Plea for the Children Coming Under the Industrial Schools Amendment Act, 1880* (London, 1884)

Horn, Pamela, 'Aspects of Child Employment, 1890-1914: Continuity and Change' in McClelland, C. Alan ed., *Children at Risk* (Hull, 1994)

Horn, Pamela, *The Rise and Fall of the Victorian Servant* (Stroud, 2004 edn)

Horn, Pamela, *The Victorian Town Child* (Stroud, 1997 edn)

Howard, John, *The State of the Prisons* (London. 1929 edn)

Hughes, Robert, *The Fatal Shore. A History of the Transportation of Convicts to Australia, 1787-1868* (London 2003 edn)

Humphery, Kim, 'Objects of Compassion: Young Male Convicts in Van Diemen's Land 1834-1850' in *Australian Historical Studies*, Vol. 25 (April 1992)

Humphries, Stephen, *Hooligans or Rebels? An Oral History of Working-Class Childhood and Youth 1889-1939* (Oxford, 1984 edn)

Humphries, Stephen, 'Steal to Survive; The Social Crime of Working Class Children 1890-1940' in *Oral History Journal*, Vol. 9. No. 1 (Spring 1981)

Ignatieff, Michael, *A Just Measure of Pain. The Penitentiary in the Industrial Revolution, 1750-1850* (London and Basingstoke, 1978)

Jasper, A. S., *A Hoxton Childhood* (London, 1969)

Jeffreys, Sheila, *The Spinster and her Enemies* (London, 1985)

Johnson, W. Branch, *The English Prison Hulks* (Chichester, 1970 edn)

Jordan, Jane and Sharp, Ingrid ed., *Child Prostitution and the Age of Consent* (London, 2003)

[Anon] '"Knife Crime": Ineffective reactions to a distracting problem? A Review of Evidence and Policy', *The Centre for Crime and Justice Studies* (London, August 2006)

King, Peter, *Crime, Justice and Discretion in England 1740-1820* (Oxford, 2000)

King, Peter, 'Decision-makers and Decision-making in the English Criminal Law, 1750-1800' in *The Historical Journal*, Vol. 27, No. 1 (1984)

King, Peter and Noel, Joan, 'The Origins of "The Problem of Juvenile Delinquency"; The Growth of Juvenile Prosecution in London in the Late Eighteenth and Early Nineteenth Centuries' in *Criminal Justice History*, Vol., IV (1993)

King, Peter, 'The Rise of Juvenile Delinquency in England 1780-1840: Changing Patterns of Perception and Prosecution' in *Past and Present*, No. 160 (August 1998)

King, Peter, 'War as a judicial resource. Press gangs and prosecution rates, 1740-1830' in Landau, Norma ed., *Law, Crime and English Society, 1660-1830* (Cambridge, 2002)

Knell, S. E. F., 'Capital Punishment: Its Administration in Relation to Juvenile Offenders in the Nineteenth Century and its Possible Administration in the Eighteenth' in *British Journal of Criminology*, Vol. 5 (1965)

Kray, Reg, *Born Fighter* (London, 1990)

Lane, Joan, *Apprenticeship in England 1600-1914* (London, 1996)

Lawson, John and Silver, Harold, *History of Education in England* (London, 1973)

Leeson, Cecil, *The Child and the War. Being Notes on Juvenile Delinquency* (London, 1917)

Leeson, Cecil, *The Probation System* (London, 1914)

Mahood, Linda, *Policing gender, class and family* (London, 1995)

Mannheim, Hermann, *Juvenile Delinquency in an English Middletown* (London, 1948)

Manton, Jo, *Mary Carpenter and the Children of the Streets* (London, 1976)

Magarey, S., 'The invention of juvenile delinquency in early nineteenth-century England' in *Labour History* [Canberra], No. 34 (May 1978)

May, Margaret, 'Innocence and Experience; The Evolution of the Concept of Juvenile Delinquency in the Mid-Nineteenth Century' in *Victorian Studies* Vol. 18, No. 1 (September 1973)

Mayhew, Henry and Binny, John, *The Criminal Prisons of London* (New York, 1968 edn) The book was first published in 1862.

Melling, Elizabeth ed., *Kentish Sources*, Vol. VI *Crime and Punishment* (Maidstone: Kent County Council, 1969)

Mercer, Malcolm, *Schooling the Poorer Child. Elementary Education in Sheffield 1560-1902* (Sheffield, 1996)

Miles, William Augustus, *A Letter to Lord John Russell concerning Juvenile Delinquency together with Suggestions concerning a Reformatory Establishment* (Shrewsbury, 1837)

Morgan, Gwenda and Rushton, Peter, *Eighteenth-Century Criminal Transportation: The Formation of the Criminal Atlantic* (Basingstoke, 2004)

Morris, Norval and Rothman, David J., ed., *The Oxford History of the Prison. The Practice of Punishment in Western Society* (New York and Oxford, 1995)

Muncie, John, *Youth and Crime*, 2nd edn (London, 2005)

Muncie, John, Hughes, Gordon and McLaughlin, Eugene, ed., *Youth Justice: Critical Readings* (London, 2006 edn)

Nicol, John, *The Life and Adventures of John Nicol, Mariner* (London, 1937 edn) The book was first published in 1822.

Oldham, Wilfrid, *Britain's Convicts to the Colonies* (Sydney, 1990)

Osgerby, Bill, *Youth in Britain since 1945* (Oxford, 1998)

Oxford, Annual Reports of the Chief Constable for the City of

Patrick, James, *A Glasgow Gang Observed* (London, 1973)

Pearson, Geoffrey, *Hooligan. A history of respectable fears* (London and Basingstoke, 1983)

Philanthropic Society, Annual Reports of

Philips, David, *Crime and Authority in Victorian England. The Black Country 1835-1860* (London, 1977)

Pinchbeck, Ivy and Hewitt, Margaret, *Children in English Society*, Vol. II. *From the Eighteenth Century to the Children Act 1948* (London, 1973)

Porter, Roy, *English Society in the Eighteenth Century* (Harmondsworth, 1994 edn)

Porter, Roy, *London. A Social History* (London, 2000 edn)

Prahms, Wendy, *Newcastle Ragged and Industrial School* (Stroud, 2006)

Radzinowicz, Leon, *A History of English Criminal Law and its Administration from 1750*, Vol. 1 (London, 1948)

Radzinowicz, Sir Leon and Hood, Roger, *A History of English Criminal Law*, Vol. 5. *The Emergence of Penal Policy* (Oxford, 1986)

Rees, Siân, *The Floating Brothel*, (London, 2002 edn)

Refuge for the Destitute, Annual Reports of

Report of the Committee for Investigating the Causes of the Alarming Increase Juvenile Delinquency in the Metropolis (London, 1816)

Rich, E., *The Education Act 1870. A study of public opinion* (London, 1970)

Richmond, Carol, *Banished! Sentences of Transportation from Oxfordshire Courts 1787-1867*, Vol. 2 (Witney, 2007)

Riley, R. C. and Eley, Philip, *Public Houses and Beerhouses in Nineteenth Century Portsmouth* (Portsmouth Papers, No. 38, 1983)

Rimmer, Joan, *Yesterday's Naughty Children. Training Ship, Girls' Reformatory and Farm School. A History of the Liverpool Reformatory Association* (Manchester, 1986)

Roberts, Robert, *A Ragged Schooling* (Manchester, 1976)

Roberts, Robert, *The Classic Slum. Salford Life in the first quarter of the century* (Manchester, 1971)

Rock, Paul and Cohen, Stanley, 'The Teddy Boy' in *The Age of Affluence*, Bogdanor, Vernon and Skidelsky, Robert ed., (London and Basingstoke, 1970)

Rook, Clarence, *The Hooligan Nights* (Oxford. 1979 edn). First published in 1899

Rose, Gordon, *Schools for Young Offenders* (London, 1967)

Rose, Sonya O., *Which People's War? National Identity and Citizenship in Britain 1939-1945* (Oxford, 2003)

Russell, Charles E. B., *Manchester Boys. Sketches of Manchester Lads at Work and Play* (Manchester, 1905)

Samuel, Raphael, *East End Underworld. Chapters in the Life of Arthur Harding,* (London, 1981)

Sanders, Wiley B. ed., *Juvenile Offenders for a Thousand Years* (Chapel Hill: University of North Carolina, 1970)

Savage Jon, *Teenage. The Creation of Youth 1822-1945* (London, 2007)

Shaw, A. G. L., *Convicts and the Colonies. A Study of Penal Transportation from Great Britain and Ireland to Australia and other parts of the British Empire* (London, 1966)

Sheppard, Francis, *London 1808-1870. The Infernal Wen* (London, 1971)

Shore, Heather, *Artful Dodgers. Youth and Crime in early Nineteenth Century London* (Woodbridge, 1999)

Shore, Heather, '"Cross coves, buzzers and general sorts of prigs": juvenile crime and the criminal "underworld" in the early nineteenth century' in *British Journal of Criminology*, special edition on *Histories of Crime and Modernity*, Vol. XXXIX (1999)

Sillitoe, Sir Percy, *Cloak Without Dagger* (London, 1955)

Silverthorne. Elizabeth ed., *Deposition Book of Richard Wyatt JP. 1767-1776* (Guildford: Surrey Record Society, Vol. 30, 1978)

Sindall, Rob, *Street Violence in the Early Nineteenth Century: Media Panic or Real Danger?* (Leicester, London and New York, 1990)

Small, Stephen, *Police and People in London. A group of young black people* (London, 1983)

Smith, David, 'Official Responses to Juvenile Delinquency in Scotland during the Second World War' in *Twentieth Century British History*, Vol. 18, No. 1, (2007)

Smith, Lyn, *Young Voices. British Children Remember the Second World War* (London, 2007)

Smith, Razor, *A few kind Words and a Loaded Gun. The Autobiography of a career criminal* (London, 2004)

Smith, William, MD, *State of the Gaols in London, Westminster and the Borough of Southwark* (London, 1776)

Smithies, Edward, *Crime in Wartime. A Social History of Crime in World War II* (London, 1982)

Society for the Improvement of Prison Discipline and for the Reformation of Juvenile Offenders, Annual Report of

Southgate, Walter, *That's the way it was. A Working Class Autobiography 1890-1950* (Oxted, 1982)

Spence, Margaret, *Hampshire and Australia 1783-1791, Crime and Transportation.* (Hampshire Papers No. 2 Hampshire County Council, 1992)

Stack, John A., 'Interests and Ideas in Nineteenth-Century Social Policy: The Mid-Victorian Reformatory School' in *Journal of Educational Administration and History*, Vol. XIV, No. 1 (January 1982)

[Anon.] *Statement of the views and Reports of the Society for the Suppression of Juvenile Vagrancy* (London, 1830)

Struthers, A. M., 'Juvenile Delinquency in Scotland' in the *American Sociological Review,* Vol 10. (1945)

Terrot, Charles, *The Maiden Tribute. A Study of the White Slave Traffic of the Nineteenth Century* (London, 1959)

Thale, Mary ed., *The Autobiography of Francis Place 1771-1854* (Cambridge, 1972)

Thomas, Donald, *An Underworld at War. Spivs, Deserters, Racketeers and Civilians in the Second World War* (London, 2003)

Thompson, Paul, 'The War with Adults' in *Oral History* Vol. 3, No. 2 (Autumn 1975)

Tobias, J. J., *Crime and Industrial Society in the 19th Century* (London, 1967)

Tuckwell, Gertrude M., *The State and its Children* (London, 1894)

Wagner, Gillian, *Children of the Empire* (London, 1982)

Walkowitz, Judith R., *City of Dreadful Delight* (London, 1992)

Walkowitz, Judith R., *Prostitution and Victorian Society. Women, Class and the State* (Cambridge, 1980)

Waller, Maureen, *London 1945. Life in the Debris of War* (London. 2004)

Watson, John A. F. *The Child and the Magistrate* (London, 1965 edn)

Weinberger, Barbara, 'Policing Juveniles: Delinquency in the Late Nineteenth and Early Twentieth Century Manchester' in *Criminal Justice History*, Vol. 14 (1993)

Whitehead, Philip and Statham, Roger,. *The History of Probation. Politics, Power and Cultural Change 1876-2005* (Crayford, Kent, 2006)

Willcock, H. D., *Mass-Observation Report on Juvenile Delinquency* (London, 1949)

Willmott, Peter, *Adolescent Boys of East London* (London 1966)

Wilson, Debbie, Sharp, Clare and Patterson, Alison, *Young People and Crime: Findings from the 2005 Offending Crime and Justice Survey* (Home Office Paper No. 17, 2006)

Wyatt, Irene, 'Juveniles Transported to Australia and Tasmania 1815-1835' in *Gloucestershire Historical Studies*, Vol. X (1979)

Wyatt, Irene, 'Some Transportees from Gloucestershire 1815-1818' in *Gloucestershire Historical Studies*, Vol. II (1969)

Wyatt, J. W., 'The Transportation of Criminals from Gloucestershire 1718-1773' in *Gloucestershire Historical Studies*, Vol. III (1969)

INDEX